Oil-Age Africa

Africa-Europe Group for Interdisciplinary Studies

VOLUME 29

The titles published in this series are listed at *brill.com/agis*

Oil-Age Africa

Critical Reflections on Oil Politics, Resource Economies and Extractive Communities

Edited by

Jannik Schritt and Annika Witte

BRILL

LEIDEN | BOSTON

Cover illustration: One of the Hausa villages near Zinder (Niger) affected by expropriation due to the construction of the Chinese-Nigerien oil refinery, which can be seen in the background of the picture. © Jannik Schritt

The Library of Congress Cataloging-in-Publication Data is available online at https://catalog.loc.gov

Typeface for the Latin, Greek, and Cyrillic scripts: "Brill". See and download: brill.com/brill-typeface.

ISSN 1574-6925
ISBN 978-90-04-53005-8 (paperback)
ISBN 978-90-04-53006-5 (e-book)

This book is printed on acid-free paper and produced in a sustainable manner.

Contents

Figures and Tables

Figures

Tables

Abbreviations

ANPE	Agence Nigérienne de la Promotion de l'Emploi
ANPN	Agence Nationale des Parcs Nationaux
ARD	l'Alliance pour le Renouveau Démocratique
AUSPE	Association des Utilisateurs de Services Publics de l'Eau
BDCs	Bulk Distribution Companies
BDG	Bloc Democratique Gabonaise
BIT	Bilateral Investment Treaties
CDS	Convention Démocratique et Sociale
CEO	Chief Executive Officer
CETA	EU-Canada Comprehensive Economic and Trade Agreement
CFA	Communauté Financière d'Afrique
CGCT	Code Général des Collectivités Territoriales
CLO	Community Liaison Officer
CNOOC	China National Offshore Oil Corporation
CNPC	China National Petroleum Corporation
CNPCIC	China National Petroleum Corporation International in Chad
COSYGA	Conference Syndicale Gabonaise
CR	Conseil Régional
CSI	Centre de Santé Intégré
CSO	Civil Society Organisation
CSR	Corporate Social Responsibility
DD	Dutch Disease
DFG	Deutsche Forschungsgemeinschaft
DG	Director-General
EACOP	East African Crude Oil Pipeline
EEPCI	ExxonMobil Exploration and Production Chad Inc
EIE	Etudes d'Impact Environnemental
EITI	Extractive Industries Transparency Initiative
EPA	Economic Partnership Agreements
FCFA	Franc de la Communauté Financière d'Afrique
FDI	Foreign Direct Investment
FPSO	Floating, Production, Storage and Offloading
GATT	General Agreement on Tariffs and Trade
GDP	Gross Domestic Product
GPL	Gaz de Pétrole Liquéfié
GREN	Groupe de Réflexion et d'Action sur les industries Extractives
GVCs	Global Value Chains
HSE	Health, Safety & Environment

HSS/E	Hygiène, Sécurité, Santé et Environnement
IEB	Inspection d'Enseignement de Base
IIA	International Investment Agreements
IMF	International Monetary Fund
ISDS	Investor State Dispute Settlement
LAPSSET	Lamu Port–South Sudan–Ethiopia Transport
LASDEL	Laboratoire d'Études et de Recherche sur les Dynamiques Sociales et le Développement Local
LCP	Local Content Policy
LCR	Local Content Rules
LDCs	Least Developed Countries
MCAS	Members of County Assembly
MNCs	Multinational Corporations
MNRG	Mouvement National de la Revolution Gabonaise
MNSD	Mouvement National pour la Société de Développement
MPPAD	Mouvement Populaire pour la Préservation des Acquis Démocratiques
MP	Member of Parliament
NDC	National Democratic Congress
NGO	Non Governmental Organisation
NPP	New Patriotic Party
NTB	Non-Tariff Barriers
ODM	Orange Democratic Movement
OMCs	Oil Marketing Companies
ONU	Organisation des Nations Unies
PAC	Programme d'Action Communautaire
PADL-N	Programme d'Appui au Développement Local – N'Guigmi
PAM	Programme Alimentaire Mondial
PDG	Parti Démocratique Gabonais
PGE	Plan de Gestion d'Environnement
PNDS	Parti Nigérien pour la Démocratie et le Socialisme
PNUD	Programme des Nations Unies pour le Développement
PPD	Public-Private Dialogue
PPP	Purchasing Power Parity
PUNGA	Parti d'Union Nationale Gabonaise
PWYP	Publish What You Pay
RDP	Rassemblement pour la Démocratie et le Progrès
REC	Regional Economic Communities
RER	Real Exchange Rate
ROTAB	Réseau des Organisations pour la Transparence et l'Analyse Budgétaire
RSD	Rassemblement Social et Démocratique

RSE	Responsabilité Sociale de l'Entreprise
RST	Rentier State Theory
SG	Secretary General
SORAZ	Société de Raffinage de Zinder
SUV	Sport Utility Vehicle
SYNATRAP	Syndicat National des Travailleurs de Pétrole
TOR	Tema Oil Refinery
TRIM	Trade Related Investment Measures
TVA	Taxe sur la Valeur Ajoutée
VRA	Volta River Authority
WTO	World Trade Organization

Notes on Contributors

Mahamidou Aboubacar Attahirou

Mahamidou Aboubacar Attahirou, doctorant à l'Université Abdou Moumouni de Niamey, est affilié au Laboratoire d'études et de recherche sur les dynamiques sociales et le développement local – LASDEL-Niamey (Niger). Il prépare une thèse de doctorat sur le pétrole et les transformations socio-économiques à Diffa (Niger).

Helmut Asche

Prof Dr Helmut Asche is an economist and sociologist. Career development:
- Assistant lecturer, Free University of Berlin; field research mainly in East Asia
- Economic advisor to the governments of Burkina Faso, Rwanda, and Kenya
- Africa chief economist at GTZ headquarters, Eschborn / Germany
- Professor for economics, politics and societies of Africa, University of Leipzig
- Honorary professor at the Department of Anthropology and African Studies, University of Mainz
- Founding director of the German Institute for Development Evaluation (DEval), Bonn.

He sits on the scientific advisory board of the German-African business association, of the Poverty Reduction, Equity and Growth Network (PEGNet) and of the Schumpeter Center for Research on Socio-Economic Change (JSEC), Friedrich Schiller University Jena.

Immo Eulenberger

Immo Eulenberger is a social anthropologist working on conflict and cooperation, energy economies, socio-ecological systems, development, evolution and future making. He is and has been working in and on Kenya, Ethiopia, South Sudan and Uganda since 2007, as lecturer and researcher with the Institute of Anthropology at the University of Leipzig and the Max-Planck Institute for Social Anthropology at Halle (Saale).

Abdoutan Harouna

Abdoutan Harouna est socio anthropologue. Il a fait ses études secondaires et universitaires à Niamey au Niger. Il est doctorant au LASDEL et à l'Université Abdou Moumouni de Niamey au Niger. Il a été en accueils en 2018 et 2019 à l'Institut d'études politiques de Bordeaux en France, dans le cadre de ses activités doctorales. Spécialiste des approches qualitatives, il a tout au long de ses 15 ans d'expérience au LASDEL, développé des compétences dans les domaines de l'enquête socio anthropologique de type qualitatif, de la facilitation, de l'administration de la recherche, ainsi que dans l'évaluation des programmes. Il a travaillé avec ODI sur plusieurs programmes de recherches. Ses centres d'intérêt en matière de recherche sont le développement local, la décentralisation, la santé, l'emploi des jeunes, et la sécurité. La radicalisation et l'insécurité ont été ces dernières axes sur lesquels il a beaucoup travaillé dans plusieurs régions du Niger (Diffa, Maradi, Tillabéri).

Monica Skaten

Monica Skaten is an Associate Professor at Western Norway University of Applied Sciences. She has researched Ghana's oil and gas industry since 2012 with particular attention to the downstream sector and politics.

Joseph Mangarella

Joseph Mangarella defended his dissertation in anthropology at Leiden University on 11 September 2019. His research interests and publications have since dealt with resource extraction, environment and sustainability, and governance in equatorial Africa. He has held teaching positions at the Université de Panthéon-Assas (Paris 2), INSEEC-Paris, and the University of Regensburg (Germany), and now works as a sustainability consultant for the World Business Council for Sustainable Development and the Czech Business Council for Sustainable Development.

Oubandoma Salissou

OUBANDOMA Salissou né le 01/01/1963 à Dogueraoua (KONNI) Niger. Après ces cours primaires à l'école primaire de Dogueraoua, il poursuit son cycle secondaire au collège d'enseignement de Konni avant de finir à l'Ecole Normale de Dosso pour sortir comme Instituteur en 1993. Après quelques années sur le terrain professionnel, il a opté pour le militantisme dans une centrale syndicale (CDTN). En 2008 il est retourné à l'Université de Niamey pour faire un Master en sociologie. De 2011 à Avril 2022, il est resté Vice président de la Haute Autorité de Lutte contre la Corruption et les Infractions Assimilées (HALCIA).

Jannik Schritt

Jannik Schritt, socio anthropologue travaillant actuellement en tant que chercheur postdoctoral dans un projet de recherche sur la translocalisation de la politique à l'Université Technique de Berlin (TU Berlin). Il a obtenu son doctorat en 2018 sur le pétrole et la politique au Niger à l'Université de Göttingen.

Il a publié sur le pétrole et la gouvernementalité, les assemblages de ressources et les manifestations liées au pétrole au Niger.

Yorbana Seign-Goura
Yorbana Seign-Goura, docteur en Sciences Sociales, a étudié dans plusieurs Universités : Université Catholique d'Afrique Centrale (Yaoundé, Cameroun), Institut des Hautes Etudes Internationales et de Développement (Genève, Suisse) et l'Université de Neuchâtel (Neuchâtel, Suisse). Il est aussi auteur de plusieurs articles sur les enjeux développementaux en Afrique dont le secteur extractif au Tchad, ainsi que du livre intitulé : Les investissements directs Chinois en Afrique. L'exemple de la China National Petroleum Corporation International Chad, Paris: L'Harmattan, 2014.

Ses centres d'intérêts sont entre autres les questions de sociologie du développement durable, la gestion des ressources naturelles, les industries extractives et les flux financiers illicites, les questions sécuritaires, commerce et développement, le management des organisations, la responsabilité sociale des entreprises et les droits humains, la migration, les relations Chine-Afrique.

Laura Smith
Laura Smith is a Lecturer in Sustainable Business at the Sustainability Research Institute in the School of Earth and Environment at the University of Leeds. Her research interests are broadly in the extractive industries and social justice, corporate responsibility and international development, with a focus on Sub-Saharan Africa.

James Van Alstine
James Van Alstine is Associate Professor in Environmental Policy at the Sustainability Research Institute in the School of Earth and Environment at the University of Leeds. His research is focused on the political ecology of resource extraction, the politics and governance of energy transitions, and opportunities for low carbon, inclusive and climate resilient development.

Geertrui Vannoppen
Geertrui Vannoppen acquired a PhD in Social and Cultural Anthropology at the KU Leuven (Belgium, 2016). Her Doctoral Research provides a spatio-temporal analysis of the Ghanaian harbor city of Sekondi-Takoradi, examining the impact of ongoing offshore oil exploitation on everyday lives and future potentialities seen and created by various actors in the city. It explores how land, property, authority, and citizenship are increasingly competed over and sought after as tradition is reinvented and identities are reshaped to make some claim

on the desired Oil City. Next to examining the role of historical documents in claims on belonging, descent, land and power, the doctoral thesis provides an analysis of a planned New Town Development in the city's periphery as a case of the changing role of traditional authorities in urban management and planning. Geertrui is now working in the private sector as a Research Consultant.

Annika Witte

Annika Witte is a social anthropologist interested in oil, risk, uncertainty and temporality as well as urban agriculture. She has conducted research in Uganda, Cameroon and Benin. For several years, she worked as a lecturer and researcher at the Institute of Social and Cultural Anthropology at the University of Göttingen. She currently works in international cooperation in Cameroon.

Opening Reflections

1

Introductory Reflections on Oil in Africa

Jannik Schritt and Annika Witte

1 Studying Oil in Africa

Over the last two decades, Africa has become increasingly important in the global competition for oil, especially between Western and Chinese oil companies. This competition was fuelled by high oil prices on the world market between 2007 and 2014 (with the exception of 2009), and political instability in the Middle East that shifted the attention to hitherto under-explored regions in Africa. Pointing to the similarities and continuities of colonial exploitation in Africa, academics and journalists have coined this competition a "new scramble for African oil" (Ghazvinian, 2007; Klare & Volman, 2006; Yates, 2012). It is through this process that many African countries have either already become new oil producing states, such as Chad, Niger and Ghana (Hicks, 2015), or discovered significant new hydrocarbon resources which are yet to be produced, such as Senegal, Liberia, Sierra Leone, Côte d'Ivoire, Togo, São Tomé and Príncipe, Uganda, Tanzania, Kenya and Mozambique (Graham & Ovadia 2019).

This development has often been analysed through old concepts from economic and political science, most notably the resource curse and the rentier state (e.g. Auty, 1993; Gelb, 1988; Karl, 1997; Ross, 2012; Yates, 1996). Developed over the last three decades, these concepts, albeit different (see below the section on 'Oil Politics and the Rentier State'), claim a number of causal relations between resource wealth and economic, social, and political transformations. Effects of particular importance include authoritarianism (Ross, 2001), economic decline (Auty, 1993), increased conflict (Humphreys, 2005), corruption (Leite & Weidmann, 1999), and gender discrimination (Ross, 2008). In particular, the resource curse concept has become so widespread in understanding oil producers that it is widely publicised outside academia. No one interested in oil production in Africa, especially in Sub-Saharan Africa, can escape confrontation with the resource curse. "Is oil in < country of concern > a blessing or a curse?" should be one of the most common questions through which oil in Africa is currently analysed. But is this simplified dichotomy truly the most interesting question to ask? Does it enable a nuanced understanding of developments in oil–producing states? While there are by now literally

 | DOI:10.1163/9789004530065_002

thousands of books, edited collections and articles on oil, nuanced qualitative ethnographic approaches to oil production are still largely underrepresented. This collection offers new insights and perspectives and, above all, critical reflections on the prevalent theories and (academic) discourses on oil in Africa. Bringing together senior and junior researchers from different disciplines with a strong focus on the social sciences and qualitative methods, this collection challenges simplified readings of the complex realities of oil politics, economics and societies on the ground through theoretical critique and qualitative-ethnographic rigour.

Most of the common approaches consider the production of new oil-induced orders from a macro-perspective based on quantitative, highly aggregated data. These data have the disadvantage of describing the relationship of only measurable and abstract entities, such as indicators for conflict, governance, or economic growth that are themselves the result of dynamic processes. Other approaches come from a historical longue durée perspective, which is based on fragmentary information and deduced from social theory. While both perspectives have brought about valuable insights into oil-induced transformations, this collection distinguishes itself by using qualitative methods and ethnographic approaches to understand how oil produces new dis/orders. It can complement the established macro-perspectives by analysing transformation processes in the making, and by capturing internal dynamics from within.

As the study of oil has been an important topic in economics and political science for several decades and an anthropology of oil has only recently begun to emerge (Behrends et al., 2011), the question arises: "What (More) Can Anthropologists Contribute to the Study of Oil?" (Behrends & Schareika, 2010). In their programmatic article, Behrends and Schareika (2010, p. 86) call for more ethnographies of oil production, arguing that "an anthropological study of oil should not only take up and make use of frameworks set by political economy, but use its particular theoretical and methodological strengths to develop new perspectives in this increasingly important field." This illustrates three important points for any anthropological study on oil: firstly, the concepts related to oil that have been well established by political science and economics should not be ignored. Secondly, empirical data should be gathered using qualitative and ethnographic methodology. Third, based on the data, a critical engagement with and advancement of theories on oil should be pursued.

Following this call, the contributions of this collection study oil-induced transformations in African oil states at the actual sites of socio-political interactions. Although taking knowledge from established political economy concepts such as the resource curse, Dutch Disease or the rentier state, the papers presented here do not, to paraphrase Gilberthorpe and Rajak (2017, p. 3), only fill the gaps of the resource curse with social details but rather they invite us to adapt the approach. The papers in this collection use ethnographic methods for theoretical advancement, and stand in conversation with the established concepts of political science and economics to engage in interdisciplinary theory building. To further interdisciplinary engagement, the collection contains contributions from social anthropology, sociology, economics, history and political science.

One central claim of this collection is that the problems known as the "oil curse" (Ross, 2012)—authoritarianism, corruption, conflict, poverty, gender inequality—are always context-specific. So far, most research on oil has only been able to look at the sociopolitical effects of oil several years or even decades after the start of production. Therefore, we contend, it has been difficult for those researchers to distinguish between oil-induced effects and other causes of social, political and economic change. That is, by looking retrospectively at oil-induced change without having a clear understanding of society and politics in those states prior to oil, scholars may be led to see oil everywhere. In other words, all kinds of social and political ills such as authoritarianism, corruption, conflict, poverty, or gender inequality may then be constructed as mono-causally connected to oil production without considering context-specific factors. Along with the rentier state perspective, Schubert (2016), for example, proposes that the new oil wealth is the cause of a "culture of immediatism" in post-war Angola. One of his main examples for such a culture of rent-seeking, complicity and co-optation is the relationships of young girls with rich and old "sugar daddies". But is this not a near universal phenomena in Africa (and beyond)? At least in Niger, it is one of the main grievances of young men unable to find a partner to marry even before oil production had started. In this sense, Joe Mangarella shows in his chapter on oil production in Gabon that what is considered a "rentier mentality" does indeed often preexist the oil production in some way. We therefore contend that the sociopolitical problems ascribed to oil by the dominant resource curse framework "should be investigated in detail against the background of each new situation—something that necessitates the use of qualitative methods" (Olivier de Sardan & Piccoli, 2018, pp. 3–4). In other words, by conducting a qualitative-ethnographic analysis of African oil states, the papers in this collection represent "the revenge of contexts" (Olivier de Sardan, 2021) that challenge mono-causal explanations and that have been underestimated or even ignored in the dominant political economy framework. In order to distinguish between pre-oil and post-oil dynamics, contextually thick qualitative-ethnographic descriptions have to be temporally situated. Then we might see that oil, instead of following a clear-cut resource curse scenario, instead appears as a "catalyst," "vehicle" or "conduit" that accelerates pre-existing dynamics slowly transforming the sociopolitical configuration in which it operates (Schritt, 2018; Anthias, 2018a, b; Nwajiaku, 2005; Watts, 2004).

2 Oil Studies Beyond the Resource Curse

True to its classic emphasis on assuming a holistic perspective, social anthropology and ethnographic approaches have moved beyond the narrow focus on oil as a substance that is converted into money. Early ethnographies of oil mostly focused on conflicts and state formation spurred by oil production (Apter, 2005; Coronil, 1997), as well as resistance to multinational oil corporations' attempts at capital accumulation and environmental destruction (Sawyer, 2004; Turner, 2004). These by-now-classic ethnographies of oil seek to understand its historical situatedness instead of seeing only pre-determined oil-driven trajectories (see also Bierschenk, 1984). In reviewing anthropological studies of oil, Reyna and Behrends (2011) have therefore argued that although these studies confirm in a way the findings of the resource curse and rentier state about violent oil realities, the authors insist that the effects of oil rents on politics and society must be analysed in the context of pre-existing patterns of domination. Moreover, all these works generally show that oil is significant not only for its monetary power, but also for its sociopolitical framing in terms of imaginaries, cultural production or identity politics. In looking at anthropological works, Behrends and Schareika (2010) have therefore suggested that "signification" as a concept marks a distinctively anthropological approach to the study of oil production.

More recent anthropological work then moved beyond the focus of the nation state and produced "global ethnographies" (Burawoy et al., 2000) to account for the influence of transnational corporations, markets and supply-chains in the making of citizenship, global inequality and capitalist formations (Appel, 2012a; Ferguson, 2005; Shever, 2012; Yessenova, 2012; Adunbi, 2015). In a review of oil and anthropology, Rogers (2015) points to materiality and temporality as newly emerging dimensions in studying oil (see also Franquesa, 2019).

Ferry and Limbert (2008), for example, theorise the temporal aspects of resource-making and resource-claiming, arguing that questions around resource discovery and its supposed ends "frame the past, present and future in certain ways; they propose or preclude certain kinds of time reckoning; they inscribe teleologies; and they are imbued with affects of time, such as nostalgia, hope, dread, and spontaneity" (Ferry & Limbert, 2008, p. 4). In this vein, Limbert (2010) shows how the end of oil was anticipated in Oman and how oil thus became visible again after years of unquestioned prosperity. Similarly, Fricke (2017) illustrates how the uncertain future of oil in Gabon conjures up diverse histories, temporalities and affects. Weszkalnys (2011; 2014; 2016) for São Tomé and Príncipe has also pointed to the importance of temporality by analysing how the expectation of oil production spurred various anticipatory practices and economies of expectation. It is also important to understand that the transition from pre-oil to production is not a sudden rupture but a transition phase that can be short or that can last for long; a phase of (infrastructural) preparations and anticipation. This phase of "not-yet-ness" is at times greatly influenced by a narrative that constructs oil as a risk to the country, based on the mono-causal explanation of the resource curse (Witte, 2018). Beneath this temporality of the pre-, the not-yet, the production and post-production phase, resource extraction is in fact a "complex mesh of multiple temporalities: durations, rhythms and cycles - with different velocities, intensities and extensions" that actors try to manipulate in line with their own strategic interests (D'Angelo & Pijpers, 2018). Manipulation of extraction temporalities becomes apparent in Monica Skaten's contribution to this volume, in which the temporality of fuel production in Ghana is tied to the election cycle. In addition to "producing temporal narratives that support or contest such organization," "extracting minerals or combustible substances means organizing temporal levels, speed and rhythms of production" (D'Angelo & Pijpers, 2018). Leonard's analysis of oil production in Chad (2016) shows that while the transnational oil industry worked at high-speed in developing its facilities and production, the Chadian government institutions could not catch up with this speed in managing the revenues. For her, this "two-speed problem" was at the heart of the failure of the World Bank-funded consortium. However, going beyond analyses that see the cause of this problem as low technical capacity in a "weak" state, Leonard shows that the high velocity was a deliberate effort to create a kind of temporal disentanglement from the residents of the oil region.

Focusing on disentanglement from a spatial and infrastructural perspective, Appel's book The Licit Life of Capitalism (2019) uses the case study of Equatorial Guinea to show how the oil industry is continuously working to create the impression of being "offshore" i.e., operating in a detached manner that is untainted by the local context, despite the industry being not only present onshore but also deeply entangled with the state. She looks at the work of abstraction, decontextualisation and standardisation of capitalism and thereby also offers a counterbalance to the resource curse theory that focusses more on the role of the producing states rather than that of the oil industry. Appel (2019) shows how (global) inequalities that become evident in analysis of oil projects are not deepened by the oil industry or global capitalism, but rather are constitutive of it. Appel's work moves beyond the resource curse framework to develop a new line of thinking which builds on Science and Technology Studies (STS) and the "material turn" more broadly (Appel et al., 2015, Richardson & Weszkalnys, 2014). Mitchell (2011, p. 5) was one of the first to prominently articulate the idea that "politics are engineered out of the flow of energy". The idea serves a heuristic purpose to look at forms of agency and control that are linked to processes of extraction, transportation, distribution and consumption of oil, and thus to overcome the narrow focus of economic and political science studies on oil rents. Oil studies following this lead thus seek to account for forms of agency and control contained in the materiality of the resources, and the technological as well as sociopolitical infrastructures surrounding oil production, be it in relation to capital accumulation (Appel, 2012a), structural violence (Appel, 2012b; Murrey, 2015), corporate social technologies (Rogers, 2012), (in)visibility of infrastructural failures (Landa, 2016), standardisation processes (Barry, 2006), or transparency and ethics (Barry, 2013).[1]

The dimensions of rents, significations, temporality, and materiality are closely interrelated, and many of the cited studies have focused on more than one of these dimensions simultaneously. In combining the various dimensions of oil, anthropologists and other social scientists have pointed to the multiplicity and heterogeneity of its manifestations by speaking, for example, of an "oil assemblage" (Appel et al., 2015; Mitchell, 2011; Richardson & Weszkalnys, 2014; Schritt, 2016; Watts, 2012).

Building on these insights, the collection advances an issue-centred approach for studying oil qualitatively and ethnographically in Africa, instead of an approach focused on pre-defined fields of social order, such as "the state," "the industry," or "the community." An issue-centred approach builds on a long tradition in anthropology, especially the Manchester School of Max Gluckman and his followers, of focusing on conflicts, social situations and events to study

1 Another focus has been on the consumer societies in the West and how capital accumulation based on the burning of fossil fuels trickled down into Western culture in terms of mobility, individualism and nuclear family life and liberalism (Huber, 2013; Strauss et al., 2013). By looking at the effects oil has on consumer societies, these studies made use of Foucauldian concepts of neoliberalism, biopower and governmentality in pointing to the production of new subjectivities in an oil-age (Boyer, 2011, 2014; Loloum et al., 2021). However, (Foucauldian) concepts developed to analyse Western societies are not easily translatable to African contexts in which the tools and technologies (like statistics, laws, rules, pictures and plans) designed to shape or reshape human life conditions to navigate their behaviour into calculable and precise ways are less developed and less widely deployed. Rather, a transnational governmentality that is at play in Africa largely shows frictions (Schritt, 2013).

social processes and change (Gluckman, 1958; van Velsen, 1967; Burawoy, 1998; Schritt, 2019).

Three aspects are central to an issue-centred approach to oil. Firstly, it is often very difficult for researchers to gain the kinds of access needed to undertake long-term ethnographic fieldwork in the oil industry, in sites such as the oil companies, refineries, the town hall, rebel groups, or worker enclaves. Therefore, the classic ethnographic approach to researching a social entity does not hold much promise in this case. However, if access to the oil industry and government institutions is possible, as seen in Monica Skaten's contribution, such an approach, especially if added to still-dominant approaches of "studying down," is a highly welcome addition to "studying up" or "studying through" (Nader, 1969), and can yield greater insights into the dynamics of oil. Moreover, an issue-centred approach, as any ethnographic approach, should use a triangulation of observations, interviews and documents. This becomes even more important as several actors in the oil assemblage produce oil-related documents themselves, such as the industry, the governments, the civil society and the media.

Secondly, issue-centred research allows researchers to focus on "mining encounters" at the intersection of (all) the relevant actors or actor groups with "different agendas, worldviews and aims within the context of mining operations" (Pijpers & Eriksen, 2018, p. 2). While oil companies and particularly extractive communities have been the focus of many ethnographies on oil and mining, the great variety of actors that pursue their own interests—such as NGO s, governments, financial institutions, churches, law firms and also researchers—create a complex social field with a variety of encounters that Nicholas Bainton and John Owen (2019) call "zones of entanglement." For example, the expropriation and compensation of farm land for the construction of the oil infrastructure generally involves not only the affected farmers and their community, but also multiple actors: the companies that construct the infrastructure; the central state that provides the legal framework for the expropriation and is responsible for measuring and compensating the land; the local state and administrative authorities that provide land titles; lawyers who plead the farmers' case; as well as civil society activists and journalists who make the cases public and political. In other words, different actors or actor groups develop a common position around a particular oil-related issue. It is especially the negotiation and contestation of such issues at stake that produce promising insights into oil-induced transformation processes. A similar argument was made some time ago for an actor-centred approach to development (Long, 1989; Long & Van der Ploeg, 1989; Elwert & Bierschenk, 1988; Bierschenk, 1988; Olivier de Sardan, 1988, 2005) .

Thirdly, the involvement, negotiation and contestation of various "strategic groups" (Elwert & Bierschenk, 1988; Bierschenk, 1988) allows the tracing of their entanglements in global regimes of power or what has been called the global "oil complex" (Watts, 2004) or "oil assemblage" (Watts, 2012). This approach avoids local or national container models that dominate the resource curse framework, especially the latest version which sees "good governance" as the solution to counter the resource curse (see the next section).

The structure of this collection is guided by the well-known concepts and representations of oil in order to clearly illustrate and situate the critical engagement offered by the contributions. The collection addresses three main themes: (a) rentier politics embedded in wider political dynamics, (b) dis/entanglement work between the transnational oil industry and the various social and political forces in the host country, and (c) oil-spurred rural-urban transformations in extractive communities.

Following this introduction, Economist Helmut Asche's discussion of structural policies in oil-rich countries makes us dig deeper into the complexities of the resource curse, rural-urban transformations, and dis/entanglement work—the opposing practices of entanglement and disentanglement of the transnational oil industry with the social, political and economic context of the host country that are simultaneously at work and aimed at profiting from the oil (Schritt & Witte, 2018, p. 431). Asche analyses the spillover effects of oil production that feed into the Dutch Disease, such as environmental degradation that forces farmers and fisherpeople to abandon occupations, and hence also abandon the primary sector. By analysing this and other complex economic effects, Asche shows that there is no blueprint for successful control of all the effects of resource wealth, and refutes any analysis that blames "failure" in resource-rich states solely on bad governance. He instead considers the complex and at times contradictory actions and effects present in resource producers, illustrating that an economics lens has as much to offer to ethnographic research as vice versa, for understanding dynamics in oil-rich countries.

3 Part 1 Oil Politics and the Rentier State

Most early scholars working on oil, especially when discussing Africa, argued that oil production and its revenues had the potential to reduce the continent's dependency on oil imports, enable infrastructural development, and allow the African economy in general to thrive (Baker, 1977; for a review on oil in Nigeria see Genova & Falola, 2003). However, in his seminal work on Iran, and in arguably an early theory from the Global South *avant la lettre*, Mahdavy

(1970) asked why oil production in the Middle East had not spurred capitalist development in line with European experiences.[2] To answer the question, Mahdavy and others after him developed the "rentier state theory". In this theory, based on classical economists such as Adam Smith and David Ricardo, "rent" is external, unearned and unproductive income for the state's government which has adverse effects on the economy and on politics by triggering the development of a minute, elite rentier class, rather than a broad, productive working class that capitalist development had created in European countries (see also Beblawi & Luciani, 1987; Beck, 1993). Although not uncontested, the causal mechanisms in a "rentier state" function roughly as follows (Yates, 1996): External oil revenues establish a "rentier mentality" or a "something for nothing" reward system for state actors, in which the only game left in town is the elites' greed to pocket as much of the oil rent as possible. The rentier mentality leads to corruption, institutional inefficiency, and an overall decline in state legitimacy, while state power is consolidated through the distribution of the oil rent to buy political loyalty. Moreover, petroleum wealth traded in US dollars reduces the foreign exchange rate, thereby making export-oriented agriculture and manufacturing internationally less competitive and thus unprofitable—a mechanism referred to as Dutch Disease. The Dutch Disease also includes the isolation of the mineral and energy resource sector (oil enclave) and negative spillovers to other sectors (see Asche in this volume). This mechanism would trigger underemployment (especially of women, who often occupy jobs in the declining manufacturing sector), poverty, rising (gender) inequality, and increased grievances, which together with greed, corruption, and institutional deficiency lead to increased conflicts.

After the predominance of the theory-driven rentier state framework formulated on single case studies, the explicitly comparative and method-driven resource curse thesis was developed, which was mostly based on econometric regression analysis by (mainstream) economists and political scientists. It discovered empirical correlations between oil wealth and all kinds of economic, political and societal "ills".[3] In explaining and "moralising" these correlations as "curse," these thinkers partly drew on causal mechanisms developed by the rentier state theory. Ross (2001, 2009), for example, explains authoritarian

2 We are grateful to Thomas Bierschenk in pointing out the early achievements of the rentier state theory as a theory from the Global South *avant la lettre* and its Marxist-inspired background.

3 Once again, we thank Thomas Bierschenk for pointing out the differences between the rentier state theory and the resource curse thesis, with the former being a theory-driven case study approach and the latter a method-driven and moralising endeavour.

tendencies in oil-rich countries mainly through the "rentier effect," "which suggests that resource-rich governments use low tax rates and patronage to dampen democratic pressures" (2001, p. 325). Others made use of an economic notion of "greed" to explain an increase of conflicts and rebellion in resource-rich countries (Collier, 2000). However, while the rentier state theory and the resource curse thesis are sometimes used interchangeably, they can also contradict each other. While the resource curse, for example, predicts that the commencement of oil extraction leads to violent conflict due to "greedy rebels" and a "weak state," the rentier state theory predicts a "rentier peace" through the purchase of political legitimacy, and the co-optation or repression of political opponents (Basedau & Lay, 2009).

Moreover, there are now contrary assertions to almost all the causal relations predicted by these concepts. Firstly, Brunnschweiler and Bulte (2008) argued that civil war created dependence on primary sector exports (but not vice versa), and that resource abundance was associated with a reduced probability of the onset of war. Secondly, in a revised version of his 2001 article on oil-based authoritarianism, Ross (2009) admitted that there was little empirical support for the causal mechanisms between resource wealth and authoritarianism he had suggested. Only the rentier effect mattered, he claimed. Moreover, in another quantitative study, Haber and Menaldo (2011) criticised the short-term focus of a large body of scholarship on the link between resource wealth and authoritarianism, and concluded that there was no such link. In fact, the authors found that oil had been a "blessing" for democratic development in many cases. Similarly, Dunning (2008) uses a game theory perspective to argue that natural resource wealth and democratic political regimes may very well go hand-in-hand. Thirdly, Cavalcanti, Mohaddes and Raissi (2011), as well as Leong and Mohaddes (2011), argued that it was not resource abundance but the trade volatility of resources that has driven negative growth effects. Finally, scholars have also suggested the opposite causal mechanism between oil and corruption, namely that the pre-existing quality of institutions is the underlying cause for any negative effects of oil to materialise, rather than oil itself creating these deficient institutions (Humphreys, Sachs & Stiglitz, 2007). These authors argue that the resource curse can be overcome by mechanisms of good governance, particularly transparency and institution building.

As such, a new paradigm seems to be emerging in political science and economics in which "governance" has become the most important factor in explaining the occurrence of the resource curse, with "good governance" becoming the solution to turn the "curse" into a "blessing" (for a review see Heinrich and Pleines (2012) who speak of "resource challenges"). Such a neoliberal reformulation of the resource curse shifts the blame away from market failures to the poor performance or bad governance of governments in the Global South, and thereby confines resource curse research to national container models. Moreover, the conflicting results of the new resource curse studies reveal that even minor changes in data selection, process and design of econometric regression analysis may lead to huge differences in outcome. A recent experimental study on quantitative methods revealed that among 73 research teams who independently conducted studies on the same hypothesis with identical starting data, excessive variation of outcomes appeared (Breznau et al., 2021). The results of this important study once more underline the need for context-sensitive qualitative-ethnographic research.

Looking at the context of oil in Africa, the literature on African politics and the state broadly agrees that many factors identified in resource curse literature as transformations stemming from oil production—authoritarianism, corruption, institutional deficiency, violent conflict, (gender) inequality—are rather general features of politics in Africa (Bayart, 1989; Chabal & Daloz, 1999; Médard, 1982). These authors share an understanding of African politics as characterised by inefficient institutions, corruption, and authoritarianism. These scholars have sought to explain common aspects of African states by using the neopatrimonial state model (Eisenstadt, 1973; Médard, 1982). The notion of neopatrimonialism draws explicitly on Weber's ideal types of authority and thereby portrays African politics as a deviation from idealised modern Western democracies. Compared to Western states, the literature of neopatrimonialism often describes African statehood as "failed" or "weak". The prime reason for the difference in conceptions of governance is typically understood as lying inside a somewhat opaque notion of "African culture" (for a critical analysis of neopatrimonialism, see e.g., Hauck et al., 2013; Olivier de Sardan, 2014; Mkandawire, 2015).

Acknowledging these competing narratives to explain African oil states, the central task for an ethnography of oil is to disentangle the historically sedimented patterns of African politics and the state, and the oil-induced transformations that occur. Moreover, as ethnography is the ideal methodology with the flexibility to deal with the informal and the unexpected, ethnographic methods enable researchers to point to the heterogeneity, fragmentation, and multiple administrative layers within African (oil) states, and to illuminate the discrepancy between the ways in which state institutions, oil managers, politicians, and bureaucrats represent the (oil) state, and how they actually "do" it (Bierschenk & Olivier de Sardan, 2019).

Ethnographies of oil politics might ask: What are the dynamics and contestations at the intersection of state administration, oil industry, local politics and civil society? Who are the new actors and structures that emerge within these configurations and how are they related to the structures that pre-exist oil production? What are the significations of oil that are developed and negotiated by and between various strategic groups in the global oil assemblage? What are the contentious politics around the issue of oil production, refinement, distribution and consumption (i.e., lawsuits, campaigning, mediatisation, demonstrations, protests, riots, rebellion)? Focusing on these and other questions, ethnographies of oil have to distinguish between pre-existing and oil-induced dynamics, and also highlight the context specifics that challenge the monocausal narrative of the resource curse thesis, even when the narrative is very popular in the research setting (Weszkalnys, 2011; Witte, 2017; Schritt, 2020).

The collection's contributions on this theme highlight the hitherto-neglected complexities of pre- and post-oil political dynamics. While the resource curse and rentier state theories are largely blind to micro-political dynamics, the historical ethnography contribution from Joe Mangarella asks if the rentier state theory is applicable to local spaces in long-standing oil producer Gabon. Tracing the development of a rentier mentality through its historical processual development, Mangarella argues for a nuanced understanding of the rentier state theory by distinguishing a pre-oil rentier mentality and a post-oil rentier mentality. He argues that a rentier mentality preexisted oil production which intensified with the influx of oil money. Moreover, he asks if the situational complexities could not better be explained by "hybrid governance" approaches, rather than with rentier state theory. As such, the contribution highlights the importance of the political context and the nature and legitimacy of the existing state in which oil production takes place.

The contribution from anthropologist Immo Eulenberger analyses the 2012 discovery and development of oil deposits in Turkana, Kenya, against the backdrop of countrywide processes such as "devolution" (decentralisation), the rise of a new middle class, and the repercussions of widespread corruption. Eulenberger points to the importance of pre-existing patterns and dynamics, arguing that oil is not a total game changer but can open a new arena for contestation. Eulenberger shows that predictions of conflict based on what happened in other nation-states, for example in South Sudan, do not hold true as such for Turkana. While land conflicts or cases of land grabbing are on the rise, they cannot be attributed to oil alone. Instead they follow from pre-existing developments such as a stark population increase, corrupt practices, or the concentrated infrastructural development funded by the development aid sector. The significance that Turkana people give these land conflicts is not uniform and does not follow common descriptions by media and civil society of land grabbing, but rather builds on their own understanding of fairness, i.e. fair compensation for land.

In a similar thematic terrain to Eulenberger's focus on devolution, Abdoutan Harouna's contribution concerning emerging oil state Niger illustrates how strategic groups in Zinder formed around the oil windfall in Niger's decentralisation efforts, and how politicians, civil society and other pressure groups in the region deployed strategies to take part in the resource wealth. Harouna's social anthropology perspective combines qualitative interviews with observations to show how the capture of oil rent is not simply an individual profit-maximisation strategy, but that it inserts itself in pre-existing patterns—in this case, regional and political logics of redistribution. Thus, oil catalyses dynamics in local and regional politics, not as sole cause, but as one opportunity to be seized in the struggle for more autonomy.

4 Part 2 Oil Industries and the Enclave Economy

As various social scientists have shown, in order to maximise profits, transnational oil companies seek a social, juridical, political, economic and spatial disembedding from the surroundings in which they are deeply entangled (Appel, 2012; Donner, 2011; Ferguson, 2005; Leonard, 2016; Yessenova, 2012; Zalik, 2009; Reed, 2009). One result of the industry's disentanglement is the "enclave economy" of oil production—identified as a major cause of economic decline in the resource curse thesis (Auty, 1993).[4] As Leonard (2016) has shown a two-speed problem for the oil production in Chad, so has Blundo (2011) identified a "two-speed bureaucracy" in the case of Forest Services in Niger and Senegal. In Chad, the oil industry out-paced the state enabling it to produce the oil in a disentangled way or, put differently, in an enclave. For Niger and Senegal, Blundo describes how the speed difference created by interventions of development projects led to bureaucratic enclaves or "bureaucratic islands of effectiveness." Thus both these authors show the possibility of creating enclaves through temporality or speed—not only through infrastructure or materiality. Disentanglement is also promoted by neoclassical economics that suggests "cutting" existing production linkages in Africa because of their inefficiency and lack of competitiveness in global markets, as they would push

4 From a historical perspective, it has been argued—against the resource curse thesis that sees the enclave economy as an effect of oil production—that the African economy in general had already inherited an enclave character from colonialism, which was designed to exploit the colonies for the development of the Empire (Mhone, 2001). From this perspective, these (post)colonial enclaves are seen as the root cause of African "underemployment" and "underdevelopment" (Mhone, 2001).

up the price of petroleum products, thereby impeding growth by burdening domestic markets with additional costs (World Bank Group, 2011, pp. 33–39).

Recently, and in contrast to transnational oil companies and neoliberal policy recommendations, "petrodevelopmental states" (Ovadia, 2016b) build on entanglement work to achieve capitalist development, especially with so-called "local content" initiatives (Ovadia, 2016a). These initiatives aim to promote economic linkages between the national economy and the foreign oil industry in order to overcome the resource curse. As a result, the oil industry is never able to fully succeed in its attempts at disentanglement: on the one hand the industry is deeply enmeshed in the capitalist logic of its origin and the final destination of its capital flows, where it is accountable to shareholders, investors, creditors and consumers; on the other hand it inevitably becomes entangled with heterogeneous social, cultural, political and economic forces in the environments in which it operates. In this sense, entanglement and disentanglement are opposing strategies and processes operating simultaneously. Consequently, oil companies walk a fine line between allowing linkages and fostering local economic development, while simultaneously appearing to investors as producing oil in disembedded enclaves untainted by the politics of host countries (Schritt & Witte, 2018). Recently, some oil companies have also embraced national content initiatives, first demanded by the producing states, as part of their "corporate social responsibility" (CSR) programme (Witte, 2018).

The practice of CSR, which typically includes engagement in local development programs, communication with local authorities, and training and education campaigns for the local population, is an important aspect of dis/entanglement work. Similar to older forms of corporate philanthropy, CSR's "gift culture" with its donations and distributions of goods to the local population has a paternalistic undertone (Rajak, 2011; Reed, 2009; Shever, 2010). Companies use CSR to showcase responsibility for their social and environmental impacts and to manage their relations with society (Blowfield & Frynas, 2005). As distinct from older forms of corporate philanthropy, CSR programmes nowadays integrate sustainability and social welfare as forms of profit maximisation into the capitalist system (Porter & Kramer, 2002). This flexibility of CSR has been described by Dolan and Rajak (2016, p. 5) as having a "chameleon-like capacity" to include new ideas in line with political-economic and social currents. While CSR practices create linkages with local authorities and neighbouring populations, critics argue that they are intended to create a stable and safe business environment, thereby disempowering local populations and delegitimising their resistance (Barnes, 2005; Kemedi, 2003). Critics also argue CSR is an attempt at "green washing" companies to present a positive image to shareholders and consumers for profit-maximisation only

(Fleshman, 2002). Others have analysed CSR in line with a new current of "expectation management" that shifts the blame for oil's detrimental effects away from both older critiques of market failures and newer forms of institutional deficiencies, towards seemingly exaggerated expectations of extractive communities (Weszkalnys, 2016, pp. 137–141).

Acknowledging the simultaneity of the dis/entanglement work[5] offers a different perspective on controversies around expectations between various strategic groups that emerge around the oil infrastructure at all levels (Nakayi & Witte, 2019; Schritt & Witte, 2018, Schritt, 2018). It is in these controversies and contested events that we can trace scale-making projects and their frictions in particular contexts (Tsing, 2000). Skaten (2017), for example, has outlined the politicisation of petroleum products and the negotiable nature of infrastructure and technology development in Ghana's everyday "politics of petrol." She argues that the trade, distribution and price of petroleum products in Ghana facilitated and shaped political and economic reciprocity between the government, the publics and profitable economic networks.

Ethnographers are well placed to study the oil industry's dis/entanglement work through its relations with its workers: How are employer-employee relations negotiated? What kind of pressure tools do the oil workers invent vis-à-vis the oil companies? What characterises the interactions and processes of boundary-making between workers and NGO actors, workers and oil company representatives, Africans and Euro-American or Chinese expatriates? Focusing on these and other questions, an ethnography of oil is able to carve out the dis/entanglement work between transnational oil companies and the various forces in the host countries.

The collection's contributions on this theme discuss how dis/entanglement work plays out in the highly politicised downstream oil and gas industry in Ghana, between the local and (inter-)national stakeholders in the Chadian oil arena, and in the CSR initiatives of a young oil production company in Uganda.

In her comparison of the Tema oil refinery and the Atuabo gas processing plant as two of Ghana's key energy infrastructure projects, African studies scholar Monica Skaten's contribution examines how markets, political considerations and the availability of infrastructure and technology are shaping the dis/entanglement of the petro-infrastructure. Building on ethnographic work among the staff of Ghana's midstream oil and gas industry, Skaten shows how the midstream industry is in various ways both entangled and disentangled

5 Instead of making disentanglement and entanglement an "either/or" question—as most of the cited literature does—we take a 'both/and" perspective, and therefore speak of "dis/entanglement."

with national politics and the national and international upstream oil industry. While the refinery on the one hand is a symbol of national pride, it does not refine the national crude. The gas processing plant on the other hand is very entangled with the national oil production, while its management is more in Chinese hands than Ghanaian ones. Pondering these different dis/entanglements, Skaten challenges the reader to think through the categorisation of upstream-midstream-downstream and the role these categories play in the dis/entanglement work of the oil industry.

The contribution from sociologist Yorbana Seign-Goura analyses dynamics in the Chadian oil arena between oil companies and oil communities relating to participation in the oil riches. Comparing various corporate social responsibility initiatives in Chad, Seign-Goura shows the ambivalent character of the oil industry's dis/entanglement work: While on the one hand CSR initiatives, that are a form of entanglement of the industry in the local setting, aim to benefit the most marginalised populations, on the other hand, they seem to reproduce this very marginalisation and can be understood as a disentanglement—as a way for the oil industry to cut any relations outside the clearly defined scope they set forth with their CSR. CSR campaigns are thus not counter-balances to the effects of oil production, but rather give superficial legitimacy to the operations of the oil industry.

The chapter from Laura Smith and James van Alstine explores the CSR initiatives of oil company Tullow Oil in Uganda as a form of dis/entanglement. It relates to the CSR programme's significant shift from philanthropic gestures in its wildcatter days towards strategic CSR as a new oil producer, reflecting Tullow's growth and growing entanglement in the international financial market. While the early CSR initiatives aimed to entangle the company with the local communities, the later strategy shift was designed to disentangle from these very communities. The changes within the company, in combination with a changing international market less favourable to oil production, necessitated a disentanglement that was locally resented. The authors conclude that CSR initiatives driven by international standards and demands overlook the simple fact that the logics of obligation and reciprocity of the giver might differ from those of the receiver - especially in an intercultural context. This contribution may offer an explanation for the contradiction raised by Seign-Goura's contribution: leaving good intentions aside, CSR is not oriented by the needs, demands or social logics of the communities it is meant to benefit, but rather by the needs and logics of the company and market demands. There remains a gap between the representation of CSR and the realities on the ground. This gap is a vital space where local actors formulate their demands of reciprocity, and respect or reject the dis/entanglement efforts.

5 Part 3 Oil Communities and Rural-Urban Transformations

According to the resource curse, Dutch Disease and rentier state framework, the massive influx of oil money traded in US dollars makes imports relatively cheaper, resulting in increasing import dependency. This import dependency leads to an increase in the urban service sector and a divestment from export-oriented agriculture into construction activities, and consequently a decline in rural standards of living, leading to a widening rural-urban divide with more and more rural people migrating to urban centres (The Economist, 1977; Yates, 2012, p. 87). Focusing on the life history of a Nigerian worker who turned from peasant to worker, Lubeck (1989), for example, illustrates how the petroleum boom spurred processes of urban proletarianisation. Similarly, Berry (1984) in her article *Oil and the Disappearing Peasantry* describes how oil production in Nigeria led to the work migration of cocoa farmers from agriculture into trade, reinforcing the importance of education and politics as a means to wealth and power. Hoinathy (2013) shows how the influx of oil workers, service providers and sex workers into the extraction zone resulted in a monetisation of social relations, such as marriage patterns (see also Behrends & Hoinathy, 2017). Seign-Goura (2017) shows how, after a decade of oil exploration, Chadian oil communities shifted their perception of oil as a gift from God, to it being the devil and the embodiment of the resource curse theory.

Also, in Uganda the presence of the oil industry during the exploration phase led to visible changes and remodelling of how people anticipated the future that was to come: People expected employment and business opportunities as well as infrastructural improvements. The hopeful expectations were counteracted by voices that warned about grave cultural and social changes with a loss of morality and increasing intercultural marriages (Witte, 2018). In the oil region, rumours and gossip about the oil workers circulated that represented them as foreign forces that came to steal local women, destroy local shrines and even ritually murder children (Witte, 2021). These rumours and gossip can be seen as risk narratives exchanged in an environment of uncertainty in a phase of not-yet-ness of Uganda's oil. They are part of what has been called "resource-making" (Ferry & Limbert, 2008, p. 4), i.e., the social and political processes through which crude oil is turned into the precious resource. Such rumours are not specific to Uganda alone: In Chad, Reyna (2011) noticed stories that depicted Exxon oil workers as "lionmen" preying on people in the Doba basin. Reyna analysed these stories as forms of resistance against imperial domination by comparing them to the old English epic of the Beowulf. As such, these stories speak of the fear and distrust caused by the arrival of the oil industry (Reyna, 2011).

However, it is not only the disappearing countryside that has become a focus for ethnographic scrutiny, but also the urbanisation processes. With his focus on petro-landscapes, petrolic-cityscapes and petro-governmentality, Watts, in his various works (2004, 2008, 2012) provides a basis to examine oil and urban forms. In focusing on the everyday realities of people living in the extraction zones, Reed (2009) explores exclusion, degradation, and violence as an inextricable part of petro-capitalism in Angola. Petro-capitalism in Angola has not only produced pockets of spectacular urbanity and astronomically high living expenses in the capital Luanda; it does so amidst rampant inequality and poverty. This is also an aspect of Schubert's (2017) ethnography of Luanda that illustrates how "New Angola" is "an essentially urban, upwardly mobile, and aspirational project" that glosses over the reality of the majority of Angolans who do not partake in the ostentatious oil wealth.

Looking at oil-related urbanisation processes ranging from a growing real estate sector, increased traffic, changing housing patterns, altered livelihoods, and a growing employment sector in Ghana's new oil-city Sekondi-Takoradi, Vannoppen (2016) shows how various actors imagined different futures for the city and its periphery, as well as for themselves and their communities. In the temporal space of the not-yet, these anticipations sparked all kinds of speculative practices that influenced new spatial urban developments and transformed socio-political institutions. The rural and urban are thus not isolated dichotomies, but are characterised by mutual flows and fluidity. Oil infrastructure such as wells and refineries are often built outside urban centres at ports or in peri-urban or even rural areas close to where the oil is found. They transform these landscapes and create connections to the urban centres through electricity grids, roads, storage and housing facilities. The longstanding flow of labour to the big urban centres is now met by a counterflow of labour, even highly skilled workers, to the rural areas. Remote areas see an influx of young men and women looking for opportunities in and around the oil industry. Casual work can be found on the increasing number of construction sites, in hotels and restaurants. Other petty activities revolve around the entertainment of truckers and other oil-related newcomers. Understanding the rural and urban as interconnected thus offers a tool to study the rural-urban interface as a network of flows of food, money, leadership, ideas, people, etc. (Lynch, 2008). Using the lens of logistics that link the onshore and the offshore, Chalfin (2019) speaks of "terraqueous urbanism" to highlight the built and interconnected environment of Ghana's oil-city Takoradi. Finally, oil extraction sites that are disconnected from their immediate surroundings by fences and military guards, are at the same time connected with distant places in Africa and beyond (USA, Europe, China) through pipelines, specific means of transport and the conversion of crude oil into money and new products (Schritt & Behrends, 2018).

Ethnographies of rural-urban transformation analyse, for example, the particular and quite different forms of dis/connection between places on a global scale in relation to the infrastructure, significations and economic models that bring forth these very dis/connections (Schritt & Behrends, 2018). More specific questions that ethnographies can address are: How does oil production, refining, distribution and consumption spur new economic activities in rural-urban interfaces? How does oil-based income affect basic social institutions like marriage, family and education in rural and urban areas? How are significations, expectations and uncertainties of oil related to all kinds of anticipatory, future-oriented and speculative practices? How are contestations against or economic activities around oil production in rural places related to contestations and management of oil in urban places? Focusing on such questions, ethnographies of oil can carve out how oil induces transformations at the rural-urban interface.

The collection's contributions on this theme highlight the ambivalence and complexities of infrastructural development generating new rural-urban interfaces, enabling mutual flows but also producing new conflicts. The contribution from social anthropologist Geertrui Vannoppen analyses the anticipatory practices of re-imagining and planning Ghana's oil city Sekondi-Takoradi that emerged when the country entered the oil age in 2012. These future imaginations included speculative practices of real estate development that tied in local and national elites, global capital and the common people in a peri-urban community. Vannoppen makes clear how infrastructural developments are not just blueprints from elsewhere copied to the African continent, but they also reflect local imaginaries of the "urban" and the "modern." Vannoppen also highlights the very different trajectories of such developments in different African countries, offering a cautionary tale to sweeping generalisations of land wrangles and dispossession wherever oil is found.

The contribution from sociologist Mahamidou Aboubacar Attahirou describes how the infrastructural development of the far eastern region of N'gourti in Niger that came with the development of the oil deposits in 2011 helped foster the dis-enclaving of the entire region hitherto neglected by the nation state. The new relevance of the region came with an improvement of existing road infrastructure and extension of mobile phone networks that literally brought N'gourti closer to the rest of Niger by reducing both travel time and costs. Combined with the availability of new employment options for the youth, the oil had remarkable impact on social life as well. Some youth were now able to afford marriage and could support their parents—moving out of their waiting situation in which so many Nigerien youth find themselves trapped (Masquelier, 2019).

The contribution from Oubandoma Salissou and Jannik Schritt analyses the transformations of the area around the Nigerien refinery close to Zinder. Salissou and Schritt show how the big hopes local people had for a better life style, known to them from some Arab oil producers, was soon replaced by a bitter disappointment: the youth gained only temporary jobs during the refinery construction; farmers received compensation payments for the land only twice, with the rest of the payment process shrouded in controversy; and investors came to build villas for the Chinese oil workers only to realise that these workers were not interested in a luxury lifestyle. The authors paint a very nuanced picture of how the arrival of the oil industry transformed the lives in the communities around the refinery, with negative effects such as environmental degradation or land price inflation, and seemingly positive effects such as more customers for small businesses and street hawkers. Salissou and Schritt's contribution points out how these transformations do not happen in rural isolation but are intricately intertwined with processes and actors based in the urban landscape.

6 Insights for (Future) Studies on Oil

Taking note of the oil studies beyond the resource curse, the contributions in this collection point to how certain concepts such as significations, temporality and materiality can be applied as "sensitizing concepts" (Blumer, 1954) in future oil research. By suggesting "directions along which to look," sensitising concepts enable the researcher to approach empirical phenomena that would otherwise remain invisible or go unnoticed (Blaumer, 1954, p. 7). These concepts are therefore to be seen as points of departure for empirical research, rather than the end product (Corbin & Strauss, 2014). The sensitising concepts are valuable as they help to overcome the narrow focus of much economic and political science study on oil rents. We believe that the combining of these concepts into an issue-centred approach to oil, as seen in these contributions, is a promising avenue for future research.

By doing so, the contributions to this collection offer a nuanced and contextually-situated understanding of oil in general and the oil-age Africa in particular. They do not offer a mono-causal prism to make sense of developments across a multitude of social, political and economic context, but instead challenge readers to think critically beyond mono-causality. The contributions show that the economic effects are not well understood and studied; nor are the social and political effects completely charted. Thus, instead of generalising the effects of oil production in the manner of the resource curse literature, the critical perspectives assembled in this collection analyse the processes at work that can be observed in oil-producing states. While the effects claimed by the resource curse literature are always context-specific, we posit that: (a) resource capture is always situated in a political game already at play, (b) the relationship between transnational oil companies and the social and political forces in the host countries can be described as dis/entanglement work, and (c) rural-urban transformations are characterised by expectations and anticipatory practices situated in complex economic, political and socio-cultural configurations.

Looking at the effects of oil rents on local, regional and national politics, the three contributions on oil politics highlight the catalysing effect oil can have on pre-existing dynamics. Rent capture is not a new phenomenon that comes with oil. Rather, oil opens just another arena for different strategic groups already at play to capture the rent according to pre-existing patterns of (re)distribution. Even in one of the most prominent examples of a rentier state, Gabon, on which Douglas Yates (1996, 2012) built his theory, rentier mentality seems to precede any oil production, casting doubt on the causal linkages claimed in the rentier state framework. The contributions here thus make the case for understanding the wider contexts of oil production and especially the history of the state in question in order to answer questions about oil-induced transformation processes.

The contributions on the oil industry show that the relationship of the industry with producer states extends beyond simple readings and are not captured entirely well by focusing only on the enclave character of the international oil industry. They point to the relevance of understanding how these multiple and at times contradictory relations are negotiated among politicians, oil industry representatives, oil workers and the affected people in the communities where oil production takes place. The effects of this dis/entanglement work are always context-specific as they are inserted in national power games, imaginaries and infrastructures, but the dis/entanglement work itself seems to be a universal feature of corporation-state-society relations.

Finally, the contributions on rural-urban transformations induced by oil-production highlight how anticipatory politics, a resource-politics nexus and infrastructural developments take centre stage. But again, they demonstrate how vitally important the context is. They show how effects of oil production are complex and how removed from reality the predictions based on the resource curse can be. We saw a "traditional chief" to be the driving force of imagining a new oil-city, the disenclaving of an entire region hitherto neglected by the state and a relatively stable region in the oil-age, despite all the catastrophic predictions and violent reputations of its inhabitants. They also show how the players involved in the developments have a much more nuanced and context-specific understanding than many of the researchers analysing the situations. It is this knowledge that qualitative and ethnographic studies tap into.

Taken together, all contributions share an understanding of oil and its connected issues as being situated in a particular context. It is by building on this understanding that we can see greater processes at work, such as the catalysing of pre-existing forces into strategic groups in the oil arena, the dis/entanglement work between oil corporations, host countries and societies, and all kinds of speculation practices that anticipate oil wealth yet to materialise. The contributions in this collection therefore aim to be exemplary in pointing the way forward for the qualitative study of oil. They are focused on particular issues at work, and while engaging with the knowledge grown from economics and political science, they have remained critical of basic assumptions of a unilinear, inevitable and deterministic social and political transformational power of oil. Instead they endeavour to follow the loose ends that don't fit into this neat narrative; to understand the spatial, social, political, material and temporal embeddedness of oil production and the new oil producers.

Acknowledgements

We would like to thank all our interview partners, peers, colleagues and friends in the field and back home who have shaped our thinking about oil with their insights. We would especially like to thank Thomas Bierschenk and the two anonymous reviewers for comments on earlier versions of this introductory chapter. The idea for this collection was born from the DFG project 'Oil and Social Change in Niger and Chad: An Anthropological Cooperative Research Project on Technologies, Signification and Processes of Creative Adaption in Relation to African Oil Production'. We would like to thank two of the project leads, namely Prof. Dr. Nikolaus Schareika and Prof. Dr. Andrea Behrends, for their funding support for a professional language editing. Our thanks also go to the language editor Lesley Branagan. Finally, we would like to thank all contributors to this collection for their patience and perseverance to see this project through with us.

References

Adunbi, O. (2015). *Oil Wealth and Insurgency in Nigeria*. Bloomington: Indiana University Press.

Anthias, P. (2018a). Indigenous Peoples and the New Extraction: From Territorial Rights to Hydrocarbon Citizenship in the Bolivian Chaco. *Latin American Perspectives*, 45(5), 136–153.

Anthias, P. (2018b). *Limits to Decolonization: Indigeneity, Territory, and Hydrocarbon Politics in the Bolivian Chaco*. Ithaca: Cornell University Press.

Appel, H. C. (2012a). Offshore Work: Oil, Modularity, and the How of Capitalism in Equatorial Guinea. *American Ethnologist*, 39(4), 692–709.

Appel, H. C. (2012b). Walls and White Elephants: Oil Extraction, Responsibility, and Infrastructural Violence in Equatorial Guinea. *Ethnography*, 13(4), 439–465.

Appel, H. C. (2019). *The Licit Life of Capitalism: US Oil in Equatorial Guinea*. Durham: Duke University Press.

Appel H., Mason A., & Watts, M. (Eds.) (2015). *Subterranean Estates: Life Worlds of Oil and Gas*. Ithaca: Cornell University Press.

Apter, A. (2005). *The Pan-African Nation: Oil and the Spectacle of Culture in Nigeria*. Chicago: University of Chicago Press.

Auty, R. M. (1993). *Sustaining Development in Mineral Economies. The Resource Curse Thesis*. London: Routledge.

Bainton, N., Owen, J. R. (2019). Zones of Entanglement: Researching Mining Arenas in Melanesia and Beyond. *The Extractive Industries and Society*, 6(3), 767–774.

Baker, J. (1977). Oil and African Development. *The Journal of Modern African Studies*, 15(2), 175–212.

Barnes, S. T. (2005). Global Flows: Terror, Oil, and Strategic Philanthropy. *African Studies Review*, 48(1), 1–23.

Barry, A. (2006). Technological Zones. *European Journal of Social Theory*, 9(2), 239–253.

Barry, A. (2013). *Material Politics. Disputes Along the Pipeline*. West Sussex: Wiley Blackwell.

Basedau, M., & Lay, J. (2009). Resource Curse or Rentier Peace? The Ambiguous Effects of Oil Wealth and Oil Dependence on Violent Conflict. *Journal of Peace Research*, 46(6), 757–776.

Bayart, J.-F. (1989). *L'Etat en Afrique. La politique du ventre*. Paris: Fayard.

Beblawi, H., & Luciani, G. (Eds.) (1987). *The Rentier State. Nation, State and Integration in the Arab World*. London: Croom Helm.

Beck, M. (1993). *Die Erdöl-Rentier-Staaten des Nahen und Mittleren Ostens. Interessen, erdölpolitische Kooperation und Entwicklungstendenzen*. Hamburg: LIT.

Behrends, A., & Hoinathy, R. (2017). The Devil's Money: A Multi-level Approach to Acceleration and Turbulence in Oil-Producing Southern Chad. *Social Analysis*, 61(3), 56–72.

Behrends, A., & Schareika, N. (2010). Significations of Oil in Africa or: What (More) Can Anthropologists Contribute to the Study of Oil? *Soumen Antropologi*, 35, 83–86.

Berry, S. (1984). Oil and the Disappearing Peasantry: Accumulation, Differentiation and Underdevelopment in Western Nigeria. *African Economic History*, (13), 1–22.

Bierschenk, T. (1984). *Weltmarkt, Stammesgesellschaft und Staatsformation in Südostarabien (Sultanat Oman)*. Saarbrücken, Fort Lauderdale: Breitenbach.

Bierschenk, T. (1988). Development Projects as Arenas of Negotiation between Strategic Groups. A Case of Study from Bénin. *Sociologia Ruralis*, 28(2–3), 146–160.

Bierschenk, T., & Olivier de Sardan, J. P. (2019). How to Study Bureaucracies Ethnographically? *Critique of Anthropology*, 39(2), 243–257.

Blowfield, M., & Frynas, J. G. (2005). Setting New Agendas: Critical Perspectives on Corporate Social Responsibility in the Developing World. *International Affairs*, 81(3), 499–513.

Blumer, H. (1954). What is Wrong with Social Theory? *American Sociological Review*, 19(1), 3–10.

Blundo, G. (2011). Une administration à deux vitesses. Projets de développement et construction de l'État au Sahel. *Etudes africaines*, 51(202–203), 427–52.

Boyer, D. (2011). Energopolitics and the Anthropology of Energy. *Anthropology News*, 52(5), 5–7.

Boyer, D. (2014). Energopower: An Introduction. *Anthropological Quarterly*, 87(2), 309–333.

Breznau, N., Rinke, E. M., Wuttke, A., Adem, M., Adriaans, J., Alvarez-Benjumea, A. et al. (2021). Observing Many Researchers Using the Same Data and Hypothesis Reveals a Hidden Universe of Uncertainty. Preprint version available at: https://doi.org/10.31222/osf.io/cd5j9.

Brunnschweiler, C. N., & Bulte, E. H. (2008). The Resource Curse Revisited. A Tale of Paradoxes and Red Herrings. *Journal of Environmental Economics and Management*, 55(3), 248–264.

Burawoy, M. (1998). The Extended Case Method. *Sociological Theory*, 16 (1), 4–33.

Burawoy, M. (ed.) (2000). *Global Ethnography: Forces, Connections, and Imaginations in a Postmodern World*. Berkeley: University of California Press.

Cavalcanti, T. V. V. de, Mohaddes, K., & Raissi, M. (2011). Does Oil Abundance Harm Growth? *Applied Economics Letters*, 18(10/12), 1181–1184.

Chabal, P., & Daloz, J.-P. (1999). *Africa Works. Disorder as Political Instrument*. London: International African Institute in association with James Currey, Oxford.

Chalfin, B. (2019). On-Shore, Off-Shore Takoradi: Terraqueous Urbanism, Logistics, and Oil Governance in Ghana. *Environment and Planning D.*, 37(5): 814–32.

Collier, P. (2000). Rebellion as a Quasi-Criminal Activity. *The Journal of Conflict Resolution*, 44(6), 839–953.

Corbin, J. M., & Strauss, A. L. (2014). *Basics of Qualitative Research: Techniques and Procedures for Developing Grounded Theory* (Fourth edition). SAGE.

Coronil, F. (1997). *The Magical State: Nature, Money and Modernity in Venezuela*. Chicago: University of Chicago Press.

D'Angelo, L., Pijpers, R. J. (2018). Mining Temporalities: An Overview. *The Extractive Industries and Society*, 5(2), 215–222.

Dolan, C., & Rajak, D. (eds.) (2016). *The Anthropology of Corporate Social Responsibility.* Oxford: Berghahn Books.

Donner, N. (2011). Notes sur la dimension immunitaire des enclaves pétrolières. *EchoGéo*, 17.

Eisenstadt, S. N. (1973). *Traditional Patrimonialism and Modern Neopatrimonialism.* Beverly Hills: Sage.

Elwert, G., Bierschenk, T., (1988). Development Aid as Intervention in Dynamic Systems. *Sociologia Ruralis*, 28 (2–3), 99–112.

Ferguson, J. (2005). Seeing Like an Oil Company: Space, Security, and Global Capital in Neoliberal Africa. *American Anthropologist*, 107(3), 377–382.

Ferry, E. & Limbert, M. E. (2008). Introduction. In: E. Ferry & M. E. Limbert (eds.), *Timely Assets: The Politics of Resources and Their Temporalities*, (pp. 3–24). Santa Fe: School for Advanced Research Press.

Fleshman, M. (2002). The International Community & the Crisis in Nigeria's Oil Producing Communities. *Review of African Political Economy*, 29(91), 153–163.

Franquesa, J. (2019). Resources: Nature, Value and Time. In J. G. Carrier (Ed.), *Elgar Research Agendas. A research Agenda for Economic Anthropology* (pp. 74–89). Cheltenham, UK: Edward Elgar Publishing.

Fricke, C. (2017). The Uncertainty of Oil: Balancing Through the Temporalities and Affects of Depletion in Gabon. *Tsantsa*, 22, 28–36.

Gelb, A. H. (ed). (1988). *Oil Windfalls. Blessing or Curse?* New York: Published for the World Bank [by] Oxford University Press.

Genova, A., & Falola, T. (2003). Oil in Nigeria: A Bibliographical Reconnaissance. *History in Africa*, 30, 133–156.

Ghazvinian, J. H. (2007). *Untapped: The Scramble for Africa's Oil.* Harcourt.

Gilberthorpe, E., & Rajak, D. (2017). The Anthropology of Extraction: Critical Perspectives on the Resource Curse. *The Journal of Development Studies*, 53(2), 186–204.

Gluckman, M. (1958). *Analysis of a Social Situation in Modern Zululand.* Manchester: University Press.

Graham, E., Ovadia, J. S. (2019). Oil Exploration and Production in Sub-Saharan Africa, 1990-Present: Trends and Developments. *The Extractive Industries and Society*, 6(2), 593–609.

Hauck, G., Kößler, R., Kumitz, D. & Wehr, I. (2013). Neopatrimonialismus? Von Sinn und Unsinn eines Diskurses. *Peripherie* 130/131, 303–26.

Haber, S., & Menaldo, V. (2011). Do Natural Resources Fuel Authoritarianism? A Reappraisal of the Resource Curse. *American Political Science Review*, 105(1), 1–26.

Heinrich, A., Pleines, H. (2012). Resource Challenges: Die politische Dimension von Ölbooms. *Neue Politische Literatur*, 57(3), 443–477.

Hicks, C. (2015). *Africa's New Oil: Power, Pipelines and Future Fortunes.* London: Zed Books.

Hoinathy, R. (2013). *Pétrole et changement social au Tchad: Rente pétrolière et monétisation des relations économiques et sociales dans la zone pétrolière de Doba.* Paris: Karthala.

Huber, M. (2013). *Lifeblood: Oil, Freedom and the Forces of Capital.* Minneapolis: University of Minnesota Press.

Humphreys, M. (2005). Natural Resources, Conflict, and Conflict Resolution. Uncovering the Mechanisms. *Journal of Conflict Resolution*, 49(4), 508–537.

Humphreys, M., Sachs, J., & Stiglitz, J. E. (2007). *Escaping the Resource Curse.* New York: Columbia University Press.

Karl, T. L. (1997). *The Paradox of Plenty. Oil Booms and Petro-states.* Berkeley: Univ. of California Press.

Kemedi, D. von. (2003). The Changing Predatory Styles of International Oil Companies in Nigeria. *Review of African Political Economy*, 30(95), 134–139.

Klare, M. T., & Volman, D. (2006). America, China & the Scramble for Africa's Oil. *Review of African Political Economy*, 33(108), 297–309.

Landa, M. S. (2016). Crude Residues: The Workings of Failing Oil Infrastructure in Poza Rica, Veracruz, Mexico. *Environment and Planning A*, 48(4), 718–735. 1–18.

Leite, C., & Weidmann, J. (1999). Does Mother Nature Corrupt? Natural Resources, Corruption and Economic Growth. *IMF Working Paper*, 99(85).

Leonard, L. (2016). *Life in the Time of Oil: A Pipeline and Poverty in Chad.* Indiana University Press.

Leong, W., & Mohaddes, K. (2011). *Institutions and the Volatility Curse.* Available at SSRN: https://ssrn.com/abstract=1885569 or http://dx.doi.org/10.2139/ssrn.1885569

Limbert, M. E. (2010). *In the Time of Oil: Piety, Memory, and Social Life in an Omani Town.* Stanford: Stanford University Press.

Loloum, T., Abram, S., & Ortar, N. (Eds.). (2021). *Ethnographies of Power: A Political Anthropology of Energy*. Berghahn Books.

Long, N. (1989). *Encounters at the Interface: A Perspective on Social Discontinuities in Rural Development.* Wageningen.

Long, N., Van der Ploeg, J. D. (1989). Demythologizing Planned Intervention: An Actor Perspective. *Sociologia Ruralis,* 29(3–4), 226–249.

Lubeck, P. (1989). Petroleum and Proletarianization: The Life History of a Muslim Nigerian Worker. *African Economic History*, (18), 99–112.

Lynch, K. (2008). Rural-Urban Interaction in the Developing World. In V. Desai & R. B. Potter (eds.), *The Companion to Development Studies* (pp. 268–271). London: Hodder Education.

Mahdavy, H. (1970). The Pattern and Problems of Economic Development in Rentier States: The Case of Iran. In M. Cook (ed.), *Studies in the Economic History of the Mid-*

dle East: From the Rise of Islam to the Present Day, (pp. 428–67). London, New York: Oxford University Press.

Masquelier, A. M. (2019). *Fada: Boredom and Belonging in Niger.* Chicago, London: The University of Chicago Press.

Médard, J. F. (1982). The Underdeveloped State in Africa: Political Clientelism or Neo-patrimonialism? In C. S. Clapham (ed.), *Private Patronage and Public Power. Political Clientelism in the Modern State,* (pp. 162–189). New York: St. Martin's Press.

Mhone, G. C. Z. (2001). Enclavity and Constrained Labour Absorptive Capacity in Southern African Economies. *ILO/SAMAT Policy Paper Series* 12.

Mitchell, T. (2011). *Carbon Democracy: Political Power in the Age of Oil.* London and New York: Verso.

Mkandawire, T. (2015). Neopatrimonialism and the Political Economy of Economic Performance in Africa: Critical Reflections. *World Politics* 67(3), 563–612.

Murrey, A. (2015). Narratives of Life and Violence Along the Chad-Cameroon Oil Pipeline. *Human Geography,* 8(1), 15–39.

Nader, L. (1969). Up the Anthropologist: Perspectives Gained From Studying Up. In D. Hymes (ed.), *Reinventing Anthropology,* (pp. 284–311). New York: Pantheon.

Nakayi, R., Witte, A., (2019). Making Cultural Heritage Claims on Profitable Land: The Case of the Ngassa Wells in Uganda's Oil Region. *Africa Spectrum,* 54(3), 222–243.

Nwajiaku, K. (2005). Between Discourse and Reality: The Politics of Oil and Ijaw Ethnic Nationalism In The Niger Delta. *Cahiers d'études africaines* 178: 457–96.

Olivier de Sardan, J.-P. (1988). Peasant Logics and Development Project Logics. *Sociologia Ruralis,* 28(2–3), 216–226.

Olivier de Sardan, J-P. (2014). Abandoning the Neo-Patrimonialist Paradigm. In L. Koechlin & T. Förster (eds.), *The Politics of Governance. Actors and Articulations in Africa and Beyond,* (pp. 75–92). Routledge.

Olivier de Sardan, J.-P. (2021). *La revanche des contextes. Des mésaventures de l'ingénierie sociale, en Afrique et au-delà.* Paris: Karthala.

Olivier de Sardan, J.-P. , & Piccoli, E. (eds). (2018). *Cash Transfers in Context. An Anthropological Perspective.* New York: Berghahn Books.

Ovadia, J. S. (2016a). *Petro-developmental State in Africa: Making Oil Work in Angola, Nigeria and the Gulf of Guinea.* London: C. Hurst & Co.

Ovadia, J. S. (2016b). Local Content Policies and Petro-development in Sub-Saharan Africa. A Comparative Analysis. *Resources Policy,* 49, 20–30.

Pijpers, R. J., Eriksen, T. H. (eds.). (2018). *Mining Encounters. Extractive Industries in an Overheated World.* London: Pluto Press.

Porter, M. E., & Kramer, M. R. (2002). The Competitive Advantage of Corporate Philanthropy. *Harvard Business Review,* 12, 1–15.

Rajak, D. (2011). *In Good Company. An Anatomy of Corporate Social Responsibility.* Stanford, California: Stanford University Press.

Reed, K. (2009). *Crude Existence. Environment and the Politics of Oil in Northern Angola.* Berkeley: University of California Press.

Reyna, S. (2011). Constituting Domination/Constructing Monsters: Imperialism, Cultural Desire, and Anti-Beowulfs in the Chadian Petro-State. In A. Behrends, S. Reyna, & G. Schlee (eds.), *Crude Domination: An Anthropology of Oil*, (pp. 132–162). Oxford: Berghahn.

Reyna S., Behrends A. (2011), The Crazy Curse and Crude Domination: Towards an Anthropology of Oil, in A. Behrends A., S.P. Reyna & G. Schlee (eds.), *Crude Domination: An Anthropology of Oil*, (pp. 3–29) New York: Berghahn Books, New York.

Richardson, T. & Weszkalnys, G. (2014). Introduction: Resource Materialities. *Anthropological Quarterly*, 87(1), 5–30.

Rogers, D. (2012). The Materiality of the Corporation: Oil, Gas, and Corporate Social Technologies in the Remaking of a Russian Region. *American Ethnologist*, 39(2), 284–296.

Rogers, D. (2015), Oil and Anthropology. *Annual Review of Anthropology*, (44), 365–380.

Ross, M. (2001). Does Oil Hinder Democracy? *World Politics*, 53(3), 325–361.

Ross, M. L. (2008). Oil, Islam, and Women. *American Political Science Review*, 102(1), 107–123.

Ross, M. (2009). *Oil and Democracy Revisited.* Retrieved from: http://www.michaelross.info/papers/working/Oil%20and%20Democracy%20Revisited.pdf [last accessed 11.2.2022].

Ross, M. L. (2012). *The Oil Curse. How Petroleum Wealth Shapes the Development of Nations*. Princeton: Princeton University Press.

Sawyer, S. (2004). *Crude Chronicles: Indigenous Politics, Multinational Oil, and Neoliberalism in Ecuador.* Durham, London: Duke University Press.

Schritt, J. (2013). Transnational Governmentality of Energy Security After 9/11: Coup D'état, Terrorism, Militarization, and Oil in Niger. In: C. Colaguori (ed.), *Security, Life, and Death: Governmentality and Biopower in the Post 9/11 Era*, (pp. 193–244), Whitby, Ontario: De Sitter Publications.

Schritt, J. (2016). From Nuclear Imperialism to Petro Democracy? Resource Assemblages and the Emergence of a New Political Configuration in Niger. *Canadian Journal of African Studies*, 50(2), 229–254.

Schritt, J. (2018). Crude Controversies: Disputes along Niger's Petro-infrastructure. *History and Anthropology*, 29(5), 645–69.

Schritt, J. (2019). An Ethnography of Public Events: Reformulating the Extended Case Method in Contemporary Social Theory. *Ethnography*, 4(1).

Schritt, J. (2020). Crude Talking: Radio and the Politics of Naming, Blaming and Claiming in Oil-age Niger. *Journal of Contemporary African Studies*, 38(3), 415–36.

Schritt, J., Behrends, A. (2018). 'Western' and 'Chinese' Oil Zones. Petro-Infrastructures and the Emergence of New Trans-territorial Spaces of Order in Niger and Chad. In: U. Engel, M. Boeckler, D. Müller-Mahn (eds.), *Spatial Practices. Territory, Border and Infrastructure in Africa*, (pp. 211–230), Boston: Brill.

Schritt, J., Witte, A. (2018). Standardized Capitalism? Negotiating the Oil Industry's Dis/entanglement in Niger and Uganda, *Economy and Society*, 47(3), 428–452.

Schubert, J. (2016). 'A Culture of Immediatism': Co-Optation and Complicity in Post-War Angola. *Ethnos*, 1–19.

Schubert, J. (2017). *Working the System: A Political Ethnography of the New Angola*. Ithaca, London: Cornell University Press.

Seign-Goura, Y. (2017). Representations of Oil in Chad: A Blessing or a Curse? *Africa Spectrum*, 52(1), 65–83.

Shever, E. (2010). Engendering the Company: Corporate Personhood and the "Face" of an Oil Company in Metropolitan Buenos Aires. *PoLAR: Political and Legal Anthropology Review*, 33(1), 26–46.

Shever, E. (2012). *Resources for Reform: Oil and Neoliberalism in Argentina*. Stanford, California: Stanford University Press.

Skaten, M. (2017). *From Refining to Smuggling: The Everyday Politics of Petrol in Ghana*. Thesis, University of Edinburgh.

Strauss, S., Rupp, S., Love, T. F. (eds.). (2013). *Cultures of Energy. Power, Practices, Technologies*. Walnut Creek, CA: Left Coast Press.

The Dutch disease. (1977, November 26). *The Economist*: 82–83.

Tsing, A. (2000). The Global Situation. *Cultural Anthropology*, 15(3), 327–360.

Turner T. E. (2004). Why Women are at War With Chevron: Nigerian Subsistence Struggles Against the International Oil Industry. *Journal of Asian and African Studies*, 39(1–2), 63–93.

Vannoppen, G. (2016). *Fuelling the Future With Concrete, Papers and Discourse: Competing Claims in the Making of an Oil City, Sekondi-Takoradi, Ghana*. Thesis, KU Leuven.

van Velsen, J. (1967). The Extended-case Method and Situational Analysis. In: A. L. Epstein (ed.), *The Craft of Social Anthropology*, (pp. 129–149), London: Tavistock.

Watts, M. (2004). Resource Curse? Governmentality, Oil and Power in the Niger Delta, Nigeria. *Geopolitics*, 9(1), 50–80.

Watts, M. (2008). Blood Oil: The Anatomy of a Petro-insurgency in the Niger Delta. *Focaal-European Journal of Anthropology*, (52), 18–38.

Watts, M. (2012). A Tale of Two Gulfs: Life, Death, and Dispossession along Two Oil Frontiers. *American Quarterly*, 64(3), 437–467.

Weszkalnys, G. (2011). Cursed Resources, or Articulations of Economic Theory in the Gulf of Guinea. *Economy and Society*, 40(3), 345–372.

Weszkalnys, G. (2014). Anticipating Oil: The Temporal Politics of a Disaster Yet to Come. *The Sociological Review*, 62(Supplement 1), 211–235.

Weszkalnys, G. (2016). A Doubtful Hope: Resource Affect in a Future Oil Economy. *Journal of Royal Anthropological Institute* 22(S1), 127–146.

Witte, A. (2017). Bright Prospects or an Ominous Future: Anticipating Oil in Uganda. *Tsantsa*, (22): 26–35.

Witte, A. (2018). *An Uncertain Future - Anticipating Oil in Uganda*. Göttingen: Göttingen University Press.

Witte, A. (2021). Rumours as Anticipatory Knowledge in a Future Petro-State. *Culture Unbound*, 13(3).

World Bank Group. (2011). *Petroleum Product Markets in Sub-Saharan Africa: Comparative Efficiency Analysis of 12 Countries*. Retrieved from https://openknowledge.worldbank.org/handle/10986/2743 [last accessed 11.2.2022].

Yates, D. A. (1996). *The Rentier State in Africa. Oil Rent Dependency and Neocolonialism in the Republic of Gabon*. Trenton: Africa World Press.

Yates, D. A. (2012). *The Scramble for African Oil. Oppression, Corruption and War for Control of Africa's Natural Resources*. London, New York: Pluto Press.

Yessenova, S. (2012). The Tengiz Oil Enclave: Labor, Business, and The State. *Political and Legal Anthropology Review*, 35(1), 94–114.

Zalik, A. (2009). Zones of Exclusion: Offshore Extraction, the Contestation of Space and Physical Displacement in the Nigerian Delta and the Mexican Gulf. *Antipode*, 41(3), 557–582.

2

Dis/Entanglement and the Resource Curse: Structural Policy in Oil-Rich Countries

Helmut Asche

1 Introduction

It is generally recognised that mineral riches theoretically endow any developing country with the financial resources to fund broad-based agricultural and industrial growth. Serious doubts about the effectiveness of the growth link between extractive industries and the rest of national economies, borne out by decades of resource squandering, seemed to have faded of late. Things apparently returned to their natural order, and resource rich countries were seen to represent primarily business opportunities, not disaster. The *Economist* conjectured after a review of African resource-rich economies that

> there is reason to think the 'resource curse' is losing its power.
> The Economist, "The twilight of the resource curse?" 2015

Shortly before this postulation, multilateral agencies had published two flagship reports which compiled knowledge from a range of experts and invited African countries to do even more to harness natural resource wealth for the benefit of inclusive economic development and structural change (AfDB, OECD & UNDP, 2013; UNECA, 2013). With the global commodities super-cycle a window of opportunity appeared wide open. Soon after publication of the two reports, however, the window closed as global commodity prices crashed. The imagery of such windows of opportunity could not have been more harshly demonstrated. Few doubt today that the excellent opportunity for inclusive growth has remained largely untapped. What are the reasons for the critical turn of events?

There are a considerable and growing number of African countries endowed with large mineral resources. While resources in the sense of reserves are in the African soil by nature, the fact that they appear as riches is not a natural but an economic fact. Historically, extreme resource wealth is a recent phenomenon in Africa, as a wider-spread occurrence when in 1973/74 oil reserves multiplied

 DOI:10.1163/9789004530065_003

in value.[1] The speed by which additional African countries until 2013, in the wake of the global commodities boom, had been identified as actual resource-rich – from Burkina Faso to Mozambique, and potentially all three East African countries Kenya, Tanzania, Uganda – gave a continental dimension to a phenomenon once limited to a handful of traditional oil producers, metal-mining states and Botswana.

The blessing of rich mineral endowments comes with the possibility of a "resource curse" or the "paradox of plenty" (Karl, 1997; Tamba, Tchatchouang & Dou'a, 2007), which has political, economic, social and ecological dimensions, among them a subset of economic problems known as the "Dutch disease" - a term coined in 1977 by the Economist to describe the decline of manufacturing and of certain agricultural exports in the Netherlands after the discovery of large natural gas reserves during the 1960s and 1970s. On a positive note, natural resource abundant countries like some so-called Neo-Europes were capable of escaping the minerals trap and use resource riches along with augmented human capital for advances in processed goods.[2] There are also some recent developing country cases worldwide which successfully manage huge mineral resources. Yet it remains one of the most egregious facts in Africa's post-independence history that not a single oil-producing country has ever put the returns to consequential developmental use, in the sense of sustained socio-economic diversification over and beyond the sectors that usually grow along with drilling.[3]

With the increasing number of actual and potential oil and gas producing countries all along the West African coast and the Great Lakes of the East, the resource curse is again on top of the international policy agenda. The aim of this chapter is to explore the economic aspects of the resource curse more narrowly put, especially what can be termed dis/entanglement: the enclave nature, yet with complex spillover effects, of the extractive industry on

---

1 The beginning of large-scale exploitation of Botswana's diamonds dates from about the same historical moment.

2 Clear cases are Australia, Canada and South Africa, despite the heavily biased social outcome, nowadays also Chile. The United States are a contested case in this respect. Some sources make the case of resource-*rich* United States, in particular after the 19th century oil discoveries, while initial North American resource *scarcity* is the theoretical workhorse of the neo-institutionalist school in comparison to South American Spanish colonies (Acemoglu & Robinson, 2012). In fact, no country made it with an oil glut *at industrial inception* – manifestly the best lubricant for rolling down the same path of resource dependence.

3 At least not in a macro-economically measurable sense. This includes the North African cases Algeria and Libya.

the one hand, and the industrial policy attempts to deal with it, on the other.[4] Moreover, the chapter marks the junctions where other disciplines, among them ethnographic research, have to explain the empirically observed practices of dis/entanglement.

2 Beyond Resource Transparency and Legal Regulation: The Extractive Industry and Structural Policy

Over the last decade or so, resource transparency and regulation issues have dominated the scene, as opacity, corruption, theft and rent-seeking are well-known nefarious dimensions of the resource problem. Initially, international efforts had a focus on rendering transparent what mining companies pay and governments receive. Paradigmatic is the Extractive Industries Transparency Initiative (EITI) launched in 2002, which set out to improve governance by calling for the full publication and verification of company payments and government revenues from oil, gas, and mining. In addition, there are initiatives like Fatal Transactions and Revenue Watch which mainly provide in-depth analysis and information. Later, initiatives broadened their scope to denounce badly negotiated contracts and to assist countries to draft better ones, along with the organisation of open tender and mining licence systems. Proper administration of mining royalties and other receipts became a major technical assistance topic (Otto, Andrews, Cawood et al., 2006). In the course of this shift, EITI's focus also widened, and the upgraded initiative EITI++ deals with the entire resource chain, from exploration and extraction to processing, managing revenues, and promoting sustainable and efficient utilisation of resource wealth. Employing a similar approach, EITI's early civil society twin Publish What You Pay (PWYP) now

> [...] aims [to achieve] full transparency in the payment, receipt and management of natural resource revenues; public disclosure of extractive contracts; and civil society participation in the monitoring of revenue expenditures.
>
> ORANJE & PARHAM, 2009, p. 28

Largely independent from the global initiatives, a number of African governments took over the last decade to renegotiate what they perceived as skewed

4 For the full range of policy challenges that resource-rich countries have to meet, see (Asche, 2018).

contract terms and to tax oil/mining company profits more heavily. This comes under the ambiguous term of "resource nationalism." Because of the fiscal intricacies it has led of late to serious conflicts with multinational companies, as in Tanzania, or has delayed new projects, such as the start of oil production in Uganda.

In order to elucidate the subsequent problem of structural policy, suppose that most royalties and taxes have been properly paid and orderly registered in the public books, and nothing big remains off-budget. The fiscal record in your African model country is impeccable. If structural issues would not matter, the main recommendation would simply read: spend everything that accrues to public coffers on good schools and clinics, proper roads and lights (similar to the initially acclaimed World Bank model for resource transparency in Chad). This would assure that in general terms 'the rest of the economy' benefits from the oil bonanza. However, the truly interesting question for resource rich countries comes after this: Does the oil or mining sector still qualify as a potential *lead sector* (in the sense of classical development economics) which – as the term indicates – can lead the whole economy to higher growth levels and modernised structures?[5] Asked inversely: Is the *lack* of deep structural change during the commodities boom merely a reflection of the fact that (a) the boom has remained too *concentrated* on the minerals sector and disentangled, hence *too isolated* from most of the economy to generate important spill-overs, for which the typical offshore oil platform is the best example? Or are there also forces at work which (b) actively depress or even marginalise other sectors? As development economists know, there are. While we do not claim to make significant new contributions to conventional wisdom about these forces, we are not aware of any empirical, econometric analyses to date that attach weights to explanatory variables behind (a) and (b) and thus their relative importance in Africa. Such a study would, however, have obvious and important consequences for policy design and economic advisory services.

2.1 *Isolation of the Mineral and Energy Resource Sector*

In the most elementary sense, the enclave character of mineral extraction in mostly foreign directed companies working with foreign technology creates a situation in which knowledge transfer or respect for domestic labour and environmental standards do not take place automatically. Foreign direct

5 Despite being the undisputable historical lead sector, the South African minerals-energy complex (MEC) is at the center of a heated national debate as to its future potential for driving economic modernization or holding it back.

investment (FDI) in the extractive industry is known for limited spillovers and technology transfers, as well as for limited willingness to re-invest profits in the host country.[6] A first consideration is thus the need for *industrial policy in the extractive industry* itself through support of skills development and technology transfer. New resource partnerships that talk nobly about supporting such technology and knowledge transfer demonstrate an awareness for the importance of the goals – without actually converting them into operational terms.

Next, the relationship between the extractive industry and adjacent branches matters. Most analyses are framed within Albert Hirschman's linkage theory (Hirschman, 1958). Hirschman distinguished four types of linkages whose strength determines, together with other factors, the lead sector quality of an industry: (1) forward (downstream) and (2) backward (upstream)production linkages, (3) consumer linkages and (4) fiscal linkages. In addition, early development economists assessed the mining sector as capital- and foreign technology-intensive, which restrains both domestic backward and consumer linkages. Even forward linkages seldom emerge on their own. Hence three of the four links appear to be generally weak. Generosity vis-à-vis foreign investors, corruption, transfer pricing and the like also weaken the theoretically important fiscal link to taxes and royalties.[7] As mineral value chains hardly expand by themselves in host countries, their governments have long employed measures of industrial policy in the periphery of the oil platforms, in order to strengthen downstream, sidestream or upstream industries. The package contains global value chain (GVC) support measures, spatial policies, as well as CSR measures, efforts to encourage social participation by local communities, and local content regulation to foster productive links.

Both policy domains for the extractive sector – within and surrounding the industry – share the general attributes of modern industrial policy, in particular the need for organised public-private search for essential inputs not available in the (domestic) market and for potential outputs which are not generated by market forces either. As with all good industrial policy, preference lies squarely

6 Though many of the once purely foreign-owned companies in the oil sector have been nationalised, this does not change the basic pattern, as the actual extraction remains mostly in foreign (company) hands. The acute problem of oil and mining companies channeling profits out of developing countries has not diminished either.

7 This finding is the theoretical entry point for today's transparency and public financial management agenda, as outlined above.

on *non-compulsory*, enabling measures. Yet there are two obvious differences between extractive and other industries:

- The extractive industry, as such, self-settles without much supportive policy as long as world market prices are at the higher end. Big oil production is no infant industry. Still in infancy, however, are the desired economic spillovers into the local labour and capital market and into adjacent sectors.
- By the very nature of the extractive industry, spillovers and links are particularly difficult to develop by just 'nudging' investors into knowledge/tech transfer and broad local sourcing for supplies.

These differences are industry-specific reasons why a second, *regulatory* set of policies is more common and arguably more justified than in other industries. One platform hosting industrial policies within and in the environment of the extracting industry involves *performance requirements* for foreign investors. Applicable to all sectors of foreign investment, e.g. in energy or water production, such performance regulation is notoriously contested with regard to the extractive industry. Often contained in oil laws, they comprise a broad range of measures and typically cover the pre-establishment and establishment phases of an investment project. The best known subset of performance requirements are *local content rules*, regulations or requirements (LCR) – to the extent that local content policy (LCP) sometimes features as family name for all such performance regulations, which is misleading. They represent systematic efforts to *re-establish entanglement* of the resource sector with the national economy in producer countries.

LCR are designed as a stimulus for domestic trade and not as trade barriers. Yet economists routinely introduce them as *non-tariff barriers* (*NTB*), which is an ideological premise, and treat them mainly as an invitation to opaque favouritism. Depending on product composition and market configuration, which are analysed mostly in partial equilibrium settings since Grossman's seminal treatment (Grossman, 1981), local content requirements do not necessarily produce a trade loss, but rather *trade diversion* between foreign and domestic suppliers with identical commercial volumes. In turn, they offer possibilities for knowledge transfer and local/regional supply chains – dynamic effects not normally covered in static partial equilibrium treatment. Despite the potentially positive economic outcome, compulsory local content rules continue to have an extremely bad reputation in market-liberal quarters, as in the broad survey of country cases by the Peterson Institute (Hufbauer, Schott, Cimino-Isaacs et al., 2013).[8] Domestic content quota in the countries covered

8 The survey contains a very critical country case study of Nigeria's oil and gas industry, based on the 2010 Nigerian Oil and Gas Content Development Act, one of the new pieces of local content legislation now *en vogue* in Africa again.

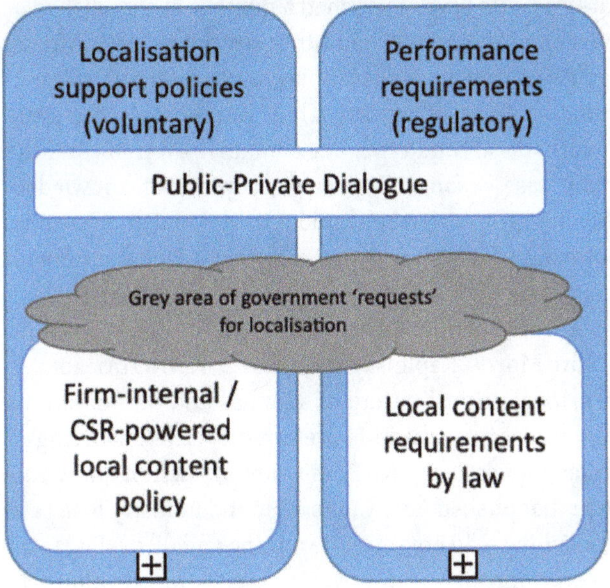

FIGURE 2.1 Industrial policy and local content measures

in the survey were typically set at unrealistically high levels, thus inviting corruption to circumvent them. While such cases still exist,[9] it is important to underline the *dual policy nature* of good local content regulation, comprising voluntary *and* regulatory action, both of which need to be addressed in frank public-private dialogue (PPD) (see diagram).

New-generation local content policy often relies on mutually agreed-upon and realistic assessment of local input production and service potential, with subsequent training for potential local suppliers, as e.g. the government of Ghana implements with technical assistance from Norway. Today, a number of multinational companies in the sector make the development of some local supplies a distinct company policy alongside their core business. Driven not only by CSR considerations, companies are voluntarily agreeing to local sourcing quotas. Hence local content rules need not always be legally prescribed. Nudging companies into more localisation may suffice for this part of outsourcing.

9 Unfortunately, old style local content rules can still be found. They work perfectly to discredit new industrial policy. The 2014/15 Petrobras scandal in Brazil was co-generated by an extremely high local content prescription of equipment and supplies for the offshore oil industry – of 85%, to create a dozen shipyards onshore, which then became a huge source of corruption and embezzlement. As expected, the Economist did not miss the opportunity to pinpoint this as a typical case of "misguided industrial policy" and noted in its reporting with satisfaction that the ruling party's "industrial policy is in full retreat" (14th February 2015).

Some leading scholars on GVCs have researched a number of established or attempted linkages between commodities and other sectors in eight African countries, such as Angola's aggressive effort to have a considerable share of metalwork for oil production done in-country. Their results show that linkages vary widely in breadth, depth and type, but contain – even beyond the established South African case – some promising examples of knowledge-intensive input links. Most importantly, they build a model which, over time, distinguishes the outsourcing of supplies that is *non-critical* for the mineral firms' core competencies from the localisation of *critical* supplies for which more consequential government action is needed to bring foreign companies to the table (Kaplinsky, 2011; Morris, Kaplinsky & Kaplan, 2012; UNIDO, 2012).[10] Depending on the non-critical/critical nature of supplies and on home/host country characteristics, vertical integration is preferred over out-sourcing of activities (Chen, Sun, Ukaejiofo et al., 2016). Both voluntary action and vigorous policies – like the one that pushed Botswana's diamond industry to accept in-country sorting and polishing – do not promote mining and oil drilling to an ideal lead sector for the economy as a whole. Nonetheless, strategic efforts to attach related or satellite activities provide at least some added value.

As with other industrial policy areas, an important question arises regarding the *legal policy space*. The first moot point here involves the local content requirements. They treat a portion of domestic products or services differently from imported ones and insofar run counter to the fundamental GATT/WTO requirement of national treatment by the General Agreement on Tariffs and Trade (GATT) and the World Trade Organization (WTO), contained in GATT article III. De facto, they erect an additional quantitative import barrier far behind the border. As long as we only consider GATT, developing countries can claim the differential treatment enshrined in article XVIII and extended in the Uruguay round to a number of additional treaties (Prieß & Berrisch, 2003, p. 162–166). Even more latitude is offered to developing countries for other investment issues not covered by the GATT. However, over the years a number of instruments of international commercial law have restricted this latitude among the contracting parties, notably Bilateral Investment Treaties (BIT) and International Investment Agreements (IIA). Increasingly, related legal claims based on these treaties have been brought before the investor state dispute

10 Because the studies concentrate on links in the industrial neighbourhood of extractive industries, they remain silent on most of the risks typically associated with the Dutch Disease and make no proposals to counteract the danger of resource sector lop-sidedness, or to support the economic sectors that suffer most because they have *no linkages at all* with the extractive industry, neither production nor consumption nor fiscal linkages.

settlement (ISDS). The South Centre provides a useful survey of this critical trend, which has led a number of oil and mineral rich developing countries to relinquish the BITs concluded so far (Mohamadieh & Uribe, 2016). Following this analysis, a range of either multi- or plurilateral agreements (TRIM) and bi-regional, regional or bilateral treaties expand the prohibition of performance requirements for foreign investments to almost everything. Globally, the EU-Canada free trade agreement (CETA) is gaining strategic importance as it clearly contains the longest list of prohibited requirements compiled so far. However, some legal scope is preserved for developing countries as long as they are not bound by BIT-like agreements.

Critically, the Economic Partnership Agreements (EPA) between the EU and African regions now carry over GATT regulations into bi-regional treaties, albeit *without* the exemption clauses still contained in the GATT. Most importantly, the *national treatment regulation* – requiring that foreign firms be treated as domestic ones and face no additional burden – is literally copy and paste from the GATT into the EPAs, effectively barring local content regulation (Asche, 2021). However, even when the remaining policy space of local content regulation is fully used, the extractive sector's characteristics of capital and technology intensity remain unchanged: both are to a large extent imported. In addition, downstream beneficiation in the mining and oil sectors is still contested for at least two reasons. Firstly, basic extraction no more qualifies an industry for further transformation of the mineral than producing cotton qualifies a country a priori as a textile manufacturer.[11] Secondly, high industry-specific economies of scale in the extractive sector and in downstream treatment can make beneficiation commercially unviable, as is presently being discussed with regard to a refinery project for Ugandan oil.

To sum up, one part of the systematic answer as to why it is important to look beyond the boundaries and the immediate neighbourhood of the minerals-energy sector stems *from the intrinsic characteristics* of this sector. Its structural isolation remains indeed very difficult to overcome.

3 Too Close to You: The Problem of Negative Spillovers

The relative isolation of the oil sector in a country's input-output structure does not completely explain the key problem raised above. The missing part of

11 See the debate in South Africa on the beneficiation of mining products, in which the Harvard team headed by Hausmann and Rodrik took the sceptics' bench opposing South African structuralists.

the answer comes with the inverse sign: the oil sector appears typically *not disentangled enough* but, by a number of transmission channels, rather *too close* to the economy at large to shield it from negative spillovers of oil.[12]

3.1 *The Basics of Dutch Disease*

The phenomenon known as Dutch Disease (DD) represents a specific subset of resource-related problems and entails a specific risk of de-industrialisation. Understanding it remains crucial for any industrial strategy. The label refers to a negative surprise which the Netherlands experienced after the onset of commercial gas exploitation in the 1960s, when a considerable appreciation of the Dutch guilder triggered a decline of the country's manufacturing industry and affected agriculture and horticulture. Exporters other than gas producers were hit by rising nominal prices, and manufacturers came under pressure by cheaper imports. The problem is thus commonly associated with a currency appreciation, but there is more. Full analysis is usually undertaken in the framework of a small open economy model, also known as the Australian Model after the economists who developed it to describe their country's economy (Corden & Neary, 1982). As the name indicates, economies in the model have two distinct features:

1. *Openness,* in that trade and capital flow across their borders and influence the domestic economy, particularly prices and money supply.
2. *Smallness,* in that neither their supply of exports nor their demand for imports has a noticeable impact on world prices, which is assumed to be true even for Australia.

Subsequently, the small open economy model also introduced a different, somewhat counter-intuitive definition of terms of trade and also of the real exchange rate. It compares two sets of national prices for tradable and non-tradable goods or services, and states that the local prices of tradables are different from world prices only by virtue of the exchange rate (with perfect competition). Terms of Trade are thus defined as national tradables prices/national non-tradables prices.

The standard model then regroups economic sectors into three categories (see figure below). *Traditional or Resource Tradables* are goods and services whose prices are determined by supply and demand on world markets, including the extractive industry. *Non-Traditional Tradables* are modern elements of

12 To an extent, this corrects the sweeping statement on the minor weight of three out of the four linkages. Forward and backward link effects are still likely to remain weak in terms of *goods* supplied to the mineral sector, but *factor* links and moves become important, as well as the consumer link. See below.

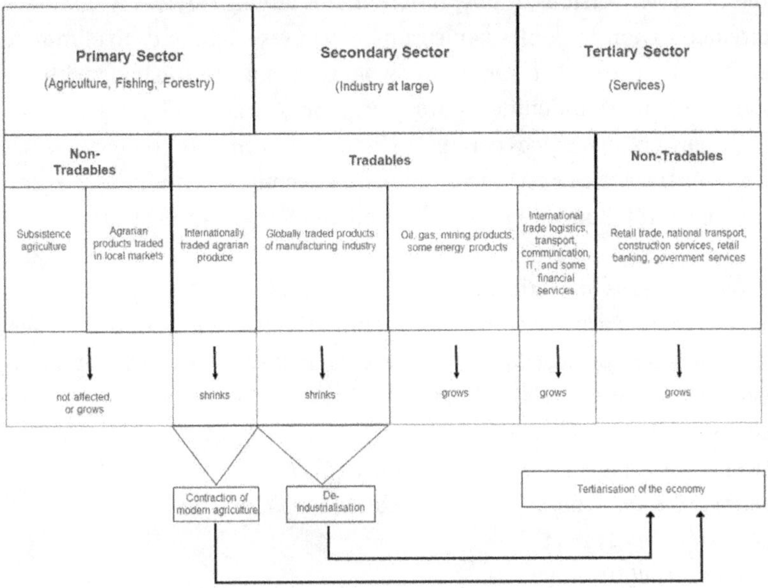

FIGURE 2.2 Tradables and non-tradables in resource-rich economies

agriculture and the manufacturing industry, the expansion of which is desirable from an economic point of view. *Non-Tradables* are goods and services such as national transport, construction, retail and household services which are either physically impossible to buy or sell abroad, or not conventionally bought and sold outside the country, mainly because of transport costs. Prices of non-tradables are determined by market forces within the economy; any shift in supply or demand will change the price of non-tradables. An obvious criterion for the classification as tradables is the exposure to competition in international trade – export-competing, import-competing, or both. Marketed outputs are considered to be non-tradable as long as they are only domestically sold. In this sense, the non-tradable part of agriculture, for instance, is broader than non-market subsistence farming. Marketed outputs such as sorghum or millet are also regarded as non-tradables as long as they are only sold domestically or in the bordering region, which makes little difference since cross-border trade does not generate a world price.

The breakdown of sectors in the figure above is not new. It always allowed to model intra- and inter-sectoral outcomes of mineral resource windfalls.[13]

13 In agriculture, intra-sectoral re-composition occurs when, under pressure from shrinking import purchasing power (in bust periods), sales of "non-traded" produce massively increase when people are forced to replace e.g. in West Africa rice by cassava.

Compared to earlier versions, it now differentiates among services which once were all treated as non-tradables while more recent research tends to eliminate the distinction altogether. Yet this is somewhat throwing out the baby with the bath water as technical difficulties to trade *some* services as well as persistently higher trade barriers for services compared to goods testimony of their still lesser tradability. What was once a stylised theorem has become an empirical question on how much contraction, de-industrialisation and tertiarisation occurs.

3.2 *Five Dutch Disease Effects*

Of particular interest are the co-variants behind the tectonic shift that generates the tertiarisation of the economy. In fact, each of these sector groupings is influenced by a vector of several effects:

1. The nominal *exchange rate effect*
2. The spending effect, also called the *price effect*
3. The resource movement effect, also called the *factor effect*
4. The *environment* effect
5. The *infrastructure* effect

The first three effects are drawn from classical DD literature. The fourth and fifth effects are our add-ons to the model. They are not systematically dealt with in seminal explanations of the economic DD vector even though their impact is physically more obvious than is the case for the three "classics." Moreover, the fourth and fifth effects economically generate covariance with the same sign.

Nominal Currency Appreciation (or the exchange rate effect) is a result of increased demand for the respective currency on world markets when there is an influx of revenue from mineral or energy resources. Tradables denominated in local currency suffer from reduced competitiveness on the export side and increased foreign competition on the import side. Volatility in the world price of commodities contributes to this effect by creating abrupt nominal exchange variation. Hence the channel has both a medium- and a short-term dimension.

The second factor, the *Spending or Price Effect,* operates through the rise in demand for non-tradable goods when the prices of these goods increase, as prices in the traded good sector are set internationally and thus cannot change. The extent to which a price rise for non-tradables will translate into higher general inflation depends primarily on two factors: the relative size of the two sectors and the nominal exchange rate (=for tradable goods). If the currency is allowed to appreciate, general inflation effects may be minimal, which is desirable for inflation targeting, but less so for structural policy. Beyond this, overall price effects depend in particular on the government spending curve and a possibly ensuing output gap, which would drive inflation.

Thirdly, the *Resource Movement or Factor Effect* refers to the re-allocation of labour, capital and even land as driven by factor price moves. During a boom time in a resource rich country, scarce human resources and capital are drawn to the newly emerging mineral riches and downstream services or construction. This constitutes a crowding-out between two parts of the private sector.[14] Higher income spurs faster domestic inflation by creating greater demand for all goods and services, and producers of tradables face rising costs in their purchases of non-tradable goods and services. The rising costs also include the wages of their workers, but producers cannot charge higher prices because they are in competition with foreign producers. As a result, they face a profit squeeze that will cause some of them to reduce production and employment.

Taken together, all three price effects (on the national currency, on goods and factors) lead to a *Real Exchange Rate* (RER) *appreciation* and engender mostly unwelcome or reverse structural change. Capital account movements often accompany and aggravate the process. The brain drain exerted by booming mineral and service sectors on the brightest minds among a country's few technically trained professionals may put a particularly severe burden on both the manufacturing sector and a government's capacity to steer further technological upgrading. The result is a lowering of political and technical absorption capacity in the private and public spheres. A final consequence relates to productivity. If the tradables sector – above all: manufacturing – plays, as widely assumed, a key role for a nation's productivity (both level and growth), then a shrinkage of modern tradables results in an economy-wide, permanent reduction of productivity. In this way, resource extraction cum tertiarisation represents the level of analysis in which entire national economies are affected by adverse specialisation. Based on both research and everyday observation, one can argue that there are two additional transmission channels that work economically in the same direction as the three previous ones.

The fourth spillover from the Dutch Disease is the detrimental Environment Effect. Risks to the environment are systematically entrenched in the physical nature of mining and drilling, even when it takes place off-shore, as incidents from Brent Spar in the North Sea to the BP oil spill in the Gulf of Mexico have shown. This is textbook market failure since high social costs are not borne by private investors unless these costs are forced upon them. The environmental dimension of the resource curse can be seen as a negative externality which is intrinsically associated with the Dutch Disease, hence with the economic dimension of the resource problem. However up to now, it did not feature

14 Some analysts also identify risks of crowding out the (non-resource) private sector through the public sector.

alongside the first three effects in the small open economies model and has thus remained peripheral to the economic core model of the Dutch Disease as discussed in the literature.[15] Macro-economically, the environment effect works very much in the same direction as the rest of the vector. As long as the social cost of environmental damage remains external instead of being internalised in the cost structure of mineral firms, it lowers costs and hence prices in the extractive industry, but drives up costs and prices in other sectors, including branches producing tradables and non-tradables. When the extractive industry drives people out of agriculture or fishing because of the proximity of platforms as in the Niger delta, it engenders adverse factor allocations as well. A full register of oil impacts would thus have to list the systematic, (mostly) adverse effects which land or water source expropriation have on local communities (= a sub-category of the factor effect) or environmental damage, with a link to the topic of oil-triggered conflicts (omitted from this text).

A fifth detrimental effect is generated by the intrinsic disposition of the extractive industry to monopolize the infrastructure needed for its proper functioning: ports, railways, access roads, power, water, and even social facilities – from schools and health care to security services. We call it the *Infrastructure Effect.* While certainly essential for the extraction process and sometimes beneficial for mine workers and others living in the vicinity, infrastructure provided by the industry itself directly and indirectly contributes to the neglect of public facilities. This occurs when the most powerful economic sector can afford to live as an enclave and/or diverts scarce infrastructure provision to itself when, for example, electricity already in short supply is absorbed mainly by the oil industry. In other cases, the industry generates its own power. Even private businesses such as housing construction that thrive in the wake of the boom are detrimentally impacted by neglected civil engineering and a lack of public transport. The other aspect is that big oil companies can afford to provide private schooling, health, and leisure to their relatively few and privileged employees (expression of capital intensity of the business). Oil thus creates what are known as exclusive *infrastructure catchment areas.* The social cost of essential public infrastructure beyond the confines of such areas is thus raised, comparable to the environment effect. As a result, oil-rich countries in Africa face an outright *infrastructure paradox:* an adverse impact on public infrastructure, which the booming sector needs less than most or all other sectors (except subsistence agriculture, but here we face endogeneity). The oil sector has less interest in public infrastructure than any other important taxpayer.

15 To make it clear: the broader literature and taxonomies on the resource curse cited contain ample references to environmental risks, but not in alignment with the three price effects.

Hence according to the "model," a composite index of per capita physical and social infrastructure is expected to be lower as a function of tax revenue levels, a vector of political economy factors and a probably binary variable if resource extraction set in before or after broad-based industrialisation (excluding countries like the Netherlands, Norway, and the United Kingdom). This is the fifth economic recourse curse effect.[16]

Taking the two latter DD effects together, it can be said that the environment effect externalises costs that should be firm-internal, while the infrastructure effect internalises facilities partly at the cost of the extractive industry that should be external or, in other words, available to the society as a whole – as a public good.

3.3 *Further Economic Effects*

In a way, all five DD effects are *price* effects – of the national currency, goods, factors, environment and infrastructure – and engender *factor* reallocations which represent unwarranted structural change. The full DD vector as presented here tends to reverse the general predictions of the *Balassa-Samuelson effect* for the special group of resource-rich developing countries. In their seminal research, Balassa, and Samuelson, focusing on productivity and wage differentials, and many other contributors examined why the law of one price and global purchasing power parity (PPP) obviously does not apply to developing countries (Samuelson, 1994). They all pointed with different explanations to the *lower* prices of non-tradables in poorer countries as the main reason for lower general price levels. They gave exemplary status to the ubiquitous cheap hairdresser working out of a roadside shack. In other words, a country's price levels are positively correlated with per capita income due to the modest prices of many services and construction in low and middle income countries. The DD diagnostic, however, calls into question or even disproves the validity of these long-debated findings as applied to a subset of economies, and there appear to be few linkages between the two bodies of research.[17] In fact, we find *two* tradables sectors in resource rich countries: one (manufacturing etc.)

16 At this point it should be clear that "Dutch disease effect" would be a misnomer insofar as, to our knowledge, neither neglect of public infrastructure nor a drain on skilled labour were associated with the original Dutch disease in the Netherlands, while the environmental effect *was*.

17 If the relevant PPP literature refers to refers to DD effects, then mostly with reference to the Netherlands itself. For a textbook summary see (Krugman, Obstfeld & Melitz, 2012). Referring to national accounts data represented in the Penn tables, Krugman et al. briefly observe that outliers are countries like Saudi Arabia with *higher* per capita incomes but *lower* price levels than the USA, in other words extremely resource-rich countries

with the features of the BS-models, i.e. lower productivity and lower wages than in advanced economies, and the other (the extractive industry) with metropolis features, i.e. high productivity, high wages and high capital intensity. The non-tradables sector in these countries does not perform like the first one (manufacturing, etc.) and thus does not entirely behave as predicted by theory. Note that the empirical degree of deviation from the theorem depends on whether you travel to Niamey or to Luanda, both in oil-rich countries.

Among the classical economic factors, the factor effect comes into play for land (removed e.g. by force from agricultural uses), capital (drawn into oil and gas), and labour. As capital for big oil extraction mostly comes from abroad, the *labour and land effects* will arguably be the most important ones, although a capital drift e.g. into domestic capital attracted by an oil bonanza should also be considered.[18] In countries with abundant unskilled labour, mass unemployment and capital-intensive extraction, the labour drain is mainly on qualified workers, technicians, and engineers.[19] Because working in the oil industry is an envisaged career path for the few students who choose engineering disciplines, it aggravates the scarcity of skilled labour, thus driving up the price of labour in these ranks.[20]

Unskilled labour in turn is drawn into certain non-tradable branches. Particularly striking manifestations of Dutch Disease are the construction booms witnessed in African capital cities and often taken as a sign of economic modernisation. However, *construction* booms in Lagos, Luanda, or Takoradi are manifestations of skewed economic growth in non-tradables rather than signs of lasting prosperity; the few accompanying industrial investments such as

---

(Krugman, Obstfeld & Melitz, 2012, p. 433). Both subgroups share the phenomenon of disproportionately high prices for non-tradables.

18 A particular expression of the capital factor effect accompanied the 2015/16 Nigerian crisis: dazzled by the golden opportunity, domestic capital bought massively into oil fields and drilling rights, financed partly by foreign credit. When the oil price and the exchange rate went down, dollar-denominated debt became doubly hard to repay – another facet of the peculiarity by which an otherwise healthy devaluation aggravates the problems of a structurally skewed economy.

19 Which is why the earlier argument of unused labour supply is hardly a valid counter against the factor effect.

20 Kingsley, the hero of Adaobi Tricia Nwaubani's acclaimed novel in Nigeria (Nwaubani, 2009) personifies another variant of the same problem. University-trained as a chemical engineer, he is geared to getting a job in the oil sector. After failing to find work in a sector already saturated with engineers, he cannot find employment in Nigeria's dwarfed manufacturing sector either. He finally turns to a booming special branch of financial services, known as advance fee fraud (AFF), in which he excels to the dismay of his solidly Christian family.

cement factories produce standard goods without much competitive appeal.[21] And this is precisely what one encounters when looking for a decent apartment or going to a modern hairdresser in Luanda (not your road side haircutter): prices are appallingly high, *despite* the construction and service boom. This is not to downplay the intermediate role played by the construction sector for some absorption of the unlimited supply of labour and some acquisition of basic technical skills. The construction boom works similarly in resource-poor Ethiopia and Rwanda.

The direct and indirect de-industrialisation resulting from the situation described above is bad for overall growth (Sachs & Warner, 1995) but especially harmful for modern manufacturing, which is, next to agriculture, one of the sectors likely to yield the most rapid capacity and employment growth. According to Corden and Neary (1982) and subsequent literature,[22] the effects of de-industrialisation can be measured against norms for sector weights at given GDP per capita levels (Chenery, Robinson & Syrquin, 1986). This means that in international comparison with other countries at the same GDP level, the proportion of a country's total GDP constituted by its manufacturing industry or non-traditional agriculture prematurely shrinks below expected levels. In this situation it becomes particularly difficult to make the inevitable adjustment back to non-boom tradable production once the mineral resources have been depleted. The decline in non-boom tradable production creates a lock-in effect that turns a foreign exchange surge into a lasting "disease."

We also encounter the notion of premature de-industrialisation in the new debate on growth and structural change. Fresh evidence seems to call the prospects for sustained growth through industrialisation into question, even for those authors otherwise in favour of this development path.[23] It has contributed much to a second, soberer reading of the *Africa Rising* narrative, but historically and doctrinally, the oil-related phenomenon came first. It started in the 1950s in Latin American and African countries, which at the time lacked either the wisdom or the necessary interplay of economic and political interests to facilitate vigorous action in favour of an ailing manufacturing industry. Policy failure thus added significantly to the phenomenon of early industrial

21 This does not imply that establishing a cement factory in a small country like Namibia is economically senseless, for the good produced comes with high international transport costs and might therefore be competitive in the domestic and surrounding markets. In fact, almost all African countries now have at least one cement factory, as part of the standard package of stand-alone industrial units, along with their brewery and grain mill. The Dangote group alone operates 18 cement plants across Africa.

22 For literature overviews see (Mildner & Lauster, 2011 and Van der Ploeg, 2011).

23 See (McMillan & Rodrik, 2014; McMillan & Harttgen, 2014; Rodrik, 2015).

decline and can be depicted on an inverted U-shaped curve of industry peaking earlier (in terms of GDP per capita) and at lower employment levels. The early de-industrialisation depressed income and demand. Avoiding or correcting this kind of policy failure in present-day oil-rich countries thus carries the potential to shift the inverted U to the right and upwards.

Unfortunately however, by adding the factors "demography" and "household consumption" to the analysis of structural change, we can model path dependence of oil-rich countries where oil plus tertiarisation of the economy lead to a *tipping point* beyond which dependency on imports of food and manufactured daily necessities has two related effects: the exchange rate stops working as a policy tool or, similarly, can no longer be allowed to work as an automatic adjuster during mineral price contraction. The economy needs the overvalued exchange rate to feed its people, obviously more so in poor populous countries. The ratchet effect of modern tradables contraction is reinforced when fuel is imported and/or fuel subsidies are perceived as the only welfare effect that the poor receive as inhabitants of an oil producing country. Beyond the tipping point, a macro-economic *poverty trap* yawns. Venezuela is probably caught in the trap; Nigeria is currently in the midst of an erratic search process to determine whether it is trapped. The body of literature on low-level equilibrium traps makes for insightful reading.[24]

Oil abundance creates not only structural imbalances at sector and subsector levels, but also *regional imbalances*, obvious both in individual countries and in regional economic communities (REC). Present even in very small open economies, regional imbalances arise most notably in big oil economies. Such imbalances can function positively in the agglomeration of regional growth poles and negatively when collusion between companies and local elites (including localised rents), environmental impact, and localised conflict is an issue, as it occurs paradigmatically with the oil spills in Nigeria's Niger delta. At an interstate level, a need for regional oil policy or for specific REC integration policy arises. Some regional economic communities in Africa have developed joint approaches to oil exploitation, including bold steps towards a common mining code, but they fail to deal with regional imbalances (Runge & Shikwati, 2011, p. 157 ff. also foregoing the opportunity to relax local content or procurement rules in favour of regional suppliers.

24 One textbook treatment of Dutch Disease with low-level equilibria under sector-differentiated returns to scale is Ros (2000), albeit strangely without exchange rate and policy implications.

4 Conclusion: On the Root Cause – It's the Economy or Politics, Stupid?

So far, we have dealt with the economic aspects of the oil curse in developing countries, especially matters of dis/entanglement. There is old and fresh argument from various disciplines, among them institutional economics, that countries with rich oil endowments are particularly ill-suited to carry out technically rational policy which benefit broader layers of society rather than small "elites." That many such governments are neo-patrimonial regimes and rely on "*limited access orders,*" following Douglas North, is invoked as proof of the difficulty. In fact, GDI and University of Cambridge authors (Altenburg, 2013) (Whitfield, Therkildsen, Buur et al., 2015) apply the stream of literature on regime types, as surveyed by Rosser fifteen years ago (Rosser, 2006), to assess the prospects for meaningful industrial policy. Such reference to regimes that limit the access to resources in favour of their respective clientele is sensible. Regimes in oil rich countries can be more corruption-prone than others, and not only in Africa, depending on other factors (see introductory chapter). This is an obvious risk for the observance of thrifty and transparent spending rules. Similarly, structural support to other industries which are possibly at the hands of competing elites may run counter to the narrow interests of the minerals power complex. Local content requirements, while an important means to re-link the oil economy with other sectors, still remain an invitation to patronage, etc. (Altenburg & Melia, 2014). Thus, while we argue that the list of *economic* difficulties in oil-rich countries is still longer than previously thought, other authors convincingly claim that the list of *political* hindrances is as long as that. The above-mentioned World Bank invitation of the ruling elites (here: of Ghana) to "*renounce the discretionary power provided by windfall revenue*" ensues consequentially, although not convincing as an economic policy means.

One cannot possibly deny the often overwhelmingly negative impact of the political and societal drivers of the resource problem, in stark contrast to the rich business opportunities in the respective countries. However, one can refute the claim according to which there has been for decades a clear set of economic rules – if not an outright blueprint – on how to fight the resource curse, so that it must have been all politics, stupid, when governments in oil-rich states, such as in Chad, stubbornly refused to play by these rules. The truth is that there has long been dos and don'ts on the shelf, mainly on fiscal and macro rules, but no complete textbook, and certainly not on structural policy. The basics of industrial policy in oil-rich countries are not yet common sense. Although we are confronted here with a classic case of generalized market failure, by adverse specialisation of the national economy as a whole, a considerable part of the literature persistently professes that the problem can be resolved by markets, by conventional fiscal and monetary policies, plus more and better public goods. Then, one wonders why real-life attempts at true structural policy in resource-rich countries so often look clumsy.

For instance, an IMF publication, reviewing the full panoply of mineral resource related policies, acknowledged the need to somehow diversify an oil-dependent economy but did not identify it as a strategic uphill battle against adverse impacts from all transmission channels (Arezki, Gylfason & Sy, 2011). That oil-rich economies urgently "need diversification" is not an interesting policy recommendation; it is stating the obvious. A decade ago, at the height of the commodities boom Collier gave a short blueprint-style summary of mineral resource-related policy measures and concluded on the infrastructure proposal:

> Typically, the non-resource export sector of LDCs faces high costs due to inadequate infrastructure for transport and power. By investing in these sectors the government can fully avoid Dutch disease.
>
> COLLIER, 2011, p. 5; my emphasis

It sure cannot, even admitting that transport and power constitute in many instances the two most binding industrial constraints. Or recall the two authoritative flagship reports on the African natural resources boom cited in the beginning. Not only that they were tragically out of date when published; none puts the links between resource abundance and selective industrial policy in clear terms, although we have shown that they are deducible as an inversion of well-known negative transmission effects. And take a more recent publication in line, the final report of the Brookings/AfDB/UNU-WIDER *Learning to Compete* project. It contains rich empirical material on African industries and has very valid policy lessons, departing from old mainstream thinking around the *Doing Business* agenda. Of course, the report recognises the special problem of resource curse and DD, and it acknowledges that the required diversification is easier said than done. The chapter "*Dealing with resource abundance*" has well thought-out ideas[25] but systematically remains in the neighbourhood of the extractive industry, in terms of sectoral and spatial policy. In the geographical coordinates of Africa's biggest oil economy, Nigeria, it does not arrive in Kano,

25 For the one on the construction industry see above.

so to speak, with its hundreds of rusting textile mills and shoe factories, but stays at the oil coast (Newman, Page, Rand et al., 2016).[26]

However, from the black box of actual *states at work* (Bierschenk & Olivier de Sardan, 2014) development-oriented authorities sometimes make a surprise appearance where one rather expects rent-seeking. Clientelistic elites at times discover their strategic interest to diversify away from oil – as successfully done in Indonesia under the Suharto regime or in Malaysia during the first reign of Premier Mahathir. At first glance unlikely candidates put also in Africa such political intentions in the right terms on paper.[27] However, they do this without textbook. Up to now, they had to operate targeted diversification *against* mainstream economics. In consequence, the evolving academic sub-discipline on natural resources in developing countries still has to rework and deepen its understanding of the interplay between economic agenda and regime types in Africa in two directions. The one is the larger-than-previously-thought economic nature of the resource curse, covered here. The other one is a question largely beyond the scope of this chapter: Which local circumstances make that some regimes in some societal arenas respond better to the complex challenge and avoid emergence of a rentier mentality, while others are mired in conflict and corruption (with number of country cases in-between the extremes)? A subset of this problematic relates to regimes which are capable to carry out ambitious structural policy as rolled out in this chapter, in the wider interest of the national economy, contrary to regimes which follow the trodden rentier path and just obey to market-liberal reform prescriptions when things go wrong.

In this regard, one element of path dependence seems clear. Countries with pre-existing "good" institutions are more likely to cope with the resource challenge. As observed in part of the literature, this represents an inversion of the chain of causality: rich mineral resources as such are not cursed (see introductory chapter). One string of the institutional turn in political economy even

26 In a similar vein, "The African Economic Transformation Masterclass" series, written by ACET and published by *African Business*, in its part 3 (March 2016), deals with natural resource management. Having number of good points, inter alia on how to manage information asymmetries in geological exploration, it mostly dwells on local content and value addition and concludes: "if the linkages cannot be made, the infamous 'resource curse' phenomenon threatens to come into play" (p. 47) – interesting but wrong, as the phenomenon also comes into play when local linkages work and may even become exacerbated by some of such entanglements.

27 See for instance the Industrialization Policy Letter for the Republic of Congo, conceiving off-mining initiatives and related public-private dialogue much in the right way. (Sassou N'Guesso, 2011) Not much has materialized out of this strategy in the following ten years.

asserts that stable institutions imported by (white) settlers to certain colonies are a reliable predictor of successful economic development, also in the presence of mineral resource riches (Acemoglu, Johnson & Robinson, 2001). Largely overlooked in the surprisingly positive reception the neo-institutional hypothesis is the fact that some settler colonies imported technological skills, tools and entrepreneurship in the first place, in fact an entire mode of production. This led to a situation where the bulk of agriculture and industry was already relatively developed when the mineral boom set in, and hence the core of the national economy proved far more resilient (Asche, 2011). South Africa falls grossly into this category, despite the negative impacts from the minerals-energy complex, described above. The ultimate cases in point are countries that were fully industrialised before an oil-gas boom commenced – Great Britain, Norway, Holland (times of Dutch Disease notwithstanding). Again, it corroborates the central topic of this volume: it is not the resource curse as such that determines a country's regime type and national fate but a number of – other – economic, geographic, social and cultural factors which ethnographers describe.

References

Acemoglu, D., Johnson, S., & Robinson, J. A. (2001). The Colonial Origins of Comparative Development: An Empirical Investigation. *American Economic Review*, 91(5), 1369–1401.

Acemoglu, D. & Robinson, J. (2012). *Why Nations Fail. The Origins of Power, Prosperity, and Poverty*. London: Profile Books.

African Development Bank, Organisation for Economic Co-operation and Development, United Nations Development Programme & Economic Commission for Africa (2013). *African Economic Outlook. Special Thematic Edition: Structural Transformation and Natural Resources*. Paris: AfDB, OECD, UNDP, ECA.

Altenburg, T. (2013). Can Industrial Policy Work under Neopatrimonial Rule? In: A. Szirmai, W. Naudé & L. Alcorta. (eds.), *Pathways to Industrialization in the Twenty-First Century* (pp. 345–372). Oxford: Oxford University Press.

Altenburg, T., & Melia, E. (2014). *Natural resource endowment and industrial development in Sub-Saharan Africa*. 12th Globelics Conference. Addis Ababa.

Arezki, R., Gylfason, T. & Sy, A. (Eds.) (2011). *Beyond the Curse. Policies to Harness the Power of Natural Resources*. Washington DC, IMF.

Asche, H. (2011). On the Colonial Origins of Statehood in Africa. A Critique of the Institutional Economics View. In N. Schareika, E. Spies and P.-Y. LeMeur (Eds.) *Auf dem Boden der Tatsachen. Festschrift für Thomas Bierschenk* (pp. 347–360). Köln, Köppe. Mainzer Beiträge zur Afrikaforschung 28.

Asche, H. (2018). *Industrial Policy Challenges in Resource-Rich Countries*. Mainz, Department of Anthropology and African Studies, University of Mainz.

Asche, H. (2021). *Regional Integration, Trade and Industry in Africa*. Heidelberg, Springer.

Bierschenk, T., & Olivier de Sardan, J.-P. (eds.) (2014). *States at work. Dynamics of African bureaucracies*. Leiden: Brill.

Chen, Y., Yuan Sun, I., Uzonna Ukaejiofo, R., Xiaoyang, T. & Bräutigam, D. (2016). Learning from China? Manufacturing, Investment, and Technology Transfer in Nigeria. *IFPRI DISCUSSION PAPER, 1565*. Washington, D.C.: International Food Policy Research Institute.

Chenery, H., Robinson, S., & Syrquin, M. (eds.) (1986). *Industrialization and Growth. A Comparative Study*. Washington DC: World Bank, Oxford University Press.

Collier, P. (2011). *Natural Resource Exploitation: Challenges and Opportunities for LDCs*. London: Commonwealth Secretariat.

Corden, M. W., & Neary, P. J. (1982). Booming Sector and De-Industrialisation in a Small Open Economy. *The Economic Journal*, 92(December), 825–848.

Grossman, G. M. (1981). The Theory of Domestic Content Protection and Content Preference. *The Quarterly Journal of Economics* 96(4), 583–603.

Hirschman, A. O. (1958). *The Strategy of Economic Development*. New Haven: Yale University Press.

Hufbauer, G. C., Schott, J. J., Cimino, C., Vieiro, M., & Wada, E. (2013). *Local Content Requirements: A Global Problem*. Washington DC: Peterson Institute for International Economics.

Kaplinsky, R. (2011). *Commodities for Industrial Development: Making Linkages Work*. Vienna: UNIDO.

Karl, T. L. (1997). *The Paradox of the Plenty: Oil Booms and the Petro State*. Berkeley: University of California Press.

Krugman, P. R., Obstfeld, M., & Melitz, M. (2012). *International Economics. Theory & Policy*. Pearson.

McMillan, M., & Rodrik, D. (2014). Globalization, Structural Change, and Productivity Growth, with an Update on Africa. *World Development*, 63, 11–32.

McMillan, M. S., & Harttgen, K. (2014). What is Driving the 'African Growth Miracle'? *NBER Working Paper Series*, 20077. Cambridge, Mass.

Mildner, S. & Lauster, G. (2011). *Curse or Blessing - Development or Misery. Scrambling to the Bottom or Scrambling to the Top. Natural Resources, Economic Growth, and Conflict: A Literature Review*. Eschborn, GIZ.

Mohamadieh, K., & Uribe, D. (2016). *The Rise of Investor-State Dispute Settlement in the Extractive Sectors: Challenges and Considerations for African Countries*. Geneva: South Centre.

Morris, M., Kaplinsky, R., & Kaplan, D. (2012). "One thing leads to another" - Commodities, linkages and industrial development. *Resources Policy*, 37, 408–416.

Newman, C., Page, J., Rand, J., Shimeles, A., Söderbom, M., & Tarp, F. (2016). *Made in Africa. Learning to Compete in Industry.* Washington DC: Brookings.

Nwaubani, A. T. (2009). *I do not come to you by chance.* New York: Hyperion.

Oranje, van M., & Parham, H. (2009). *Publishing What We Learned: An Assessment of the Publish What You Pay Coalition.* PWYP.

Otto, J., Andrews, C., Cawood, F., Doggett, M., Guj, P., Stermole, Stermole, F., & Tilton, J. (2006). *Mining Royalties. A Global Study of Their Impact on Investors, Government, and Civil Society.* Washington DC: World Bank.

Prieß, H.-J., & Berrisch, G. (2003). WTO-Handbuch. München: Beck.

Rodrik, D. (2015). Premature Deindustrialization. *NBER Working Paper*, 20935.

Ros, J. (2000). *Development Theory and the Economics of Growth.* Ann Arbor: University of Michigan Press.

Rosser, A. (2006). The Political Economy of the Resource Curse: A Literature Survey. Brighton, IDS, *IDS Working Paper,* 268.

Runge, J., & Shikwati, J. (Eds.) (2011). *Geological Resources and Good Governance in Sub-Saharan Africa.* Balkema: Taylor & Francis.

Sachs, J. D. & Warner, A. M. (1995). *Natural Resource Abundance and Economic Growth.* Cambridge / Mass., National Bureau of Economic Research.

Samuelson, P. A. (1994). Facets of Balassa-Samuelson Thirty Years Later*. *Review of International Economics* 2(3): 201–226.

Sassou N'Guesso, D. (2011). *Industrialization Policy Letter.* Brazzaville, Presidence of the Republic of Congo.

Tamba, I., Tchatchouang, J. C., & Dou'a, R. (Eds.) (2007). *L'Afrique Centrale, le paradoxe de la richesse: Industries extractives, gouvernance et développement social dans les pays de la CEMAC.* Yaoundé: Presses Universitaires d'Afrique.

The Economist (January 10th 2015). The twilight of the resource curse?, p. 32.

UNECA (2013). Making the Most of Africa's Commodities: Industrializing for Growth, Jobs and Economic Transformation: Africa's industrialisation imperative. *ECA policy brief,* 8(4), Addis Ababa.

UNIDO (2012). *Promoting Industrial Diversification in Resource Intensive Economies. The Experiences of Sub-Saharan Africa and Central Asia Regions.* Vienna: UNIDO.

Van der Ploeg, F. (2011). Natural Resources: Curse or Blessing? *Journal of Economic Literature* 49(2): 366–420.

Whitfield, L., Therkildsen, O., Buur, L., & Kjær, A. M. (2015). *The Politics of African Industrial Policy: A Comparative Perspective.* Cambridge: Cambridge University Press.

PART 1

Oil Politics and the Rentier State

3

Rural Rentierism? The Rentier State Theory and Its Applicability to Local Spaces in Gabon

Joseph N. Mangarella

1 Introduction

Rentier theories are powerful and compelling analytical tools for explaining certain political pathologies in states heavily dependent on oil exports for government income, and thereby offer an elegant, universalist, and non-essentialist explanation for patterns of corruption based on government-controlled oil rents (Beblawi & Luciani, 1987; Mahdavy, 1970; Yates, 1996). This analytical framework, which posits that "rentiers" occupy the instruments of state for their own gain, especially points to diminished public accountability, an ensuing decline in state legitimacy, and rent-seeking behaviour by state officials. However, many questions have since arisen which cast doubt on the supposed universality of the framework. For one, rentier theory predicts a relatively high degree of political stability, while oil rents—proceeds to state budgets from oil extraction—have caused regional conflict and instability in several African rentier states (Basedau & Lay, 2009). Another debate considers whether rentier theory has overlooked confounding factors and omitted variables in reaching conclusions that significant oil rents lead to pathologies in sub-Saharan Africa, as these outcomes are also faced by a wide variety of non-rentier African states, and manifest differently depending on the different sources of data (Bayart, 1989; Mamdani, 1996).

This chapter addresses these analytical issues by longitudinally applying rentier state theory to rural and peri-urban spaces which have so far mostly been neglected in literature on rentierism that focuses almost exclusively on political elites. But if the theory of the rentier state is to prove valid, it needs to also apply to the vast majority of subjects living in areas marginalised by the state. To test the rentier state theory, a qualitative case study design was chosen for this study, using primary, secondary, and archival sources in order to trace the processual outcomes of rentier effects (see section 2) on the oil-bearing community of Gamba—the historic oil town of Gabon situated close to the Ndougou lagoon about 600km south of the capital Libreville—from before the advent of oil to 2015. Before oil was discovered, Ndougou was enclaved

 | DOI:10.1163/9789004530065_004

and relatively isolated from transportation networks. An historical research approach is possible given that the town of Gamba has been home to the Shell Gabon Upstream terminal since the 1960s, after Shell Gabon's discovery of the onshore Gamba well in 1963. Since the 1980s, Gamba has been the seat of ever-expanding operations, including the discovery of the gigantic onshore Rabi-Kounga oil field in 1985 and subsequent production (beginning 1989) which contributed substantially to Gabon's rentierism. Gamba is therefore also an extreme case of local rentierism, in which rentier effects can be critically observed over the course of several decades.

The chapter concludes that while a "rentier mentality" appeared to result from the discovery of vast reserves in the 1980s (in contrast to the effects of less productive wells in existence there since the 1960s), the same mentality most likely existed prior to large-scale oil production in Gabon, based on oral history and archives. Thus, rentier state theory can only partially explain a perceived increase in corruption and a growing accountability deficit, while other factors—including decentralisation and anomic trends resulting from the breakdown of social solidarity without efforts at balancing from the state—appeared to hold sway. Moreover, the concept of "the state" in a region such as Gamba is highly problematic, since one has to distinguish the prefectoral state (executive, governors, prefects, chiefs) from the electoral, decentralised assemblies, which often operate independently of, and at odds with, the prefectoral state. Lastly, I consider the applicability of rentierism to local spaces, arguing that this is in part possible since it makes claims on individuals with reasonable access to incomes derived from oil rents. However, resource rentierism conceptions in general are more usefully positioned as subtheories of ethnography-based explanations of corruption and low political accountability. Other approaches, such as hybrid governance, may be better suited to the task of determining the causes of corruption and low accountability. The conclusion thus aims to deepen our knowledge of how rentierism plays out at the local level, and begs further understanding of the relationship between state-level macroanalyses and local manifestations.

2 Testing the Rentier State Theory (RST)

Since Mahdavy (1970) and Beblawi and Luciani (1987) introduced their theoretical foundations, many rentier theorists have applied these frameworks to not only the Middle East but also to Africa. Rentier theorists use the specific case of oil rent dependence to explain how elites, encouraged by weak law enforcement, exercise self-enrichment and self-empowerment to the detriment of democratic and rule-of-law values. Rentier theory embodies an organised research programme with defined concepts and a theoretical commitment to universalist and structuralist thinking. Oil dependence represents an extreme form of dependence due to the unparalleled cash flows and central management of oil revenues. However, Rentier State Theory (RST) has been criticised as "conceptual overstretch," where several intervening variables between the cause (oil) and the effect (democracy) are often ignored—as has been demonstrated in RST's application to the Middle East—and where falsifiability is difficult to achieve thanks to disagreements over definitions and causal mechanisms (Ross 2001, p. 331).

Thankfully, Yates (2012)—among the first scholars to explicitly apply RST to Africa—has since responded to some of these shortcomings. After surveying the literature, Yates lays out the causal logic of RST as follows: Dependency is created by a significant inflow of oil rent. (There is no consensus as to how much oil rent is needed to produce rentier effects, though Beblawi and Luciani (1987) set the threshold at 40% of all government receipts.) Within the political—as opposed to economic—dimensions of rentier theory, the state achieves financial autonomy from its subjects as a result of significant inflows of oil rent. This financial autonomy necessarily relieves the government of the burden of taxation and deteriorates the rentier state's extractive capacity. Three qualified rentier effects result from the absence of taxation. Firstly, the government ceases to be accountable to its subjects as the government and its bureaucracy no longer depend on the bulk of the population for their sustenance. This in turn limits *democratic participation*, which becomes a futile exercise. Thirdly, unaccountable governments inevitably face a decline in state *legitimacy*. Lastly, the financial autonomy of the state not only relieves the government of the burden of taxation, but also engenders a "rentier mentality," or broad-based rent-seeking in lieu of more economically productive pursuits. Government office is sought for its potential monetary rewards, and office-holding becomes an end unto itself. This in turn leads to widespread inefficiency and *corruption*.[1] Generally speaking, the more dependent a state is on oil for its financial sustenance, the more vulnerable it is to these outcomes (Yates, 2012, p. 87). These five rentier effects—low accountability, limited democratic participation, decline in state legitimacy, rentier mentality, and corruption—are all testable and, if demonstrated, would bear witness to the robustness of RST.

Rentier state theory is arguably grand theory, and this fact might lead some to argue against its applicability to rural and peri-urban spaces. It deals with

1 All of these rentier effects are well represented in RST literature. See Ross' literature review, for example (2001, pp. 332–336).

abstract concepts (e.g., "rentier mentality," "political accountability," "state legitimacy") and builds upon itself syllogistically, often sacrificing specifics for analytical cohesion. There are two reasons, however, for why I argue for the valid application of RST to localities. First, the human behavioural assumptions underlying the axes of rentier theory are fairly consistent throughout, and are indeed applicable to rural and peri-urban spaces. Corruption is held to be the illegal personal gain through public office, legitimacy rests on the ability of a Weberian state to answer to its citizens, and democratic participation effectively amounts to civil society. Behaviourally, individuals are maximisers facing constraints, albeit less than those in states with strong institutions. A rentier mentality should permeate all corners of society where there is perceived access to easy riches. Second, limited democratic participation, decline in state legitimacy, and corruption are conditions sustained by individuals who themselves reside anywhere. If the state is an apparatus subsidised and sponsored by the main organs of statehood in a capital city, then most municipal government concerns matters of the state. Therefore, the theorised incentive to instrumentalise public positions for personal profit remains. Grand theories are there to be qualified, not proven correct.

A newer generation of rentier theorists objected to the "uni-contextual" bent of orthodox RST, arguing quite reasonably that conflict, corruption, and low accountability in African states cannot be solely explained by oil. Other determining factors such as ethnic cleavages and post-colonial institutions must be explored (Tar, 2008, pp. 27–49), as well as the participation of multinational corporations and "subaltern groups" who compete with those who have captured the state for a piece of the rent (Omeje, 2008). When all these intervening variables are considered, however, the thrust of oil rentier theories becomes so diluted as to become almost meaningless, as Ross (2001) hinted in his introductory survey. There can indeed be wide variations in democratic outcomes among African states qualifying as rentier states—for example, Gabon has fared much better in this regard than its neighbour, Equatorial Guinea. And perhaps more importantly, the state itself—that which ceases to be accountable, experiences a decline in legitimacy, etc.—is seldom adequately defined, as this chapter will make clear. Problematizing the state opens several other dimensions of political reality—e.g., government-company duopolies and competing arms of statehood—that simply cannot be discussed with RST's broad strokes.

The chapter therefore concludes that alternative theories may be better positioned to explain the inconsistent rentier effects present at local levels, even in the most extreme of cases like the oil-rich Ndougou lagoon. "Hybrid governance" theories in particular have emerged to characterise subnational spaces as "local political arenas" where absentee states (such as rentier states without the need for extractive capacity or legitimacy) and the lack of national norm-setting from above may result in the creation of "sedimentation" of local public authorities. Moving away from hybridists' earlier attempts to redefine the "failed state," scholars like Christian Lund, Thomas Bierschenk, and Jean-Pierre Olivier de Sardan provide evidence to demonstrate the proliferation of public authorities filling the vacuum left by the state. Rather than always having a positive outcome, the situation is often given to incongruent legislation and initiatives, opportunistic rent-seekers, and lack of trust (Lund, 2006; Bierschenk & Olivier de Sardan, 1997). Given the emphasis on similar premises (absent states) while positing alternative causal mechanisms of democratic decline, hybrid governance is a worthwhile body of research to explore in application to African oil states.

The chapter proceeds by describing the historical development of certain rentier effects (state legitimacy, public accountability, rentier mentality, corruption, and legitimacy) in three separate time periods. Section 2.1.3 begins before the first wells were drilled, establishing a baseline for comparison with Section 2.1.4, when Gabon could be characterized as an incipient rentier state. Section 2.1.5 details rentier effects when Gamba and the Ndougou lagoon could be described as an extreme case of oil-rent dependence at local levels, after the discovery and exploitation of the giant Rabi-Kounga oilfield. The conclusions in Section 2.1.6 qualify RST according to this evidence, and suggest future lines of research.

3 Rentier Effects before Oil in Gabon (1950–1967)

Gabon suffered weak political accountability well before independence and oil rents, rendering difficult *ab initio* any attempt to establish a causal link between oil rents and future instances of weak accountability. Leon M'ba, the country's first president, achieved his status not as much through popular mandate as through backroom deals and the courting of key French business interests, notably the foresters. After a surprising and most likely fraudulent victory in the Territorial Assembly elections of 1957 (Ballard, 1964, pp. 289–349; Yates, 1996, p. 103), M'ba was appointed Vice President of the Government Council by the French Governor, setting up M'ba's succession to the Presidency upon independence in 1960. Historian Florence Bernault (1996, p. 262) identified M'ba's initial appointment as the moment when "Gabon went from a representative regime, albeit quite imperfect, to a regime of backstage manoeuvring."

At the onset of independence, backstage manoeuvring quickly devolved into authoritarianism. With the help of foresters connected to Paris, M'ba began coopting opposition parties in a broader effort to win a "yes" vote for the 1958 referendum on the French Fifth Republic's Constitution. Refusing to join the efforts of the ruling Bloc Démocratique Gabonaise (BDG), the Parti d'Union Nationale Gabonaise (PUNGA)—the most prominent and strident of the opposition—was targeted in legislation which granted M'ba unprecedented police powers. After the government failed to retain a departmental status within France and Gabon became independent in March 1960, PUNGA's leader was apprehended in Paris. Intimidation tactics encouraged more opposition to switch ranks, while several PUNGA members, including party co-founder René-Paul Sousatte himself, would eventually do the same. A series of laws enacted in May 1960 regulated public gatherings and targeted "subversive" activity, and were key to opposition party co-optation (Bernault, 1996, p. 296).

Shortly thereafter, M'ba declared a state of emergency, carried out arrests of his opponents, and dissolved the National Assembly. With near impunity and forester backing, M'ba was able to hand-pick the single electoral list of 1961 (Bernault, 1996, p. 306). M'ba's attempted consolidation of power eventually led to the suppressed coup attempt of 1964, during which the French authorities unilaterally invoked the Cooperation Accords, thus inviting French military assistance. M'ba was reinstalled, and surrounded by French agents led by the infamous network of French adviser Jacques Foccart, began imprisoning his opponents. The same "Clan des Gabonais" composed of Jacques Foccart's shadowy network of business associates who suppressed the coup would eventually groom Omar Bongo for succession in 1967 (Yates, 1996, pp. 113–114).

In the countryside, the formal political relationship between peasants and government had already been set by colonialism, and many of the notoriously despotic French colonial commandants de cercle[2] had been more or less reproduced in prefects and local administrators, many of whom remained European at independence (Bernault, 1996, p. 298). Chiefs in particular had not escaped widespread suspicion among villagers that they worked as informants to higher authorities (Bernault, 1996, p. 327), and villagers had plenty of reasons to believe this. Dissenting administrative chiefs were indeed either replaced or co-opted (Bernault, 1996, p. 269), a fate which befell chiefs in Nyanga province (the administrative unit surrounding Gamba) who in 1965 resisted attempts by the regime to forcefully regroup villages (Bernault, 1996, p. 352). After the failed coup attempt in 1964, BDG chapters had been created in all villages, oftentimes

2 The commandant de cercle presided over the smallest unit of French colonial administration.

invoking bitter memories of colonial taxation and census-taking. Henceforth M'ba became known as the "eater" of people (Bernault, 1996, p. 353).

Shortly before independence in 1960, and presumably as a means to facilitate the transition to self-governance, rural collectivities (*collectivités rurales*) and representative municipal structures (*communes de moyen exercice*) were added as quasi-corporate entities with a degree of financial autonomy. With respect to the municipal councils, only the larger cities benefited from formal republican structures and near-complete autonomy, as mayors were chosen by council members elected via universal suffrage. Smaller cities had their mayors appointed directly by the President's cabinet in Libreville. Universally elected members of the collectivities could collect the tax *vicinale* and disburse the proceeds towards local projects, but they could be—and often were—vetoed by the government-appointed sous-prefects. Furthermore, decisions reached by the rural collectivity were only executed after approval by the Interior Ministry in Libreville, entailing a process which commonly took as long as two months (Garandeau, 2010, p. 826). When funds were insufficient, rural collectivities simply exacted a form of forced labour upon their constituents; villagers were required to provide both labour and materials (Garandeau, 2010, pp. 848–872). Such issues were among the many reasons the government adopted the forced village regrouping policy in 1963–1964, one which was enforced with little to no consultation with the very cantons subject to removal or consolidation (Garandeau, 2010, pp. 848–872).

Gabon had therefore satisfied none of the requirements for the enjoyment of vertical (politicians to electors) or horizontal (checks and balances) accountability (see O'Donnell, 1998 for different forms of accountability). M'ba not only headed an authoritarian regime with a rarely contested grip on affairs at every level, but he had also become increasingly unpopular in the years leading up to the 1964 attempted coup until his death in 1967. What remains to be seen is whether the increasing financial autonomy—or, more accurately, the increasing assurance of financial autonomy based on oil rents—of the state in the 1970s had any discernible effect on public accountability, from the countryside of the Ndougou lagoon to the capital in Libreville.

4 Rentier Effects after Gamba Oil Field Development but before the Discovery of Rabi-Kounga (1967–1989)

4.1 *National Accountability*

The creation of a one-party state, in conjunction with French assistance and generous amounts of petrodollars after the Gamba oil field development in the 1960s and thereafter, helped sustain a regime entirely noxious to public accountability. Following the BDG practice, committees of its successor party, the Parti Démocratique Gabonais (PDG), were placed at each level of government, where success in politics depended entirely on being a militant party member. Dialogue and tolerance naturally gave way to cut-throat intraparty competition where people regularly denounced each other to get ahead (Garandeau, 2010, p. 197). The infamous Garde Republicain, commanded by French and staffed by those belonging to Bongo's ancestral ethnic group (the Teke), were charged with rooting out political dissidents (Yates, 1996, p. 121). Whereas many political forces and opponents were folded into the PDG, including L'Union des Femmes, L'Union de la Jeunesse, and the Conférence Syndicale Gabonaise (COSYGA) in 1973, many intransigent critics were either intimidated or assassinated. As a ranking member of Libreville's Franc-Maçonnerie lodge and leader of the Njobi secret society, Bongo was able to enlist the support of Bob Denard, a French mercenary, in orchestrating the September 1971 assassination of Germain Mba, leader of the Mouvement National de la Révolution Gabonaise (MNRG) (Yates, 1996, p. 122). In addition, Marxist student groups at the National University of Gabon were arrested in 1972 after creating the Parti Gabonais de Travail and not released until 1976. After their release, some maintained a healthy distance from politics while others joined the PDG (N'Nah, 2006, p. 208). In February 1973, Bongo succeeded in his incumbency (this would be his first election) by winning 99.59% of the vote—nearly a statistical impossibility.

While high oil prices and rising interest rates in the early 1970s negatively impacted most of equatorial Africa and ended nearly three decades of growth, the government in Gabon was among the minority states to have benefited. As external debt rose, so did oil receipts, allowing the regime to pursue an "anarchic" development plan which focused on constructing hospitals, schools, and even athletic centres in cities. The countryside, however, remained practically unchanged, facilitating a rural exodus which would eventually shift the country's geospatial demographics so that Libreville and Port-Gentil would balloon in population while villages were left to decay (N'Nah, 2006, p. 200). As oil prices began showing signs of stagnation and decline in 1976, Gabon was left with soaring external debt (~XAF 500 billion) as oil receipts were practically squandered and embezzled (N'Nah, 2006, p. 201).

4.2 *Local Accountability*

Throughout the first oil boom (1973–1977), misguided development policies and failed efforts at *regroupement*—government efforts to agglomerate rural villages into larger communities—led to the pluralisation of local collectivities and bureaucratic strain. This, in turn, led to decentralisation reforms in 1975. But despite the creation of departmental councils and consultative committees of chiefs, the reforms merely extended party and central administrative control to the lowest geo-political tiers (Garandeau, 2010, pp. 893–938). Thus, local accountability had suffered prior to the introduction of oil and stagnated throughout the late 1970s, and what little historical information exists on today's Département de Ndougou (the administrative district circumscribing the Ndougou lagoon) during this time largely reflects the nationwide trend. In 1967, the Canton of Sette Cama became the autonomous district of Sette Cama/Gamba within the Ndougou department after petitioning by Shell. In 1975–1976, the seat of the sous-prefect of the newly created Department of the Ndougou was permanently transferred to Gamba, near Shell's major upstream oil terminal (see map). This reportedly acted against the interests of the area's local elites who agitated to keep their primary source of employment and resources in their centuries-old trading post. Nevertheless, the Prefect of the larger Ogooué-Maritime province happily reported in 1968 that "all villagers" in the District Autonome de Sette Cama/Gamba were in favour of the BDG (Saulnerond, 1968).

Seemingly contrary to rentier theories, Shell's presence throughout the 1970s appeared to expose other, informal channels of vertical accountability; in other words, oil rents appeared to accentuate the benefits of neo-patrimonialism without overly impacting formal corruption. As the clan largely remained the mechanism through which most grievances were expressed and resolved, Shell had to contend with as many as five families whose elite members were prominent in rural collectivities. As opposed to the prefects, local politicians and administrative chiefs were often clan heads. In fact, it is likely that both the BDG and later the PDG made sure of this when composing electoral lists (Ossendo, personal communication). It is also likely that these older forms of solidarity resulted in goods and services for the local population. The Boukousso clan chief who had negotiated Shell's exploration zones near the Gamba terminal had also demanded that Shell provide medical assistance, schooling, and work to members of his family. According to one local elite, Shell was financing up to 90% of the lagoon's medical fees during this era (Penga, 2nd Maire adjointe, personal communication, August 2015). The provision arrangements also allegedly benefited Shell, who could thus write off portions of its legal allowances to the Gabonese state (Ndoutoungu, Ex-advisor at Ministry of Hydrocarbons, personal communication, July 2015).

As Shell was contracted to build and develop the town of Gamba in conjunction with other state entities, the existence of a Shell-state duopoly is undeniable. The official visit of President Omar Bongo to Gamba in 1971 made clear the

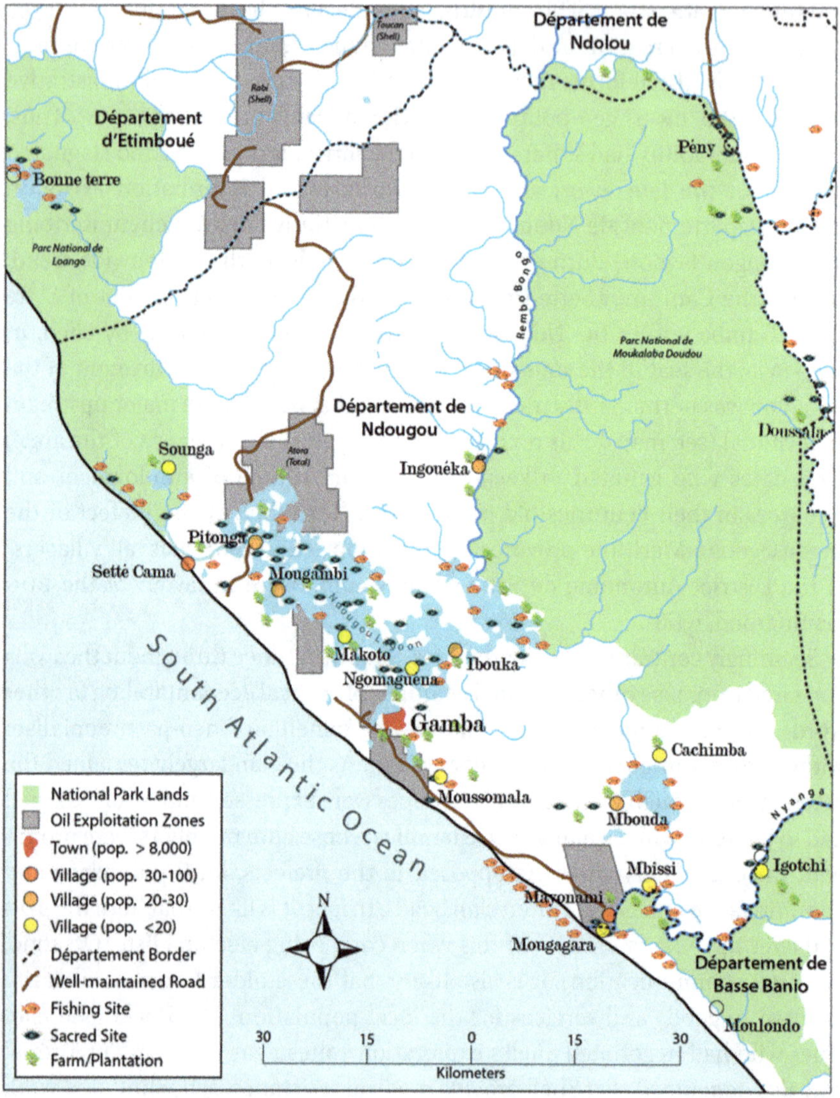

FIGURE 3.1 The Ndougou Lagoon, author's illustration derived from the World Wildlife Fund, Shell Social Performance Plan, and the Plan de Développement Local du Département du Ndougou et de la Commune de Gamba, 2012

duopoly, and it seems from most ensuing decisions that Shell was given *carte blanche* to continue with its overall development. In this sense, Shell served as a proxy state, influencing national decision-making and taking over state responsibilities at the local level. For example, the sous-prefect reported to Libreville in 1969 that the breakdown of their government-owned jeep forced local administrators to rely on Shell. Despite the repentant tone, however, the sous-prefect was quick to extend gratitude for Shell's hosting of a recent Christmas party.[3] Sometimes, however, local assemblies and clans were not responsive to popular will, or Shell was unresponsive to clan demands. When the famed hunter/guide Maurice Patry petitioned the collectivity to exclude fishermen from his touristic hunting sites, the petition was granted, which is still recalled bitterly by many villagers of Sette Cama who do not benefit personally from today's refashioned safari lodge. Shell was also granted exclusive operating rights over the provisions of the harbour at Mayonami against the wishes of the canton chief and many of the fishers using the harbour. As an external actor, Shell's generosity was limited by a calculated program of buffering contestation (Ratanga-Atoz, personal communication, July 2015) and the minimal and rather vague requirements demanded by the state.

4.3 *The Legitimacy of the State in the Ndougou*

Under rentier theories, such limited state accountability (if one dissociates Shell and the state as a single, authoritative duopoly) should be met with a decline in state legitimacy. If such a decline took place in more contested regions of Gabon such as the Woleu-Ntem—where ethnic Fang had traditionally fought to preserve autonomy and influence in Libreville—it clearly did not in much of the Ndougou lagoon. In fact, the legitimacy of the state in the Ndougou may have increased for reasons not necessarily having anything to do with oil production. Interlocutors near-universally expressed appreciation for the policies of Omar Bongo, vis-à-vis both his predecessor Leon M'ba and his successor Ali Bongo. One interlocutor invoked the prevailing national sentiment, which was that Leon M'ba simply continued French colonial practices and was thus incapable of overturning said unjust practices such as allowing "whites" to remain in administrative positions.[4] Omar Bongo, on the other

3 "[P]our mes differents déplacements je suis obligé de me vouer à la Shell—solution inélégante s'agissante de déplacement pour l'adminisration du District." *Fiche d'Activités du Mois de Décembre, 1969, District Autonome de Sette-Cama/Gamba*, by Revignet-Ingueza, Le Sous-Préfet du District Autonome de Sette Cama-Gamba, January 1, 1970, Carton 2385, Région de l'Ogooué-Maritime, Fiches mensuelles d'activités du mois de Décembre, 1969, Archives Nationales du Gabon, Libreville, Gabon.

4 In 1969, the sous-prefect of Sette Cama/Gamba lamented that much of the population believed the country to be "*encore dirigé par les 'BLANCS*.'" (original capitalisation) - *Fiche d'Activités du Mois de Décembre, 1969, District Autonome de Sette-Cama/Gamba*, by Revignet-Ingueza, Le Sous-Préfet du District Autonome de Sette Cama-Gamba, January 1, 1970, Carton 2385, Région de l'Ogooué-Maritime, Fiches mensuelles d'activités du mois de Décembre, 1969, Archives Nationales du Gabon, Libreville, Gabon.

hand, ended the "suffering" (Chef de village of Mougagara, personal communication, August 2015) and perhaps even colonial practices by instituting Gabonisation in the 1970s, according to one local elite (Moussavu, personal communication, August 2015).

In addition to favourable attitudes towards the policies of Omar Bongo, the Gabonese state benefited from a form of legitimacy derived from power and force which was unmistakably linked to Gabon's pre-colonial and colonial past. A form of administrative legitimacy—a tacit and normative idea (Schatzberg, 2002, p. 1)—prevailed in the Ndougou thanks in no small part to the imposition of customary chiefs and the associative power they derived from higher French administration. As under French colonialism, chiefs in the Ndougou enjoyed a conscious follow-up attempt by the Bongo regime to replicate traditional legitimacy wherever possible by appointing as chiefs those who descended from customary chiefs and other forms of traditional authority. But Joseph Tonda also claims that over time these same people acquired the legitimacy of party and state and were thus "representative" (Tonda, personal communication, July 2015). Another interlocutor makes the same claim, invoking an "administrative legitimacy" derived from habituation to these forms of representatives, and the power they were historically able to wield (Ratanga-Atoz, personal communication, July 2015). Such was the case in the Ndougou, where administrative chiefs were more often than not clan heads in an area where matriclans and family hierarchy predominated. In a seeming confirmation of Mamdani's (1996) idea of the bifurcated state, the Ndougou was ruled "cost-effectively" by utilising "natural" forms of governance when and wherever possible. The use of colonial forms of legitimacy by post-colonial regimes may also be substantiated by reference to an old Loumbou terms signifying "chief of state" being developed and modified to designate the "highest authority in the country," which itself had not existed until 1960 (Mouvoungu, personal communication, July 2015).

4.4 *Rentier Mentality and Corruption in the Ndougou*

Two components of rentier theory which do in fact resonate in the Ndougou are the oft-remarked "rentier mentality" and consequent corruption, though it is unclear such outcomes derive from oil as such rather than collective impressions of relative scarcity. One prominent opposition figure based in Libreville shared a prevalent opinion among non-southern Gabonese that southerners were "lazy people" thanks to the easy riches of oil (Essangui, personal communication, July 2015). But as explained previously, though the Ndougou was enclaved and relatively isolated from transportation networks prior to Shell's arrival, many local family members had connections in the region's capital of Port-Gentil, and thus had a self-awareness of their own well-being relative to those inhabiting more urban spaces. It is therefore unsurprising that upon Shell's arrival, a previously held affinity for money (Tonda, personal communication, July 2015) was on display as locals agitated for unskilled work and jockeyed for positions within the company or local government. Money was a means towards escaping the kind of isolation from which so many rural Gabonese sought to free themselves at independence. Political clientelism from this perspective becomes a means to escape isolation and aspire to a standard of living sustainable in a monetised economy where jobs and opportunities are often scarce. Though not as efficient a means to redistribution as transparent and state-driven methods, little opposition to political clientelism existed during this time (Secretary General of City Hall, personal communication, August 2015).

Another explanation for a persistent rentier mentality might be based on deep-rooted socio-political culture. The southern matriclans of Gabon were by and large tributary extensions of the pre-colonial Loango kingdom based in Buali (Diosso), present-day Congo-Brazzaville. Clientelism in this sense is a pre-existing mode of organising social and political spaces, and one which easy money from oil might only lubricate. The opposition figure cited above admitted that southerners bore "laziness" as a cultural in comparison to his native Fang (Essangui, personal communication, July 2015). The logic behind a cultural argument is that matriclans of the south, where the oilfields are located, and perhaps the Baloumbou in particular, thrived on greater control over widespread clients whilst utilising the legitimating influence of the Maloango in Buali, the king of the Loango kingdom (Martin, 2002). As a result, social and political advancement came through gathering dependents and clients, rather than other forms of materially productive labour. According to a Libreville-based jurist originally from southern Gabon, "those [villagers in the Ndougou lagoon] who don't have relatives in Gamba become the clients of those who do" (Nambo, personal communication, July 2015). Also, village elites choose to go into politics so that "those of his village become his clients," a process compounded by the inflow of oil money into Gamba (Nambo, personal communication, July 2015). With oil, there is then enough money within the state apparatus to also keep chiefs in the system, while in the south these chiefs retain their legitimacy thanks to the region's particular history (Mpaga, personal communication, July 2015). Models of deference to chiefs and administrative authority most likely lead to comments such as: "If the chief says do something, you do it. If the prefect says do it, you do it. The Loumbou are like that." (Koumba, personal communication, July 2015).

Such arguments support the notion that rather than instigate an exogenously derived form of political clientelism, Shell's arrival ushered in material and symbolic goods which would allow a pre-existing system to intensify. The inadequacy of this contention, however, lies in the unaddressed determinants of clientelism itself. Cultural aspects have been considered, but explanations based on these run the risks of banality and tautology. Further on in the chapter we will consider more dynamic explanations of political clientelism in the Ndougou.

5 Rentier Effects after the Discovery Rabi-Kounga (Since 1989)

5.1 *Local Accountability*

After years of waste and mismanagement of oil receipts, Gabon fell into a debt crisis during the latter part of the 1980s, which led to the conclusion of an IMF austerity plan. Frozen wages and other cuts led to strikes, notably at the SOGARA refinery in Port Gentil. Rioting, however, did not result in the PDG's ouster, as it won a slim majority in parliament in 1990. The elections were alleged to have been fraudulent (Yates, 1996). On 15 March 1991, parliament approved a new constitution inaugurating the third republic in Gabon and introducing a host of formal power-sharing arrangements, and checks and balances. The president would be elected for five years and permitted another term, while a free press was nominally recognised. But little had changed in reality, leading to more general strikes and successful attempts by Bongo at co-optation. OPEC-led production cuts led to more strikes that same year, culminating in more half-hearted reforms that ultimately buttressed Bongo's legitimacy (N'Nah, 2006). It was during this time that development wells at the gigantic Rabi-Kounga oilfield, serviced by staff and industries in Gamba, came on-stream (1989), with production peaking in the late 1990s. Rabi-Kounga would thereafter provide roughly half of Gabonese total production, which peaked in 1997 at 364,000 b/d and dropped to 230,000 b/d in 2007.

Despite an unmistakable accountability deficit, political stability became more or less the norm in Gabon from the mid-1990s to 2009, with the PDG winning commanding majorities. Three years after the presidential election of Omar Bongo's son, Ali Bongo shook up the old order in 2012 by consolidating his cabinet and limiting the number of ministries. In doing so, many of Omar Bongo's former clients were either cast aside or overlooked. The long-time opponent of the dynasty and director of the environmental NGO Brainforest, Marc-Ona Essangui, claims that this was a conscious attempt by Ali to create a small inner circle answerable only to him (Yates, 2013). Such actions helped fuel the events of 2016, when scores of protesters swept Libreville in support of Jean Ping, Ali's officially defeated opponent in the presidential elections, as well as in the hapless coup attempt of 2019.

5.2 *Local Politicians*

In conversations with public officials and through direct observation, it is unclear whether any systematic relationship of vertical accountability to the local population was established in Gamba and the Ndougou. Assessing the commitment of the electorate of elected officials is no easy task, but several anecdotes paint a variegated picture of how local politicians view their roles. Gamba's first mayor, Doctor Sisso, is both accessible and conscientious, and as the clinic's only certified physician, appears to care deeply for the well-being of patients and the community as a whole (Sisso, personal communication, August 2015). Similarly, the third mayor (2003–2008) was candid and attempted to initiate several public works projects, while also railing against the "egocentrism" of those in state government and the atmosphere of "politique du ventre" (Senator, personal communication, August 2015). In contrast, the second mayor (1999–2003) and current senator was evasive during interviews and reaffirmed from his grandiose villa's living room that he was ambitious and desired to move up the political ladder (Senator, personal communication, August 2015). The fourth and contemporary mayor (2008–2013, 2013–2018) was unavailable for interview, but her *Directrice du Cabinet* and *Chargé de Mission* reaffirmed her commitment to the goals set out in the region's local development plan PDL (Chargé de mission to the mayoral cabinet director, personal communication, August 2015), while the Secretary General of City Hall (an unelected civil servant) praised the mayor for organising town hall meetings (Secretary General of City Hall, personal communication, August 2015). At the same time, one of the maires adjoints who had run against the sitting PDG mayor lamented that people often voted only according to their "mood" (Maire Adjoint, personal communication, August 2015).

Members of the departmental council proved just as varied in their approach to governance. A retired member stated during an interview that the council's function was to transmit law between the state and the people. As councillors they did not "take initiatives" and they needed to explain "Why the law, how to respect it, how to apply it." When asked if people used electoral pressure to dictate the course of policy, he replied in the negative. "They were accepting because it was the state. It's the intellectuals who analyse.... There is no problem. All Gabonese complain ... people complain, but it's Shell who hires. They approach the elected.... Shell has a community liaison to take grievances" (Former Vice President of Departmental Council and ex-assemblyman, personal communication, July 2015). Paternalism like this was not unusual. One interlocutor stated that when constituents attempted to form associations in the past for the purpose of either siphoning state resources or expressing a list of grievances, local politicians stepped in to "take advantage of it in bad faith" (Gamba local radio, July 2015), evidence that contradicts other assertions that southerners were reticent and passive. On the other hand, plenty of reports suggest that even local politicians found it sufficient to capture the electorate with t-shirts and even cash handouts. Other more civic-minded constituents complained that "we vote and vote and nothing changes" (Inhabitant Ingouéka, personal communication, September 2015) or that "politicians don't bring anything" (Mbouity, personal communication, August 2015).

Ignoring for the moment some of the prima facie positive initiatives taken by local representatives, much of the accountability deficit may be due to party control emanating from Libreville and/or Port Gentil. It is generally accepted that the PDG often imposes local authorities against the wishes of locals (Tonda, personal communication, July 2015), in spite of the rhetoric championing of multipartism. The brother of the Ndougou's cantonal chief, a certified nurse, claimed that the PDG "controls everything". According to him, a minister will visit individuals and assess party affiliation, and if he or she believes they are members of the opposition, said minister will make promises but never deliver anything (Younger brother of Chef de Canton of the Ndougou, personal communication, July 2015). Even members of the nominal opposition such as ADERE (unofficially an allied party to the PDG) feel pressure to bend to the ruling party. One villager in Ingouéka related a recent story whereby a militant ADERE council member from Ibouka was invited by the PDG "bosses" in Port-Gentil to discuss issues of common interest. When the youthful opposition member returned, he was recast as a loyal member of the PDG (Inhabitant of Ingouéka, personal communication, September 2015). The Secretary General of the Departmental Council added that often local politicians will return from trips to the United States or Europe ambitious to change things. But once they are given positions, "they stop militating." In addition, and in a blow to horizontal accountability, he said that the prefect rarely exercised his veto over decisions of the council, because they are the majority party anyway (Ossendo, personal communication, August 2015).

In a nutshell, formal political accountability generally suffered in the Ndougou, yet it also varied according to the institution and individual, which seemingly confirms Mamdani's thesis on local spaces which remain relatively unincorporated by the state (Mamdani, 1996).

5.3 *National Politicians*

Locally elected officials, given their proximity to their own constituents as well as the kindred links they share with much of the population, do not on the whole appear entirely unaccountable and distant. Indeed, they remain accessible as members of the community, and like any political class, are not at all homogenous. The same, however, cannot be said for the senators and assemblymen and women who represent the region in the chambers of Libreville. The historian Ratanga-Atoz claims that the regime will refuse to put in place intellectuals as either chiefs or on electoral lists if either they do not belong to the party or if they are too intellectual, as intellectuals are perceived as having "too much knowledge". At the time of the interview, Ratanga-Atoz's former student was the minister of the interior and though once his pupil, Ratanga-Atoz could no longer "tell [the minister] anything". Nor does the state regime appreciate personal initiative, according to the historian. Referring to his nephew who was responsible for the construction of a bridge in Mayumba but who was not permitted to inaugurate it (in lieu of President Bongo): "If you rise alone, you are bad, you are a sorcerer." Instead, the state prefers candidates who "have been there a while" and who will not ask questions (Ratanga-Atoz, personal communication, July 2015).

According to villagers, the state is also hopelessly distant, which also seems to contribute to a certain fatalism prevalent for the last couple of decades. In a group discussion, the villagers of Ibouka complained that not only is the state unhelpful and rarely if ever responds to their communal demands, but their own deputies and senators remained completely inaccessible (Inhabitants Ibouka, personal communication, August 2015). The Senator himself admitted that national politicians only return to Gamba for certain holidays such as the independence celebration in August, preferring to remain in Libreville most of the time (Senator of Gamba, personal communication, August 2015). Furthermore, there is a consensus among most of the population of the Ndougou that the oil money all goes to "the top," and that they never see it.

Though clearly more aloof than their local counterparts, national politicians do respect some forms of accountability which may not be considered formal. Ingouéka and Mougambi are two cases in point. Ingouéka is the furthest removed from Gamba of all lagunar villages and is located to the north on the river Bongo, yet by many accounts the best provided for. Its media centre still operates, its primary school is staffed, its medical dispensary still provisioned, and many houses are fashioned with coveted wooden planks. According to the village elites including the cantonal chief, this is because their deputy was well-meaning and sensitive to the plight of his constituents, and thus kept getting voted into office (Inhabitants of Ibouka, personal communication, August 2015). In Mougambi, at least the vestiges of decent infrastructure remain, including a rare water pump. The village elite insists that this was possible because of a successful national politician who remained true to his native village (Notable of Mougambi, personal communication, August 2015). In honour of the late politician, the village erected an impressive mausoleum overlooking the lagoon, and kept his mansion intact and uninhabited. Though perhaps an informal expression of accountability, this variant of "pork-barrel" politics is not unknown to Western democracies, most notably the United States of America.

5.4 *The Prefectoral State*

As we have seen, the "state" in Gabon may also refer to the executive branch, including the provincial governors, prefects, and chiefs. One can therefore speak of executive accountability, even if the lines of accountability linking the executive to the population are circuitous and indirect. For instance, the Secretary General of the City Hall reaffirmed the state's commitment to respecting "customary" land ownership. Although the law clearly states that land formally belongs to the state, and it is clear that the state reserves the power of exclusion, the state almost always assures that land is unoccupied before embarking upon public development schemes. The hesitance to readily confiscate land, even if profitable on behalf of a multinational corporation, reveals accountability (Secretary General of City Hall, personal communication, August 2015).

The prefect in the Ndougou wields considerable power over local affairs that extend beyond the legislative veto, such as controlling and monitoring agencies such as the gendarmes, the Brigade de Faune, and the Agence Nationale des Parcs Nationaux (ANPN). He is also marginally accountable. Since administering a region which provides nearly half of the government's revenue necessitates close attention to local dynamics, prefects have been and are regarded by the local population as a final measure in case of difficulty. When Maurice Patry, the acclaimed hunter/guide (see above), succeeded in petitioning the departmental assembly to exclude fishermen from his touristic hunting areas, the prefect assured the citizens of Sette Cama that they could quietly continue. When the prefect selects chiefs or settles disputes, it is with local political dynamics in mind. Even in Gamba, the process of chief selection is a familiar affair, where quartier chiefs are still typically family heads (Fisherman of Soungha, personal communication, August 2015), despite a glaring formal accountability deficit. For example, the Government Relations director of Shell-Gabon suggested that the prefect overstepped authority by negotiating certain matters with Shell, which are the prerogatives of local assemblies (Koumba, Shell Government Relations, personal communication, August 2015), which include locally elected councillors to the Mairie and Departmental Council whose primary role appears to be determining the use of budget outlays.

As members of their respective communities, cantonal chiefs, regroupement chiefs, and village chiefs are almost all locals. They nearly all had at one point been employed by Shell-Gabon. Most villagers will cite their chiefs as the people to whom they would turn if they had any minor problems, whether it be financial or cases of larceny or adultery (Gamba local radio reporter, personal communication, August 2015). Exceptions to this relative accountability, however, include at least one absentee chief to whom villagers attribute their lack of resources and dilapidated structures. Another more pernicious example is one cantonal chief who is often accused of confiscating public goods (boats, mattresses, lamps, etc.) for personal use (Mboumba, Housemaid of case de passage in Pitonga, personal communication, August 2015). A strict hierarchy also encourages blind loyalty (Ratanga-Atoz, personal communication, July 2015), sometimes at the expense of village priorities. An NGO worker in Sette Cama warned that chiefs may refrain from open discussion because they are unsure as to whether their interviewer is a spying party member (Head of NGO Ibonga, personal communication, July 2015). One chief expressed fear of being killed if he continued with his harsh criticism of the government in Libreville (Chef de village of Mougagara, personal communication, August 2015). In fact, the most vocal elites tend to be those whose applications for chiefdom have gone unanswered or are mired in bureaucracy. The chief-elect of Mayonami is heavily preferred by the population, which dislikes Shell's occupation of the provisions harbour and the restrictions it naturally imposes on their fishing activities. The chief-elect of Mougambi was also the most virulently critical of the regime, and was likewise awaiting confirmation of his chiefly status.

In sum, the concept of "accountability" in the Ndougou must be disambiguated, as the decentralised assemblies were held to be relatively unaccountable to their constituents, while the unelected prefectoral officers were quite responsive to popular will. Rentier theory, therefore, must account for this kind of discrepancy in order to effectively describe the evolution of political events in rentier states and spaces.

5.5 *The Legitimacy of the State in the Ndougou*

The legitimacy of the Gabonese state in and around Gamba does not rise and fall with strict political accountability, as much as it may with other factors. First, the legitimacy of the state in the Ndougou must be disaggregated. Regarding the newly decentralized collectivities, evidence above already points to waning legitimacy. Unlike the prefectoral arm of the state, the Mairie and the Departmental Council are relatively new bodies with relatively limited resources at their disposal. In discussions with their electorate, a consensus had emerged that the decentralised elected officials do not truly represent them, and that the same officials accomplish little. In this particular case, it could very well be that a lack of direct accountability by locally elected officials and their reputation for confiscation has indeed led to an attitude of dismissiveness by the electorate. In this sense, colonial forms of legitimacy predominate.

In another sense, the legitimacy of the prefectoral state (the executive arm) seems comparatively unaffected. As already mentioned, the prefect is widely acknowledged as the rightful decider to whom people can turn in times of desperation. This may be because the prefectoral arm is justifiably regarded as the true sovereign, with direct links to the regime in Libreville. The 17 August 2015 Independence Day celebrations in Gamba were quite revealing in this regard. Seated in the grandstands overlooking the parade processions were the prefect and chiefs, whom were given pride of place. Marching were gendarmes and contingents of the army, proudly displaying the Gabonese flag to a cheering crowd. The mood reflected what many interlocutors felt about their state in private discussions, which was a certain pride linked to having just been born within Gabon's territorial boundaries. The chief of Mougagara excused himself for meeting me at his son's house, because normally in his official capacity he convened meetings "at my house, because that's where the Gabonese flag is" (Chef de village of Mougagara, personal communication, August 2015). In Ingouéka, north on the river Bongo, the cantonal chief proudly displayed a picture commemorating his first appointment as chief, with Omar Bongo at his side, despite the chief's critiques of the state during a group discussion that same day. And in the Shell cafeteria which feeds Shell-Gabon's interns in Plaine 3 of Gamba, a characteristic portrait of Ali Bongo hangs overhead, which all interns, including those who could be described as politically conscious, considered entirely justified. An administrative legitimacy indeed exists and accords with the verbal analysis of Joseph Tonda (Ratanga-Atoz, personal communication, July 2015). Electoral legitimacy, however, is woefully lacking in comparison.

5.6 *Rentier Mentality and Corruption in the Ndougou*

A former mayor, who wished to remain anonymous, reached an agreement with a certain company to build a road for the price of XAF 1 billion after several rounds of negotiation. Shortly thereafter, the Minister of the Interior intervened and demanded that the price remain above XAF 1.8 billion. The former mayor left it to interpretation to determine whether or not the minister had an interest in the company, declining to comment further for fear of retribution. Similarly, George Mpaga of the non-governmental organisation ROLBG, which is said to be close to the political opposition, explains that the system of awarding public contracts is a familial system of governance run by a strict hierarchy, and this hierarchy is reproduced among even the lowest levels, such as the Ndougou. It is for Mpaga a means of "controlling the population," whose people are themselves neither informed nor conscious of their citizenship (Mpaga, personal communication, July 2015). A discussion with an advisor at the US Embassy touched upon a reciprocal mentality, which extended as well to the intelligentsia. The system of patronage mastered by Omar Bongo, however, was being undermined by Ali's reforms, which threatened "political stability" (Sherry, Political and Economic Advisor, US Embassy, personal communication, July 2015). But the Secretary General of Gamba's City Hall on two separate occasions railed against chronic "political clientelism" and the clan being at the base of the local power structure. The Secretary General of the Departmental Conseil, in turn, mentioned that in just a few short years he had already witnessed first-hand the nepotism which prevails in the system of awarding public contracts. Elected officials use their positions, he said, to extract benefits for members of their family, while voters were swayed by mere T-shirts and cash handouts (Ossendo, personal communication, August 2015). Shell's Government Relations Director also bemoaned a culture of corruption in Gabonese politics, offering that "somewhere along the way it gets corrupt" (Koumba, Shell Government Relations, personal communication, August 2015).

As these voices of experts and activists—many of whom are based in Libreville—show, they are all largely convinced that a rentier mentality is unique to southern Gabon, though there is no consensus as to whether this is due to oil rents. There is no consensus as to whether the corruption within government derives from the dominance of political families, echoing the assertion that although "there aren't traditional means, … there may be traditional ends" in a "progressive adaptation" (Nambo, personal communication, July 2015), or whether corruption sprang first from oil rents and quick monetisation of the local economy.

A clue is thankfully given by the interpersonal relations which characterise the non-rentier class of individuals in the Ndougou. Firstly, the few elected politicians—mostly national—who remit goods and services to their native villages are the most celebrated, and unsurprisingly are the least likely to attract criticism. Secondly, some chiefs, though not uniform in behaviour, do in fact display rent-seeking behaviour, most exemplified by the Ndougou cantonal chief described above, who at one point suggested he "needed" me to "rise more easily," since he had already surpassed the optimal age for "success": "If you were not here," he added, "what would I do?" (Chef de canton of the Ndougou, personal communication, August 2015). Rent-seeking and clientelism were rampant amongst many of the population as well. Dieudonné, an employee at the local radio station, admitted to having given part of his salary to the senator who had helped secure him his job. This, he contended, was "fair" (Radio news reporter, August 2015, personal communication). Agents of the prefect also regularly requested "tips" to complement their salaries, explaining in curt terms that it was simply the way things were done. Thirdly, it is almost always the case that locals who are not employed as gardeners, caterers, cleaners, or as manual labour by Shell or one of its contractors, are officially or unofficially employed by one of the state's agencies or decentralised institutions. The prefecture was among these sources of local employment, as at any hour of the day there were self-described drivers, security guards, and other assistants loitering outside the prefecture and the prefect's spacious home just next door. The same phenomenon was a regular occurrence at both decentralised institutions. Common to all institutions was a prevailing atmosphere of inactivity and inertness, despite the lavishly furnished buildings replete with leather sofas and mahogany tables and desks. One could reasonably conclude that a bloated bureaucracy was the culprit.

Added to a bloated bureaucracy were several local ministerial divisions present in Gamba, but by all observable accounts inoperative. Ali Bongo's development and diversification programme Gabon Emergent occupies a small building next to the high school, and on most days seemed unoccupied. Though they marched in the Independence Day celebrations, they were unable to describe in detail any accomplishments towards local development in the area). A government-sponsored AIDS clinic, located in the neighbourhood Plaine Bienvenue, was likewise unoccupied. A local branch of Gabon Telecom, the national provider with a substantial office building next to the radio station in Plaine 3, never responded to Shell's requests to improve its internet bandwidth capacity. Evidence abounded that energies were deflected away from economic productivity and towards personal enrichment.

Another way to trace an evolution in rentier mentality is to compare the modalities and opinions of youth to older generations. From this perspective at least, one might conclude that a rentier mentality among the population itself has become more pronounced. Older generations in the Ndougou—even those who had been formerly employed by Shell—are in large numbers still active on their respective communal plantations, while the youth prefer to seek out well-paid jobs in the oil industry. However, such a behaviour cannot mono-causally relate to oil, as we observe such processes elsewhere as well, where it is foremost the youth who seek urban and globalised lifestyles. Even if we concede that a rentier mentality was aggravated by oil, its attributes share many characteristics in common with the larger phenomena of urbanisation and consumerism.

6 Conclusion

By and large, corruption in the Ndougou did not appear to coincide with the relative dependence of the state on Shell-Gabon. Even as the state was relieved of its taxation burden and bore little interest in the Ndougou, the prefectoral state in tandem with Shell and a handful of national politicians remained legitimate. By their very nature, the related concepts of rentier mentality, corruption, and bureaucratic inefficiency are hard to prove with anything other than anecdotal and hearsay evidence. But an abundance of such evidence, including perceptions by experts or those acquainted with the day-to-day business in and around Gamba, can lead to a plausible conclusion. Proceeding with this assumption, one can conclude that a rentier mentality does indeed exist in the Ndougou, but directly linking it to external oil rents has been demonstrated to present other analytical difficulties which rentierism may not be equipped to deal with. Rentier mentalities were aggravated but certainly can be traced to pre-existing norms. Although the decentralised state was entirely illegitimate, its illegitimacy did not coincide with oil production, but rather with the institution of decentralisation itself.

Yet, although rentierism did not follow its proscribed axioms at this local level, the rationale of self-interest is compelling. Many in the Ndougou are self-interested, as everywhere, but are circumscribed by certain realities which preclude social and economic advancement. At the state level, therefore, rentierism still applies. In states with extraverted regimes (Bayart, 1989), it is almost by definition that actors in capital cities would not seek to incorporate the periphery. There is consequently no need to incorporate populations which have no bearing on the success of elite classes. Classes are self-sustaining and oil is far away from the population. As shown here, a rentier mentality can and does indeed become aggravated at all levels of society in rentier states, and is concordant with older models in places such as the Ndougou. Though rentier behaviour was found to be only modestly related to oil production in the Ndougou, it cannot be easily refuted that self-interested politicians understand the benefits of political promotions. Energies are therefore more likely turned towards self-aggrandisement and recognition, than towards collective projects.

However, instead of oil production, it might rather be the colonial and postcolonial (African) state in general, as Mbembe (2001) claims, which uses its capacity to fragment the population, while co-opting diverse people into a political game that is always about some form of personal enrichment. It might also be a symptom of hybrid governance, where the lack of norm-setting encourages the proliferation of institutions of public authority, leading then to what hybridists variously call "opportunism," and what rentier state theorists call "rentier mentality." Hybrid governance has the potential to resolve the Ndougou lagoon's other inconsistent rentier effects, where legitimacy was reserved for the prefectoral state in its duopoly with Shell-Gabon, and withheld from the decentralized assemblies which often were at odds with the former. Hybrid governance allows for the possibility that rentier mentalities may coexist with prefectoral state legitimacy, while RST does not. One hypothesis that deserves more research is that rentier states, or those highly dependent on oil receipts, are more prone to incongruent and competing institutions of public authority. With further research, it might very well be proven that the fundamental causal mechanisms leading to our five rentier effects in local arenas lie in such alternative constructs, especially those that collapse definitions of state and authority.

Acknowledgements

First and foremost, I'd like to thank each and every interviewee that took time out of their busy days to provide me with crucial information and data for the completion of this chapter. In particular, I'd like to thank Lionel Ikogou Renamy, accomplished researcher in his own right, for helping to facilitate very successful fieldwork trips. I'd also like to thank Klaas van Walraven and Jan Abbink, my doctoral supervisors, for their encouragement and guidance. My wife, Alžběta also contributed useful commentary, while Lesley Branagan provided excellent language editing. Lastly, I'd like to thank this volume's editors, Annika Witte and Jannik Schritt, for their suggestions and limitless patience.

References

Ballard, J. (1964). *The Development of Political Parties in French Equatorial Africa* [Ph.D. dissertation]. Fletcher School, Medford/Somerville, pp. 289–349.

Basedau, M., & Lay, J. (2009): Resource Curse or Rentier Peace? The Ambiguous Effects of Oil Wealth and Oil Dependence on Violent Conflict. *Journal of Peace Research* 46(6),757–776.

Bayart, J-F. (1989). L'Etat en Afrique: *La politique du ventre. L'espace du politique*. Paris: Fayard.

Beblawi, H., & Luciani, G. (Eds.) (1987). The Rentier State. Nation, State and Integration in the Arab World. London: Croom Helm.

Bernault, F. (1996). *Démocraties ambiguës en Afrique Centrale: Congo-Brazzaville, Gabon, 1940–1965. Les Afriques*. Paris: Éd. Karthala.

Bierschenk, T. & Olivier De Sardan, J-P (1997). Local Powers and a Distant State in Rural Central African Republic, *Journal of Modern African Studies*, 35, 441–468.

Garandeau, V. (2010). *La décentralisation au Gabon: une réforme inachevée*. Etudes africaines. Paris: Harmattan.

Lund, C. (2006).Twilight Institutions: Public Authority and Local Politics in Africa, *Development and Change*, 37 (4), 685–705.

Mahdavy, H. (1970). The Pattern and Problems of Economic Development in Rentier States: The Case of Iran. In M. Cook (Ed.), *Studies in the Economic History of the Middle East: From the Rise of Islam to the Present Day* (pp. 428–67). London, New York: Oxford U.P.

Mamdani, M. (1996). *Citizen and Subject: Contemporary Africa and the Legacy of Late Colonialism*. Princeton, N.J. Princeton University Press.

Martin, P. M. (2002). *Leisure and Society in Colonial Brazzaville*. Cambridge: Cambridge University Press.

Mbembe, A. (2001). *On the Postcolony*. Berkeley: University of California Press.

N'Nah, N. M. (2006). *Histoire Du Gabon - Des Origines À L'aube Du XXIème Siècle*. Paris: Harmattan.

O'Donnell, G. A. (1998). Horizontal Accountability in new Democracies. *Journal of Democracy*, 9(3), 112–126.

Omeje, K. (2008, Ed.). Extractive Economies and Conflicts in the Global South. Hampshire: Ashgate.

Ross, M.L. (2001). Does Oil Hinder Democracy? *World Politics*, 53 (April), 325–361.

Schatzberg, M. G. (2002). *Political Legitimacy in Middle Africa: Father, Family, Food*. Bloomington: Indiana University Press.

Tar, U.A. (2008). Rentier Politics, Extractive Economies and Conflict in the Global South: Emerging Ramifications and Theoretical Exploration. In K. Omeje (Ed.) *Extractive Economies and Conflicts in the Global South* (pp. 27–49). Hampshire: Ashgate.

Yates, D. A. (1996). *The Rentier State in Africa: Oil Rent Dependency and Neocolonialism in the Republic of Gabon*. Trenton, NJ: Africa World Press.

Yates, D. A. (2012). *The Scramble for African Oil: Oppression, Corruption and War for Control of Africa's Natural Resources*. London, New York: Pluto Press.

Yates, D. A. (2013). Gabon. In A. Mehler, H. Melber & K. van Walraven, *Africa Yearbook 9: Politics, Economy and Society South of the Sahara in 2012*. Leiden: Koninklijke Brill NV.

4

"Night Milk": Energy Development and Conflict in Kenya's Turkana County

Immo Eulenberger

1 Introduction

> We are people of the cow, we live of white milk and we get and drink it for all to see. But now they have found the black milk of the earth under our land, and they want to milk it in darkness with so many hands, we can't even know.
>
> TURKANA PASTORALIST, Lokichar 2015

In 2012, Tullow Oil and the Government of Kenya announced the discovery of significant oil deposits in Turkana County, an 'ultra-marginal' dryland region with a pastoralist society I have been studying since 2008. In this region, where indicators point to extreme poverty, armed violence is part of normal life and the impact of socio-economic and ecological change is at its most severe (Eulenberger et al., 2018). Nevertheless, oil seems to "cause," at least so far, significantly fewer problems than elsewhere, most strikingly across its embattled northern frontier in South Sudan (Pinaud, 2014; Waal, 2014), provoking the question what it takes for a coveted resource to become (or, as I will suggest, rather contribute to the emergence of) a curse associated with escalating conflict, economic decline and anti-democratic dynamics.

This chapter aims to contribute to ethnographies of resource extraction that look at its impact on transformation processes shaping the life of local people in distinct socio-cultural environments. Engaging with resource curse, rentier economy and neo-patrimonialism theorems, it shares the interest of recent work in the political anthropology of energy that interprets: how pre-existing socio-political conditions and dynamics shape the impact of energy resources like oil and renewables; which powers are at play; and what triggers or counteracts conflict escalation. It makes a case for anthropology's holistic tradition that allows us to recognise hierarchies of significance and urgency from long-term perspectives that interrelate social and ecological, elite and non-elite, individual, regional and global costs and benefits, both as local phenomena

 | DOI:10.1163/9789004530065_005

and as part of larger assemblages, including socio-ecological systems, energy economies and transformation dynamics.

Many studies referenced here point to the fact that costs of large-scale transformations are commonly borne by populations with insufficient influence or the knowledge necessary to stop them. Looking at interlinking economies and the risks and opportunities associated with oil from a future-centred holistic perspective, we can contribute to their empowerment by providing systemic contextual knowledge where it matters most and give more discursive power to their interests, attention to the ecosystems they rely on and practical recognition to the treasures of cultural capacity that enable them to use their environment sustainably, efficiently and equitably.

Thus, the next section looks at influential debates from this perspective before I focus on the interplay of "pre-existing conditions" with energy extraction-related dynamics in the Turkana context.

2 Debates

2.1 *Resources and Conflict*

One of the main concerns of the resource curse literature is the increase in the severity and destructiveness of conflicts associated with resource wealth (Berdal & Malone, 2000). Even research on the prehistory of intergroup violence seems to indicate that it occurred first and foremost where important resources were concentrated, and history certainly has many documented examples of that pattern (Fry, 2013; Helbling, 2006; Meller et al., 2015). Consequently, inquiries into reasons of serious conflict often look to resources coveted by antagonistic opponents. Following such functionalist leads, inquiries of markedly different academic affiliations into the resource-violence nexus abound, including in regard to East African pastoralist areas (for example, see Homer-Dixon, 1999; Lind & Sturman, 2002; Van Baalen & Mobjörk, 2016). Close analyses of conflict frequency in relation to degrees of resource scarcity in the region both contradicted one another and refuted assumptions of simple correlations. However, they also reveal that the heuristic value of quantitative data depends very much on a thorough understanding of the socio-ecological, political and historical context (Adano et al., 2012; Ember et al., 2014; Eulenberger, forthcoming).

On the other hand, the (somewhat under-published) view that humans normally try to avoid violence and conflict that sees "peace always lurking under the surface" (Bregman, 2020) could easily muster an even greater number of examples for cases where interaction around coveted resources is organised in predominantly peaceful ways (Eulenberger, forthcoming; Fry, 2013), raising the question of why resource contests escalate where they do.

For the Omo-Turkana region, the bottom line is that resources are central in violent conflict—perhaps most conspicuously because the impact of environmental factors, such as recurrent periods of extreme scarcity, is strong, even though its pathways are complex (Adem et al., 2012). Fortunately, ethnological and historical analyses provide a wealth of material allowing for a holistic understanding of their dynamics, thanks to extensive communication with the people concerned (see for example, McCabe, 2004; Mulugeta, 2016; Mkutu, 2017; Okumu, 2017; Schlee, 2011).

At the same time, predilection for change and modernisation phenomena has promoted notions of pernicious trends, e.g., from once pro-social "redistributive raiding" to now purely destructive "predatory raiding," "warlords," and modern weaponry as "change agent" (resonating concerns of the privileged). These interpretations have produced "grey" literature teeming with clichés, errors and rash conclusions that can nevertheless exercise significant influence on high-level decision making. Research can only inform policies and practice adequately if sound holistic analysis enables it to discern the relative importance of phenomena and factors to join the key dots. Yet, while pastoralist war(fare) and civil war in the study region have received remarkable attention, the much greater damage done by social and environmental violence perpetrated in the name of "development" and "modernisation" (see for example, Gabbert et al., 2021; Stevenson & Buffavand, 2018) is under-regarded and in need of urgent action.

2.2 *Resources & Rents*

Just as policy-oriented publications on conflicts in the region focus on grievances, so too do studies that examine the impact of oil (e.g., Johannes et al., 2015; Mkutu, 2016; Nanok & Onyango, 2017). On the other hand, influential work on conflict economies suggests that persistence and intensity of armed conflict are related to its (perceived) economic attractiveness (Ballentine, 2003), as are elite strategies generating the "oil curse" (Behrends, 2011), partisan governance (Tilly, 1985), corruption (Andvig & Barasa, 2014) and organised crime.

The core argument of the resource curse theorem is simple and plausible: As oil (and other important resources, including renewables) can be extracted in segregated enclaves (Appel, 2019; Ferguson, 2005)—which are often run by foreign companies who bring in most of the investments, technology, know-how and expert staff—production and profits don't depend on local or national improvements. Putting it in a language of collective rational choice: Elites capturing the derived economic and social power are far more likely to reap high personal returns when they invest in securing their privileges, than when they invest in socially and ecologically exquisite but delicate systems of local production—be they agricultural, manufacturing or other—for fickle markets prone to crisis and embattled by myriad competitors (Auty, 1993; Gary et al., 2003).

It should not be forgotten that, as individuals, such elites commonly live in highly competitive environments. People seeking to replace those further up abound, and those at the top are often where they are because they are more competitive and/or better at this competition—and not necessarily because they care more for moral principles, the public good or long-term effects. Where "dog eats dog," both cooperation (alliance) and deterrence (violence, repression and intimidation) are key and complementary strategies. Players use them in very different forms and doses but, generally speaking, as oil extraction commonly requires little cooperation of local and national populations, oil wealth allows for higher degrees of elite aggressiveness in accumulating stakes (Behrends et al., 2011). Chad (Behrends & Hoinathy, 2017) and the Sudans (Eulenberger, 2015; Simone, 2018) are daunting examples that illustrate the brutality with which this power can be used to gain or protect access to privileges.

However, it has been pointed out that the ills often attributed to the "resource curse" also occur where the usual suspects (such as oil and gems) are missing. The image of Africa in global imaginaries is *in general* characterised by tropes of deficiency and state failure, reflecting the fact that they affect "resource-rich" and "resource-poor" countries alike. A much-noted exception is Botswana, which derives most of its GDP from mineral exports (Livingston, 2019).

The undeniable governance problems afflicting much of the continent, including extreme inequality, rampant corruption, violence and authoritarian patterns, have been described as the "neopatrimonial" system: private interests pervade public institutions and create clientelist networks that allocate resources and positions according to requirements of individual and partisan struggles for shares, and not according to the interests of the wider public, competencies and the achievement of official goals (Bach, 2013; Erdmann & Engel, 2006).

While this analysis is in itself valid and important, neopatrimonialism and clientelism do not explain why violent conflict explodes in some oil boom cases, such as the Sudans or Nigeria, and not in others, including Turkana, because these phenomena are just as pervasive in the latter as in the former. Thus, the striking contrast of these situations requires further explanation. Pertinent anthropological studies indicate that the actual occurrence of conflict is best explained from the historical dynamics acting on (and from within) a region's socio-political structures, and not by economic mathematics (Behrends & Schareika, 2011; Schritt, 2018; Witte, 2018).

Another problem is the widespread notion that corruption is related to what is referred to as "African culture." The ethnocentricity of this projection is not only revealed by its occurrence across continents and the North/South divide, but also by its absence from "traditional" African cultures like Turkana pastoralism where grass-roots democracy has prevented the emergence and entrenchment of classes, anti-social elite power and resource-grabbing for millennia.

The cited anthropological studies show that, instead of exoticizing political practices as non-standard cultures, or getting absorbed by grievance discourses or using narrow economist lenses, it is more productive to have a circumspect look at how economic, ecological and political pressures interact with power dynamics, historical, cultural and social factors, aspiration and opportunity landscapes in the dynamics in which oil economies emerge.

In concord with these studies, this chapter argues that, on the one hand, valuable and easily extractable resources raise the stakes of social contest and, in many cases, intensification and continuation of armed conflict can be plausibly related to the struggle for access to the benefits. Especially where the strategic use of organised violence, clientelism and corruption are already entrenched barriers to democratic grass-roots power, opportunities for elites with privileged access to distributive and decision-making mechanisms to multiply their income and power can grow dramatically. Resource rents allow this without the difficult task of raising income levels through an increase in sustainable productivity of local economies.

On the other hand, cases like Turkana could be cited to argue that traditions of outspokenness and egalitarian self-assertiveness, cooperativeness, and restraint on intra-social violence can have strong de-escalating effects, both within extraction area communities and between communities and the state, and that chances to access benefits can have such effects even when they are only partly on the licit, public and standard-compliant side of social interaction.

The most basic conclusion that can be drawn from research on the conflict-resource nexus is that context matters. In the following section, I sketch out those context matters that are particularly important here.

3 Context Matters

3.1 *Turkana – Ultra-Marginality & Democratic Power*

Turkana county is one of Kenya's driest regions and officially its poorest.[1] Reputed for famine and inter-ethnic conflict, it is part of a pastoralist belt

1 In the 2015–16 Integrated Household Budget Survey (KNBS 2018), Turkana had the highest poverty rate of all counties (at 79.4%), while Nairobi had the lowest rate at 16.7%.

between Somalia and the Sahel where communities have adapted to aridity and periodic resource scarcity by way of highly mobile livestock economies, material minimalism and decentral organisation. High political autonomy of local groups with large herds of cattle, sheep, goats and camels exists alongside a warrior culture and livestock raiding, today powered by AK47 and G3 assault rifles (for literature on the wider region, see Eulenberger et al., 2019; Eulenberger, forthcoming).

Before the discovery of oil deposits, this harsh dry land—sandwiched between some of the "least developed" and most culturally conservative parts of Ethiopia, South Sudan and Uganda—was to most Kenyans what Africa is to most non-Africans: an anti-place, epitome of remoteness, "backwardness," disaster, poverty, and war. Indeed, uncounted Turkana live with their herds beyond the reach of motorised modernity. The only tarmac road is the one that connects Kenya and South Sudan; but it remained, until very recently, a sea of potholes with waylaying pirates lurking at the entry and exit points of the county. Pastoralists continue to fight one another with automatic weapons along ethnic frontiers, while the needs of the growing population exceed the capacity of pastoralism to provide for them, which leaves them with little choice but to depend on semi-reliable food aid. Local economies are frequently ravaged by disaster, and policies are often at odds with local realities.

But while all this is true, an important fact largely remains absent from public awareness: nomadic pastoralism has been remarkably successful in using both sophisticated indigenous knowledge and practices, including of resource and conflict management, and *ariàng* (non-pastoralist, "cultural outsider," "modern") resources. It remains the single most productive and sustainable use of local resources and a bulwark of grass-roots democracy in an environment otherwise prone to soaring accumulation of economic and political power (Eulenberger et al., 2018).

While remaining economically and culturally distinct, Turkana pastoralist society has developed a pragmatic symbiosis with the state and money economies, but it also constitutes a source of social and mental self-empowerment that keeps them at bay, including thanks to its cultural influence on the growing non-pastoralist sectors of Turkana society. At the same time, modernisation efforts led to the rapid multiplication of a school-educated but largely jobless population, who inhabit the mushrooming permanent settlements with no similarly efficient, sustainable and equitable systems of production and social regulation (Eulenberger et al., 2018).

3.3 *Night Milk*

In Kenya's rough economic environment, where millions struggle to meet basic needs and a vibrant and ambitious middle class strives for upward mobility, an entrenched culture of corruption is widely perceived as spoiling "normal" people's chances to ensure a fair distribution of social wealth. In this context, the prospect of petro-dollars was met with both excitement and scepticism, including in Turkana itself (Johannes et al., 2015, p. 12ff.). Public imagination associates oil with amenities and prosperity—things everyone desires and millions are in desperate need of. A bonanza feeling flared up and people from all over Turkana and other parts of Kenya flocked to the main sites of the ensuing little flush of opportunities, triggering increased competition. As Tullow Oil tried to warm up with both the national government (in direct talks) and local people (through outreach programs), elites and their networks—but also more egalitarian and democratic local associations—were quick to develop strong pressuring devices. In the twilight of business opportunities, legal limbo and neopatrimonial thickets, many hands scrambled to milk the ghost of the black gold, with land rights emerging as a new field of contestation, machinations, resistance and search for new models. In contrast to pastoralists who harness the patchy vegetation through milk, blood and meat, the *ariàng* ["modern people"] tap into global resource flows with this "night milk" that transforms social into economic and symbolic capital, joining the global commodification of 'everything' in the pursuit of individual and collective status.

3.4 *Aid, Water & Land*

While, in this region, oil, land and water are only recently emerging as objects of national and international grabbing economies, aid and development-induced poverty have long evolved into elite devices for the milking of resource flows. After a century of infrastructure development and relief, production and consumption have largely been uncoupled in Turkana. While pastoralism remains the best adapted, most efficient and sustainable use of local resources, a 50-fold population increase since the colonial conquest a mere century ago has made it impossible to sustain a majority of the county's population without massive transfers of energy, food and funds.

Turkana's ecological conditions make agriculture and manufacturing too costly for investors outside the aid sector. However, a transition to a renewable energy regime might change the region's outlook, as the potential of solar and wind power extraction is high (Eulenberger et al., 2022). Nomadic livestock production and fish from Lake Turkana are the only major profitable industries so far, but both are under threat from agro-industrial schemes across the Ethiopian border (Eulenberger, 2019; Hodbod et al., 2019; Stevenson, 2018), where dams along the Omo are threatening to unleash a different kind of resource curse: based on the availability of water and new infrastructure constructed by foreign, especially Chinese, capital and intervention. The use of

Omo water—which constitutes 80% of Lake Turkana—for industrial biofuel and cotton production threatens to dry up the world's largest desert lake and to devastate the livelihoods of innumerable pastoralists, fishermen and value chain stakeholders. The Kenyan government and local elites, however, derive their income from international cash flows rather than from local economies, therefore these threats face conspicuously scant opposition,[2] and those likely to be most affected are hardly aware of them. The economic, ecological and social value of the region's pastoralist cultures continues to be neglected by decision makers both in the regional sphere and internationally.

Dryland pastoralism requires maximum mobility. As rainfall patterns are highly unstable and often highly localised, so is biomass production. This led to the evolution of socio-cultural systems that allow access to fodder and water across ecological zones where they happen to be available. Land rights beyond settlements are therefore communal. In Turkana County, this is even reflected by the legal status of land, with the exception of a small percentage of privately-owned plots in and around settlements, as Community Trust Land (Odhiambo, 2013; Odote, 2013). In the "more attractive" parts of Kenya, land was already privatised during colonial rule (often to be allocated to European settlers) or after independence, leading to large-scale loss of once-communal lands to economically and politically privileged actors (Galaty, 2014).

The communal status of most land in Turkana has sustained a fairness-based commons economy as strong and vibrant. Among active and "cultural" pastoralists (those outside the pastoralist economy who remain attached to pastoralist culture), the spirit of engaged collective care for maintaining the collective benefits of an established egalitarian order is very much alive. People violating restrictions and rules are challenged immediately. If found persisting, "the community," i.e. the best possible selection of locals that can be assembled ad hoc, will stop them and hold them responsible. This encompassing system of local ownership and cooperative control forms a striking contrast to the modern sphere, where people—whom pastoralists refer to as *ariàng* [modernised]—often don't feel responsible for sustaining perishable resources or for keeping up with official norms and regulations. They know that others will, in most cases, either not care or shy away from the social and psychological costs of sanctioning transgressions, especially when transgressors are in some way powerful.

---

2 Notable exceptions are the local NGO Friends of Lake Turkana, and the scholars who form the Lands of the Future (https://www.eth.mpg.de/lof), and Omo-Turkana Research Networks (OTuRN).

Land rights have become a central field of social conflict for several reasons. First, as the population has grown from 30,000 to 1.5 million over the last century, space has naturally become a less abundant resource per capita.[3] As only a part of that growth could be accommodated by the pastoralist economy, sedentary populations have grown around infrastructure hubs of roads, water points, food distribution centres, administration and service provision sites that governments and NGOs have built over the years. Though this growing density has entailed conflicts over plots that could not have occurred when people lived as nomads, these have not escalated to a state of crisis, as land is still abundant enough in most of Turkana to resolve the issues by moving into unsettled spots nearby.

This brings us to the second reason: "Development" as a process of infrastructural concentration. As it creates hubs of activity and transport arteries connecting them, development concentrates resources and movement in core zones where the use and the value of land change in correlation with one another. In Turkana, the county headquarters, Lodwar, is in the lead of this process, followed by Kakuma, which is a small Turkana town combined with Kenya's second-largest refugee camp that hosts over 100,000 refugees (Rodgers, 2020), and Lokichar, the administrative and economic centre of Turkana South sub-county where most oilfields are located (see map). The emergence of oil triggered a rush on ungazetted land in the hope of profitable re-sales, on-site business or compensation for land. The anticipated construction of a Lamu Port–South Sudan–Ethiopia Transport (LAPSSET) corridor (Browne, 2015; Mosley & Watson, 2016) and trans-national oil pipelines in Turkana caused a similar effect.

Thirdly, unprecedented amounts of resources came into Turkana due to both the oil development activities and the decentralisation of government funds by the 2010 reforms of Kenya's administrative system ("devolution"), shifting funding to county-level contests, at the same time as the commercial value and the relative scarcity of land were rising sharply. The eagerness of elites to buy land grew accordingly (Lind, 2018; Mkutu et al., 2014; Orr, 2019).

Lastly, the mixture of extreme population growth, extreme poverty, GDP growth-oriented policies and the availability of enormous national and international financial resources for interventions (concomitant with irresponsible penuriousness in relation to investment in adequate understanding) leads to increasing demands for land for transformation projects. Officially promoted

3 Although it remains a sensitive topic, scale and pace are increasingly recognised by policy makers and researchers as a major challenge (e.g., Galaty, 2014; Turkana County Government, 2013).

to "improve food security," "combat poverty," "reduce marginalisation," "boost development," etc., such projects often result in the reallocation of usage rights from equitable, time-tested and sustainable systems to elite-controlled schemes whose "side-effects" outweigh overall benefits but can be externalised to people and species without the power to prevent them (Buffavand, 2016; Escobar, 2011).

The land requirements for oil exploration and production and prospects of large-scale infrastructure development triggered a rush on unregistered land. (Almost all land in Turkana, except plots in the main (para)urban centres, is unregistered.) However, people are very keen to protect their own and their associates' rights to land and land-based resources, especially biomass and water.

In interviews on emerging patterns of land grabbing, rural interviewees said that they wouldn't accept anyone taking a larger stretch of land for himself and fencing it. "Only someone really rich" (*ekabaràn*, a term traditionally connoting an owner of large herds) would be able to stake such a claim by acquiring a title deed from the county government. But even then, people would insist that such a transfer of ownership would not be valid if the person had not obtained local consent. Exceptions are made for people hailing from the area who both consult "the community," i.e., the group holding customary land rights, and act at the bureaucratic level. Even outsiders could be accepted to acquire and use a reasonably limited piece of land, provided they reciprocate with a substantial contribution, e.g., a borehole or a community building.

From the massive international resource flows that drive infrastructure development, the notion of compensation emerged as a coveted new source of income, especially for well-informed and well-connected people. The idea of compensation has come to pervade locals' ways of thinking about justice in their engagement with the waves of top-down development that impact on their lives. That "development" is something you should be compensated for speaks volumes about its character.

3.5 *Devolution*

Before Tullow Oil and the Kenyan government signed contracts in 2012, the latter had transformed the political landscape through "devolution," a more decentralised distribution system that shifts considerable financial and decision-making power from the national to the regional level, especially to the new county governments. Introduced in 2010, it was the product of a long and popular political struggle for more autonomy and resources that, in 2007/8, had brought Kenya to the brink of the civil war it had been so fortunate to avoid since independence. Particularly in geographically, politically and economically marginal regions like Turkana, this redistribution was often framed as compensation for decades of negligence (see for example, AfriCOG, 2014, Nyanjom, 2014). In the 2013 elections, Kenyans could, for the first time, elect their own local governments in 47 newly-formed counties, in form of governors and county assemblies.

In contrast to many other counties, Turkana is (with the exception of a few scattered proto-urban centres) a basically mono-ethnic region, and although colonial and post-colonial rule had sub-divided it repeatedly, the strength of Turkana cultural identity had always kept a strong ethnic self-consciousness across all other social divides. Devolution made it an administrative unit for the first time since its forced integration into statehood. It now had its own parliament and elected president (governor)—a role that outshone the once all-powerful centrally appointed (and non-local) Commissioner—and a county government with numerous ministries at Lodwar, the main centre of modern life and power since colonial days. Turkana could not only start making policies on their own, those in the government and in politics also had unprecedented amounts of money at their disposal to implement them and to employ a good part of the rapidly growing, restive and ambitious intelligentsia.

While the official reason for devolution was "to bring the government closer to the people," at a less explicit level it was an attempt to deal with a collective action problem the elites in power now faced: how to maintain a political system that favoured them, and at the same time avoid the serious trouble more disadvantaged players could cause. For example, in the 2007–08 post-election crisis factions clashed—especially alliances around long-dominant Kikuyu and Kalenjin elites from the populous and productive central highlands—and both local and national positions came under fierce attack. With devolution, these elites managed to keep control over the national government and associated powers by pacifying regional power complexes. Devolution created a whole new landscape of opportunities for the acquisition of political, social and economic clout, attracting particularly those with the strongest competitive drive among local and regional elites, whose focus now shifted increasingly away from national battles (D'Arcy & Cornell, 2016; Kiambati, 2020).

Simultaneously, the massive raise of the stakes at the county level intensified political competition in Turkana, further compounded by the oil finds. Long before actual oil sales, the anticipation of oil profits increased the capacity of Turkana to attract economic and political capital through national transfers. Not only was Turkana allocated the largest budget after the capital Nairobi—even though it ranks only 14th in terms of population (Ongiri, 2015)—allies of both the main opposition party and the ruling coalition received huge transfusions. The 2017 elections indicated that politics in Turkana had become somewhat more violent and much more expensive.

As the new county government was run by a governor belonging to the main opposition party, the Orange Democratic Movement (ODM), politicians allied with the Jubilee coalition controlling Kenya's central government received massive support and were able to maintain strong influence as national Members of Parliament (MPs) or Members of County Assembly (MCAs) representing sub-counties and lower-level constituencies (Eulenberger et al., 2018).

In Kenya, where sources of state revenue have always been much more diverse than in typical oil and rentier states (Beblawi & Luciani, 1987; Kimenyi et al, 2016), any political coalition needs support from the growing middle class. Kenyan middle-class culture includes expectations of a global lifestyle featuring cars, certain types of houses and identity-based expenditure patterns. Even though considered the strongest in the region, the Kenyan economy does not, however, create enough lucrative jobs in the commercial sector to accommodate their aspirations. Therefore, devolution works as a massive job creation programme for the most competitive and advantaged—those best at using their political, cultural and social capital. Upward mobility in a capitalist consumer culture is expensive. Where and what to buy, where and how to move matters, as it generates symbolic capital that is convertible into social and thus economic capital and the ultimate wellbeing that people derive from recognition. Thus, Lodwar and other centres of provincial elite life saw a staggering rise in national flights, with as many as five different airlines frequenting the stone-strewn tire-killing airstrip, a flood of SUVs, large expensive houses, the mushrooming of diners and clubs, and modern fences asserting new private property rights where people's goat and sheep had been freely roaming only yesterday (see photos).

A few ultra-visible and prestigious projects, such as the tarring of at least the most centric and essential of Lodwar's alternately dusty or muddy streets, were pushed through and earned much acclaim from a public used to seeing even the crumbs of public funds "magically" disappear, which strengthened the governor's bid for a second term. Some also stress the construction of a multitude of new schools and pre-schools, standard icons of *maendeleo* (Kiswahili for development). A tiny but shiny solar-powered irrigation scheme worth $US 0.7 million at Napuu, where some needy Lodwarians plant kale or water melon, was celebrated.[4] Yet my interlocutors agreed that the strongest factors

4 Not long after the festive inauguration of the irrigation scheme, millions of litres of precious water were left to disappear in muddy puddles because nobody cared to replace the dozens of broken valves. Apparently, funds were lacking for a simple padlock or the *c.*€ 30 to pay a watchman to prevent the semi-feral goats from gobbling the crops at night (Eulenberger, 2019).

FIGURE 4.1 Map of oil production in Kenya. Editors' illustration based on UN map no. 4187
SOURCE: HTTPS://WWW.UN.ORG/GEOSPATIAL/CONTENT/KENYA

in most candidate's bids for office were: the means, tenders and positions that candidates offered to supporters; their skill to make the right promises to the right people; and their aptitude to strategically decide the terms of investment, i.e., in whom to invest, how much, at what point in time, and whom to leave out or punish. These factors were much the same as before the advent of oil

FIGURE 4.2 Modern fences enclosing new private property
PHOTO BY IMMO EULENBERGER

FIGURE 4.3 People's goats and sheep roaming freely
PHOTO BY IMMO EULENBERGER

and devolution. (For similar dynamics unfolding around oil and decentralisation in Niger see the chapter of Harouna, this collection.).

3.6 *Corruption*

Kenya has long been a darling of the international development community, thanks to: its status as a rather stable state welcoming expats, their investments and amelioration schemes; a diversified economy with negligible importance of mineral exports; a bustling service sector cross-cutting class boundaries; and a vibrant civil society—all of which are features that contrast with those of archetypal rogue petro-states. So, if classic resource curse theory has explained the oligarchic rule and crony economies that scar oil-producing neighbours like the Sudans or Chad, the Kenyan government's reliance on taxes, agricultural and manufacturing production and the country's overall functionality indicates that such ills can have different backgrounds. Kenya, too, has serious problems with cronyism, lacking accountability, dominance of illicit pathways to accumulation of political capital, and with infringements on civil and human rights. That does not diminish the importance of Kenya's relative freedom from the troubles plaguing most of its neighbours, such as the reverberations of decades of civil war and rule of force, or the significance of the greater freedom of expression, stronger democracy and better infrastructure. Nevertheless, the contrast between mass poverty and extreme elite wealth is extreme, the threats faced by those trying to hold the powerful accountable are often serious, and development policy mistakes prove to be especially disastrous in areas like Turkana, posing a heavy burden on the majority of the population, on political morality, the environment and the future (D'Arcy, 2019).

At the root of these problems is a culture of resource capture reaching back to repression-based land grabbing by European settlers, entrepreneurs and government institutions during the colonial period, which was continued by their Western-educated successors after independence. This culture spread across social boundaries by way of behavioural economies that punish actors' integrity where it forfeits partisan benefits and where it insists in the face of power.

From natural resources to business and education opportunities to international aid, working things out in a business-like manner has become a trait of Kenya's political, socio-economic and administrative system. Consequently, it is not surprising that much of the funds and resources meant for development disappeared in spectacular quantities from national and county governments alike (D'Arcy & Cornell, 2016; Manji, 2020).

In her seminal 2009 account of corruption in Kenya, Michaela Wrong points out that the amount of aid Kenya received roughly equalled the amount embezzled by government players and their business allies, suggesting that resource curse debates should consider a wider range of resources instead of limiting their focus to minerals (Bierschenk et al., 2002; Collier, 2006). The conspicuous indifference of Turkana and other elites towards the enormous human, ecological and economic costs of extreme population growth, systemic corruption and ill-conceived development policies may, thus, look like a perfectly rational approach from individual and partisan *homo oeconomicus* perspectives. In this sense, poverty and crisis have—through aid and embezzlement—long become a crucial resource base for local and national elites alike. If public office, development and aid can be considered "cursed" resources, Kenya has been accursed long ago, and oil adds just more fuel to a running problem engine. People in Kenya complain remarkably often about corruption and cases are sometimes prosecuted – but this is part of the system, as this is usually directed against members of rival networks. Politicians are under considerable pressure to provide supporters with financial and social resources. Claims and promises are part and parcel of the game, and reciprocity is inevitably uncertain in an environment where resources are insufficient to satisfy even the major part of demands and expectations. Working strictly within the confines of full legality and ethical correctness is a self-defeating strategy in a context where electoral support depends on agents and brokers who trade support for resources and who won't be made into suckers (as game theory calls players investing in a cooperative relationship without receiving commensurate returns). Apart from income for personal needs, they also need to be provided with incentives to be passed on to those whose votes they aim to mobilise.

"He should give us at least those hundred shillings (circa €1), as we will likely not see much of him again before the next elections" is a popular statement about politicians. For rural Turkana, this gift of a bill or two is important, not so much because they can buy food or booze for a day but because they materialise a relationship, a portion of attention and recognition. A person denying them this token would not primarily be seen as integer, but as mean and stingy, which amounts to the opposite of moral integrity in Turkana pastoralist culture where sharing surplus through asking and giving gifts is at the heart of both the economic system and collective morality. And if a candidate could really not afford these hundred shillings: Would he actually be able to achieve more for his supporters than he was able to achieve for himself? But given that the costs of a campaign are determined by the necessity to convince a multitude of constituents of one's capability by investing large amounts of money in vote acquisition: how can a candidate obtain the money necessary to afford it? Wages are low, few make enough money from businesses, and success depends on social capital among office holders. Consequently, candidates who succeed without access to diverted money are rare.

Turkana pastoralists often don't see much benefit in otherwise celebrated achievements like schools and roads, as these have little impact on their lives. The most important things people expect of their representatives is the food aid they so often rely on and—in the frontier zones, where pastoralists are armed—bullets without which they would fall prey to better equipped neighbours. Failure of "our people in the government" to provide them is deeply resented and sometimes punished at the ballot box. For schooling youth, the same is true regarding the patronage they depend on to pay the €5000 or so in fees alone required for a degree, in a context where poor families often have to survive on less than €50 per month. Here, Tullow's flagship stipend scheme, hailed for helping promising Turkana youth overcome financial barriers to success, was an injection of capital that enjoyed considerable popularity among elites, though an injection into a system imbued with clientelism. School and college fees are main fields for politicians and churches to create ties of loyalty and reciprocal obligation; even external sponsorship programs find it difficult to escape clientelist currents that direct funds strategically to families, clans and brokers where returns can be expected, which, in turn, enlarges power disparities. A large part of the funds Tullow dedicated to Corporate Social Responsibility went into these very generous stipends. While having a well-informed, understanding and connected intelligentsia is important for the pursuit of the common interests of a community like the Turkana, proportionality issues arise due to the fact that such stipend schemes benefit only a few individuals pertaining to, or bound to pertain to, the top strata of Turkana *ariàng* society. The same funds could have enabled many more of the less privileged to access education at more moderate rates, which would better equip more people to gain a foothold in the national labour market – a market whose importance for Turkana is increasing as unemployment and poverty continue to grow parallel to the size of the population while prospects for good jobs remain bleak.

3.7 *Environment*

Oil development might easily not only fail to improve the situation for the inhabitants, but instead worsen it significantly. Concerns are about loss of land, vegetation, biodiversity, soil and "cultural sites," displacement from water sources, grazing lands and routes and overgrazing of alternative sites due to the fencing of well pads and a processing facility, roads, a future pipeline and "local climate change" (KCSPOG, 2014). While this may sound somewhat exaggerated given that, for example, the 280 prospected wells clustered into 25 well pads would occupy only 40 hectares in total, the government of Kenya could not be said to dispel concerns when it issued two gazette notices in February 2019 that decreed the compulsory acquisition of 6,000 ha (60 km^{2}) for oil development in Turkana's south and 200 km^{2} for the LAPSSET transport corridor project—both acquisitions decreed without the consent of the County Government, which then took the National Land Commission to court. This case exposes conflicts between elite factions and a dangerous disconnection from local social realities.

The most serious impact oil is bound to have is probably the one on water. Water is of key importance for everyone in the drylands, and active pastoralists depend on it for their livelihoods (Debay, 2009). On the one hand, ground water sources could be contaminated and thus lost. The strongest, least evitable and to laymen least obvious issue, however, is the enormous demand for water to maintain sufficient oil flow pressure. So far, oil extraction is very limited and can be serviced from boreholes and even bowsers ferrying water from the Turkwel River, but once it gets into full swing, water consumption will skyrocket to unprecedented levels (Mkutu et al., 2019). During my visit in May 2019, Tullow, the government of Kenya and the County Government agreed to pump the water stored by the Turkwel Gorge dam to the oil fields. The consequences are still utterly unclear, as a large part of the county's population depends on the water of the Turkwel, including in Lodwar. The "hit" will not only be felt by the irrigation projects established, maintained and cyclically resuscitated in the name of food security and development over the last seven decades (Akall, 2020), but the significant decrease of surface and underground water flow will affect the pastoralist economies of an infinitely larger area.

Tullow has created a dense network of water points in its main areas of activity. When it had to temporarily close down local operations after attacks on its facilities by protesting mobs of "wild" locals—a notion in Kenya most strongly associated with Turkana and kindred pastoralist (i.e., least "modernized" and best-armed) groups—their closure generated substantial pressure on the local population. Reports suggest, however, that much of the semi-violent collective action was actually organised by politicians seeking to increase their and their networks' shares in the oil cake, recruiting people for protests with promises and hand-outs. Though not unprecedented, the hiring of lumpen street violence is certainly a push towards a very dangerous slope. And there are other threats to security, too.

3.8 *Security*

In this region, pastoralist societies are based on intense cooperation within independent and mobile family units, amicable resource sharing within neighbourhoods and stern adherence to solidarity norms and predation taboos within ethnic units, reinforced by cross-cutting institutions such as territorial sections, age and generation sets and clans. Frontier sections can maintain cooperative alliances with neighbouring ethnic groups, thus extending the taboos, and individuals frequently have friends across the boundary, but inter-tribal relations are more often than not characterised by mutual hostility, armed and lethal raids and counter-raids. Intra-ethnic relations, however, are entirely peaceful, based on culturally engrained norms of solidarity, fairness and equity (Eulenberger, 2013, 2015). Despite the rise in "modern" resources, the traditional taboos on intra-ethnic violence remained largely intact, not least because modern Turkana elites remain bound to these pastoralist norms in return for popular acceptance. In their contests to harness support, politicians cooperate across party lines to enable self-protection in borderlands where only armed pastoralists are capable of providing security efficiently.

Seeking security, Tullow, thus, recruited local pastoralists who, officially licensed as "National Police Reserve" (NPR), combine renown military skills, courage and proactive attitude that few soldiers or regular police officers can boast, simultaneously preventing the common protest against "hiring outsiders". In the southern oil zones along the Pokot frontier, however, where Turkana have long been at a relative disadvantage (Bollig, 1990), the well-funded security demands of the emerging energy enterprise led to a drain of top-level providers, i.e., the warriors acting as NPR, from critical frontline positions (Lokiyo, 2014; Mkutu & Wandera, 2016). Spikes in attacks and incursions by Pokot raiders and herds were perceived as the results of this drain of martial capital, and only fierce counter-attacks by an unusually large coalition of Turkana warriors (including sections ranging as far as the South Sudanese and Ethiopian borders) brought them to a halt (Eulenberger et al., 2019; Noonan & Kevlihan, 2018).

The oil finds also contributed to international commotion around the Elemi Triangle, the disputed border region with South Sudan and Ethiopia, where population growth, decades of civil war and problematic transformation schemes fuel violent competition between pastoralist groups for borderland resources (Eulenberger, 2016; Snel, 2022). On the positive side, a tradition of amicable cooperation between their national and local governments ensures so far that local conflicts don't translate into national conflicts; democratic mechanisms curtail social disintegration in Turkana and a strong culture of collective action helps local people here to a remarkable degree to secure rights and protect the natural and ecological resources they depend upon. Terrorism—such as that by the Somali-based group al Shabaab which poses a threat to fossil fuel extraction in Kenya's east—has not materialised so far in Turkana, not least because Turkana people who adopt *ariàng* modernity normally become Christians and have no separatist agenda or cultural ambitions that deviate from the mainstream. Despite this relatively stable scenario, some politicians have capitalised on the rampant destitution for "anti-security" strategies. By using mob attacks to pressure for concessions and hiring goons to eliminate rivals, beat up opponents, protesters or paupers claiming land, they pose a threat to the intra-Turkana taboo on serious and predatory violence that has contained social disintegration for so long. With the pervasive culture of backroom deals, such "criminal modernisation" is dangerous, not least because Turkana pastoralists have proven that they can defeat and kill government forces even when the warriors are heavily outnumbered, while the latter tend to take revenge on innocent civilians, thus undermining trust, amity and cooperation between people and state (Eulenberger, 2019, 2013; Vasquez, 2013).

4 Energy Perspectives: Pastoralism, Oil & Renewables

In view of the considerable attention given to armed violence and the dangerous lack of recognition of the problems of dominant approaches to development, it is paramount to realise that, as regrettable as this violence is, its impact is dwarfed by the threats arising from investment in "the wrong things". To understand the impact of oil production and development in their wider context, it is helpful to consider energy perspectives on economic interrelations that connect local, regional and international dimensions.

In drylands, pastoralism makes efficient use of the solar energy converted into biomass as much as water is temporarily and spatially available (Coughenour et al., 1985). Turkana's integration into national and global economies, however, went along with massive energy transfers in the form of food and fuels, material and labour, driven by colonial, national and international interests in control, infrastructure development, short- and medium-term stability and the prevention of lethal starvation. The oil finds simply reinforced this pattern to facilitate commercial operations and to prevent costly disruptions by disgruntled locals and unsatisfied power players.

At the global level, all production of fossil fuel can be regarded as problematic in as far as its consumption adds to man-made climate change, to which drylands and disempowered populations are particularly susceptible (Krätli et al., 2012). As it is, nevertheless, very unlikely that Kenya could be persuaded to leave the oil in the ground (Bos & Gupta, 2016), it would make sense to at least invest oil revenues in ways that counteract the mentioned risks. Apart from pastoralism, two economic fields offer particularly conspicuous chances for sustainable income: transport and renewables.

Turkana is well-positioned to connect South Sudan and Western Ethiopia with the Kenyan coast, but it is currently outcompeted by longer-yet-better-developed routes, namely from Juba to Uganda, and from Addis to Nairobi via Moyale. If realised, LAPSSET could change that, but its realisation is more than uncertain, due to: the enormous costs that can be anticipated (including embezzlement and compensation schemes); the limited prospects for quick amortisation; and the current disinterest from sufficiently potent donors.

Nevertheless, reduced versions that feature a Nairobi-Turkana-Juba railway but forgo problematic components (such as the Lamu port, the Lamu-Isiolo corridor and the pipeline) have a good chance to benefit adjacent populations, to reduce energy costs of trans-regional flows, and to increase international traffic and facilitate oil development with positive long-term "side effects." A high-voltage power line could help develop the region's vast potential for renewable energy production.

The drylands of the region, long figured as unproductive money dumps, are emerging as a new frontier of the global energy transition. While the mentioned biofuel production in the Lower Omo must be disqualified as ecologically, economically and socially destructive, the natural conditions for the production of electricity from solar power (George et al., 2019; Lomax et al., 2021), wind (Indeje et al., 2001) and geothermal power (Kombe & Muguthu, 2018) are strikingly favourable and potentially less problematic than the exportation of the ultra-scarce water resources in form of sugar-based biofuel. However, conflicts around and management problems with Africa's largest wind park in a Turkana-majority area (Cormack & Kurewa, 2018; Eulenberger et al., 2022) or geothermal development at the Turkana-East Pokot frontier (Greiner, 2020; Mkutu & Wandera, 2016, p. 20) suggest that it is important to closely and equitably involve local communities, explore how production can be decentralised and integrate local families as (co-)owners and guardians of the infrastructure in democratic and conflict-sensitive ways, especially as this is most likely the economic field with the highest potential of sustainable GDP growth in this region.

At the same time, it is important to make sure that ensuing opportunities are not used in ideology-based detrimental ways, including the expansion of irrigated food- and cash-crop agriculture that offsets small gains in local production in the best-watered 10% of the region with far larger losses occuring in the remaining 90% due to the alienation of resources that pastoralists rely upon for herd survival during dry periods (Eulenberger, 2019). And none of the measures under discussion has a chance of leading to sustainable improvement without investments in social security that free locals from the necessity to multiply offspring to increase chances of kinship-based income—which leads to a growth of aid-dependent pauper populations bound to outpace any possible growth in production (Hall et al., 2017; Livingston, 2019; Zinkina & Korotayev, 2014).

5 Conclusion and Outlook

To identify the main threats posed by oil, it is important to disentangle pre-existing dynamics from oil-induced transformations. The Niger Delta

(Eberlein, 2006) and Chad (Behrends & Hoinathy, 2017) appear to be prime examples for links between extractive resource wealth and conflict, and the discovery and production of oil in the south of Sudan in the 1980s contributed to the outbreak, atrociousness and persistence of a civil war that led to the south's secession but has never really ended (Pendle, 2015; Rolandsen, 2015; Craze & Marko, 2022). Spectacular escalations of inter-ethnic violence along the Turkana-Pokot frontier are suspected of being fuelled by prospects of oil and geo-thermal development (Noonan & Kevlihan, 2018). Based on such experiences, Patey (2014) speculates that "political interference" will significantly increase in Kenya, including on the national level, once oil production takes off. The bonanza has so far almost exclusively been based on the prospects of future oil sale profits and investments made in anticipation of such profits, as actual production remains very low, while these prospects have concurrently fuelled concerns that conflicts over the disputed Elemi Triangle between Kenya, South Sudan and Ethiopia could escalate (Eulenberger, 2016).

However, the situation in Turkana has a number of advantages compared to prominent 'oil problem cases' like the Niger Delta or (South) Sudan. Although the wider environment is strikingly violent (featuring frequent inter-ethnic clashes and livestock raiding), this violence is almost exclusively limited to ethnic frontier zones and pastoralist issues; the traditional taboo on intra-ethnic fighting continues to function remarkably well, very much in contrast to the decades of ferocious factional fighting poisoning the socio-political environment in Chad and the Sudans. Importantly, there is also a strong culture of self-confident and forceful demand among the Turkana, both pastoralist and *ariàng* [modernized], which has helped to push for increased shares of all kinds of benefits. This is, however, only possible because Kenyan politics has not been militarised by civil wars; after the gradual defeat of Moi's authoritarianism in the 1990s, a level of democratic freedom was achieved that can be well utilised to defend local and non-elite interests, in comparison to the conditions of the more oppressive regimes in Kenya's neighbourhood and amongst African oil states.

Despite this, fundamental problems have also become visible. The most momentous one is arguably the overall development path that Kenya shares with many other countries. Growth is perceived as an unlimited possibility of tapping new resources and a process that will eventually lead everyone to the kind of life the economically privileged inflict on the planet. However, the people in the Global North and the well-off in the Global South who are able to live it bank on the support of millions who will never be able to do the same (Livingston, 2019). The acquiescence of the majority is based on promises that suggest introducing Northern technologies and methods of organisation will bring them Western-style wealth. However, the privileged commonly manage to use their disproportionate influence on transformation processes to make sure the gains are not distributed too evenly, as this would endanger the disproportionality of their share. This continued inequality is their only hope for continued access to such consumerist comforts in a world that would collapse if everyone would consume as they (we) do.

Political elites in Turkana and similar places commonly gain popular support by playing the advocate of "the community," their constituents, or at least a sufficiently influential faction. This raises the problem who "the community" actually is, who qualifies as a member, who should be considered and who is entitled to speak and negotiate in its name. This is a long-standing and widespread problem, yet it has never been so urgent for Turkana, which is now facing a boom of transactions conducted in the mode of well-established patterns of clientelism, corruption and trajectories of future-making, which are bound to worsen the situation. The resulting escalation of contradictions, scarcities and conflicts could cause severe damage to structures that kept Turkana society internally peaceful and cooperative to this day.

At the discourse level, all actors employ a language of development and justice. Turkana—elites, school-educated working class and pastoralists alike—use grievance discourses to stake their claims. Nomads and paupers point to their hunger, the school leavers to jobs, projects and tenders, and the top players passionately engage in ethical algebra regarding the differential allocation of millions of dollars in benefits in the name of their community and in the interest of their accumulation enterprises. The national government points to revenue invested into the region's progress and entrusted to its autonomous county government. Tapping the new resources for personal networks is a top priority for anyone with political ambitions. Established methods of tactical exclusion and inclusion have become exacerbated in parallel to the rise in available funds, not unlike in the Sudan in the 1980s but, at least so far, in a much less extreme manner.

The problems posed by curse-like paths development has taken are even more consequential (in Turkana and elsewhere). From this perspective, oil adds more fuel to a vehicle headed into the wrong direction.[5] The Omo-Turkana

5 This is obviously not a 'normatively neutral' statement – but doing social science value-free is neither achievable nor desirable. Research on problematic social facts generates moral obligations to consider implications for human and environmental well-being (Eulenberger, forthcoming) and to point out these implications wherever that is feasible and holds potential to benefit the public. From an ethical perspective, to not do so is a neglect of the opportunity to prevent harm. It is thus a disservice to the people concerned and those who contributed to our work, even though it would shield us from ideology-based academic criticism and interest-based 'stakeholder' scorn.

Region is but an extreme showpiece of the threats posed by a flawed approach to future-making that decreases landscape-scale productivity for the sake of unsustainable short-term gains and increased local extraction. The bio-fuel production schemes across the Ethiopian border that damage the highly efficient and adaptive, self-determined and equitable social-ecological systems of millions of people have become a widely known cautionary tale, but they are just the tip of the iceberg the region is headed towards. Transformation policies in Turkana and other parts of Kenya, and indeed the world over, suffer in many regards from the same flaws. This is only possible because powerful international cooperation networks, including Northern and Southern governments, donors and charities, NGOs and businesses, continue to ignore both the sustainable efficiency and critical social benefits of indigenous socio-ecological systems, as well as the diagnoses provided by well-informed experts, such as those cited here. Instead, these networks remain guided by global ideologies of growth and modernisation used by privileged minorities to manufacture consent. They do so by dangling carrots of material amenities and relative advantage, while in fact they sow inequality and grow dependent and disempowered populations – in tandem with the assets of elites exploiting their dependency and disempowerment.[6]

Fortunately, researchers, practitioners, and locals are in dialogue, important questions are being asked and discourses are gradually changing. The relative freedom of such coalitions provides spaces for developing inclusive holistic analyses that can help re-orient, design and implement interventions whose costs do not outweigh benefits to disastrous degrees. To counter destructive transformation dynamics, it is important: to understand the interplay of factors from landscape-scale perspectives; to keep track of ecological, social and cultural costs; and to take a longue durée view on the desirability of interrelated outcomes of interventions and infrastructural change. So far, dominant transformation ideologies, policies and practices too often fail to do so. Socio-ecological research can be a corrective, e.g., by shedding light on long-term effects, on democratic assemblages with considerable potential to empower people at grass-roots levels, and to mechanisms generating pressure in the opposite direction.

Closer contact with non-elite majorities and familiarity with their sophistication as experts of their own environments (a rarity in the global development

---

6 Causes for this 'wrong' direction are not just external, as local assemblages and dynamics obviously contribute to the challenges. But ignoring the strong impact of external factors would be heuristically reckless and a disservice to those interested in understanding these problems.

apparatus), draws our attention to points of view that contextualise energy development and benefit distribution as part of a larger picture where the equitable, careful and inclusive use of land and water, renewable energy resources and ecosystem productivity are the main concern. There is enormous potential for synergy between the socio-ecological expertise and democratic power of local populations, the technical expertise and financial power of development actors and the cross-cutting expertise and analytic power of socioecological research. Making use of it is not just a matter of common sense. In the long run, it is a matter of disaster prevention.

Acknowledgements

I would like to thank Annika Witte, Augustine Lokwang, Boniface Samal, Egbert Wesselink, Jannik Schritt, Jacob Lolelea, Jed Stevenson, Lawrence Etoot, Lesley Branagan, Matthew Osborne, Rebecca Loru, Sara Ketelaar, Shauna LaTosky, Simon Simonse, Sindy Schug, and Ursula Rao for their support. This work was supported by FORMAS 2017–01941 Integrering av konfliktanalys i projekt för förnybar energi: möjligheter att främja och upprätthålla fred.

References

Adano, W., Dietz, T., & Witsenburg, K. (2012). Natural Resources and Conflicts: Theoretical Flaws and Empirical Evidence from Northern Kenya. In K. Witsenburg & F. Zaal (eds.), *Spaces of Insecurity: Human Agency in Violent Conflicts in Kenya,* (pp. 141–166). Leiden University, African Studies Centre.

Adem, T. A., Ember, C., Skoggard, I., Jones, E., & Faas, A. (2012). Dangerous Geography: Spatial Distribution of Livestock Raiding in Northwestern Kenya. *Ethnology,* 51(1/2), 1–29.

AFRICOG. (2014). Mixed Blessing? Promoting Good Governance in Kenya's Extractive Industries. Africa Centre for Open Governance. http://www.africog.org/reports/extractive_industries.

Akall, G. (2020). 'Farmer-Led Irrigation Investments: How Local Innovators Are Transforming Failed Irrigation Schemes'. In J. Lind, D. Okenwa & I. Scoones (eds.), *Land, Investment & Politics: Reconfiguring Eastern Africa's Pastoral Drylands,* (pp. 155–65), Boydell & Brewer, James Currey.

Andvig, J., & Barasa, T. (2014). 'Grabbing by Strangers: Crime and Policing in Kenya'. In T. Søreide (ed.), *Corruption, Grabbing and Development,* (pp. 83–92), Elgar.

Auty, R. (1993). *Sustaining Development in Mineral Economies: The Resource Curse Thesis.* Routledge.

Appel, H. (2019). *The Licit Life of Capitalism: US Oil in Equatorial Guinea*. Durham: Duke University Press.

Bach, D. (2013). *Neopatrimonialism in Africa and Beyond*. Taylor & Francis.

Ballentine, K., & Sherman, J. (eds.). (2003). *The Political Economy of Armed Conflict: Beyond Greed and Grievance*. Rienner.

Beblawi, H., & Luciani, G. (Eds.) (1987). *The Rentier State. Nation, State and Integration in the Arab World*. London: Croom Helm.

Behrends, A. (2011). Fighting for Oil When There Is No Oil Yet: The Darfur-Chad Border. In A. Behrends, S. P. Reyna, & G. Schlee (eds.), *Crude Domination*, (pp. 39–56), Berghahn.

Behrends, A., & Schareika, N. (2011). Öl, Staat, Ressourcenfluch. In N. Schareika, E. Spies, & P.-Y. Le Meur (eds.), *Auf dem Boden der Tatsachen: Festschrift für Thomas Bierschenk*, (pp. 465–476). Köppe.

Behrends, A., Reyna, S., & Schlee, G. (eds.). (2011). *Crude Domination: An Anthropology of Oil*. Berghahn.

Behrends, A., & Hoinathy, R. (2017). The Devil's Money: A Multi-level Approach to Acceleration and Turbulence in Oil-producing Southern Chad. *Social Analysis*, 61(3), 56–72.

Berdal, M. R. & Malone, D. (Eds.). (2000). *Greed & Grievance: Economic Agendas in Civil Wars*. Rienner.

Bierschenk, T., Chauveau, J., & Olivier de Sardan, J.-P. (2002). *Local Development Brokers in Africa: The Rise of a New Social Category*. Universität Mainz, Institut für Ethnologie & Afrikastudien.

Bollig, M. (1990). Ethnic Conflicts in North-West Kenya: Pokot-Turkana Raiding 1969–1984. *Zeitschrift für Ethnologie*, 115, 73–90.

Bos, K., & Gupta, J. (2016). Inclusive Development, Oil Extraction and Climate Change: A Multilevel Analysis of Kenya. *International Journal of Sustainable Development & World Ecology*, 23(6), 482–492.

Bregman, R. (2020). *Humankind: A Hopeful History*. Bloomsbury Publishing.

Browne, A. J. (2015). *LAPSSET: The History and Politics of an Eastern African Megaproject*. Rift Valley Institute.

Buffavand, L. (2016). "The Land Does Not like Them": Contesting Dispossession in Cosmological Terms in Mela, South-West Ethiopia. *Journal of Eastern African Studies* 10(3), 476–93.

Collier, P. (2006). Is Aid Oil? An Analysis of Whether Africa Can Absorb More Aid. *World Development*, 34(9), 1482–1497.

Cormack, Z., & Kurewa, A. (2018). The Changing Value of Land in Northern Kenya: The Case of Lake Turkana Wind Power. *Critical African Studies*, 10(1), 89–107.

Coughenour, M., Ellis, J., Swift, M., Coppock, D., Galvin, K., McCabe, T., and Hart, T. (1985). 'Energy Extraction and Use in a Nomadic Pastoral Ecosystem'. *Science* 230(4726), 619–25.

Craze, J., & Marko, F. D. (2022, January 6). Death by Peace: How South Sudan's Peace Agreement Ate the Grassroots. *African Arguments*. https://africanarguments.org/2022/01/death-by-peace-how-south-sudans-peace-agreement-ate-the-grassroots/ [last accessed 19 February 2022].

D'Arcy, M. (2019). 'Big Men' and Poor Voters: Political Corruption and Elections in Kenya. In I. Amundsen (ed.), *Political Corruption in Africa* (pp. 52–70). Elgar.

D'Arcy, M., & Cornell, A. (2016). Devolution and Corruption in Kenya: Everyone's Turn to Eat? *African Affairs*, 115(459), 246–273.

Debay, T. W. (2009). *Climate Change and Transboundary Water Resource Conflicts in Africa*. Institute for Security Studies.

Eberlein, R. (2006). On the Road to the State's Perdition? Authority and Sovereignty in the Niger Delta. *Journal of Modern African Studies*, 44(4), 573–596.

Ember, C. R., Skoggard, I., Adem, T. A., & Faas, A. J. (2014). Rain and Raids Revisited: Disaggregating Ethnic Group Livestock Raiding in the Ethiopian-Kenyan Border Region. *Civil Wars*, 16(3), 300–327.

Erdmann, G., & Engel, U. (2006). 'Neopatrimonialism Revisited - Beyond a Catch-All Concept'. *GIGA Working Paper Series* 16.

Escobar, A. (2011). *Encountering Development: The Making and Unmaking of the Third World*. Princeton University Press.

Eulenberger, I. (2013). Pastoralists, Conflicts and Politics: Aspects of South Sudan's 'Kenyan Frontier'. In C. Vaughan, M. Schomerus, & L. de Vries (eds.), *The Borderlands of South Sudan*, (pp. 67–88). Palgrave Macmillan.

Eulenberger, I. (2015). Gifts, Guns and Govvermen: South Sudan and Its Southeast. In S. Calkins, E. Ille, & R. Rottenburg (eds.), *Emerging Orders in the Sudans*, (pp. 153–96). Langaa.

Eulenberger, I. (2016). The Ilemi Triangle. Internal Report. Pax Netherlands.

Eulenberger, I. (2019). Energy Economics, Climate Change and Renewables in East African Drylands. Karamoja Resilience Support Unit, Working paper https://karamojaresilience.org/wp-content/uploads/2021/07/14ec3c_901b2ec4c6594faabcaf8d968398oc2c.pdf.

Eulenberger, I. (forthcoming). *Conflict, Environment & Future-making: Violence, Collective Action Problems & Development in a Pastoralist Trans-border Region of Kenya, Ethiopia, South Sudan and Uganda*, Dissertation. Martin Luther University & Max Planck Institute for Social Anthropology.

Eulenberger, I., Kamski, B., & Longole, H. (2018). Pastoralist Civil Societies: Cooperative Empowerment across Boundaries in Borderlands of Kenya, Uganda and Ethiopia. Arnold Bergstraesser Institute, Robert Bosch Stiftung. https://www.bosch-stiftung.de/en/publication/pastoralist-civil-societies.

Eulenberger, I., Feyissa, D., Iyer, P., Gebresenbet, F., Adugna, F., Tefera, S., Hoehne, M., Lokwang, A., Eaton, D., Meckelburg, A., Wassie, M. (2019). Borderlands of Eastern

Africa. Borderlands Working Group / DRC, https://www.bkhub.org/publications/agenda-setting-report-for-the-borderlands-working-group/.

Eulenberger, I., Gebeyehu, A. K., LaTosky, S., Mulugeta, M. F., Kurewa, A., Samal, B., Boru, H. (2022). Energy development frontiers in the Omo-Turkana Region: Potentials & Challenges. Stockholm Environmental Institute.

Ferguson, J. (2005). Seeing like an Oil Company: Space, Security, and Global Capital in Neoliberal Africa. *American Anthropologist*, 107(3), 377–382.

Fry, D. (ed.) (2013). *War, Peace, and Human Nature*. Oxford University Press.

Gabbert, E., Gebresenbet, F., Galaty, J., & Schlee, G. (2021). *Lands of the Future: Anthropological Perspectives on Pastoralism, Land Deals and Tropes of Modernity in Eastern Africa*. Berghahn.

Galaty, J. (2014). 'Unused' Land and Unfulfilled Promises: Justifications for Displacing Communities in East Africa. *Nomadic Peoples*, 18(1), 80–93.

Gary, I., Karl, T., & Oliveira, R. (2003). *Bottom of the Barrel: Africa's Oil Boom and the Poor*. CRS.

George, A., Boxiong, S., Arowo, M., Ndolo, P., Chepsaigutt-Chebet, and Shimmon, J. (2019). Review of Solar Energy Development in Kenya: Opportunities and Challenges. *Renewable Energy Focus*, 29(June), 123–40.

Greiner, C. (2020). Negotiating Access to Land & Resources at the Geothermal Frontier in Baringo, Kenya. In J. Lind, D. Okenwa, & I. Scoones (eds.), *Land, Investment & Politics*, (pp. 101–109). Currey.

Hall, C., Dawson, T., Macdiarmid, J., Matthews, R. and Smith, P. (2017). The Impact of Population Growth and Climate Change on Food Security in Africa: Looking Ahead to 2050, *International Journal of Agricultural Sustainability*, 15(2), 124–35.

Helbling, J. (2006). *Tribale Kriege: Konflikte in Gesellschaften ohne Zentralgewalt*. Campus.

Hodbod, J., Stevenson, E. G. J., Akall, G., Akuja, T., Angelei, I., Bedasso, E. A., Buffavand, L., Derbyshire, S., Eulenberger, I., Gownaris, N., Kamski, B., Kurewa, A., Lokuruka, M., Mulugeta, M. F., Okenwa, D., Rodgers, C., & Tebbs, E. (2019). *Social-ecological Change in the Omo-Turkana Basin: A Synthesis of Current Developments*. Ambio.

Homer-Dixon, T. F. (1999). *Environment, Scarcity, and Violence*. Princeton University Press.

Indeje, M., Semazzi, F., Xie, L., and Ogallo L. (2001). Mechanistic Model Simulations of the East African Climate Using NCAR Regional Climate Model: Influence of Large-Scale Orography on the Turkana Low-Level Jet. *Journal of Climate*, 14(12), 2710–24.

Johannes, E., Zulu, L. & Kalipeni, E. (2015). Oil Discovery in Turkana County, Kenya: A Source of Conflict or Development? *African Geographical Review*, 34(2), 142–64.

KCSPOG. (2014). *Setting the Agenda for the Development of Kenya's Oil and Gas Resources*. Kenya Civil Society Platform on Oil and Gas (KCSPOG).

Kiambati, K. (2020). The Levels of Transparency and County Service Delivery in Kenya. *International Journal of Research in Business and Social Science* (2147–4478), 9(3), 14–25.

Kimenyi, M., Mwega, F., & Ndung'u, N. (2016). Kenya: Economic Growth, Labor Market Dynamics, and Prospects for a Demographic Dividend. In H. Bhorat & F. Tarp (eds.), *Africa's Lions: Growth Traps and Opportunities for Six African Economies* (pp. 109–144), Brookings Institution Press.

KNBS. (2018). Kenya Integrated Household Budget Survey 2015–2016. Kenya National Bureau of Statistics (KNBS). http://statistics.knbs.or.ke/nada/index.php/catalog/88.

Kombe, E., & Muguthu, J. (2018). Geothermal Energy Development in East Africa: Barriers and Strategies. *Journal of Energy Research and Reviews*, 2(1), 1–6.

Krätli, S., Hülsebusch, C., Brooks, S., & Kaufmann, B. (2012). Pastoralism: A Critical Asset for Food Security Under Global Climate Change. *Animal Frontiers*, 3(1), 42–50.

Lind, J. (2018). Devolution, Shifting Centre-Periphery Relationships and Conflict in Northern Kenya. *Political Geography* 63, 135–147.

Lind, J., & Sturman, K. (eds.). (2002). *Scarcity and Surfeit: The Ecology of Africa's Conflicts*. Institute for Security Studies.

Livingston, J. (2019). *Self-Devouring Growth: A Planetary Parable as Told from Southern Africa*. Durham: Duke University Press.

Lokiyo, E. L. (2014) *Trans-Border Conflict Between the Turkana and Pokot in Kainuk and Alale Divisions, Kenya: 1995–2013*. Kenyatta University Nairobi.

Lomax, J., Osborne, M., Aminga, V., Mirumachi, N., & Johnson, O. (2021). Causal Pathways in the Political Economy of Climate Adaptation: Winners and Losers in Turkana, Kenya Solar Mini-grid Projects. *Energy Research & Social Science*, 82, 102296.

Manji, A. (2020). *The Struggle for Land and Justice in Kenya*. Boydell & Brewer.

McCabe, T. (2004). *Cattle Bring Us to Our Enemies: Turkana Ecology, Politics, and Raiding in a Disequilibrium System*. Ann Arbor: University of Michigan Press.

Meller, H., Schefzik, M. (eds.). (2015). *Krieg - eine archäologische Spurensuche*. Landesmuseum für Vorgeschichte.

Mkutu, K. (2016, September 14). Avoiding the Local Resource Curse in Turkana, Kenya. *Horn of Africa Bulletin*. https://life-peace.org/hab/avoiding-the-local-resource-curse-in-turkana-kenya/.

Mkutu, K. A. (2017). Oil and Emerging Conflict Dynamics in the Ateker Cluster: The Case of Turkana, Kenya. *Nomadic Peoples*, 21(1), 34–62.

Mkutu, K., Marani, M. & Ruteere, M. (2014). *Securing the Counties: Options for Security After Devolution in Kenya*. http://erepository.uonbi.ac.ke:8080/xmlui/handle/11295/85852.

Mkutu, K., & Wandera, G. (2016). *Conflict, Security and the Extractive Industries in Turkana, Kenya. USIU-Africa & Kenya* School of Government (KSG).

Mkutu, K., Mkutu, T., Marani, M. & Ekitela, A. L. (2019). New Oil Developments in a Remote Area: Environmental Justice and Participation in Turkana, Kenya. *Journal of Environment & Development*, 28(3), 223–252.

Mosley, J., & Watson, E. E. (2016). Frontier Transformations: Development Visions, Spaces and Processes in Northern Kenya and Southern Ethiopia. *Journal of Eastern African Studies*, 10(3), 452–475.

Mulugeta, M. F. (2016). Statehood, Small Arms and Security Governance in Southwest Ethiopia. In S. Okello & M. Gebremichael (eds.), *African-Centred Solutions: Building Peace and Security in Africa* (pp. 103–133). Institute for Peace and Security Studies (IPSS).

Nanok, J. K., & Onyango, C. O. (2017). A Socio-Economic and Environmental Analysis of the Effects of Oil Exploration on the Local Community in Lokichar, Turkana County, Kenya. *International Journal of Management, Economics and Social Sciences*, 6(3), 144–156.

Noonan, O., & Kevlihan, R. (2018). Managing Conflict in North-West Kenya: The Siege of Loregon and its Aftermath. *Conflict, Security & Development*, 18(2), 137–157.

Nyanjom, O. (2014). Remarginalising Kenyan Pastoralists: The Hidden Curse of National Growth and Development. *African Study Monographs*, 50, 43–72.

Odhiambo, M. O. (2013). The ASAL Policy of Kenya. *Nomadic Peoples*, 17(1), 158–165.

Odote, C. (2013). The Dawn of Uhuru? Implications of Constitutional Recognition of Communal Land Rights in Pastoral Areas of Kenya. *Nomadic Peoples*, 17(1), 87–105.

Okumu, W. (2017). *Meanings of Violence and Its Impacts on the Socio-Political Relations among the Turkana and Samburu of Baragoi, Northern Kenya*. Dissertation, Universität zu Köln (Cologne).

Ongiri, I. (2015, February 10). Nairobi and Turkana to Get Biggest Share of County Cash from July. Daily Nation.

Orr, D. W. (2019). Renegotiating the Periphery: Oil Discovery, Devolution, and Political Contestation in Kenya. *The Extractive Industries and Society*, 6(1), 136–144.

Patey, L. A. (2014). Kenya — An African Oil Upstart in Transition. Oxford Institute for Energy Studies. http://www.oxfordenergy.org/2014/10/kenya-an-african-oil-upstart-in-transition-2/.

Pendle, N. (2015). 'They Are Now Community Police': Negotiating the Boundaries and Nature of the Government in South Sudan through the Identity of Militarised Cattle-keepers. *International Journal on Minority and Group Rights*, 22(3), 410–434.

Pinaud, C. (2014). South Sudan: Civil War, Predation and the Making of a Military Aristocracy. *African Affairs*, 113(451), 192–211.

Rodgers, C. (2020). Hosting Refugees as an Investment in Development: Grand Designs versus Local Expectations in Turkana County, Kenya. In J. Lind, D. Okenwa, & I. Scoones (eds.), *Land, Investment & Politics*, (pp. 89–100), Boydell & Brewer.

Rolandsen, Ø. H. (2015). Another Civil War in South Sudan: The Failure of Guerrilla Government? *Journal of Eastern African Studies*, 9(1), 163–174.

Schlee, G. (2011). Suggestions for a Second Reading: An Alternative Perspective on Contested Resources as an Explanation for Conflict. In A. Behrends et al. (eds.), *Crude domination,* (pp. 298–302). Berghahn.

Schritt, J. (2018). Crude Controversies: Disputes Along Niger's Petro-infrastructure. *History and Anthropology*, 29(5): 645–669.

Simone, S. de. (2018). Playing the 'Fragile State' Card: The SPLM and State Extraversion in South Sudan. *Journal of Modern African Studies*, 56(3), 395–420.

Snel, E. (2022). The Ilemi Triangle: Understanding a pastoralist border area. Pax Netherlands. https://paxforpeace.nl/news/overview/the-ilemi-triangle-understanding-a-pastoralist-border-area.

Stevenson, E. G. J. (2018). Plantation Development in the Turkana Basin: The Making of a New Desert? *Land*, 7(1), 16.

Stevenson, E. G. J., & Buffavand, L. (2018). "Do Our Bodies Know Their Ways?" Villagization, Food Insecurity, and Ill-Being in Ethiopia's Lower Omo Valley. *African Studies Review*, 61(1), 109–133.

Tilly, C. (1985). War Making and State Making as Organized Crime. In P. B. Evans, D. Rueschemeyer &T. Skocpol (eds.), *Bringing the State Back* (pp. 169–191), Cambridge University Press.

van Baalen, S., & Mobjörk, M. (2016). *A coming anarchy? Pathways from Climate Change to Violent Conflict in East Africa.* Stockholm University. http://urn.kb.se/resolve?urn=urn:nbn:se:su:diva-130294.

Vasquez, P. I. (2013). Kenya at a Crossroads: Hopes and Fears Concerning the Development of Oil and Gas Reserves. *International Development Policy*, 4.3.

Waal, A. de. (2014). When Kleptocracy Becomes Insolvent: Brute Causes of the Civil War in South Sudan. *African Affairs*, 113(452), 347–369.

Witte, A. (2018). *An Uncertain Future – Anticipating Oil in Uganda.* Göttingen University Press.

Zinkina, J., and Korotayev, A. (2014). Explosive Population Growth in Tropical Africa: Crucial Omission in Development Forecasts—Emerging Risks and Way Out. *World Futures,* 70 (2): 120–39.

5

Captage régional et politique de la rente pétrolière: Les collectivités territoriales face à la raffinerie du pétrole à Zinder (Niger)

Harouna Abdoutan

1 Introduction

À l'image de la majorité des États ouest-africains, le Niger s'est engagé dans un processus de démocratisation et de décentralisation au début des années 1990 qui a conduit à la mise en place des collectivités territoriales et d'autorités élues (Olivier de Sardan & Tidjani Alou, 2009). Après la communalisation en 2004, ce sont les élections de janvier 2011 qui consacrent l'aboutissement du processus de décentralisation, avec la mise en place effective des collectivités territoriales. La décentralisation, en cours au Niger, modifie en profondeur les rapports administratifs entre le centre et la périphérie (Guesnier, 1986). Elle est associée au développement local (Mback, 2001) et considérée comme un aspect important de son processus. Certains analystes de l'échec de l'État central comme Wunsch et Olowu, (1990), cités par Darbon & Crouzel (2009), mettent en avant les potentialités associées à la décentralisation pour favoriser la démocratisation et le développement local. L'un des défis pour les collectivités territoriales est de favoriser l'initiative locale dans la conception et la mise en œuvre de l'action publique (Tidjani Alou, 2009). Cependant, il faut rappeler que la décentralisation au Niger est mise en œuvre dans un contexte de désengagement de l'État, avec des collectivités territoriales, dans leur majorité, sans ressources propres (Olivier de Sardan & Tidjani Alou, 2009). Pour être effectif, un transfert de compétences et de ressources doit accompagner la réforme. Au Niger, il est un des principes fondamentaux de la libre administration des collectivités territoriales posé par la constitution et le Code Général des Collectivités Territoriales (CGCT). Le transfert de compétences va changer la nature des rapports avec l'administration de l'État qui passent de la tutelle à un rôle de conseil (Coulmin, 1986). Comme presque partout en Afrique, les collectivités territoriales tirent principalement leurs ressources des recettes fiscales, des remises accordées par l'État, des fonds d'équipement et de dotation. Depuis leur mise en place, les conseils régionaux au Niger fonctionnent seulement avec la dotation annuelle de l'État, faute de transfert de compétences. C'est

 | DOI:10.1163/9789004530065_006

dans ce contexte qu'a commencé, dans la région de Zinder, le raffinage du pétrole.

Le 28 novembre 2011 le Niger a inauguré, à Zinder, sa première raffinerie de pétrole. La raffinerie est exploitée par la Société de Raffinage de Zinder (SORAZ).[1] L'accès aux redevances pétrolières pour impulser le développement économique régional est un véritable défi pour les collectivités territoriales. Le raffinage du pétrole à Zinder est au cœur des dynamiques politiques et locales du pays (Tidjani Alou, 2001). Aussi, l'implantation de la SORAZ et la mise en place effective des organes de la décentralisation au Niger nous permettent, à travers cet article, d'étudier les transformations sociales et politiques induites par le raffinage du pétrole à Zinder. Basé sur la théorie de « l'état rentier » selon laquelle les revenus du pétrole établissent une « mentalité rentière » dans laquelle l'unique logique restante dans le jeu politique est l'avidité des élites à empocher le plus possible de la « rente pétrolière » (Beblawi & Luciani, 1987; Mahdavy, 1970; Ovadia, 2013; Yates, 1996), l'article retrace les stratégies développées par les acteurs sociaux et politiques pour capter la « rente » ou la « manne pétrolière » dans un contexte de décentralisation. Nous soutenons que le captage de la manne pétrolière suit une logique politique et régionaliste qui reflète le processus de la décentralisation au Niger. En d'autres termes, les effets de la production pétrolière ne peuvent être compris que dans le contexte de dynamiques sociopolitiques préexistantes. Nous pouvons voir ici une capture élitaire des rentes pétrolières, non, comme souvent, par les acteurs nationaux, mais par les acteurs locaux. Les acteurs locaux pourraient tirer parti de la décentralisation et de leur longue tradition de contestation de l'État central pour se tailler une place de choix.

La présente étude s'appuie sur des travaux de recherche menés durant trois mois (un premier séjour en février et un deuxième en mai et juin 2013) dans la ville de Zinder dans le cadre du programme de recherche du LASDEL[2] « Oil and Social Change in Niger and Chad ».[3] La collecte des données de terrain a été effectuée suivant « la rigueur qualitative » de la socio-anthropologie, combinant à la fois entretiens et observations (Olivier de Sardan, 2008). L'entretien est focalisé sur « les groupes stratégiques » dans « l'arène politique locale »

1 La SORAZ est une entreprise de la China National Petroleum Compagnie (CNPC). La CNPC est majoritaire à 60% de capital et l'État du Niger pour 40% des parts (Sahel dimanche, 2012, p. 12).

2 Le LASDEL (Laboratoire d'Études et de Recherche sur les Dynamiques Sociales et le Développement Local) est un laboratoire de recherche en sciences sociales basé à Niamey au Niger. Pour plus de renseignements sur le LASDEL : www.lasdel.net.

3 Un projet de recherche en collaboration avec les universités de Göttingen, Mayence et Halle, financé par la Fondation allemande pour la recherche (DFG) dans le cadre du programme prioritaire 1448 « Adaptation et créativité en Afrique ».

(Elwert & Bierschenk, 1988; Bierschenk & Olivier de Sardan, 1998) autour du pétrole à Zinder. Les groupes stratégiques se caractérisent par le fait qu'ils n'existent pas a priori, mais se forment par rapport à un enjeu précis (dans ce cas : la rente du pétrole) sur la base d'intérêts et stratégies communs (ibid.). Cependant, les groupes stratégiques n'émergent pas simplement d'un vide. Ils sont souvent basés sur des constellations sociopolitiques préexistantes telles que les partis politiques, les chefs administratifs, la société civile, etc. Ainsi, certaines questions liées à la formation des groupes stratégiques sont de savoir quels sont les nouveaux acteurs émergeants, comment les acteurs bien établis s'approprient l'enjeu ou comment ils se regroupent et se transforment.

Dans le cadre de cette recherche, nous avons identifié les groupes stratégiques suivants : les élus locaux, les agents de la SORAZ, la société civile, les médias, la population de la ville de Zinder ainsi que les autorités administratives, coutumières et religieuses. Un guide d'entretien a été élaboré à partir des indicateurs de recherche. Ces indicateurs sont des thématiques de l'étude autour desquels ont été articulées et formulées les questions posées aux enquêtés. Les aspects abordés varient selon le groupe stratégique considéré. Au total, une trentaine d'entretiens a été réalisée. Parallèlement aux entretiens, nous avons fait des observations directes au niveau de l'exécutif du conseil régional, à l'auto-gare d'Agadez (Tacha Agadez) et à la tribune de Zinder. Ces observations nous ont permis de voir les activités quotidiennes de l'exécutif au niveau du conseil régional, et de voir au niveau de l'auto-gare, de la tribune et du parking des camionneurs les activités annexes qui se sont développées avec l'implantation de cette raffinerie ainsi que les interactions que cela mobilise.

Dans la première partie de ce travail, nous évoquons l'enjeu de la mise en place des régions collectivités territoriales et la responsabilité qui leur incombe dans la promotion des initiatives locales pour impulser le développement économique et social dans leurs entités. Dans la deuxième partie, nous abordons l'espoir des collectivités territoriales à Zinder fondé par l'exploitation du pétrole en vue de stimuler un développement régional. Les mobilisations sociales organisées autour de la manne pétrolière nous permettent d'observer les conflits induits par l'exploitation pétrolière. Enfin, dans la troisième partie, nous montrons les différentes stratégies développées par les différents acteurs, au niveau local, dans le but de capter la manne pétrolière.

2 Bref historique du processus de la décentralisation et l'exploitation du pétrole au Niger

Au Niger, la constitution du 8 novembre 1960 a déjà déterminé les principes fondamentaux de la libre administration des collectivités territoriales, de leurs compétences et de leurs ressources. Les arrondissements et les communes, érigés en collectivités territoriales, étaient dotés d'une personnalité morale et d'une autonomie financière. Ils ont à leur tête des organes délibérants. Mais, comme le dit Otayek (2009, p. 127), « les premières collectivités mises en place ne sont que des simples extensions du pouvoir central ». Dans la pratique, les collectivités locales restent sous la tutelle des autorités administratives, leurs exécutifs étant nommés par le pouvoir central. C'est finalement avec l'avènement de la Ve République que la décentralisation a été adaptée et mise en œuvre lors des premières élections municipales de 2004. Toutefois, il a fallu attendre les élections de janvier 2011 pour voir l'aboutissement du processus de décentralisation, avec la mise en place effective des collectivités territoriales. La région reçoit la compétence la plus large en matière d'animation et de planification du développement économique (Pecqueur, 1998, p. 108). En effet, elle devient le lieu privilégié d'élaboration des politiques d'aménagement et d'action économique.

En 2008, le président Tandja Mamadou a signé une production-accord-partage avec China National Petroleum Corporation (CNPC). Cette convention a conduit, en 2011 à Zinder, à l'inauguration de la première raffinerie de pétrole du Niger. Rappelons cependant qu'avant la signature de cette convention, le Niger a une histoire de 50 ans d'exploration pétrolière (Schritt, 2018). Les

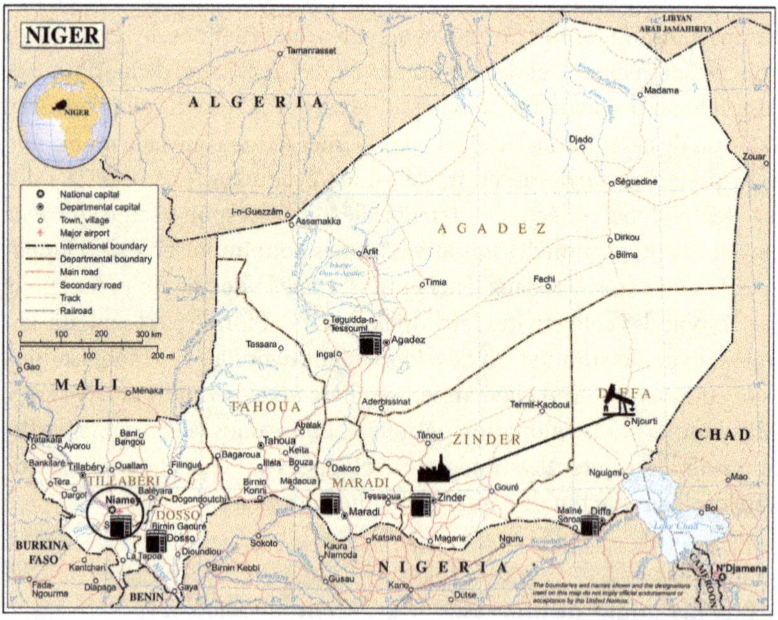

FIGURE 5.1 L'infrastructure pétrolière au Niger montrant les puits, la raffinerie, le centre de consommation (cercle), et les six dépôts de carburant : Diffa, Zinder, Maradi, Dosso, Sorey (Niamey) et Agadez
SCHRITT, 2018, P. 653

premières explorations confiées à des compagnies françaises et américaines datent de 1958. Si l'existence de gisements ne faisait aucun doute, des tentatives d'exploitation ont eu lieu en 1984. Les rapports coûts d'exploitation/rentabilité ont « laissé ce dossier dans les tiroirs » durant des décennies.

3 L'implantation de la SORAZ en contexte de décentralisation au Niger

La région collectivité territoriale est apparue pour la première fois dans le paysage institutionnel du Niger avec les élections locales et régionales du 11 janvier 2011. Sa vocation est essentiellement économique, sociale et culturelle (Code Général des Collectivités Territoriales (CGCT), art. 98). Elle apparaît, ainsi, dans l'échelon politique et administratif national comme le dernier palier à même de comprendre et d'assurer des responsabilités politiques dans un pays en construction. L'un des grands enjeux des collectivités territoriales est de promouvoir les initiatives au niveau local afin d'impulser le développement local et régional. Conformément au Code Général des Collectivités Territoriales du Niger, les Conseils Régionaux créent des commissions spécialisées dont la mission est d'assurer la coordination technique des actions de développement au sein de leur entité territoriale, de donner leur avis sur les programmes de développement prévus, de suivre les opérations en cours et l'état des réalisations. Ces commissions sont censées permettre aux régions collectivités territoriales de « négocier » le tournant d'un État centralisateur à une autonomie administrative et économique. Comment les régions pourront-elles trouver les moyens de suppléer l'État au niveau local ?

Quant à la SORAZ (Société de Raffinage de Zinder), elle a été mise en service le 28 novembre 2011, lors de la double cérémonie de lancement des activités de production pétrolière au Niger et l'inauguration de la raffinerie de pétrole de Zinder. Elle est située à 52 km du chef-lieu de région sur la route de Tanout. C'était sous le haut patronage du président de la République du Niger que ces opérations ont été lancées. D'une capacité de 20.000 barils par jour (soit 1.000.000 tonnes par an), la raffinerie est en mesure de produire les dérivés que sont le gaz ; le pétrole liquéfié (GPL), 69.900 tonnes par an ; l'essence super, 306.200 tonnes par an et le gasoil, 505.400 tonnes par an. La raffinerie est composée de cinq (5) parties : un complexe de raffinage d'une capacité de 1.000.000 tonnes par an, une centrale électrique de 24 mégawatts, un centre de vente de produits pétroliers, un complexe d'approvisionnement en eau de la raffinerie et une base vie du personnel. Cette production permettra au Niger non seulement de satisfaire ses besoins en produits pétroliers raffinés, mais aussi d'en exporter, ce qui, dans les deux cas, permettra de soutenir la croissance économique du pays. Le pétrole du Niger est exploité dans la région de Diffa mais raffiné dans celle de Zinder. Au Niger, la loi n° 2007-01 du 31 janvier 2007 portant sur le code pétrolier prévoit 15% des recettes pétrolières pour « le budget des communes de la région concernée par les opérations pétrolières, pour le financement du développement local » (Code Pétrolier du Niger 2007, art. 146). L'implantation de la SORAZ a été prometteuse aussi bien au niveau de l'État central qu'au niveau de l'État local :

> Au vu des dynamiques politiques autour du pétrole, il y'a des dynamiques qui se jouent autour de l'État. C'est par exemple tout ce qui se crée. La mise en place d'un ministère chargé de pétrole, la réorganisation des grandes sociétés publiques pour prendre en charge la nouvelle donne. Mais, finalement ce n'est pas seulement l'État central qui change mais aussi toutes les opportunités qui s'offrent à l'État local. Les structures locales, conseils régionaux, conseil municipal, etc.[4]

Faute d'un transfert des compétences aux régions, comme nous allons le montrer ci-après, cette raffinerie est perçue par les collectivités territoriales de la région comme « une manne importante qui leur tombe dessus » qui leur permettra de réaliser beaucoup d'investissements. Les redevances issues du raffinage de pétrole dans la région de Zinder constituent des ressources importantes sur lesquelles les autorités centrales et régionales fondent beaucoup d'espoir.

4 De l'espoir fondé sur l'exploitation pétrolière : les rapports entre la SORAZ et le Conseil Régional (CR)

Dans ses dispositions, le code pétrolier prévoit 15% pour le budget des communes de la région concernée par les opérations pétrolières pour le financement du développement local. Avec l'exploitation de l'uranium au Niger, les communes de la région d'Agadez ont bénéficié de la redevance minière. Selon Abdoul Kader (2008, p. 5) les communes de la région d'Agadez ont « bénéficié d'une enveloppe de 1,57 milliard de francs [USD 3.45 million][5].» Cette enveloppe a été répartie entre les collectivités territoriales de la région d'Agadez en fonction de certains critères : critère de proximité avec les mines, critère de population, critère de superficie de la commune, critère de l'impact

4 Propos tenus par Mahaman Tidjani Alou à la 3e conférence biennale du programme SPP 1448 à Postdam, septembre–octobre 2016.

5 Taux de change du 1.1.2008.

environnemental, critère d'investissement des partenaires sur place, critère de mobilisation des ressources internes et critère d'infrastructures existantes dans la commune. C'est dans cette optique que les collectivités territoriales de la région de Zinder, mais également de celle de Diffa, avaient nourri beaucoup d'espoir avec l'exploitation (Diffa) et le raffinage (Zinder) du pétrole.

Les ressources issues de l'exploitation du pétrole sont même perçues comme un médicament découvert pour soigner une maladie incurable comme le témoignent les propos de cet interlocuteur[6] : « mun warké wanga kalanzir da mun ka samu » (nous sommes guéris avec ce pétrole que nous avons eu). Dans l'entendement des exécutifs du Conseil Régional, du Conseil de la Ville et des Arrondissements Communaux à Zinder, leurs différentes structures allaient bénéficier des redevances pétrolières à l'image de collectivités territoriales de la région d'Agadez qui bénéficiaient des redevances liées à l'exploitation de l'Uranium. « Mais la SORAZ est considérée actuellement comme faisant partie des grandes industries au Niger » (Cadre de la SORAZ, mai 2013). À ce titre, elle verse annuellement les taxes et impôts y afférant à la Direction Générale des Impôts du Niger. Cette situation ajoutée à l'absence de transfert des compétences forme l'un des obstacles majeurs pour les collectivités territoriales de Zinder dans le but de bénéficier directement de la « manne pétrolière ».

> D'un point de vue fiscale, c'est-à-dire TVA et taxes, la SORAZ représente plus de quatre (4) milliards [de francs CFA (USD 7.941.600)][7] par mois mais elle est inscrite dans le domaine des grandes entreprises ce qui fait qu'elle verse tout cet argent à Niamey. Si c'était versé à la région de Zinder, ça allait changer beaucoup de choses j'en suis sûr !
>
> Interview, Directeur Relations Publiques SORAZ, juin 2013

Mais dans tous les cas, les redevances prévues par les textes, c'est-à-dire le code pétrolier, ne concernent que le premier palier des collectivités territoriales, à savoir la commune. L'article 146 du code pétrolier ne fait pas cas de la région collectivité territoriale dans la répartition des redevances pétrolières.

> Les redevances, il y a une loi qui règle les questions. La loi qui était jusqu'ici en vigueur n'a pas prévu les régions comme collectivités, mais maintenant, c'est en train d'être corrigé et même sur ce que la région va avoir sur le brut ou le raffiné.
>
> Interview, SG Conseil Régional de Zinder, juin 2013

---

6 Un maire dans la ville de Zinder.

7 Taux de change du 1.6.2013.

Ainsi, à l'état des dispositions législatives actuelles, la région de Zinder n'est pas concernée par les 15% prévus par l'article 146 du code pétrolier du Niger car elle n'abrite que la raffinerie. Selon les personnes rencontrées, aucune disposition légale et réglementaire n'est prévue pour que les collectivités à Zinder bénéficient de ces ressources.

> Il n'y a pas de cadre légal et réglementaire pour que les collectivités bénéficient directement des apports de la SORAZ. Il y a une loi de 2007 ou 2008 [référence au code pétrolier du Niger], qui donne des avantages aux collectivités mais la loi dit la zone d'exploitation pas la zone de raffinage. Ce qui fait que la région de Zinder à l'heure actuelle ne peut pas profiter de ça directement. Ça a été calqué sur ce qui se fait avec les compagnies d'uranium, or là-bas, ce sont les zones d'exploitation. L'autre obstacle, c'est que la loi n'a pas prévu ce que les conseils régionaux, comme collectivités territoriales, doivent avoir, mais seulement les communes, je pense que la loi est dans les circuits entre le gouvernement et l'assemblée.
>
> Interview, Directeur Relations Publiques SORAZ, juin 2013

Mais, dans le cadre de ses activités courantes, notamment à travers ses commissions spécialisées, le Conseil Régional est entré en contact avec la SORAZ. En effet, deux commissions spécialisées du Conseil Régional, notamment la commission du développement rural et de l'environnement et la commission chargée des affaires économiques, ont conduit des missions sur le site de la SORAZ. L'objectif de ces missions est de voir dans quelles mesures la SORAZ peut aider à créer de petites industries à Zinder. Malgré ces initiatives des élus régionaux, les rapports avec la direction de la SORAZ ne se sont pas améliorés. En effet, selon certains membres des commissions ayant effectué des missions dans cette société, ils étaient confrontés, ajouté à l'absence des cadres, à la difficulté d'accès aux documents. En effet, la majorité des documents de la société sont écrits en mandarin.

> Le document d'étude d'impact environnemental préalablement rédigé par les chinois est en langue chinoise, il n'a jamais fait l'objet de publication, de traduction, encore moins d'atelier de validation. Le flou à ce sujet reste et demeure. C'est pourquoi il est plus que nécessaire de lever cette opacité.
>
> Interview, président de la commission développement rural et de l'environnement Conseil Régional de Zinder, juin 2013

De manière générale, pour Aoun (2008, p. 88) l'industrie pétrolière est depuis de « nombreuses décennies caractérisées par une opacité très lourde ». Et cette absence d'ouverture dans la collaboration au niveau de la SORAZ traduit en une certaine opacité dans la gestion de la raffinerie de manière générale et dans la connaissance des ressources financières issues de la vente du pétrole en particulier. Nous retrouvons dans le discours de certains interlocuteurs l'expression de cette opacité :

> Au Niger, le pétrole, c'est une gestion obscure. Depuis que la raffinerie a commencé, qui peut te dire le bilan qui a été fait sur la quantité de gasoil, d'essence produite et vendue ? Parce qu'il n'y a pas une transparence. Comment on peut croire que le Nigérien a une raffinerie et qu'il achète le carburant à plus de 500f CFA. Alors que le carburant quitte la raffinerie, va au Nigeria, revient au Niger, on le vend à moins de 500f CFA.[8]
>
> Interview, 2e vice-président Conseil Régional de Zinder, février 2013

Dans le cadre de la construction de son siège, le Conseil Régional a adressé une demande de financement, restée lettre morte, à la SORAZ. Mais, la SORAZ a tout de même octroyé une aide d'une valeur de huit cent mille francs [USD 1,444] lors d'une tournée-prise de contact que le Conseil Régional a organisée après sa mise en place.

Ainsi, comme nous avons pu le constater, les interactions entre la SORAZ et le Conseil Régional de Zinder n'ont pas d'ancrage juridique. Cela se répercute sur les rapports que les deux institutions entretiennent. Néanmoins, les différents acteurs politiques au niveau local et régional développent des stratégies pour capter la manne pétrolière.

5 Aux stratégies développées par les différents acteurs pour capter la manne pétrolière

Trois principaux acteurs ont joué un rôle dans l'élaboration et la mise en place de ces stratégies : les élus locaux, la société civile et les médias privés et

8 Selon les informations que nous avons recueillies, le carburant est acheté à environ 350f CFA au niveau de la SORAZ. Une fois que les camionneurs nigérians le ramènent dans leur pays, l'État Nigérian subventionne l'essence, de sorte qu'il est vendu dans les stations-service du Nigeria pour l'équivalent de 300 à 350f CFA. Les contrebandiers nigériens passent la frontière, l'achètent là bas et le font traverser la frontière jusqu'au Niger. Au Niger, il est ensuite vendu au marché noir à 350–400f CFA. Alors que le même carburant est vendu dans les stations-service au Niger à 540f le litre

associatifs. Les élus locaux, les organisations de la société civile et les médias animaient déjà, en fonction des évènements, les débats publics dans la ville de Zinder avant l'ouverture de la SORAZ. Mais c'est l'exploitation pétrolière et les enjeux qui en ont découlé qui avaient permis à ces acteurs d'animer encore plus les débats publics.

5.1 *Les élus locaux*

La région de Zinder compte de nombreux partis politiques. Cependant, à l'issu des élections régionales de 2011, seules sept formations politiques sont représentées, à travers des conseillers élus, au Conseil régional. Il s'agit de 12 conseillers pour la Convention Démocratique et Sociale (CDS), 9 pour le Parti Nigérien pour la Démocratie et le Socialisme (PNDS) ; 8, pour le Mouvement National pour la Société de Développement (MNSD) ; 5 pour l'Alliance pour le Renouveau Démocratique (ARD) ; 3 pour le Lumana FA ; 2 pour le Rassemblement pour la Démocratie et le Progrès (RDP) et enfin 2 pour le Rassemblement Social et Démocratique (RSD). Les conseillers élus sont les représentants des populations au niveau des collectivités territoriales. À ce titre, et selon la loi, le Conseil Régional prend « les mesures nécessaires pour promouvoir le développement économique, social, éducatif, sanitaire, scientifique, culturel et sportif de la région » (CGCT, Art. 104). Dans une perspective d'intérêt général, les élus locaux de la ville de Zinder ont mis de côté leur appartenance politique, qui les divisait habituellement, pour s'inscrire dans une logique d'intérêt commun afin de faire aboutir leurs revendications. La SORAZ étant pourvoyeuse d'emplois, les conseillers élus ont fait front commun pour exiger le recrutement à la SORAZ des jeunes de la région de Zinder. En effet, on peut mettre à l'actif de ces derniers la participation à l'organisation de plusieurs déclarations publiques en collaboration avec les organisations de la société civile.

> Nos activités revendicatives ont permis de mettre en place un comité présidé par le gouvernorat dans le lequel sont aussi représentés le conseil régional, le conseil de ville, les représentants des sans-emplois, la section de l'Agence Nigérienne de la Promotion de l'Emploi (ANPE), les services techniques et la société civile. Ce comité a eu pour rôle dans un premier temps de répertorier tous les candidats ayant déposés leurs dossiers pour le concours de recrutement à la SORAZ. Ce comité a donc suivi pas à pas l'organisation du concours et, à l'annonce des résultats, une copie de la liste des admis, environs 192, a été transmise à tous les membres de ce comité pour contrôler l'insertion progressive des candidats, en fonction de la demande au niveau de la SORAZ.
>
> Interview, 1er vice-président Conseil de ville de Zinder, juin 2013

L'implication des élus locaux dans l'organisation du concours et l'affichage de la liste des candidats retenus peut contribuer à la légitimation de l'institution et à leur implication dans le développement de leur localité. Par cet acte, les élus locaux ont, d'une certaine manière, conforté leur appellation de représentants des populations.

5.2 *La société civile*

Un de nos interlocuteurs nous a révélé que « la ville de Zinder a une tradition de contestation des régimes qui se sont succédés au Niger.». Selon lui, cette situation trouve son fondement dans le transfert de la capitale du Niger de Zinder à Niamey en 1926. Il est à rappeler qu'au Niger, la politique coloniale française a dès le début favorisé l'ouest du pays par rapport à l'est (Lund, 2009; Danda, 2004; Ibrahim, 1994). Dans le cadre de l'exploitation du pétrole à Zinder, les rôles de la société civile et des élus locaux (supra) ont été déterminants, notamment dans le cadre du recrutement et de la nomination des agents à la SORAZ. Pilotée par Alternative Espace Citoyen et le Mouvement Populaire pour la Préservation des Acquis Démocratiques (MPPAD), la société civile à Zinder a organisé plusieurs mouvements sociaux et rendu publiques plusieurs déclarations après l'inauguration de la SORAZ.

> Les Zinderois ont considéré que la raffinerie est pour eux puisqu'elle est chez eux, parce qu'au fond l'installation de la raffinerie est politique...Ils ne sont pas d'accord que ceux qui travaillent dans le pétrole viennent des autres régions. Ils veulent que ce soient les gens de leur région qui aient un accès prioritaire à l'emploi.[9]

À la suite de ces manifestations, un mémorandum a été élaboré puis soumis au Président de la République lors de son passage à Zinder pour l'inauguration de la raffinerie. Une série de manifestations, dont des marches, meetings, débats, etc., a été organisée dans la même lancée (Schritt, 2019a; 2020). Ces mouvements ont été soulevés par l'annonce de la hausse du prix du carburant à la pompe, mais surtout, selon la teneur de certaines déclarations, à cause de « la marginalisation des ressortissants de Zinder dans le recrutement à la SORAZ ».

> A partir de la fin du mois de novembre jusqu'au début décembre 2011, nous avons tenu des réunions pour préparer nos mouvements. Ça se faisait ici

9 Propos tenus par Professeur Mahaman Tidjani Alou à la 3e conférence biennale du programme SPP 1448 à Postdam, septembre–octobre 2016.

> chez moi mais c'est surtout le 6 et 7 décembre qu'il y a eu les mouvements de grande envergure, où tout le monde à Zinder a participé, parce que ça nous concerne tous. Nous avons rendu une déclaration et la manifestation a été réprimée par les forces de l'ordre et il y a eu les morts là.
>
> Interview, président du MPPAD de Zinder, Mai 2013

> Ce qu'on a fait pendant ce temps c'est de donner la parole à tous ceux qui veulent la prendre pour un débat objectif et franc sur la question. (…) Cela a obligé les autorités à prendre en charge le problème, parce que le gouverneur, le Sultan se sont impliqués quand on avait médiatisé ça. Donc, notre objectif c'était de porter le problème sur le terrain public où ça concerne tout le monde. Parce que tant que le problème est géré dans les bureaux, il y a moins de chance à ce qu'il trouve une issue favorable.
>
> Interview, Coordonnateur Alternative Espace Citoyen de Zinder, Février 2013

Selon de nombreux observateurs, ces différentes manifestations ont porté leurs fruits. En effet, suite à ces manifestations, de nombreux opérateurs,[10] ressortissants de Zinder, ont été recrutés à la SORAZ. Outre cela, à l'échelle nationale, les mouvements de Zinder et ceux organisés notamment à Niamey par les organisations de la société civile ont servi d'argumentaire pour l'Assemblée Nationale afin d'interpeller le ministre du pétrole.[11] Le ministre a été notamment entendu au sujet de la commercialisation du pétrole raffiné et du prix du carburant à la pompe. Dans la ville de Zinder, se sont surtout les débats organisés autour du prix du pétrole qui ont été les plus houleux. L'interpellation du ministre du pétrole et les différents débats organisés ont permis de réduire de 30f CFA le prix du carburant à la pompe.

> Moi, je crois qu'on a réussi, parce que grâce à nous, des jeunes de Zinder ont eu du travail et le pouvoir de Niamey nous a sentis. Ils savent que Zinder est toujours là, on ne va pas baisser les bras.
>
> Interview, président du MPPAD, juin 2013

Les radios et télévisions privées et associatives ont également joué un rôle important, en couvrant non seulement toutes manifestations mais en

---

10 C'est le qualificatif utilisé pour désigner les ouvriers à la SORAZ.

11 Le 04 novembre 2012, le ministre du pétrole a été interpellé à l'Assemblée Nationale relativement à la commercialisation du pétrole raffiné par la SORAZ qui est vendu à des prix jugés excessifs par les consommateurs.

organisant aussi des débats publics pour « donner la parole » aux organisateurs des manifestations et aux représentants des populations.

5.3 *Les groupes Alternative, Dunia, Gaskia et Ténéré*

Outre la radio associative Alternative, les radios et télévisions privées Dunia, Gaskia et Ténéré[12] ont joué un rôle important en couvrant les meetings et les manifestations organisés, et en élaborant des émissions spéciales dans le but de couvrir les évènements ou d'organiser des débats. Les médias, plus spécifiquement ici les radios et télévisions privées, sont des espaces où les élus locaux, la société civile et d'autres acteurs se retrouvent pour débattre des attentes de la décentralisation et de la SORAZ. Des débats sont organisés sur des thèmes tels que la présence des camionneurs qui viennent chercher le carburant à la SORAZ dans la ville de Zinder, les accidents causés par les camionneurs, les artères de la ville de Zinder que les engins obstruent, les taxes que les camions, qui viennent chercher le carburant, permettent de générer, l'importance du contrôle citoyen, etc. Ainsi, à travers ces multiples espaces de dialogues et de discussions, les médias à Zinder ont joué un rôle important dans l'animation des débats publics autour de la SORAZ. Ils ont été également des espaces d'appel à la mobilisation générale en vue d'une marche ou d'un meeting.

> Nous travaillons en étroite collaboration avec les journalistes. C'est impossible actuellement de faire quelque chose sans les impliquer. Tu vois lui,[13] il est de Anfani, chaque soir, il vient ici causer avec moi et il n'est pas le seul.
>
> Interview, président du MPPAD, février 2013

Sur les antennes de TV Gaskia, télévision locale qui émet à Zinder,[14] de nombreuses émissions sont organisées et diffusées. Les animateurs de cette télévision ont organisé, par exemple, des débats sur le prix de parking des camionneurs. Ce prix a fait l'objet de plusieurs manifestations, de contestations et de débats sur les ondes locales. En effet, les camionneurs venus dans la ville pour chercher le carburant, restaient stationnés pendant des jours à attendre leur tour de passage aux pompes de la société. Les délais d'attente

---

12 Ce sont ceux que nous avons rencontré mais il y'en a d'autres tous aussi actifs.

13 Quand j'étais arrivé pour mon rendez-vous d'entretien, j'avais trouvé le président du MPPAD en compagnie d'un homme avec qui il discutait. Le monsieur s'était mis de côté pour nous laisser discuter.

14 En 2013, la TV Gaskia couvre seulement la ville de Zinder, cette situation a peut-être changé.

étaient longs et coûteux pour ces derniers qui payaient chaque jour 1000f CFA pour le parking. À la suite des débats et des manifestations, le prix de parking pour les camionneurs étrangers a été réduit de moitié, à savoir de 1000f CFA à 500f CFA par jour.

Les mouvements sociaux émanant des acteurs de la société civile et des partis politiques ont eu un double objectif. Pour les premiers, les mouvements ont permis de recruter des jeunes de la ville dans la société. Pour les seconds, il s'agit des stratégies développées pour récompenser leurs militants. Nous allons aborder ce point dans la partie suivante.

6 Les stratégies de captage de la manne du pétrole

Nous avons identifié deux types de stratégies : la politisation et la régionalisation des postes au niveau de la SORAZ. Ces deux stratégies, comme nous le verront plus loin, sont imbriquées.

6.1 *Le captage politique*

La manne pétrolière représente un enjeu autour duquel gravitent plusieurs acteurs. Elle procure des revenus élevés entraînant des luttes pour leur contrôle. L'argent du pétrole attise les convoitises et génère des comportements de recherche de rente (Meilleur, 2010, p. 116). Quant à la SORAZ, l'enjeu pour les acteurs politiques est de récompenser leurs militants en plaçant certains dans cette société. Une récompense politique qui a pour objectifs non seulement d'aider les militants, mais également d'aider financièrement le parti (à travers ces derniers). On assiste ainsi à une main mise des partis politiques sur les postes rentiers. Et comme il est courant de remarquer au niveau de ces postes, ce ne sont pas des techniciens mais plutôt des politiciens reconvertis qui sont nommés. Ainsi, dans l'organigramme de la SORAZ, le poste le plus haut placé occupé par un Nigérien est celui de Directeur Général Adjoint, le Directeur général étant chinois. Le poste de directeur adjoint est occupé par un militant du parti qui a apporté son soutien, en 2011, au deuxième tour des élections présidentielles au Président de la République.

> Il y a des postes pour chaque parti politique de la majorité, en tout cas les deux principaux partis au pouvoir. Par exemple, de toute façon, ça, tout le monde le sait, le DG adjoint, c'est le gars de Lumana FA pour, le poste de Directeur de Relations publiques, c'est pour le PNDS. C'est d'ailleurs le président régional du PNDS de Zinder qui occupe ce poste.
>
> Interview, agent à la SORAZ, juin 2013

Outre ces nominations à des postes « rentiers », certains opérateurs (des ouvriers nigériens) ont été recrutés suite à la pression exercée par des élus locaux. En effet, après la déclaration qui a permis la nomination de cadres ressortissants de Zinder et de Diffa à la SORAZ, plusieurs opérateurs ont été aussi recrutés avec l'appui de ces derniers. Ce qu'il faut comprendre, ce n'est pas le recrutement en soi, mais la pression exercée par les élus de la ville de Zinder. La configuration politique actuelle des Conseils des Arrondissements Communaux, du Conseil de Ville et du Conseil Régional fait que la ville de Zinder est à dominance Convention Démocratique et Sociale (CDS), c'est-à-dire l'un des principaux partis de l'opposition du régime au pouvoir en place.[15] Par exemple, sur les 77 conseillers que comptent les cinq Arrondissements Communaux de la Ville de Zinder, une quarantaine est élue au nom de ce parti politique. Ainsi ces derniers, avec le soutien des autres partis alliés (MNSD et ARD) et de la société civile, dont le chef de file n'est autre que le président du MPPAD, ont rendu des déclarations pour revendiquer un recrutement de « in damagaram » (habitants de Zinder) à la SORAZ. Ces mobilisations ont eu le mérite d'avoir eu des répercussions dans l'administration de la SORAZ et au ministère de tutelle. Ainsi, politiquement, ces partis, bien qu'ils soient de l'opposition, ont instrumentalisé les actions de la société civile à des fins politiques en vue de récompenser leurs militants. Ils ont, au cours de nombreux débats organisés sur les médias, mis en valeur leur lutte pour le recrutement des « enfants de la région » à la SORAZ. Ces actions leur garantissent de la confiance et une certaine reconnaissance des électeurs en vue des prochaines élections.

> Les élus locaux ont rendu déclaration sur déclaration et ont organisé plusieurs débats sur les radios et la télé Gaskia pour dénoncer le non recrutement des jeunes de Zinder. Les chinois ont compris vite ça et ils ont pris leurs enfants pour les mettre dans la société et depuis, les chinois ont eu la paix.
>
> Interview, agent à la SORAZ, juin 2013

Il est essentiel d'analyser les manœuvres politiques qu'il y a eu sous deux angles. Les élus locaux ont certes amené l'administration de la SORAZ à recruter des jeunes de Zinder, plus de la moitié des jeunes opérateurs ont ainsi été recrutés suite à ces mouvements. Mais il est tout de même à noter qu'à la faveur de cette situation, la société a également profité de la situation pour redorer son image auprès des collectifs et de tous les acteurs de la société civile, c'est du

15 La CDS et le MNSD sont les deux principaux partis d'opposition au cours de la période durant laquelle cette enquête a eu lieu.

« gagnant-gagnant ». Ce cas montre une fois de plus comment les demandes de contenu local enchevêtrent l'industrie pétrolière dans le contexte local et comment, dans ce cas, les investisseurs chinois ont accepté ces enchevêtrements car ils sont plus favorables à leur commerce que les actions d'une population en colère (Skaten, cette édition). Au-delà des manœuvres politiques ayant pour but la nomination des membres de leurs partis à la SORAZ, les politiciens ont aussi créé des postes pour chaque région afin de placer « leurs gens ».

6.2 *Le captage régional*

Ici, l'enjeu pour les acteurs est de créer des postes à la SORAZ, ce par région. L'un des arguments avancés par les différents interlocuteurs que nous avons rencontrés est de donner des postes pour toutes les régions concernées par l'exploitation et le raffinage du pétrole. En fait, il s'agit ici de créer des postes pour les régions de Diffa et de Zinder. Ainsi, il y a eu deux postes pour chacune des régions. À titre d'exemple, on peut citer le poste de directeur adjoint des achats pour N'Gourti, et celui de Directeur Adjoint d'Hygiène, Sécurité, Santé et Environnement (HSS/E) pour Diffa. Il y a eu deux directeurs adjoints d'achat, tous deux de N'Gourti, et les deux Directeurs d'HSS/E viennent également de Diffa.[16] Ces postes sont dits « rentiers » parce que, par exemple, toutes les commandes de la société sont gérées par la Direction des Achats et tous les marchés concernant les produits pour assurer l'hygiène, la santé, la sécurité et l'environnement sont attribués par ladite direction. La région de Zinder a eu par exemple le poste de directeur des relations publiques. C'est aussi un poste « rentier » car le directeur des relations publiques a un budget propre pour « bien vendre » la SORAZ au niveau national et international. Là également, les personnes sont placées au niveau de ces postes en fonction de leur appartenance politique, c'est-à-dire que les membres de la coalition au pouvoir ont été recrutés (PNDS et Lumana FA). L'argent capté servirait entre autres à aider financièrement les partis politiques.

> Avec les mouvements que vous connaissez, il y a eu des recrutements au niveau des opérateurs mais aussi des nominations au niveau des cadres de la SORAZ, bon, entre moi et toi, les cadres ce sont des postes qu'on a donnés aux régions.
>
> Interview, agent de la SORAZ, Juin 2013

Les mouvements de contestation initiés dans la ville de Zinder ont permis une attribution, pour les deux régions concernées par l'exploitation et le raffinage

16 Le partage de certains postes aux régions de Diffa et Zinder se justifie par le fait que ce sont les deux régions qui sont concernées par l'exploitation du pétrole au Niger.

du pétrole, de poste au niveau de la SORAZ. Là également, les personnes sont placées au niveau de ces postes en fonction de leur appartenance politique.

7 Discussion

Selon Danda (2004, p. 13), la région apparaît dans le champ politico-administratif nigérien, comme l'échelon disposant d'une capacité potentielle à produire une catégorie dirigeante mieux à même de comprendre et à assurer des responsabilités politiques pour un pays en construction. En devenant une collectivité territoriale à part entière, selon Bernard Pecqueur, « la région reçoit la compétence la plus large en matière d'animation et de planification du développement économique » (1998, p. 108). Aussi, pour Tidjani Alou, la mise en place de ces organes décentralisés devrait permettre, non seulement de « multiplier les points d'ancrage de l'État dans les espaces locaux » (2009, p. 189), mais aussi de favoriser une meilleure mobilisation et une meilleure gestion des ressources sur leurs espaces territoriaux afin d'impulser le développement régional. C'est pour cela que l'implantation de la SORAZ dans la région de Zinder constitue un grand espoir pour le développement de cette région. Aussi, il n'est pas étonnant qu'au Niger, et particulièrement dans les régions de Diffa et de Zinder, les ressources issues de l'exploitation du pétrole soient perçues comme une solution à la pauvreté des populations en général et aux problèmes de ressources auxquels sont confrontées les collectivités territoriales. Les propos tenus par ce chef de quartier le traduisent assez bien : « Mun warke wanga kalanzir da mun ka samu » (nous sommes guéris avec ce pétrole que nous avons eu). Ces propos tenus par un de nos interlocuteurs[17] nous permettent de mesurer l'espoir fondé sur le raffinage du pétrole par la SORAZ. En effet, en voyant la manne pétrolière comme un remède d'une maladie, les acteurs régionaux avaient cru que leurs structures bénéficieraient des redevances pétrolières à l'image de collectivités territoriales de la région d'Agadez qui bénéficient des redevances liées à l'exploitation de l'uranium. Cependant, faute de cadre légal, les collectivités territoriales ne peuvent pas bénéficier directement des apports de la SORAZ.

Face à cette situation, une des options choisies par les acteurs locaux est de développer des stratégies pour capter la manne. Ainsi, les revendications pour le recrutement des ressortissants de Zinder à la SORAZ, la baisse du prix du carburant ont été, pour ces derniers, des passerelles pour bénéficier directement ou indirectement des ressources issues de l'exploitation du pétrole. Les

17 Un chef de quartier dans le 2e arrondissement communal à Zinder.

contestations initiées par les élus et par la société civile locale pour revendiquer le recrutement des ressortissants de Zinder à la SORAZ ont transformé le caractère et l'ampleur des mouvements sociaux. En portant le problème sur la scène publique et en impliquant la politique dans sa gestion, les élus locaux et la société civile à Zinder ont donné davantage de poids à leurs revendications. L'implication des médias a été également déterminante dans cette lutte.

Le lien entre la solidité des institutions, la croissance et le développement dans les pays exportateurs de ressources naturelles a été fait par de nombreux auteurs, notamment Aoun (2008, p. 194 ; Humphreys et al., 2007). Même si la situation est ici à un échelon plus local, elle permet de faire le parallèle avec la mobilisation des élus locaux à Zinder pour contrôler le processus de recrutement des agents à la SORAZ. On peut, en effet, dire qu'à travers les actes qu'ils ont posés, les élus locaux et la société civile à Zinder ont joué plus ou moins un rôle de contre-pouvoir vis-à-vis de la gouvernance de la SORAZ. Ils se sont associés pour organiser des marches, des débats dans le but d'expliquer à la population les enjeux de développement liés à l'exploitation du pétrole et surtout d'exiger le recrutement des jeunes de la région à la SORAZ. Dans ce cadre précis, ils ont plutôt participé à défendre les intérêts des citoyens de la région de Zinder, à influencer les processus de décision et à promouvoir la participation des couches défavorisées ou marginalisées dans la gestion des affaires publiques. Les différents acteurs qui gravitent autour de l'exploitation du pétrole ont développé des stratégies pour profiter des opportunités, à savoir la distribution des emplois (recrutement des militants des partis), le rehaussement de l'économie locale (création d'emplois), les opportunités d'affaires (les marchés donnés aux fournisseurs locaux), etc. Ainsi, comme nous l'avons vu plus haut, ces stratégies vont du captage politique au captage régional. Les deux stratégies ont permis à certains acteurs de bénéficier directement ou indirectement des ressources liées à l'exploitation pétrolière (Schritt, 2019b). Mais il est tout de même important de relever que les groupes de pression, qui se sont organisés pour dénoncer une marginalisation des ressortissants de la région au niveau de la SORAZ, se sont également créés, dans une certaine mesure, « pour mieux accéder aux postes politiques et aux dividendes tirés de l'exploitation pétrolière » (Fanchette, 2006 , p. 192). Cependant, une analyse plus générale de ce qui s'est passé à Zinder mais également dans d'autres régions du Niger peut montrer que la solidité des institutions démocratiques peut permettre d'influer la gestion des ressources.[18]

18 Il y a eu des mouvements de revendications dans le cadre de l'exploitation de l'or à Samira dans la région de Tillabéry, il y en a eu également avec l'exploitation de l'uranium dans la région d'Agadez.

La raffinerie a permis de créer des opportunités d'emploi pour les jeunes, un développement de l'économie locale mais elle a également favorisé l'implantation de plusieurs unités industrielles dans la ville de Zinder. En définitive, on peut dire que les revendications autour de l'exploitation pétrolière ont permis de créer de l'emploi, et tant aux élus locaux qu'à la société civile d'exister. Mais nous savons, avec Carbonnier (2007, p. 91), que dans la pratique, « il est impossible pour des acteurs de la société civile [et des élus locaux] d'appréhender l'ensemble des paiements et des revenus perçus par un gouvernement au titre de la production et de la vente d'hydrocarbures ». Les contrats de partage de production et les systèmes de redevances sont opaques et complexes. Ainsi, dans le cadre de l'exploitation du pétrole à Zinder, malgré tous les débats et les mouvements sociaux autour de cette exploitation du pétrole, les issues politiques de recours pour la gestion des conflits entre la société et la partie nigérienne ont toujours tourné en faveur des chinois.

> Et apparemment le gouvernement nigérien n'a eu aucune capacité d'influer sur cette situation là, dans laquelle il ne semble pas avoir grand pouvoir parce que toute dynamique de la compagnie c'est de rembourser les prêts qui ont été contractés à la Chine pour construire la raffinerie.[19]

8 Conclusion

Cet article a permis en premier lieu de mettre en évidence, dans le cadre de la décentralisation en cours au Niger, la place prépondérante occupée par la région collectivité territoriale. Il s'est agi ensuite de montrer les attentes engendrées par le raffinage du pétrole dans la région de Zinder dans un contexte de désengagement de l'État et de la mise en place effective des organes de la décentralisation au Niger. Grâce à leur statut d'élus locaux ou régionaux, les conseillers ont été l'avant-garde de la lutte, ils ont porté le débat au niveau du gouvernorat. Cet article a aussi permis de montrer les interactions entre le conseil régional et la SORAZ mais également les mouvements populaires qu'avait suscités l'exploitation pétrolière à Zinder. Enfin, il a mis en lumière les enjeux autour du raffinage du pétrole dans la ville de Zinder. Les stratégies développées, les positionnements politiques et régionaux nous ont permis de percevoir la réalité de l'exploitation du pétrole au Niger. La

19 Propos tenus par Professeur Mahaman Tidjani Alou à la 3e conférence biennale du programme SPP 1448 à Postdam, septembre–octobre 2016.

présence de la SORAZ dans la région a contribué à créer de l'emploi dans la ville de Zinder, mais elle a également permis à certains acteurs politiques de profiter de la rente pétrolière. Comme nous l'avons montré, cette captation de la manne pétrolière reflète une logique politique et régionale qui s'inscrit dans le processus de la décentralisation au Niger.

Depuis le 2 avril 2014, une loi transmise par le gouvernement de la 7e République a été adoptée par l'Assemblée Nationale sur les transferts des retombées liées au raffinage du pétrole aux communes mais également à la région qui abrite la raffinerie. Est-ce qu'avec un transfert effectif des compétences et des redevances pétrolières au niveau régional, l'apport de SORAZ permettra au conseil régional de Zinder de faire face à ses nouvelles responsabilités ?

Remerciements

Je tiens à remercier ici toutes les personnes qui m'ont inspiré, aidé et soutenu dans la rédaction de cet article.

Références

Abdoul Kader, A. (2008). La Commune d'In Gall (3), *LASDEL Etudes et Travaux* 73.

Aoun, M.-C. (2008). *La rente pétrolière et le développement économique des pays exportateurs.* Thèse de doctorat, Université Paris Dauphine, Paris, France.

Beblawi, H., & Luciani, G. (Eds.) (1987). *The Rentier State. Nation, State and Integration in the Arab world.* London: Croom Helm.

Bierschenk, T. & Olivier de Sardan, J.-P. (1998). *Les pouvoirs au village. Le Bénin rural entre démocratisation et décentralisation.* Paris, Karthala.

Carbonnier, G. (2007). Comment conjurer la malédiction des ressources pétrolières. *Annuaire Suisse de Politique de Développement*, 26(2), 93–98.

Code général des collectivités territoriales (2011). République du Niger.

Coulmin, P. (1986). *La décentralisation. La dynamique du développement local.* Paris: Syros/Adels.

Danda, M. (2004). *Politique de décentralisation, développement régional et identités locales au Niger : le cas du Damagaram.* Thèse de doctorat de science politique, Université de Montesquieu, Bordeaux IV, France.

Darbon, D. & Crouzel, I. (2009). Administration publiques et politiques publiques des Afriques. In: M. Gazibo & C. Thiriot (eds.), *Le politique en Afrique. État des débats et piste de recherche,* (pp. 71–101). Paris: Karthala.

Elwert, G. & Bierschenk, T. (1988). Development Aid as Intervention in Dynamic Systems. *Sociologia Ruralis,* 28(2–3): 99–112.

Fanchette, S. (2006). Le delta du Niger (Nigeria): Rivalités de pouvoir, revendications territoriales et exploitation pétrolière ou les ferments de la violence. *Hérodote*, 121, 190–220.

Guesnier, B. (1986). *Le développement local et la décentralisation.* Paris: ERESA.

Humphreys, M., Sachs, J. & Stiglitz, J.E. (2007). *Escaping the Resource Curse.* New York: Columbia University Press.

Lund, C. (2002). Démocratisation précaire et dynamiques locales au Niger : micro-politiques à Zinder, *Development and Change,* 32(5), 845–869.

Lund, C. (2009). Les dynamiques politiques locales face à une démocratisation fragile (Zinder). In: Olivier de Sardan, J.-P., Tidjani Alou, M. (eds.): *Les pouvoirs locaux au Niger*, (pp. 89–112), Paris: Karthala.

Mahdavy, H. (1970). The Pattern and Problems of Economic Development in Rentier States: The Case of Iran. In: Cook, M. (ed.), *Studies in the Economic History of the Middle East: From the Rise of Islam to the Present Day* (pp. 428–467). London: Oxford UniversityPress.

Meilleur, K. (2010). Les pratiques de la RSE revisitées par un examen de la malédiction des ressources: contribution de la littérature sur la région du delta du Niger. *Canadian Journal of African Studies,* 44(2), 362–396.

Ministère des mines et de l'énergie (2007). Code pétrolier du Niger, Niamey, République du Niger. Loi n°2007-01.

Montazer-Zohour, M. (1975). L'impact des revenus pétroliers sur le développement économiques des pays du Moyen-Orient. *Études Internationales*, 6(4), 529–554.

Nach Mback, C. (2003). *Démocratisation et décentralisation. Genèse et dynamiques comparés des processus de décentralisation en Afrique subsaharienne.* Paris: Karthala.

Olivier de Sardan, J.-P. (2008). *La rigueur du qualitatif. Les contraintes empiriques de l'interprétation socio-anthropologique.* Louvain-La neuve, Academia-Bruylant.

Olivier de Sardan, J.-P. & Tidjani Alou, M. (2009). *Les pouvoirs locaux au Niger. A la veille de la décentralisation.* Paris: Codesria-Karthala.

Ovadia, J. S. 2013. The Nigerian "One Percent" and the Management of National Oil Wealth Through Nigerian Content. *Science and Society,* 77(3), 315–341.

Otayek, R. (2009). Décentralisation et résilience des autoritarismes en Afrique : une relation de cause à effet ? In: M. Camau & G. Massardier, *Démocraties et autoritarismes. Fragmentation et hybridation des régimes*, (pp. 121–140). Paris, Karthala.

Pecqueur, B. (1998). *Le développement local : pour une économie des territoires.* Paris: Syros/Alternatives, 2e Edition.

Sahel dimanche (9 novembre 2012 Novembre 9), 1514, p. 12.

Schritt, J. (2018). Crude controversies: Disputes along Niger's Petro-Infrastructure. *History and Anthropology*, 29(5), 645–669.

Schritt, J. (2019a). Urban Protest in Oil-Age Niger: Towards a Notion of 'Contentious Assemblages'. *Sociologus*, 69(1), 19–35.

Schritt, J. (2019b) Well-Oiled Protest: Adding Fuel to Political Conflicts in Niger. *African Studies Revue* 62(2), 49–71.

Schritt, J. (2020). Crude Talking: Radio and the Politics of Naming, Blaming and Claiming in Oil-Age Niger. *Journal of Contemporary African Studies*, 38(3), 415–36.

Tidjani Alou , M. (2001). La dynamique de l'Etat postcolonial au Niger. In K. Idrissa (ed.), *Le Niger: État et démocratie* (pp. 85–126). L'Harmattan.

Tidjani Alou, M. (2009). Décentralisation en Afrique : état des lieux de la recherche en sciences sociales, In: M. Gazibou & C. Thiriot (eds.), *Le politique en Afrique : État des débats et pistes de recherches*, (pp. 185–207). Paris: Karthala.

Wunsch, J. S., & Olowu, D. (eds.). (1990). *The Failure of the Centralized State: Institutions and Self-governance in Africa.* Westview Press.

Yates, D. (1996). *The Rentier State in Africa: Oil Rent Dependency and Neocolonialism in the Republic of Gabon.* Trenton, NJ: Africa World Press.

PART 2

The Oil Industry and the Enclave Economy

6

Dis/Entangling Ghana's Oil and Gas Industry: Economics, Politics and Infrastructure

Monica Skaten

1 Introduction

This chapter draws on ethnographic material from two of Ghana's key energy facilities – Tema Oil Refinery (TOR) and Atuabo Gas Processing Plant. These facilities could – and arguably should – add value to petroleum extraction in Ghana and the larger West African region, since infrastructure and human capacity are available for processing, and there is no shortage of markets for consumption of such petroleum products. In fact, there are regular electricity and fuel shortages, which slow down domestic and industrial activity.

The oil refinery was built in the early 1960s in collaboration with Italian capital and human resources. It was seen as an important part of Ghana's state-building project. Following its nationalisation in the 1970s, the refinery has become an integral part of the domestic political landscape, supplying fuel to key state enterprises and being used for political patronage, thus building up considerable debts (Skaten, 2017, p. 77). Ahead of production in 2010 the oil refinery was refining imported crude oil and small amounts from the Ghanaian Saltpond oil field. Commercial quantities of crude oil were discovered in Ghana in 2007, and citizens had high expectations for a new era for the refinery. However, the consortium operating the Jubilee oilfield off Ghana's shores claimed that the TOR lacked the technical capacity to refine the oil (Skaten, 2018a).

In contrast to TOR, the Ataubo Gas Processing Plant, opened in 2016, does not lack raw material. The same Jubilee consortium supplies the plant with natural gas without payment. However, in the plant's few years of existence, it has not been utilised to its full potential. We can observe several challenges that have hampered its development, including delays in project completion, difficulties in Chinese-Ghanaian cooperation and political polarisation getting in the way of maximising output.

In this context, this chapter examines some of the challenges that the Ghanaian workers face in connection with Ghana's relatively new offshore oil and gas industry. Everyday working-life for engineers and technicians at the

 | DOI:10.1163/9789004530065_007

FIGURE 6.1 Map of oil production in Ghana showing the approximate location of Atuabo gas processing plant (west coast) and Tema oil refinery (east coast). Editors' illustration based on UN map no. 4186
SOURCE: HTTPS://WWW.UN.ORG/GEOSPATIAL/CONTENT/GHANA

processing plant sites is characterised by the pervasiveness of rumour, politics, insecurity and cultural challenges. This chapter seeks to expand knowledge of the everyday workings and socio-political realities of petroleum industries in West Africa with the use of ethnographic data. The paper demonstrates how the offshore industry is alternately entangled with, and disentangled from, domestic industrial activity, and how this is experienced, battled and renegotiated by those working in the domestic industry. Dis/entanglement manifests in different ways, driven by economic arguments, political considerations, and the availability and narratives surrounding the petroleum industry, infrastructure and technology.

2 Conceptualising Dis/Entanglement in Ghana's Oil and Gas Industry

Appel (2012) and Ferguson (2005) argue that upstream industries in Equatorial Guinea and Angola operate as enclaves, and that oil money only reaches the political elites, with minimal redistribution amongst the populace. These scholars shed light on the ways in which multinational oil companies work actively to disentangle themselves from onshore political, economic and social environments. Multinational oil corporations are entangled with financial centres in the north and disentangled from the everyday socio-political realities in the south. This is made possible through oil contracts that facilitate the circulation of rigs, manpower and crude oil internationally, whilst minimising contact with the host country and its residents. Others, such as Barry (2006), have argued that spatial disentanglement and standardisation in the oil industry, particularly at early stages, are contested and may produce a range of effects that in fact entangle the industry.

Watts' (2012) concept of the "oil assemblage," developed from his earlier concept of the "oil complex" (Watts, 2005), seeks to draw together the full multiplicity of actors involved in oil and gas industries. Watts proposes a framework that accounts for the prosaic workings of the oil apparatus on a localised level (Watts, 2012, p. 439), making it possible to account for ways in which disentanglement and entanglement remain present in the same project or country. Watts views the global oil production network as a regime of accumulation and a mode of regulation. The properties of the wider oil assemblage are in some sense generic and normalised, while modular pieces of infrastructure, capital systems and technology travel globally. However, oil and gas are always discovered in a specific space and time and subsequently inserted into a very "localised political economy," according to Watts (2012, p. 440). Building on this and Tsing's (2015) notion of "capitalism as assemblages," Schritt and Witte (2018, p. 3) argue that assemblages of heterogeneous elements shape negotiations of the oil industries' standards and industries' dis/entanglement in new oil states. They point to the influence of "the ownership structure of the oil companies, economic theories, contractual agreements, strategies of capitalist profit-making, conditions set by the governments of oil states, local content laws and the agency of various forces in the extractive community […]" in Niger and Uganda that makes dis/entanglement a useful framework to understand realities in new oil states.

Building on Ovadia's (2016) work on petrodevelopmental states as well as scholars' attention to the oil industries' standardisation (Appel, 2012; Barry, 2006; Witte, 2018), Schritt and Witte argue that capitalist assemblages represent zones of inclusion and exclusion. Through measures such as local content policies, economic linkages are promoted between the industry and the national economy, while at the same time parts of the industry legitimise global practices of standardisation to separate the democratic western capitalist economies from the non-western political regimes, characterised by informality, corruption, patrimonialism and at times violence (Barry, 2006, p. 249).

In Ghana's relatively new offshore oil and gas industry, and in the case of its two onshore state-owned processing plants, the dis/entanglement framework becomes a productive lens. Overall, Ghana's petroleum industry cannot be seen exclusively as an enclave separated from political, economic and social life in Ghana. However, the tension and ambiguity around the forces of disentanglement were a considerable concern for my informants. At Tema oil refinery and Atuabo Processing Plant, we can categorise dis/entanglement as: (1) economic dis/entanglement, (2) political dis/entanglement, and (3) infrastructural and technological dis/entanglement. An ethnographic inquiry into oil assemblages and the various layers of dis/entanglement, demonstrates, firstly, that the "enclave theory" is not a productive framework for analysing oil states such as Ghana; secondly, how disentanglement and entanglement practices vary in space and time, according to factors such as oil contracts, domestic politics, international financial institutions, availability of workforce and so on (not only do they vary, but they also depend on continuous developments within the local political landscape, political legacies and available infrastructure); and finally, that there are also impacts from disentanglement and industry standardisation on economic development and domestic industry. This article first presents empirical findings from an ethnographic study of the two processing plants, and then analyses this data through the lens of dis/entanglement.

3 The Tema Oil Refinery

The Tema oil refinery (TOR) is Ghana's iconic oil refinery, occupying a central place in the public imaginary, as it is a continuously politicised state enterprise.

Built in 1963, in Tema, the refinery had an original refining capacity of 45,000 barrels per day. To date, the refinery struggles with alleged corruption, breakdowns and a cast-aside status on the global trade and refining scene. Based on a decade of observation of the refinery, including multiple visits in 2013 and 2014, it is safe to say that its operational uptime is linked to domestic politics, and particularly the political calendar. Ahead of elections, it gets a boost in investment from the government and starts to refine, while the rest of the time the refinery remains dormant (Skaten, 2018a). This kind of politicised operation in Ghana is not limited to the petroleum industry (for mining, see Ntwusu, 2018).

The refinery is part of the looming historical legacy of Ghana's first president, Kwame Nkrumah, who initiated the construction of the refinery, and many other grandiose infrastructural projects, in pursuit of a grand industrial vision. The refinery was constructed and managed by the Italian national oil company, Agip Minera (Nkrumah, 1963). TOR's technologically modern infrastructure in the early 1960s signalled expectations and hope of Ghanaian modernisation. The refinery was set up to be the backbone of the Ghanaian economy, pumping fuel to industries and agriculture, securing freedom from energy imperialists, and realising the socialist dreams of Nkrumah's independent Ghana.

The refinery remains a key infrastructural entity for the popular vote in Ghana's democracy, but it has to date not refined any of Ghana's domestic crude oil. Workers at the refinery lobby for the refinery's potential in the new industry (particularly through the labour union); however, their efforts have been constrained to date by hierarchies and profits driving international trade and refining practices.

The large, attached tank-system for storage of petroleum products has been rented out to private import companies since industry-wide privatisation reforms in the mid-2000s. These companies supply most of Ghana's consumption of petroleum products. Moreover, early in the production phase of the Jubilee-field, the operator of the field claimed that the refinery does not have the technical capacity to refine crude oil from Ghana's first commercial oil and gas field. A rather complex picture of justifications for why the refinery remains disentangled from Ghana's new upstream petroleum industry emerges, beneficial for an industry elite of private entrepreneurs in Ghana's downstream petroleum sector and the consortia of companies extracting oil offshore and exporting it to refineries outside Africa.

The following section presents vignettes from rather dull days at the refinery (2013–2014). While there has since been production at the refinery, it continues to experience longer downtimes. These vignettes demonstrate the dis/entanglement experienced by my informants in a web of national and international influences. While the "new" crude oil does not reach the refinery, the competitive political environment in Ghana and the role of state-owned enterprises continue to make the refinery relevant.

4 Where Is the Crude Oil?

It was a regular day at the refinery in December 2013. One of the engineers and I were enjoying some shade from the distillation tower. I asked him when he thought we would get some crude oil to refine. He shook his head and said, "Unless I see it with my own eyes, I cannot tell you." He went on to tell me about an incident that had happened two months earlier, when they had a vessel coming to the Tema Harbour, supposedly loaded with crude oil for the refinery. "By our own efforts, we had bought [crude oil] from some other place," he said, indicating that it was not the government who had supplied them with either the crude oil or the credit to purchase it. The comment reflected the tense relationship between the workers at the refinery, in particular the labour union, and the politicians in the current government's administration.

I was surprised by this information, since I had been at the refinery at the time he was talking about – and to my knowledge, there had not been any refining. My face expressed confusion. "You see, I'm coming [to the point]," he said laughing. "The vessel came, and as it was about to discharge, they [harbour staff] realised that the vessel was too big for the offshore mooring dock. So they did the ocean transfer. When they had transferred it into two different vessels, the vessels took off. And the product [crude oil] was gone." "Where did the vessels go?" I asked. "All we heard was that some other place needed the crude oil more than the oil refinery. One vessel turned to Spain and one to Cameroon," he continued. "We had the LC [Letter of Credit] to buy the crude oil, the vessel came right up to the discharging point, and then one goes for Spain and one for Cameroon. Can you believe it?" his laughter came to an abrupt halt, and he added in a disheartened tone:

> You have seen it. We know how to refine. We are not useless engineers here [at the refinery]. What is this, sitting here? For people to think we are useless, like all of them. So you should know that, this industry, what we call the oil and gas industry, the forces we are battling with are not small. We find ourselves not able to do anything.

To make sense of this conversation – similar to many other conversations I had with engineers at the refinery – we require an understanding of the contemporary dynamics of Ghana's petroleum industry and the refinery's place in it.

The downstream industry, which the refinery technically belongs to, has undergone a privatisation reform since the mid-2000s. The industry has been structured in various ways since Ghana's independence, but the refinery has always, until now, been an integral part of providing petroleum products to the oil marketing companies that will then supply to filling stations. Either the refinery has been the sole importer of petroleum products or it has refined petroleum products for sale. After the reform, private import companies were allowed to import finished petroleum products and sell directly to oil marketing companies (OMCs). These private bulk distribution companies (BDCs) have grown from a handful to more than thirty since the initiation of the reform. With the refinery being idle at the same time as there has been a growth in private companies and market consumption of petroleum products, the large storage system at the refinery has been rented out to these private companies.

Many of my discussions with workers at the refinery were about the BDCs and OMCs. Not only were they taking over the market share of the refinery, but they were also using the refinery's tank farm and pipeline system to do so. The refinery had rented out storage tanks to private companies as an additional source of revenue generation. However, at this point – when the refinery was dormant, and all the storage space was up for rent – the workers viewed the practice as suspicious. "Could the refinery be left intentionally dormant so the private companies would make money?" was a question that came up from time to time. The engineers were further agitated by the fact that the cost of the rental of storage space was set by the National Petroleum Authority, the industry's regulator, at what the workers thought was a suspiciously low price. If this was not enough, to add further fuel to the issue, the private companies were mainly run by former politicians, some of whom had even had board management roles at the refinery. Several industry observers noted in interviews that private import companies were run by political patrons who engaged in a reciprocal relationship with the political elite where fuel and state contracts were exchanged. This was not the case for all of these companies, but for a fair number of them established after the reform.

The refinery in its current state, instead of being the centrepiece of the industry that every company relied on, had to fight for its own existence. Stories like the one about the vessels going to Spain and Cameroon were common and mixed with claims about national politics and international interests. Transparency about the actual reasons for shutdown at the refinery remained absent, so rumours and theories continued to develop. One significant blow for the refinery was when it became clear that it would not refine crude oil from Ghana's own Jubilee Field in 2011.

The claim that the refinery was not able to refine Jubilee oil was based on accusations that the refinery was not "technologically equipped" to refine the specific composition of hydrocarbons that made up the Jubilee crude oil. The consortium of oil companies operating the Jubilee Field held a press conference in Tamale, where they stated that TOR was not able to refine the Jubilee oil produced in Ghana. The statement was prompted when a journalist asked about the refinery's role in the new upstream petroleum industry, and how local industries would be incorporated. A Ghanaian engineer with Tullow Oil Ghana told the journalist that the refinery needed to be retrofitted to be able to refine the type of crude oil produced by the Jubilee Field. He claimed that the refinery was only able to refine lower quality types of crude oil and that it lacked the technical capacity at this point. He further pointed out that retrofitting of the refinery would be very expensive, and that it might become counterproductive as new oil discoveries in Ghana could produce other types of crude oil (Ghana web, 2011).

Retrofitting the refinery meant overhauling and updating the refining equipment and machinery, implying that the refinery was not sufficiently modern. Given the recent South Korean modernisation project and the fact that nothing more than maintenance had been carried out since 2008, the workers at the refinery received this information with great frustration. Several informants said that the news made them sad and frustrated. A meeting of the TOR union ensued. They remembered it as a heated meeting, where all the "Jubilee frustration" that had gathered over the years came to a boil. Some people were saying they knew this would happen; others just could not believe that a Ghanaian could say such a dismissive thing about the refinery. At the meeting it was agreed that the only thing they could do for now – since organising a strike was out of the question at the inoperative refinery – was to contact the media. Everyone who knew journalists called and tried to get newspapers and radio programmes to talk about their version of the story. (This outreach to media resulted in articles like Modern Ghana, 2011. Continued work by the engineers to spread their side of the story can be seen at Ghana web, 2014a).

My informants agreed that it was good to produce some counterclaims to the false statements about the refinery, but they had their doubts about whether anyone would believe them. One of my informants said that the Ghanaian people, in general, wanted the refinery to work, but, for good reasons, people were suspicious about the state of the refinery and the amount of corruption that would prevail if politicians (who control the state-owned enterprise) got their hands on the new oil. When the Minister of Energy at the time, Emmanuel Kofi Buah, again confirmed TOR's inability to refine Jubilee oil – thereby legitimising the claim of the Tullow engineer (Nyavor, 2014) – it did not make the situation any better. Most engineers believed that the current government was anything but supportive of the refinery's operations. Rumours about privatisation became more pressing when President John Dramani Mahama stated in his annual State of the Nation address that the government was closing in on a joint venture agreement between the refinery and Petro-Saudi (IMANI, 2014).

At the refinery, there was a strong emphasis on workers' technical prowess. A favourite point of reference was the 2009 visit of President Barack Obama to Ghana. The US President visited Ghana, and his Air Force One personnel came to the refinery to test the aviation fuel that the refinery produced. Engineers in the lab would frequently refer to the visit as a stamp of approval for the quality of their work. The aviation fuel was tested and approved, and used by Obama for his trips around Africa. Other African heads of state, prominent individuals and industries throughout West Africa also relied on the services of the refinery. These and other success stories from the past were frequently discussed with me in interviews and informal conversations, promoting a positive image of the refinery and the engineers there.

Claims about the refinery being outdated, disappearing batches of crude oil, rumours about politically linked private companies, erratic threats of privatisation, and a dire state of production were impacting everyday working life at the refinery when I conducted fieldwork there. With the absence of crude oil to refine, speculations and rumours infiltrated social interactions at the refinery and fuelled a strong sense of uncertainty among the workers. Notwithstanding this prevailing uncertainty, there was also a sense of security regarding the future of the refinery as a state-owned enterprise, the individual job security and the refinery's role in the domestic political landscape.

There was a fundamental belief in the refinery's role as a force for economic development, but the current situation produced a sense of confusion. Explanations were found in the "political." The political became a way of explaining the inexplicable, those actions or inactions that went against one's beliefs and desires. For the most part, the political was described as something that was working against refinery workers. However, my informants were not shy about sharing how they also embodied the political, and felt a modicum of power. This political agency emerged particularly in response to rumours of privatisation. The following conversation with another engineer exemplifies this sense of politics:

Monica: What happened to the private partnership between Petro-Saudi and Tema Oil Refinery?

Emmanuel: Which one was that?

Monica: I read about it in the news a few months ago. [*President*] *Mahama said they were doing the final negotiations.*

Emmanuel: You see. This is what they do. They lie. We heard this story, but our managers did not know anything. How can you say we are going into a partnership, and the people working, me, I am running the machines, I don't know.

Pause.

Emmanuel: Monique I will tell you this much. They cannot touch us. It is political. They can let us sit and wait. But we are the ones who can make kerosene for the fishing communities at Election Day – if we strike, there will be a shortage. They cannot touch us.

Another pause.

Emmanuel: These partnerships with what-what Saudi people. It's not the first one and it will not be the last. They sometimes say these things to show that they are working on our industry.

In this conversation, Emmanuel reveals a sense of safety he feels against privatisation. Threats of privatisation met resistance among workers at the refinery and the general public. He implies that the government would, from time to time, make announcements about changes to the industry, public-private partnerships, caps on subsidy spending and so on, but that these were rarely acted upon. These announcements, according to him, were more for the sake of theatre, than to broadcast actual plans. Already in 1996, the IMF reported that the government had agreed to prepare TOR for sale (IMF, 2000, p. 8) as part of wider structural adjustment programmes. Subsequently, IMF reports and press statements where the refinery is mentioned have referred to caps on spending, and the prospect of privatisation has been proposed as a way to address accumulated debts which strain the national budget (IMF, 1999, p. 48, IMF, 2008, p. 32). International monetary institutions continue to lack any vision for African refining as a force for economic development (World Bank, 2011). However, the refinery continues as a state enterprise.

Debt was central to any discussion about the refinery in Ghana. The numbers were usually unverified and conflicting, coming from various sources; but the overall weight of debt was not in question. Everyone knew that there was debt and that it was significant. The debate centred on the question of whether the debt was due to the refinery's financial mismanagement – as was often argued by the media or "experts" – or whether it was due to a tendency among government ministries to use the refinery as their personal filling station, helping themselves to petroleum products without paying, which was the view held by the workforce at the plant. While some of the usage by politicians could be justified, such as fuelling the ambulance fleet during times of shortage elsewhere, other usages, such as for personal travel or political campaigning, were not legitimate in the view of my informants.

The workers at the refinery deployed their political agency by engaging in union lobbying and debates in the media, thus underscoring their technical capabilities and seeking to shore up the political importance of the refinery for Ghana. The missing cargo became one of the examples of how refinery workers were unable to control or impact the refinery's operations, but the continued existence of the refinery as a state enterprise – even as IMF and others were advocating for privatisation – gave the workers faith in their importance and status as a political entity with significance for the state.

Ahead of the Ghanaian general election in 2016, it seemed like the winds had turned for the refinery. While President Mahama stated in the annual address of the nation in 2014 that the refinery was in final negotiation with PetroSaudi over a merger (Ghana web, 2014b), he was quoted during a visit to the refinery, in 2016, saying, "Government has no intention of selling the Tema Oil Refinery and we will rather assist the refinery to re-establish itself as a vibrant state enterprise in petroleum production" (Benaba, 2016). The President said that the government was planning to build a new crude distillation unit, expanding the capacity of the refinery and re-establishing it as a viable entity and one of the foremost state enterprises in Ghana (TOR, 2016a; TOR, 2017b). My key informants at the refinery confirmed that it was operating again, and that the atmosphere had changed. Emmanuel did, however, point out that they were suspicious about this turn of events in an election year, and wondered whether it was just a political move to keep the current administration in power. The New Patriotic Party and Nana Akufo-Addo won the 2016 election. In January 2017, there was an explosion in a crude distillation unit and the refinery was reduced to a refining capacity of 25,000 bpd. However, the new management of the refinery were able to attract new customers and at the end of 2019 it was reported that the refinery had signed a deal to refine

11 million barrels of crude oil from private oil trading companies. Shortly after this announcement, the managing director stepped down and was replaced by a former U.S-based banker. The new managing director resigned in April 2020 after the US Security and Exchange Commission filed a lawsuit against him for allegedly bribing Ghanaian government officials to secure a Turkish company a power deal in Ghana (Nettey, 2020; Ibukun, 2020).

5 The Transformative Powers of Gas Processing

Across new oil and gas producing countries in sub-Saharan Africa, there is an increasing tendency for operators and governments alike to focus on the gas aspect of the discovery. With the help of national governments, multinational oil companies tell a dramatic narrative of transformative gas industries in Africa, which provide an abundance of electricity and clean cooking. While the crude oil is shipped away without much complication, the natural gas found in the same deposits is more expensive to transport. The alternative to flaring the gas is to build domestic or regional processing plants, either offshore (as planned in Mozambique) or onshore close to the extraction site, like Atuabo, in Ghana.

The Atuabo Gas Processing Plant shared quite a few similarities with the Tema oil refinery when it was built. It was built with foreign expertise and capital – in this case, with a Chinese government loan, and with oversight of its construction and operations by China's state oil company, SINOPEC. The plant was promoted as an industrial development project which would benefit the Ghanaian public and industries, with gas derived from the newly discovered Jubilee Field generating electricity. The plant's creation has further been attributed to the progressive vision of the late President John Atta Mills. As such, like the refinery, the gas processing plant was envisioned to create economic linkages and promote prosperity in a series of important economic sectors, starting with the energy sector and continuing with those reliant on gas power. By replacing wood burning in cooking, natural gas had the environmental benefits of reducing carbon emissions and deforestation and the health benefit of reducing respiratory disease.

The initial plan was that the plant would begin operating in June 2013, but continued delays saw the gas flowing through the pipelines for the first time only in early 2015. The delay was scrutinised by civil society organisations and the public, because gas was being flared offshore, and extensive power cuts had been carried out across the national grid. The gas had been provided for free by the Jubilee Partners, but the infrastructure, the pipelines, and the plant had to be built by the Ghanaians (hence the Chinese partnership). Schritt and

Behrends (2018) show how the "Chinese factor" enables, in some cases, African economies to connect upstream extraction with downstream production. In both Niger and Chad, oil refineries have been built for the domestic market with a capacity that the World Bank deems uneconomic (less than 100,000 bdp).

6 At the Atuabo Gas Processing Plant

The Atuabo gas processing plant is located on a previous farm area, along Ghana's southwestern coastline, strategically placed 45 km from the Jubilee Field's floating, production, storage and offloading (FPSO) facility. Entering the secured industry area, you go through a security gate and a small reception, and then to the right you see a quadrangle office complex, and, straight ahead, the plant itself. The main machinery at the plant is grey with marks of various colours while the tanks are white. The office complex consists of three engineering offices, offices for managers (at the time, engineering manager, plant director, and HSE manager) and the food court. The engineering offices are divided by departments: electrical, mechanical and process engineering. Ghanaians and Chinese engineers share the offices.

While the offices have a blend of the two nationalities, a special division within the rooms is obvious, Ghanaian on one side of the room and Chinese on the other, at their work stations and computers. Work is divided along national lines as well, engineering teams working together are mostly completely Ghanaian or Chinese. Ghanaians working on the plant are a mix of Ghana Gas personnel, sub-contractors and a range of "local hires" for cleaning, security, etc. One can clearly distinguish them by the colour of their overalls as well as allocated office places in the main building. They meet in the morning for plant safety briefings in the main building, during lunch in the food court and while conducting the various work tasks in the plant over the course of a day. While the Ghanaians in the plant have their work routine, the Chinese have a slightly different one. They all start at the same time, the Chinese have early lunch before they have a one hour break intended for mid-day sleeping. After returning to work, they finish their day at the same time as the Ghanaians. The differences in work hours only come up as a point of tension when discussing other problems between the two nationalities.

When I first visited the plant in July 2015, it was operating on and off. The Chinese were doing most of the technical work on the plant; they had, after all, been part of the construction and knew the plant intimately. The Ghanaian engineers were complaining that the Chinese engineers kept delaying the completion of the "knowledge transfer programme" – a scheme to provide training to Ghana Gas personnel, which was part of the Chinese contract. The Ghanaian workers suspected that it was an intentional bid by the Chinese to sabotage the training in order to get their contracts extended. On separate occasions, Ghana Gas personnel had been "stood up" by their Chinese colleagues when they had arranged to undertake work together. One informant explained the following:

> The people [Chinese engineers] agreed to meet at 3 pm. We were waiting at the safety point when we saw them returning from the plant. We were expecting them to come from the office. They said that they had already checked the equipment and that we could come with them next time. We were disappointed but [with] language [difficulties] and all, it's difficult to find out why they do this.

There were similar stories from other engineers. At points when collaboration between the two nationalities were planned, the Chinese engineers would make an excuse for cancelling the plans last minute, either because the work had already been done or due to some other work-related happening. Schritt (2018, p. 266) sees similar developments in Niger, where Nigerien workers at the refinery accuse the Chinese of systematically blocking knowledge transfer. Instead of working together, Chinese staff would issue a "fetch and carry" order to the Nigerien workers, hampering their opportunity to learn from the Chinese. Nigerien workers saw it as deliberate actions to hinder the "indigenisation" of the industry.

While some informants attributed parts of the unfortunate development to communication, others were firm in their argument about sabotage. They had an overall picture of the Chinese as people who did not want to leave the plant, as per the contract, because they wanted to keep their jobs and not return to China. "They have everything they want: jobs, secluded housing area, Chinese food. They even import women, prostitutes," an engineer claimed, as part of his explanation for why the Chinese were not interested in completing the knowledge transfer programme. Several other engineers, even among the managerial level at Ghana Gas, expressed this view.

In between the arguments about communication and economic rationale, there was another less pleasant sentiment. Several of the workers in Ghana Gas had experienced racial slurs and a demeaning attitude from the Chinese workers. This had been attended to by the management of the plant, and had improved somewhat. Just before my stay at Atuabo, however, there had been an incident that sparked a new discussion about racism at the plant. In this incident, the management of the plant pointed out that drinking water consumption at the offices was too high. There had been recruitment as well as the addition of a subcontractor, which had increased the number of workers at the plant, and obvious to most, the drinking water consumption had increased. The financial department in Accra was not happy and urged the plant management to find a solution. Some of the Chinese engineers then suggested that the bottled drinking water should be reserved for the Chinese nationals, while the Ghanaians could drink the cheaper and sometimes filthy "sachet water" or tap water. To this the Ghanaians reacted with outrage, seeing this as another example of the Chinese' inherent racism, related to their reluctance to train the Ghanaians as per the contract.

While Ghanaian takeover at the plant was hindered by the challenges of interracial cooperation and, possibly, Chinese workers' attempts to sabotage knowledge transfer, there was also another problem for the Ghanaians. Many of the engineering roles at Atuabo were filled by what my informants referred to as "political recruitment." This is a common phenomenon in Ghana's industry (and society in general) and basically refers loosely to people being hired for positions based on their social networks, likely kin relations to people in position of power.

Even though the plant was located in a remote area of the western region, it was still the national gas company, and therefore a very attractive place of work for young Ghanaians. Salaries were decent and the experience could lead to a job with a multinational oil company. The majority of engineers at the plant were qualified (with engineering degrees), but due to multiple avenues of recruitment, it was evident that some were more motivated to do the job than others. It was common to see people spending hours on the computer playing games or downloading videos. There was some talk about whether specific managers or the director were in the right place. However, the main issue was that there were no trained Ghanaian technicians, only engineers, who observed some of the work being done by Chinese technicians, but were not trained to do that particular work. As one engineer expressed: "We are the plant engineers, we make sure that the machinery is up to date [...]. We don't do the bolts and knots. That is a technician's job." Whether the engineer's statement was one that the human resources department of Ghana Gas had considered was not something I could get an answer to. But the reality on the ground was that the engineers at Atuabo Gas Processing plant were not (at the time of my fieldwork) able to carry out the everyday operations of the plant.

The challenges at Atuabo were not just on the ground; they were also related to the political environment and industry partners. Like the refinery and other state-owned enterprises, key managerial personnel changed with a change in government (if not more frequently). That was the case when, in 2016, the

National Democratic Congress (NDC) lost the election to the New Patriotic Party (NPP). The new politically appointed management inherited a plant that had severe cash-flow problems. The plant's largest customer, the Volta River Authority (VRA), was in charge of providing state-owned electricity companies with power. A media report suggested that the VRA owed Ghana Gas US$ 500 million (Nyavor, 2014). On their side, the VRA stated that they would be unable to pay up until the electricity companies had settled their outstanding bills. The electricity companies blamed the consumers for failing to pay for the power they used. Raising tariffs or forcefully collecting money owed by Ghanaian citizens would directly contradict the gas industry's bold promise and be politically damaging to whichever party dared to broach the subject.

Taken together, intercultural relations, economics and politics impact on the performance of the processing plant and the extractive industry. As I have argued elsewhere, Ghana's competitive democracy and politicians' pursuit of political legacies have major impacts on the new petroleum industry. The two main political parties have different strategies for the development of infrastructure and awarding of contracts. As Ghana's "Fourth Republic" has demonstrated thus far, changes in government happen at frequent intervals, and a period of scrutinising the previous administration leaves the domestic elite and international investors and actors vulnerable to contract termination or legal challenges (Skaten, 2018b).

7 Dis/Entanglement at Tema Oil Refinery and Atuabo Gas Processing Plant

In general, we do not question the entanglement of downstream industries – they are naturally a part of their localities and dependent on consumers of petroleum products. A refinery, however, is located between the upstream and downstream sectors, refining crude oil from production fields and dependent on transportation and marketers for the sale of petroleum products. The crude oil can be imported from anywhere. An oil refinery that refines the oil extracted in domestic territory can be considered the ultimate economic entanglement – with a connection between upstream and downstream industries even if the upstream industry is operated by multinational oil companies and the downstream is mainly national. While Ghana today produces around 288,000 bpd per day, with the Ghana National Petroleum Corporation's mandatory 10% ownership in all production fields, crude oil is still not sold to the refinery from domestic offshore production. The jubilee consortium has made a claim about the outdated state of the refinery, but this is highly contested and not proven as noted above. Subsequently, fields that have come on-stream after the Jubilee Field have not engaged in a public debate about whether they should supply the refinery. As such, this early debate about TOR's technological ability has to date hindered the further development of closer connections between Ghana's upstream oil production and downstream state-owned infrastructures.

The consortium of oil and gas companies operating the Jubilee Field had no obligation to sell or provide the refinery with crude oil. Access to Jubilee crude oil could have been agreed upon during the negotiation of the Product Sharing Agreements; but as Ghana had very little to offer in the negotiations, in terms of capital and petroleum infrastructure for extraction, there was not much to bargain with. The track record and capacity of the refinery might also have made it difficult to convince the oil consortium to agree to such terms. The disconnect between Ghana's upstream industry, which oversees the extraction of crude oil, and its downstream industry, the refinery in Tema, is not exceptional. Over the last few decades, the refinement of crude oil has become focused around hubs in Asia, Europe and North-America, with large scale, high-tech refineries. The ease of sea cargo trade, the availability of special economic zones, and the general flow of raw materials globally has encouraged this sort of centralisation (Bridge & Billion, 2013, pp. 51–52). Jubilee crude oil is shipped for refining in France and other parts of Europe and Asia through the Swiss oil trading company (Vitol, 2010).

In contrast to the Tema refinery, which was cut off from economic linkages with the new crude oil industry, Atuabo gas processing plant became a crucial point of entanglement. Natural gas was provided to the Atuabo plant for free, which would avoid flaring at the FPSO. Construction and initial start-up was carried out with the Chinese national petroleum company, SINOPEC. Afterwards, the Ghana national gas company was supposed to run the plant, which was projected to have a far-reaching economic impact in Ghana. Instead, we have seen a non-functioning Ghanaian take-over of the plant, several parts of the plant remaining unconstructed, and a customer base with an unreliable payment record.

The leading discourse, supported by market dynamics and institutions such as the World Bank, remains that crude oil is not profitable for small African refineries, but that gas, conveniently enough, can lead to transformative economic development. While we should support the development of national gas industries, it does not justify the total abandonment of petroleum product refinement in sub-Saharan Africa. Crude oil and petroleum products become just another example of the many raw materials exported from the continent and re-imported as more valuable commodities.

It is more useful to talk about the ways things are politicised, than to look for political disentanglements in Ghana. Kosmos Energy, the American multinational company that led the discovery of the oil and gas in commercial quantities in Ghana, were involved in a lengthy political process after the change in government in 2008 (Skaten, 2018b). Kosmos Energy entered Ghana through a Ghanaian company tightly connected to one of the political parties, and therefore did not manage to distance itself from party-political affiliation. Domestic and international investigations into alleged corruption claims ensued. This case reflects ways in which political entanglement materialises in Ghana's upstream industry. Elsewhere, I have described in detail how the two competing political parties in Ghana affect the industry by overturning each other's policies and changing key personnel in the petroleum sector after a change in government (Skaten, 2018b).

While the refinery might be economically disentangled from Ghana's upstream industry, it remains deeply entangled in domestic politics. Neither of Ghana's two main political parties want to shut down or privatise the refinery, because it is useful to have a refinery (crude extracted from the smaller Saltpond oilfield or Western African neighbours can be used) for both private and state reasons. Moreover, the refinery represents something symbolically important in Ghana. The past glory of integrated energy systems was again made relevant with discovery of oil in offshore waters. Engineers at the refinery engage in the public debate about the role of the refinery and believe the refinery embodies political power through its historical legacy and mere existence, despite recommendations to privatise it. Since the discovery of the Jubilee Field, and later with the inception of TEN, Sankofa and soon the Pecan oil fields, operations have been run like an enclave in relation to the refinery. The lack of modern equipment makes it possible to justify rejecting domestic refining, even if the reasons are just as likely to be economic (streamlining trade to large refineries and markets in Europe and Asia). As such, the new players are able to disentangle the upstream crude production from the refinery on both economic and technological grounds. The new energy infrastructure in Atuabo, whatever its significance to new political legacies and economic linkages, casts a temporary shadow over the possible gains of refining domestically. But the refinery's place in the national political landscape remains important, and while the disentanglement remains obvious, I would argue that the refinery's role cannot be discounted for the foreseeable future. Past and future political legacies and high stakes in the new offshore industry could re-establish the importance of the refinery for economic development in Ghana.

The availability of infrastructure enables the domestic entanglement of crude oil and gas from offshore extraction with downstream processing.

However, as we have seen in the case of TOR, disputing the technology available at the refinery became a way to disentangle the upstream industry from Ghana's downstream domestic industry. By presenting the old, non-modern refining apparatus as unable to refine the "new," "high grade" oil produced by international companies such as at the Jubilee Field, a well-known dichotomy emerges of semi-functional African industries versus streamlined and economically profitable Western industries.

The new gas processing plant represents local content, local industry, and gas-fuelled solutions to long-standing electricity challenges, as well as other benefits arriving from the entanglement of the new offshore industry. However, even when these things are entangled, there are still challenges to the future of gas-driven economic development in Ghana. The presence of the infrastructure enables possibilities, but just like with the disentanglement of the oil refinery, dis/entanglement of gas processing is not a stable state of affairs. Political and economic rationales, whether international or national, local considerations and other factors make these solutions complex. As this chapter has shown, dis/entanglement can manifest in different ways and cannot be boiled down to either entangled or disentangled; it varies according to the economic sphere, political involvement and the availability and perceived standards of infrastructure and technology.

8 Conclusion

On the face of it, the upstream-downstream classification suggests the organisation of economic flow, or it appears to be an explanatory model of the transformation of crude oil and gas into petroleum products. This classification was used to justify the transportation of oil extracted from the Jubilee Field to Europe for refining, rather than to the Ghanaian domestic refinery. With refining industries often located in the Global North, the upstream-downstream classification serves to uphold political dynamics that enforce structures of inequality in trade and industry and between workers in upstream and downstream industries, reflecting and reproducing inequality in global capitalism more broadly.

While the refinery and gas plant are two very different entities in terms of their technical capabilities, with opposite problems – one has no crude oil, whereas the other has free natural gas – they are also strikingly similar, in terms of the rhetoric behind their construction and their roles as catalysts for economic development. They are both shaped by their context and run according to Ghanaian political life. Yet the focus on the socioeconomic benefits of natural gas has allowed the Atuabo Gas Processing Plant to be taken as a sufficient solution to the "development" imperative, overshadowing the value added of crude oil and allowing the refinery to be forgotten. While Ghana has infrastructure, human capacity, the natural resources and the technology available to process both its oil and gas, the reality remains that these local entities come with a risk to profit for international companies. Gas is more expensive to transport and can therefore be supplied to the Ghanaians, while crude oil is transported to the Global North from West Africa using systems that have been developed for decades. Complete disentanglement, however, is not the reality on the ground, but something that is an everyday threat to the industry, which can be seen through the everyday relationships at the energy facilities and engagement with politics.

Acknowledgements

The author would like to express gratitude to informants, gatekeepers, and friends in Ghana for making fieldwork in the industry possible. Part of the project was funded by the Fund for Women Graduates (FFWG).

References

Appel, H. (2012). Offshore Work: Oil, Modularity, and how of Capitalism in Equatorial Guinea. *Journal of American Ethnological Society*, 34(4), 692–709.

Barry, A. (2006). Technological Zones. *European Journal of Social Theory*, 9(2), 239–253.

Benaba, G-R. (2016). TOR is not for Sale – President Mahama. Ghana News Agency. Retrieved, 2017, January 24, from http://www.ghananewsagency.org/politics/tor-is-not-for-salepresident-mahama--103659

Bridge, G., & Le Billion, P. (2012). *Oil*. Cambridge: Polity Press.

Ferguson, J. (2005). Seeing Like an Oil Company: Space, Security, and Global Capital in Neoliberal Africa. *American Anthropologist*, 107(3), 377–381.

Ghana Web (2011). Tema Oil Refinery Cannot Refine Jubilee Oil. Retrieved, 2017, January 24, from http://www.ghanaweb.com/GhanaHomePage/NewsArchive/Tema-Oil-Refinery-cannot-refine-Jubilee-Oil-208228.

Ghana web (2014a). Politicians Working Against TOR. Retrieved, 2016, March 5, from http://www.ghanaweb.com/GhanaHomePage/NewsArchive/Politiciansworking - against-TOR-319226.

Ghana web (2014b). TOR Will Need $200 Million to Refine Jubilee Crude. Retrieved, 2017, January 24, from http://www.ghanaweb.com/GhanaHomePage/business/TORwill-need-200million-to-refine-Jubilee-crude-320693.

Ibukun, J. (2020). Ex-Goldman Banker Quits Ghana Refinery After SEC Bribe Claim. Retrieved, 2020, October 17, from https://news.bloomberglaw.com/securities-law/ex-goldman-banker-quits-ghana-oil-refinery-after-sec-bribe-claim.

IMANI (2014). IMANI Report: Evidence-based Support for Ghana to Ratify the EPA. Myjoyonline, Retrieved 2017, January 24, from http://www.myjoyonline.com/business/2014/April-14th/imani-reportevidence-based-support-for-ghana-to-ratify-the-epa.php.

IMF (1999). Ghana—Enhanced Structural Adjustment Facility Economic and Financial Policy Framework Paper, 1998–2000. Retrieved 2017, January 24, from https://www.imf.org/external/np/pfp/ghana/ghana0.htm.

IMF (2000). Interim Poverty Reduction Strategy Paper 2000 – 2002. Retrieved 2017, January 24, from https://www.imf.org/external/NP/prsp/2000/gha/01/063000.pdf.

IMF (2008). Fuel and Food Price Subsidies: Issues and Reform Options. Retrieved 2016, March 12, https://www.imf.org/en/Publications/Policy-Papers/Issues/2016/12/31/Fueland-Food-Price-Subsidies-Issues-and-Reform-Options-PP4293.

Modern Ghana (2011). TOR Rejects Claims it Can't Refine Crude Oil From Jubilee Field. Retrieved, 2017, January 24, from https://www.modernghana.com/news/329774/1/tor-rejects-claims-it-cantrefine-crude-oil-from-jubilee-field.html.

Nettey, N. (2020). TOR MD, Asante Berko Resigns After Bribery Allegations in US. Retrieved, 2020, October 17, from https://citibusinessnews.com/tor-md-asante-berko-resigns-after-bribery-allegations-in-us.

Nkrumah, K. (1963). Formal Opening of the Oil Refinery. Retrieved 2015, March 24, from http://nkrumahinfobank.org/article.php?id=439&c=51.

Ntwusu, S. (2018) 10,000 Miners, 10,000 Votes: Politics and Mining in Ghana. *Africa* 88 (4), 863–866.

Nyavor, G. (2014). Gov't Under Pressure to Pay Debts Owed Petroleum Importers. Joyonline. Retrieved 2017, January 24, from http://www.myjoyonline.com/business/2014/august-14th/govt-under-pressure-to-release-funds-to-pay-debts-owed-petroleumimporters.php.

Ovadia, J. (2016). *The Petrodevelopmental State in Africa: Making Oil Work in Angola, Nigeria and the Gulf of Guinea*. London: Hurst.

Schritt, J. (2018). Contesting The Oil Zone: Local Content Issues in Niger's Oil Industry. *Energy Research & Social Science*, 41, 259–269.

Schritt, J., & Behrends, A. (2018). 'Western' and 'Chinese' Oil Zones: Petro-Infrastructure and the Emergence of New Trans-Territorial Spaces of Order in Niger and Chad. In U. Engel, M. Boeckler & D. Müller-Mahn (Eds.), *Spatial Practices: Territory, Border and Infrastructure in Africa* (pp. 211–230). Leiden: Brill.

Schritt, J. & Witte, A. (2018). Standardized Capitalism? Negotiating the Oil Industry's Dis/entanglement in Niger and Uganda. *Economy and Society* 47:3, 428–452.

Skaten, M. (2017), From Refining to Smuggling: The Everyday Politics of Petrol in Ghana. PhD Thesis, University of Edinburgh.

Skaten, M. (2018b) Ghana's Oil Industry: Steady Growth in a Challenging Environment. Oxford Institute of Energy Studies, Working paper no. 77.

Skaten, M. (2020). Political Legacies in Ghana's Petroleum Industry. In J. Schubert, U. Engel and E. Macamo (Eds.), *Extractive Industries and Changing State Dynamics in Africa: Beyond the Resource Curse*. Routledge studies in African development (pp. 148–166). London: Routledge.

TOR (2016a) President Pledges Governments Support to TOR. Retrieved 2017, January 24, from http://www.tor.com.gh/2016/05/10/president-pledges-governmentssupport-to-tor/.

TOR (2017). Before it All Began. Retrieved 2016, December 15, from http://www.tor.com.gh/about-tor/history/.

Tsing, A. L. (2005). *Friction: An Ethnography of Global Connection*. Princeton: Princeton University Press.

Vitol (2010). Vitol Appointed as Exclusive Marketer of Tullow Oil's Jubilee Production. Retrieved 2017, January 24, from http://www.vitol.com/vitol-appointed-asexclusive-marketer-of-tullow-oils-jubilee-production/.

Watts, M. (2005). Righteous Oil? Human Rights, The Oil Complex and Corporate Social Responsibility. *Annual Review for of Environment and Resources*, 30(1), 373–407.

Watts, M. (2012). A Tale of Two Gulfs: Life, Death and Dispossession Along Two Oil Frontiers. *American Quarterly*, 64 (3), 437–467.

Witte, A. (2018). *An Uncertain Future: Anticipating Oil in Uganda*. Göttingen: Göttingen University Press.

World Bank Group. (2011). Petroleum Product Markets in Sub-Saharan Africa: Comparative Efficiency Analysis of 12 Countries. Retrieved from http://documents.worldbank.org/curated/en/767991468202165845/Petroleumproduct-markets-inSub-Saharan-Africacomparative-efficiency-analysis-of-twelvecountries.

7

La responsabilité sociale des entreprises comme dés/enchevêtrement : L'industrie pétrolière au Tchad

Yorbana Seign-Goura

1 Introduction

Sur la base d'intérêts et de stratégies communs, le captage des ressources met en jeu une arène de plusieurs acteurs ou « groupes stratégiques » (Bierschenk, 1988). Pour l'exploitation du pétrole, cette aventure crée une « arène pétrolière » dans les pays dans lesquels les différents groupes stratégiques essayent de capter la rente pétrolière comme c'est le cas du Tchad depuis deux décennies. Mais la chaîne de valeur extractive qui s'étend de l'exploration à la valorisation de ladite ressource est source de dynamiques globales économique, sociale, politique et culturelle. Ces enjeux de transformations structurelles issues des jeux de pouvoir entre les groupes stratégiques se déroulent notamment entre l'État, les multinationales, les institutions internationales, la société civile et les communautés locales. Ils renvoient encore à plusieurs sous-groupes tels que les autorités traditionnelles, les jeunes, les politiciens locaux, les travailleurs, les communautés religieuses etc. qui composent, selon Watts (2005, p. 54), « le complexe pétrolier ». Depuis 2003, le Tchad est entré dans le concert des pays producteurs de pétrole et a consolidé sa place à travers le projet de développement de l'oléoduc Tchad-Cameroun en 2000, le projet Rônier en 2011, les projets de Badila et Mangara en 2014 et récemment encore en 2019, le Projet Daniela dans le bassin de Bongor (Voir ces zones pétrolifères ci-dessous, sur la carte du Tchad).

Le but de ce travail est de comprendre comment les dynamiques de pouvoir entre les groupes stratégiques, ainsi que la gouvernance de ce qu'ils attendent des projets pétroliers, produisent des changements structurels perçus subjectivement comme positifs ou négatifs par les acteurs du complexe pétrolier. Autrement dit, il s'agit de saisir les enjeux de pouvoir entre les groupes stratégiques autour des pratiques de la responsabilité sociale des entreprises (désormais RSE) dans l'industrie extractive au Tchad. Ainsi, nous avons mis en exergue une analyse critique partant de la notion de la responsabilité sociale de l'entreprise comme pratique de dés/enchevêtrement pour comprendre

 | DOI:10.1163/9789004530065_008

cette situation dynamique d'exploitation pétrolière. Alors que la RSE est saluée par les compagnies pétrolières et ses partisans comme une nouvelle forme d'enchevêtrement qui suit des considérations humanistes et est censée faire progresser le développement durable, les critiques objectent que l'enchevêtrement est principalement de nature symbolique et sert à échapper à la responsabilité de redistribution des avantages tirés des projets pétroliers. Ainsi, selon eux, la RSE continue de servir la maximisation des profits comme une forme de dés/enchevêtrement.

Ainsi, cette contribution est basée sur la méthode qualitative. La démarche qualitative adoptée pour cette recherche a consisté en une triangulation des données (Olivier de Sardan, 2008). Nous avons collecté des informations soit de première main par des entretiens sur le terrain et des observations directes sur les sites pétroliers de Komé ainsi que dans les bassins de Bongor, Badila et Mangara, soit de seconde main, comme des entrevues, des discours ou des verbatim. Aussi, une partie des données est issue de la documentation sur les pratiques des entreprises, à travers leurs rapports d'activités, de la littérature trouvée sur le sujet au Tchad et ailleurs, des documents académiques et des journaux de la place. Nous avons aussi pu avoir des entretiens avec les groupes stratégiques que sont les autorités locales, les travailleurs sur les chantiers pétroliers, les représentants de la société civile etc. Les données mobilisées dans le cadre de cette étude ont été rassemblées entre 2015 et 2020, lors de séjours réguliers au Tchad pour la collecte d'information dans le cadre d'une thèse doctorale sur la gouvernance pétrolière au Tchad. Pour cette étude portant sur les pratiques RSE des entreprises pétrolières, nous avons procédé à une analyse de contenu de la documentation et des discours à l'issue des données collectées dans ce cadre. Les tendances discutées ci-dessous ressortent de nos analyses.

Ainsi, dans le cadre de ce travail, nous déclinerons le contexte de l'exploitation pétrolière au Tchad et le cadre critique de lecture des projets extractifs que sont la RSE et les groupes stratégiques. Nous procéderons par la suite à l'analyse des initiatives RSE dans les projets pétroliers comme pratiques de dés/enchevêtrement, puis nous discuterons les dynamismes issus de la chaîne de valeur extractive et des enjeux de pouvoir qu'ils sous-tendent. Nous conclurons ce travail par une mise en perspective globale de la raison d'être des projets extractifs au Tchad et ailleurs dans le monde.

2 Contexte de l'exploitation pétrolière au Tchad

Comme la plupart des pays d'Afrique Subsaharienne, le Tchad a obtenu son indépendance dans les années 1960. Au début des années 1970, les premières réserves de pétrole furent découvertes dans le Sud du pays. Cependant, compte tenu de l'instabilité institutionnelle du pays, ce n'est qu'en 2000 que la valorisation desdites ressources a commencé et a fait du pétrole la principale source de revenus d'un pays dont l'économie reposait jusque-là sur l'agriculture et notamment la culture du coton. Le processus ayant conduit à l'exploitation pétrolière a été marqué par des dynamiques et jeux de pouvoir entre les différents groupes stratégiques des projets pétroliers. D'une part, certains acteurs tels l'État et les multinationales ont été les initiateurs des projets et d'autre part les organisations de la société civile, les communautés locales n'ont fait leur apparition dans le processus que tardivement pour consolider l'arène pétrolière. Comme le fait remarquer Appel (2012), au-delà de l'argent qu'engendre l'industrie pétrolière et auquel s'intéressent très souvent les recherches, nous allons nous intéresser aux pratiques des multinationales et à leur perception au niveau local.

En effet, après les troubles politiques ayant secoué le Tchad après la décennie des indépendances en Afrique (pendant les années 60), des multinationales telles Shell, Chevron et Exxon se sont intéressées au pétrole en s'approchant de l'État pour des négociations en vue de son exploitation (Petry & Bambé, 2005, p. 22). Lesdites négociations furent interrompues par les soubresauts politiques qui ont frappé le pays en 1979 ainsi que par la gouvernance tumultueuse pendant la décennie suivante. Mais en 1988, à l'issue d'un avenant entre l'État et Esso, il a été décidé de poursuivre la prospection, en vue d'une exploitation des réserves découvertes. Cependant, l'échiquier politique du Tchad a connu encore des changements avec la prise du pouvoir en 1990 par celui qui deviendra plus tard président, Idriss Deby Itno, jusqu'à sa mort en 2021.

Le consortium monté pour l'exploitation pétrolière connut aussi des perturbations avec le départ de Chevron et son remplacement par Elf. Ainsi le consortium des multinationales s'est constitué de Shell, Elf et ExxonMobil possédant respectivement 40%, 20% et 40% des actions. Mais en 1999, on vit le départ successif d'Elf et de Shell puis leur replacement par Chevron et Petronas. Après tous les soubresauts politiques, la transformation et la formation des sociétés pétrolières, l'aventure de l'exploitation pétrolière du Tchad devait donc continuer avec un Consortium composé des sociétés ExxonMobil (45% des actions), Chevron Texaco (35%) et Petronas (25%). Le Tchad étant un pays sans accès à la mer, il a fallu trouver un accord avec le Cameroun pour faire transiter son pétrole brut par le port de Kribi sur les côtes ouest du Cameroun.

Le projet d'exploitation du pétrole Tchadien reçut aussi le soutien de la Banque Mondiale, ce qui allait donner une tournure historique à cette aventure car cette dernière imposa des normes qui devaient guider le projet. Les conditionnalités imposées par la Banque Mondiale aux parties, à savoir les multinationales et l'État, devaient aboutir à une gestion responsable devant conjecturer le phénomène de la malédiction des ressources naturelles (Gary & Reisch, 2004, IAG 2009). Le financement du, ainsi nommé, Projet de l'oléoduc Tchad-Cameroun, évalué à 4,2 milliards de Dollars, fit de lui l'un des investissements privés le plus important d'Afrique en ce début de siècle en 2000 (Gary & Reisch, 2004). Cependant, le but principal du projet assigné à l'État et aux autres parties prenantes fut l'utilisation de la rente pétrolière pour la lutte contre la pauvreté. Les faits en amont du projet devaient garantir les conditions d'exploitation respectant les normes sociales, environnementales et économiques responsables. La composition du consortium pétrolier, sa recomposition et restructuration ainsi que les soubresauts politiques locaux montrent les jeux de pouvoir des groupes stratégiques qui composent l'arène pétrolière. Les uns et les autres sortent de l'arène ou y restent selon l'échec ou la réussite de la stratégie de pouvoir développée pour maintenir et développer leurs intérêts dans l'arène.

Les débuts de l'aventure pétrolière au Tchad, notamment la phase d'octroi des permis d'exploration puis d'exploitation, ainsi que la négociation des avenants ont uniquement impliqué l'État et les multinationales en bilatéral vu le contexte politique de parti unique. Les autres groupes stratégiques sont intervenus plus tard dans la chaîne de valeur extractive. Autrement dit, sur le plan formel, le Projet d'Exploitation Pétrolière et d'Oléoduc Tchad-Cameroun a posé les bases institutionnelles pour une gouvernance responsable du secteur pétrolier au Tchad. Ceci s'observe notamment à travers la loi n° 001 (relative à la gestion des revenus pétroliers) votée par l'Assemblée nationale du Tchad en 1999 et la documentation relative au Plan de Gestion de l'Environnement, les Études d'Impact Environnemental, fournis par ExxonMobil Exploration and Production Chad Inc[1] (désormais EEPCI) en dizaine de volumes et des documents annexes qui devaient servir de guide pour les autres activités extractives au Tchad (GIC, 2009, p. 12).

Après le projet de Doba sont apparus les projets du Bassin de Bongor puis ceux de Badila et Mangara toujours dans le sud du Tchad. EEPCI, CNPCIC (China National Petroleum Corporation International In Chad) et Glencore se partagent donc le pétrole tchadien. (Cf. Carte du Tchad indiquant les différentes zones ou régions pétrolières, ci-dessous). Leurs défis seraient donc de gérer les contraintes imposées par le contexte des normes internationales de la Banque Mondiale et de satisfaire les attentes des différents groupes stratégiques du

1 EEPCI signifiant ExxonMobil Exploration and Production Chad Inc, désigne le consortium pétrolier au Tchad dirigé par ExxonMobil. EEPCI est aussi appelé localement Essochad. Dans ce travail nous utiliserons les deux noms interchangeablement.

FIGURE 7.1 Production de pétrole au Chad. Illustration des éditeurs basée sur la carte du Chad de l'ONU no. 3788
HTTPS://WWW.UN.ORG/DEPTS/CARTOGRAPHIC/MAP/PROFILE/CHAD.PDF

complexe pétrolier. Au vu de ce contexte, nous pensons que le concept de responsabilité sociale des entreprises et ses pratiques en termes d'enchevêtrement et de dés/enchevêtrement des projets pétroliers dans les zones productrices peuvent être mobilisés pour comprendre les dynamiques du secteur pétrolier au Tchad depuis plus de deux décennies.

3 La responsabilité sociale des entreprises comme dés/enchevêtrement

Le concept de la « responsabilité sociale de l'entreprise » (RSE) est appréhendé dans le milieu académique comme une notion polysémique, ce qui lui vaut une pluralité de définitions et d'interprétations. Dahlsrud (2008) recense une trentaine de définitions qui présentent des nuances. Ainsi, une socio-histoire de la RSE renvoie aux initiatives allant de la philanthropie d'entreprise à celles de responsabilités éthiques relatives à la promotion du développement durable dans la société contemporaine (Baba, 2018). La notion de RSE a vu son émergence dans la perspective du débat sur le rôle de l'entreprise dans la société globale. Ainsi, les divergences épistémologiques de sa définition vont aussi entrainer une diversité dans ses applications. Les pratiques RSE naviguent donc entre des appréhensions humanistes et les perspectives critiques de responsabilités éthiques et sociétales des entreprises (ibid.). Ces différentes définitions et perspectives mettent en évidence les négociations complexes entre les pratiques d'enchevêtrement et de dés/enchevêtrement inhérentes à l'industrie pétrolière comme suit :

Des perspectives appréciatives mettent l'accent sur la dimension humaniste et le développement durable. Le concept de RSE selon Carroll (1991, p. 43), par exemple, est l'exécution simultanée et donc holistique des responsabilités économiques, légales, éthiques et philanthropiques (discrétionnaires) de l'entreprise. Les responsabilités économiques consistent en la poursuite de l'objectif de rentabilité, et donc de la satisfaction des intérêts économiques de l'entreprise. Les responsabilités légales consistent à respecter ce qui est prescrit par la loi, celles qui sont éthiques poussent les entreprises à faire ce qui est bon, juste et honnête sans y être contraintes par les dispositions légales, et celles qui sont philanthropiques ou discrétionnaires mettent l'accent sur l'engagement volontaire des entreprises à la résolution des problématiques économiques, sociales et environnementales de la société (Ben Rhouma & al., 2018).

Quelques années plus tôt, Carroll (1979) avait défini le concept de RSE sous une forme pyramidale de responsabilités économiques, légales, éthiques et discrétionnaires, la philanthropie étant située dans la responsabilité discrétionnaire de l'entreprise. Aussi, les modèles d'initiatives RSE conçus par Ritu et al. (2001) se déclinent en modèles philanthropique, juridique, libéral et éthique. Ces modèles en vigueur en Inde intègrent les différentes responsabilités sous la forme pyramidale conçues par Carroll en 1979. Dans la pratique, tous ces modèles ne sont pas exclusifs et ils représentent aussi l'évolution qu'a connue le concept de la RSE depuis son origine jusqu'aujourd'hui et qui reflète le passage de la conceptualisation de la RSE comme de la philanthropie à l'intégration des dimensions du développement durable (Bon, 2009; Dahlsrud, 2008; Garriga & Melé, 2004). Vue comme des pratiques humanistes destinées à un développement durable, la RSE est représentée comme un enchevêtrement local symbiotique : Les multinationales du pétrole font face à leurs responsabilités économiques, légales, éthiques et discrétionnaires, et contribuent ainsi au développement durable.

C'est dans le sillage des responsabilités définies par la pyramide de la RSE de Caroll qu'ont émergé les modèles de RSE soient-ils, libéraux, éthiques, philanthropiques ou discrétionnaires, légaux ou juridiques.

Des perspectives critiques, cependant, mettent l'accent sur le dés/enchevêtrement selon lequel les entreprises, par le biais de programmes de RSE, ne se montrent pas seulement responsables de leurs impacts sociaux et environnementaux (enchevêtrement) mais cherchent plutôt à tirer profit de leur relation avec la société en posant des actes de bienveillance(dés/enchevêtrement) (Blowfield & Frynas, 2005). Les perspectives critiques de la RSE font une lecture des structures de pouvoir qui sous-tendent les initiatives des entreprises en faisant souvent référence à la généalogie néolibérale de la RSE (Gond & Nyberg, 2017, p. 1129). Les tenants de cette perspective soutiennent d'une part, dans la lignée du marxisme, que les pratiques RSE permettent de maintenir le statu quo dans la société, de maintenir l'ordre social existant, et d'autre part la société devient une marchandise, le statu de salariat va s'étendre, et les entreprises capitalistes vont conforter leur domination, d'après Hanlon (2008, p. 166).

Une autre perspective critique de la RSE se base sur une lecture de la RSE comme discours et constitution symbolique du pouvoir dont les tenants et aboutissants épistémologiques sont entre autres les analyses de l'interactionnisme symbolique avec Shamir (2005), le post-colonialisme avec Banerjee (2000) ou les approches de Foucault (1977) sur la surveillance et la gouvernementalité (Vallentin & Murillo, 2012) dans le but de décrypter les processus par lesquels les rapports de pouvoir sont véhiculés. Selon Gond et Nyberg (2017), et à travers les analyses de Banerjee (2000), cette dernière perspective est aussi celle qui a montré, pour le cas de la mine de Jabiluka en Australie, comment le RSE a contribué à la manipulation des communautés locales afin de permettre l'instauration d'une nouvelle forme de colonisation.

Ces notions de dés/enchevêtrement mises en perspective par rapport à l'avènement de l'ère pétrolière au Tchad pourraient signifier que, dans le complexe pétrolier, les groupes stratégiques, à savoir, entre autres, l'État, les entreprises et les communautés locales, la société civile et les institutions internationales impliquées dans lesdits projets, cherchent à valoriser une ressource qu'est le pétrole à travers les activités de la chaîne de valeur extractive en tenant compte des enjeux sociaux, économiques et environnementaux matérialisés par les initiatives RSE. Autrement dit, les pratiques RSE sont interpellées ici dans les projets pétroliers au Tchad en raison de leur influence locale. En observant comment les initiatives RSE s'intègrent dans les projets pétroliers au Tchad à travers les pratiques initiées sous les différents registres philanthropiques, juridiques, libéraux et éthiques, nous étudions empiriquement quels groupes stratégiques bénéficient des pratiques de RSE respectives. Nous montrons comment la question d'enchevêtrement et de dés/enchevêtrement est au cœur des initiatives RSE, ou tout au long de la chaîne de valeur extractive, et les dynamiques de pouvoir soutenus par les discours et pratiques dans les projets pétroliers ayant pour but la lutte contre la pauvreté au Tchad. L'agencement de ce travail soutient l'hypothèse selon laquelle les communautés locales constituent le maillon faible du complexe pétrolier au Tchad et ont par conséquent, ce comparativement aux autres groupes stratégiques, un accès limité aux avantages que procure l'exploitation pétrolière.

4 Les initiatives RSE au Tchad

Les initiatives RSE sont les produits des dispositifs de gestion environnemental et social. A l'origine, ces pratiques RSE, financées par les multinationales et les entreprises de sous-traitance, sont relatives aux initiatives de formation des communautés locales, des projets relatifs à la santé, de l'emploi, des campagnes de sensibilisation publique ou de construction des infrastructures dans la région productrice (Cash, 2012). Ces initiatives montrent combien la société pétrolière s'intéresse aux enjeux locaux de développement et exprime son enchevêtrement au niveau local comme une entreprise citoyenne. Le consortium chapeauté par ExxonMobil dans le cadre du Projet de l'oléoduc Tchad-Cameroun, à partir de ces pratiques, a construit un modèle d'initiatives RSE au Tchad. On retrouve les mêmes types d'initiatives RSE développées par la CNPCIC et Glencore dans leurs zones d'exploitation pétrolière dans le pays. Mais il y a lieu de se demander si les mêmes initiatives produisent aussi les mêmes effets dans les contrées d'implantation des entreprises pétrolières au Tchad, à savoir EEPCI à Doba, CNPCIC à Koudalwa et Glencore à Badila et Mangara.

Malgré le manque de structures politiques officielles et institutionnelles réelles de promotion de la RSE dans les projets extractifs au Tchad, des pratiques sont promues toutes azimut et mobilisées sous divers registres (philanthropique, éthique, légal, volontaire ou discrétionnaire) par les multinationales. Les pratiques RSE sont accompagnées de discours d'enchantement et de désenchantement dans les zones productrices par les différents groupes stratégiques. En nous basant sur la pyramide de la responsabilité sociale de Carroll (1979) et les modèles RSE développés par Ritu et al (2001), nous avons pu faire un panorama des initiatives RSE adoptées par les entreprises pétrolières (Voir les images 1, 2 et 3). Ces initiatives RSE permettent de justifier les pratiques d'enchevêtrement ou de dés/enchevêtrement des entreprises multinationales dans les zones productrices de pétrole au Tchad.

5 Les illustrations des initiatives RSE dans les zones productrices du pétrole au Tchad

Dans leurs pratiques, les multinationales pétrolières au Tchad mobilisent des initiatives RSE qui participent, selon elles, au premier but du projet affiché qui est l'élimination de la pauvreté. Ainsi, sous les différents modèles RSE implémentés, des activités sont menées par les différentes entreprises afin de légitimer leur présence sinon leur enchevêtrement dans les contrées productives. Dans ce qui suit, nous examinons de plus près les différents modèles et nous nous interrogeons sur leurs effets tout au long de la chaîne de valeur extractive.

5.1 *Le modèle philanthropique*

Les trois entreprises se sont adonnées à la construction d'écoles, de magasins servant de greniers communautaires, de puits d'eau potable, de moulins etc. qui seront remis aux populations locales sous forme de dons des sociétés pétrolières (voir les images ci-dessous). Les dons de matériels agricoles ainsi que de fournitures scolaires sont aussi fréquents dans les zones riveraines et parfois dans la capitale du pays. Glencore donne les détails de ses initiatives en ces termes : 396m^3 de dons ont été remis à la communauté, notamment sous forme de déchets de bois, de ferraille, de matériaux de construction, de bouteilles en verre et de canettes vides (CNPCIC, 2014, 2016; EEPCI, 2019; Glencore, 2016, 2017).

Faces à ces initiatives RSE, les populations locales dénoncent une situation d'injustice dans la répartition de la rente pétrolière. Elles estiment que les entreprises et l'État acquièrent des sommes d'argent astronomiques

FIGURE 7.2 Tableau signalant la présence d'un moulin offert par Glencore au village de Ngarda
SOURCE: SEIGN-GOURA, 2016

issues de leurs ressources alors que, elles, n'ont droit qu'aux miettes se déclinant en compensations minables, en rebuts de bois ou autres biens

FIGURE 7.3 Etablissement scolaire offert par la ESSO, Petronas et SHT
SOURCE: SEIGN-GOURA, 2016

des chantiers pétroliers, ou encore en emplois de subalternes distribués sous couvert de dons et de philanthropie. Ce sentiment d'injustice dans le cadre du partage des avantages de la rente pétrolière ressort ici dans les propos d'un de nos interlocuteurs, ancien travailleur sur le site pétrolier à Doba :

> Nous n'avons droit qu'aux miettes dans ces projets alors que les entreprises et l'État raflent des millions. Toutes les choses qu'on nous donne individuellement ou collectivement à savoir les déchets de bois, les futs vides, les bâtiments scolaires etc…, ce n'est rien. Vous trouvez normal ce que ces gens-là (entreprises et État) font. C'est de l'injustice pure et simple. Et en plus, on ne peut rien faire.
>
> ENTRETIEN G, Doba 2016

Cette situation d'injustice est aussi dénoncée par les membres de la société civile qui aident les populations des contrées pétrolifères à développer des stratégies pour un accès plus équitable aux bienfaits de l'exploitation pétrolière. L'équation néolibérale à l'origine des projets pétroliers au Tchad à savoir les multinationales qui investissent leurs capitaux, la rente pétrolière qui est partagée entre les groupes stratégiques et l'effet de ruissellement qui atténue la pauvreté dans le pays n'a pas fonctionné comme prévu. Les propos de l'interlocuteur de la société civile rapportés ci-dessous éclairent cette perception :

> Vous voyez, l'histoire est en train de nous donner raison. Nous disions, il y a une dizaine d'années, que les conditions n'étaient pas réunies pour une exploitation responsable du pétrole au Tchad. On ne nous a pas écouté et voilà que l'histoire nous donne raison.
>
> ENTRETIEN. P, N'Djamena 2015

Autrement dit, les initiatives RSE philanthropiques perçues comme marginales, et loin des bonnes pratiques, par les populations locales, participent à la marginalisation des populations locales face aux enjeux de partage de la rente pétrolière entre les groupes stratégiques participant aux projets pétroliers dans les zones productrices. Dans la perspective de la gestion des risques, les multinationales pétrolières ont néanmoins mis en place une politique qui, selon leur argumentation, navigue entre la philanthropie et la gestion des risques sociaux et environnementaux. Cependant, et paradoxalement, elle crée une perception d'inégalité, d'injustice et d'appauvrissement entre les communautés locales qui revendiquent une implication locale dans l'industrie extractive, donc davantage d'accès aux bénéfices au lieu de leur marginalisation. Il semblerait donc que, pour se déresponsabiliser des obligations juridiques ou morales, les entreprises présentent leurs pratiques RSE comme relevant de la philanthropie et se déclinant en donations qu'il s'agisse des rebuts ou du matériel non-essentiel pour l'entreprise.

5.2 *Le modèle juridique*

Sous ce registre, on retrouve des initiatives justifiées comme des initiatives RSE, mais qui en principe se font pour respecter les obligations juridiques issues des contrats entre l'État et les sociétés pétrolières et qui ressortent dans les dispositifs normatifs des Études d'Impact Environnemental (EIE), Plan de Gestion d'Environnement (PGE), la législation du travail etc. Il s'agit des plans de compensation, de restauration des carrières et de réinstallation des populations qu'exigent les législations nationales et internationales dans les situations où le système de gestion environnemental et social est déficitaire. Alors qu'elles cherchent à se conformer à ces normes juridiques, les entreprises présentent aussi leurs initiatives comme relevant de la RSE planifiée. Ainsi, dans leurs rapports annuels, sont évoqués des dizaines de milliers de francs versés aux populations en termes de compensations individuelles ou communautaires, de surfaces restaurées et remises aux populations locales ou de coûts de la réinstallation d'une famille dans une zone hors de danger. EEPCI évoque 6,3 Millions de dollars US de compensations communautaires en 2015, la CNPCIC a dépensé 300,000 USD pour la construction de 24 puits d'eau pour 25000 habitants de 21 villages qui dépendaient des eaux de mare dans sa zone d'activité en 2015, tandis que Glencore dit avoir recruté 760 habitants de la zone pétrolifère, dont 74 femmes pour différentes catégories de travail : signaleurs (hommes/femmes), aides à la construction, coupe des herbes et nettoyage (EEPCI, 2016; CNPCIC, 2016; Glencore, 2016).

Comment ces pratiques de la RSE juridiques sont-elles perçues par les communautés locales ? Un travailleur pétrolier pense que l'exploitation pétrolière en soi est une bonne chose car tout le monde est gagnant dans cette activité :

> Le pétrole coule, mais l'argent rentre aussi dans nos poches. Tout le monde gagne : l'État, les entreprises pétrolières, les entreprises de sous-traitance, les salariés, les populations locales, etc. Le pétrole, c'est ça du vrai business…On aurait pu exploiter cela depuis longtemps.
>
> ENTRETIEN F, N'Djamena 2016

Même si ici le travailleur proclame une situation gagnant-gagnant du secteur extractif qui soutient la logique néolibérale selon laquelle il y a un effet positif du fait des avantages issus de l'effet de ruissellement dans un modèle d'investissement capitaliste, un de ces avantages étant la rente pétrolière, on peut se demander s'il y a vraiment de l'équité dans le système de partage des avantages et des risques issus de l'exploitation pétrolière entre les acteurs du complexe pétrolier. Ce questionnement est aussi révélé dans les propos ci-dessous émanant d'un autre observateur qui se plaint que les travailleurs du pétrole sont encore plus mal lotis qu'avant l'exploitation du pétrole :

> Le bilan après une décennie d'exploitation pétrolière est que le Tchad est devenu le cimetière des travailleurs pétroliers. Ceux qui ne sont pas morts, ont fini par le divorce ou la clochardisation ou une vie de misère. Beaucoup d'entre eux n'imaginaient pas une telle récession due à la fluctuation du prix du pétrole. L'ère de l'embellie pétrolière est terminée, c'est la fin de l'Eldorado pétrolier. Ça a duré moins de dix ans et les dégâts sont énormes.
>
> ENTRETIEN. B, N'Djamena 2016

On observe donc que les uns (communautés locales et autres groupes apartés) se contentent des initiatives RSE dont les coûts sont minables, alors que les autres (État, entreprises) se partagent d'énormes revenus engendrés par les retours sur investissements, les royalties et autres. Cette injustice dans le partage de la rente pétrolière dans le complexe pétrolier est une illustration des enjeux de pouvoir présents au sein des groupes participant à la gouvernance ou dans l'arène pétrolière. Dans cette arène, les uns et les autres développent des stratégies pour capter la rente pétrolière, qu'elle soit minime ou gargantuesque. Le cadre institutionnel de la répartition des avantages issus des projets pétroliers (régime fiscal, royalties, dividende revenant à la région productrice, bénéfices issus du pétrole etc.) garantit une répartition structurelle et donc inégale de la rente pétrolière entre les groupes stratégiques participant aux projets.

5.3 *Le modèle libéral*

Ce modèle fait référence à l'utilitarisme qu'impose le modèle d'économie libérale. Les initiatives déclinées par les entreprises font partie de leur business model mais celles-ci les présentent comme des initiatives RSE utiles aux communautés locales et aux autres groupes stratégiques participant aux projets extractifs. Il s'agit du respect des normes de régulation environnementale ainsi que des normes sécuritaires et sanitaires dont la négligence engendrerait des coûts pour les entreprises pétrolières ou un risque pour la poursuite de leur activité. La rigueur des managers quant à l'implémentation de ces mesures sur les chantiers pétroliers montre combien ces initiatives sont capitales, autant pour lesdites sociétés que pour les communautés locales. En effet, il a été observé dans les rapports d'EEPCI qu'une violation des normes de sécurité, considérée comme grave, ouvre la voie à des sanctions allant d'avertissements au renvoi immédiat du chantier pour les travailleurs locaux, et au rapatriement immédiat pour les expatriés. Aussi, les entreprises félicitent très souvent leurs employés pour des heures de travail sans incidents, sinon sans accident fatal, pour des déversements accidentels d'hydrocarbures maitrisés, pour des voleurs arrêtés ou encore pour des campagnes de sensibilisation des populations locales. Les rapports réguliers des départements de l'environnement, socio-économique ou de sécurité valorisent souvent ces initiatives relatives à la protection de l'environnement et à la sécurité des biens et des personnes sur les chantiers pétroliers. Des cadeaux symboliques, mais ayant parfois une valeur financière considérable, sont distribués aux employés en récompense de leur conduite responsable en matière de sécurité.

Dans son rapport annuel de 2018, Essochad, se félicite d'avoir réalisé une réduction de 50% des vols– entre 2006 et 2016, il y avait un à deux cas de vols par jour dans ses installations), ou d'avoir assuré un support continu des communautés locales et des forces de sécurité, et d'entretenir d'excellentes collaboration avec les autorités locales de la zone pétrolifère (EEPCI, 2019). Dans la même lignée des pratiques RSE, la CNPCIC valorise ses résultats relatifs au domaine de la santé, de l'environnement et de la sécurité en termes de formation : en 2015, la société a organisé 190 formations, 1906 personnes y ont assisté tandis que ses entreprises de sous-traitance ont fait leurs propres formations pour 6153 bénéficiaires (CNPCIC, 2016). Ou encore, concernant la sécurité, elle dit avoir révisé plus de trente plans d'urgence, et avoir fait 150 exercices d'urgence (CNPCIC, 2016). Glencore se félicite aussi de ses performances en 2016 (Glencore, 2017). Cela concerne plusieurs domaines : le domaine de la sécurité avec un an de travail sans accident ayant entrainé des arrêts de travail (LTI) et la diminution de la fréquence totale des blessures enregistrées (TRI) ; Le domaine de l'acquisition de terres avec 14 personnes concernées et payées 8 638 dollars américains ; le domaine des dégâts réparés avec 51 réclamations liées à des dommages matériels qui ont été jugées recevables et payées 16 103 dollars pour 8, 32 hectares.

Au niveau local, la perception de ce dispositif libéral et des initiatives RSE est mitigée comme constaté dans les propos de nos interlocuteurs représentant une catégorie des communautés locales :

> Nous étions sans problème, sans le pétrole. Et Satan nous a envoyé le pétrole avec tous ces Blancs.
>
> ENTRETIEN O, Komé 2016

> Et croire qu'on nous a promis que le projet pétrolier durerait 30 ans. Ils nous ont eus.
>
> ENTRETIEN Q, Doba 2015

Les entreprises se défendent par des initiatives RSE qui valorisent la conformité aux normes, les activités discrétionnaires qui sont au-delà des normes prescrites et à l'avantage des communautés locales. Sous ce modèle, les initiatives RSE s'intègrent dans la perspective de gestion des risques liés au système d'exploitation capitaliste. Un risque non géré par ce dispositif de sécurité dans lequel le monitoring du Plan de Gestion Environnemental constitue un coût pour l'entreprise. Un coût qui impacterait l'objectif de maximisation des profits que garantissent les dispositifs Santé, Sécurité et Environnement en place dans les zones pétrolifères.

5.4 *Le modèle éthique*

Ce modèle fait théoriquement référence aux initiatives développées par les entreprises pour des raisons sous-entendues éthiques qu'elles considèrent devoir à la société d'une manière globale. Dans le contexte tchadien, les projets extractifs se situent dans des zones rurales qui manquent cruellement d'infrastructures de base dans les domaines de la santé, de l'éducation et du transport. En côtoyant ces populations locales démunies, et si elles ont une sensibilité éthique, les entreprises pétrolières peuvent, grâce à leur important pouvoir financier, intervenir à travers des initiatives pouvant atténuer les difficultés et les manquements des communautés locales. La construction de centres de santé et d'infrastructures routières pour faciliter les mobilités, la construction de barrages hydroélectriques sont d'une grande utilité pour les populations locales et c'est en ce sens que ces initiatives devraient être promues.

Dans le contexte des initiatives RSE au Tchad, les œuvres à usage communautaire, notamment la construction des puits d'eau potable, des moulins et des magasins par les multinationales pétrolières, peuvent rentrer dans ce modèle-là.

Comment ces pratiques du modèle de la RSE éthique sont-elles perçues par les communautés locales ? Les cliniques sur les chantiers ne sont pas ouvertes aux populations riveraines qui en ont réellement besoin. Or, dans ces contrées, l'État brille par son absence dans l'offre de services publics relatifs à la santé, à l'éducation, aux infrastructures de transport et à d'autres besoins élémentaires. L'État ne manque pourtant pas d'assurer son rôle de garant de la sécurité des biens et du personnel des multinationales pétrolières dans lesdites zones afin que l'extraction du pétrole se fasse sans gêne et sans risque. Les propos ci-dessous de ces interlocuteurs de la société civile illustrent bien la perception de ces initiatives :

> Le pétrole du Tchad a été vilipendé aux sociétés étrangères par un club d'amis. Qui était aux négociations des contrats ? Personne, sinon le président de l'époque avec sa clique d'amis ou de protégés.
>
> ENTRETIEN G, Doba 2016

> Ce sont les intérêts qui priment ici avec le pétrole. Ces entreprises ne sont pas là pour nos beaux yeux et pour la construction des infrastructures pour notre développement. Dites-moi ce qu'elles ont fait en une décennie ? Rien, sinon prendre notre pétrole et nous le revendre cher.
>
> ENTRETIEN Y, Koudalwa 2016

Autrement dit, au Tchad, les multinationales pétrolières se sont contentées d'aménager les routes utiles pour leurs travaux aux détriments de celles pouvant désenclaver un village entouré de puits de pétrole afin de permettre les communications avec les autres villages des zones pétrolières ou d'accéder en sécurité aux villes proches pour écouler leurs marchandises par exemple. Les pistes arrangées sont utiles aux entreprises ou à leurs employés dans la zone pétrolifère alors que celles utiles aux populations sont délaissées dans un état lamentable, les rendant parfois impraticables en saison des pluies. Ces investissements intéressés des entreprises pétrolières et leur non-intervention dans certains espaces qu'elles jugent appartenir à l'État illustrent aussi leur engagement et désengagement stratégique par rapport aux zones productrices dans lesquelles elles interviennent. Face aux revendications des communautés locales dans les zones pétrolières de Komé, des champs Rôniers, de Badila et Mangara, les entreprises pétrolières se déresponsabilisent des responsabilités sociétales prétextant qu'elles paient déjà des impôts à l'État à qui il revient de prendre ses responsabilités. Il n'est pas fortuit de se demander si le modèle de RSE éthique est implémenté dans le contexte Tchadien au regard de ces pratiques et justifications.

6 Discussion

Toutes ces initiatives RSE illustrent donc que, dans ce contexte d'État-absent ou fragile dans l'offre de services publics de base dans les zones pétrolifères et de multinationales fuyant leurs responsabilités face aux attentes des populations locales et au partage de la manne issue de leurs terroirs, la responsabilité sociale des entreprises semble être aussi une voie de partage de la rente adoptée par ces dernières. Les quatre registres d'initiatives RSE (du modèle éthique, philanthropique, libéral au juridique) coexistent dans le secteur pétrolier au Tchad. Leur mise en œuvre est aussi une illustration des jeux de pouvoir existant dans l'arène pétrolière pour l'accès aux avantages qu'engendre l'exploitation du pétrole.

Le jeu de pouvoir aboutit donc à un jeu d'intégration ou d'exclusion selon la capacité de chaque partie prenante à valoriser ses ressources financières, institutionnelles ou informationnelles. Dans le contexte tchadien, une exigence légale de la mise en œuvre explicite d'une politique RSE n'existe pas mais, implicitement, dans les diverses normes exigeant des recrutements locaux et des politiques de compensation, la formation, les achats locaux, la sous-traitance des entreprises locales, le transfert de technologies etc. signifient qu'elle se profile. De pareilles exigences sont implicitement reparties dans les normes tels le Code du travail, le Code pétrolier, dans une certaine mesure les lois sur la gestion de l'environnement au Tchad, et donnent ainsi un pouvoir à l'État pour agir et demander leur implémentation par les multinationales. Leur mise en œuvre est aléatoire du fait de la méconnaissance de ces politiques par les communautés locales, de l'absence de mécanismes de mise en œuvre et de contrôle desdites normes et du fait de stratégies de camouflage adoptées par les entreprises par le biais de l'asymétrie d'information sur les projets pétroliers. On notera par exemple qu'au Tchad, les entreprises pétrolières n'évoquent pas les standards internationaux qui encadrent les pratiques RSE, à savoir le pacte global des Nations Unies, la Déclaration tripartite de l'Organisation Internationale du Travail, ISO 26 000, les normes sociales et environnementales de la Société Financière internationales etc. Les communautés locales ignorant ces normes, aucune revendication légale n'est faite et, les entreprises et les communautés locales mettent sur le dos de la philanthropie les initiatives RSE. Les sociétés civiles sensibilisent les communautés locales à ce propos. Cependant, la manipulation du savoir constitue un des pouvoirs qu'utilisent les entreprises au détriment des communautés locales.

Le dispositif institutionnel régissant le secteur extractif en adoptant ces dispositions relatives aux initiatives RSE garantit ainsi l'enchevêtrement du secteur pétrolier dans le contexte local. Ainsi, les pratiques des multinationales pétrolières au Tchad nous permettent d'apprécier l'élasticité du concept de RSE (Rajak, 2011a). Ce dernier est différemment apprécié par les acteurs du complexe pétrolier. Alors que les communautés locales attendent beaucoup des multinationales pour l'amélioration de leurs conditions de vie, ces dernières se contentent de quelques initiatives minimales mobilisées selon le contexte comme relevant de la philanthropie, par conformité aux normes, ou pour des raisons éthiques. La RSE brasse donc, dans ce contexte, le formel et l'informel, et comme l'appréhendent Gossling et Vocht (2007), elle pourrait être considérée comme une tentative d'assurer un équilibre entre les impératifs économiques, environnementaux et sociaux. Pour autant, la RSE ne renonce pas aux attentes des actionnaires et elle tente de restituer à la société ce que les entreprises lui ont retiré. Autrement dit, les initiatives sociales des entreprises auprès des communautés locales doivent tout d'abord servir leurs propres intérêts économiques. Dans cette perspective, les entreprises suivent les logiques utilitaristes et instrumentales du modèle économique néolibéral. Le fonctionnement en enclave des entreprises pétrolières est un aspect de leur dés/enchevêtrement au niveau local. Aussi, ces initiatives, au-delà de leurs mimétismes d'une entreprise à une autre, peuvent être considérées comme des stratégies entrepreneuriales pour se légitimer et pour éviter tout risque de mécontentement (sabotage, manifestation, etc) pouvant résulter en coûts pour ces dernières. A propos du délaissement du volet de la santé, Calain (2008) cite un expert qui dit ceci :

> ...it appeared that in this project, decisions were based largely on cost and profit considerations, giving only passing attention to environmental and social aspects, and little or no decision-making power to the affected populations.

Cette citation illustre à merveille la logique capitaliste qui se niche derrière les initiatives RSE alors qu'officiellement, elles sont présentées comme des gratuités ou des actes philanthropiques. Cela signifie donc que même la philanthropie paie dans les entreprises pétrolières. Les pratiques RSE et les discours qui les accompagnent, tels que présentés dans cette étude, suscitent assez de débats sur la contribution réelle des entreprises aux maux globaux de la société et des communautés des régions productrices vivant souvent dans des conditions précaires. On retrouve parmi ces maux la lutte contre la pauvreté et la perspective dans laquelle ont été envisagés les projets pétroliers au Tchad.

Ainsi, les quatre registres de la RSE et les discours des groupes stratégiques qui les accompagnent dans les zones pétrolières nous montrent combien l'approche instrumentale de la RSE est valorisée par les entreprises dans leur philosophie d'affaire basée sur la recherche du profit et non la philanthropie. Ces pratiques permettent aussi de gérer les risques socio-économiques, environnementaux et éthiques par la valorisation des normes dont leur négligence pourrait mettre en péril les activités des entreprises dans les différentes contrées productrices de pétrole.

Quant aux initiatives relevant du registre des modèles RSE, certains auteurs pensent que l'adoption de ces modèles par les entreprises permettent au système capitaliste de se réinventer pour un capitalisme dit responsable. Les initiatives vertueuses se justifient par la volonté des entreprises de perpétuer leurs activités sans risque à travers la chaîne de valeur extractive. Il y a donc ici, à travers ces pratiques RSE, un « marché de la vertu », pour reprendre le terme utilisé par Vogel (2005), pour designer la prolifération et la justification des initiatives RSE par les entreprises mues par le système capitaliste. Les modèles juridiques et économiques de la RSE s'imposent aux entreprises pour gérer les risques tandis que ceux dits philanthropique et éthique relèvent des pratiques socialement acceptées ou attendues des entreprises par la société. Dans les projets pétroliers au Tchad, l'instrumentalisation des initiatives RSE mise en place par les entreprises pétrolières participe à la justification d'un système d'exploitation capitaliste du secteur extractif permettant aux entreprises de se déresponsabiliser des enjeux sociaux, économiques et politiques locaux et de perpétuer la logique du marché. C'est aussi ce que relève Coll (2012, p. 367) en ces termes :

> The oil project did, however, allow ExxonMobil and its partners to generate several billions of dollars of topline revenue, to forge a path to profitability just as world oil prices spiked, and embed themselves with Deby's regime, positioning the corporation for additional oil deals beyond those covered by original bargain.

Autrement dit, le rapport enchevêtrement / désenchevêtrement observé dans les projets pétroliers est l'issu des pratiques des entreprises sur le terrain. Généralement, ces multinationales occidentales et asiatiques se livrent à des pratiques RSE parfois déconnectées des attentes locales. Rajak (2011b), Shever (2010), Reed (2009), Watts (2005) citent les initiatives RSE qui vont des programmes de développement local, en passant par les campagnes de sensibilisation des populations locales, les dons, aux bonnes relations avec les autorités. Ces initiatives rejoignent ainsi les registres des initiatives RSE observées dans les projets pétroliers au Tchad (cf. images 1, 2, 3 relatives aux initiatives RSE). Mais pour les sociétés pétrolières, il s'agit en réalité de gérer le système de gestion environnementale et sociale de l'entreprise et de garder de bons rapports avec l'État afin de perpétuer leur activité comme le fait remarquer Blowfield & Frynas (2005). Ces pratiques RSE amènent certains auteurs à dire que les politiques de durabilité et de protection de l'environnement ne sont que des formes de maximisation du profit (Porter & Kramer, 2002) ou de « greenwashing » dans un système capitaliste dont la logique est basée sur la destruction de l'environnement ou des ressources de la terre. Les populations locales des zones pétrolifères sont donc entraînées dans ces logiques capitalistes de profit sur les ressources de leur territoire qui signifient pour elles, marginalisation, exclusion et destruction de leur environnement. A travers les initiatives RSE, les communautés locales sont parfois marginalisées car les entreprises instrumentalisent les RSE sous forme de dons, de protection des populations locales et de l'environnement au lieu de prendre leurs responsabilités face aux conséquences locales et globales de leur activité.

Entre discours et pratiques RSE, celles de philanthropie et de responsabilités sociales, économiques et environnementales des entreprises, la notion de RSE prend la forme d'un mot caméléon (Dolan & Rajak, 2016, p. 5), soit pour camoufler les situations d'irresponsabilités des entreprises et les présenter sous forme d'initiatives de développement local, soit pour montrer combien les entreprises pétrolières assument leurs responsabilités sociales, voire éthiques au nom dudit capitalisme responsable. Ailleurs, comme au Nigeria, les motivations de ces initiatives RSE, comme relevées par Frynas (2005) dans le cadre des industries extractives, se déclinent entre autres en recherche d'avantages compétitifs, le maintien d'un travail stable, une politique de gestion des perceptions extérieures et le maintien du bien-être des employés des multinationales. Une situation qui se révèle similaire au Tchad.

Cette vision traduit ainsi l'agenda international de la RSE imposé par une vision des pays du Nord sur les sociétés africaines, comme instrument du développement durable et de la lutte contre la pauvreté sans prise en compte des réelles préoccupations des communautés locales des pays du Sud (Idemudia, 2011, p. 2). Le principe prépondérant dans l'arène extractive est ici la recherche de profit et non la promotion du développement local ou la lutte contre la pauvreté, des objectifs publiquement affichés. La RSE brasse donc, dans ce contexte, le formel et l'informel.

Ces dernières pratiques peuvent parfois masquer les intentions réelles des entreprises et apparaissent comme une théâtralisation de la vertu à travers les initiatives RSE (Rajak, 2011a). Des pratiques qui cachent les situations de marginalisation des populations locales ayant un accès limité aux avantages qu'offre l'exploitation des ressources de leur territoire par un système dit capitaliste, sous couvert des initiatives de RSE. Ces constats rejoignent ainsi l'hypothèse émise au départ de cette recherche et, dans une certaine mesure, la confirment dans le cadre des projets pétroliers au Tchad.

7 Conclusion

L'avènement des projets pétroliers au Tchad se situe dans un contexte particulier, celui de la lutte contre la pauvreté, attribué au premier projet ayant commencé dans les années 2000. Conjurer la malédiction pétrolière par les entreprises pétrolières est un phénomène ayant paradoxalement des effets néfastes dans les sphères économique, sociale et politique des pays riches en ressources naturelles et il reste un dilemme sinon un travail de Sisyphe. Les pays faisant exception et donc ayant pu profiter de l'exploitation des ressources naturelles, à l'instar du pétrole, avec un changement social positif, sont entre autres la Norvège, le Botswana, l'Australie, le Chili, le Canada pour ne citer que ceux-là, aussi rares soient-ils. Si ces pays ont pu conjurer la « malédiction pétrolière », c'est grâce, dit-on, aux institutions et aux bonnes politiques, qu'elles soient économiques, sociales ou politiques. Le Tchad s'est donc vu obligé de s'aligner en théorie à ce diktat pour faire de ses projets pétroliers une source de développement et donc de changement social positif. Sur le plan formel, tout a été fait pour une exploitation pétrolière responsable afin d'atteindre l'objectif de la lutte contre la pauvreté. La mise en œuvre de ce plan, notamment à travers le Projet de développement de l'Oléoduc Tchad Cameroun, le projet Rônier et ceux de Badila et Mangara, s'est heurtée aux logiques, représentations et attentes divergentes des groupes stratégiques du complexe pétrolier. Pour reprendre Vogel (2005), Rajak (2011b) et Frynas (2005), la vertu contre la pauvreté et le phénomène de sa théâtralisation par les initiatives RSE furent les fausses promesses du développement. Il s'est donc créée une dynamique de pouvoir entre les groupes stratégiques dont les communautés locales semblent être marginalisées par les structures de pouvoir régissant la gouvernance pétrolière dans le complexe pétrolier. Leur marginalisation ne se situe pas seulement dans des changements structurels causés par la présence des multinationales mais aussi dans les logiques capitalistes de profit qui sous-tendent l'exploitation du pétrole. Le concept de la RSE comme des/enchevêtrement nous a permis de saisir les dysfonctionnements structurels causés par le phénomène d'exploitation pétrolière dans les projets pétroliers et de mettre en exergue les formes de marginalisation, de pouvoir et de résistance des communautés locales faces aux dégradations environnementales, aux politiques de compensations, sinon de partage de la rente pétrolière. Les enjeux sociaux, économiques, culturels et politiques sont au cœur du partage des bénéfices mais aussi des méfaits – souvent inéquitables – de la rente pétrolière entre les groupes stratégiques. Autrement dit, le pétrole avec ses promesses, attentes et représentations crée des divisions entre les groupes stratégiques qui vont des multinationales, en passant par les sociétés civiles et l'État, aux populations locales. Les politiques de contenu local avec des dispositions impératives ne peuvent-elles pas participer à équilibrer ces rapports de pouvoir et ces dynamiques de partage de la rente entre les groupes stratégiques ?

Mais ces divisions existent-elles uniquement entre les critiques et les supporters des projets extractifs, les groupes stratégiques inclus dans le ou exclus du partage des bénéfices économiques des ressources naturelles, comme le font remarquer Aguilar-González et al. (2018) dans le cas du secteur minier au Guatemala, ou bien sont-elles révélatrices des maux profonds liés au système capitaliste d'extraction, de l'injustice environnementale, d'une situation d'iniquité envers une catégorie des groupes stratégiques, « un maillon faible » du complexe pétrolier que sont les communautés locales dans le cadre des projets pétroliers au Tchad et ailleurs ? Avec les pratiques de marginalisation et la résistance des communautés locales, les projets pétroliers sont au cœur d'une dynamique de changement social dont l'issue est incertaine. Mais pour le cas tchadien, le dispositif préparé par la Banque Mondiale et ses alliés a raté son objectif de lutte contre la pauvreté et a perpétué un système de partage inéquitable inhérent au système capitaliste. Dans ce contexte, la réussite dans le futur serait peut-être en fonction de la recherche d'un équilibre entre la recherche du profit, le bien-être des humains, et la protection de la planète dans un pays du Sud. Ce qui reste est un système à inventer sinon à expérimenter s'il existe déjà dans ce monde défié par la transition énergétique due au changement climatique dont est à l'origine le secteur extractif.

Références

Aguilar-González, B., G. Navas, C, Brun, A. Aguilar-Umaña, & Cerdán, P. (2018). Socio-ecological Distribution of Conflicts in the Mining Sector in Guatemala (2005–2013): Deep-rooted Injustice and Weak Environmental Governance. *The Extractive Industries and Society,* 5(3), 240–254.

Appel, H. (2012). Offshore Work: Oil, Modularity, and the How of Capitalism in Equatorial Guinea. *American Ethnologist,* 39, 692–709.

Baba, S. (2018). Analyse sociohistorique et épistémologique de la recherche en responsabilité sociale des entreprises. *Management international / International Management / Gestiòn Internacional,* 22(2), 96–111.

Banerjee, S. B. (2000). Whose Land Is It Anyway? National Interest, Indigenous Stakeholders, and Colonial Discourses. The Case of the Jabiluka Uranium Mine. *Organization and the Environment,* 13, 3–18.

Ben Rhouma, A., Koleva, P. & Schaltegger, S. (2018). RSE, management responsable et isomorphisme institutionnel: une analyse à partir des résultats d'une enquête internationale, *Management International* 22(3), 65–78.

Bierschenk, T. (1988). Development Projects as Arenas of Negotiation between Strategic Groups. A case of Study from Bénin. *Sociologia Ruralis,* 28(2–3), 146–160.

Blowfield, M., & Frynas, J. G. (2005). Editorial Setting New Agendas: Critical Perspectives on Corporate Social Responsibility in the Developing World. *International affairs*, 81(3), 499–513.

Bon, V. (2009). Les outils de la durabilité et de la RSE. Spécificités et récurrences. *Management & Avenir*, 6(26), 224–240. Retrieved 2019, October 2, from https://www.cairn.inforevue-management-et-avenir-2009-6-page-224.htm.

Calain, P., (2008). Oil for health in sub-Saharan Africa: Health Systems in a 'Resource Curse' Environment. *Globalization and Health*, 4(10).

Carroll, A.B. (1979). A Three-Dimensional Conceptual Model of Corporate Performance. *The Academy of Management Review*, 4(4), 497–505.

Carroll, A.B. (1991). The Pyramid of Corporate Social Responsibility: Toward the Moral Management of Organizational Stakeholders. *Business Horizons*, 34(4), 39–48.

Cash, Audrey C. (2012). Corporate Social Responsibility and Petroleum Development in Sub-Saharan Africa: The Case of Chad. *Resources Policy*, 37(2), 144–151.

CNPCIC (2014). CNPCIC 2013 Conférence de revue annuelle, Documentation, N'Djamena, Tchad.

CNPCIC (2016). CNPCIC 2015 Conférence de revue annuelle, Documentation, N'Djamena, Tchad.

Coll, S. (2012). *Private Empire: ExxonMobil and American Power*. New York: Penguin.

Dahlsrud, A. (2008). How Corporate Social Responsibility Is Defined: An Analysis of 37 Definitions. *Corporate Social Responsibility and Environmental Management*, 15, 1–13.

Dolan, C. & Rajak, D. (2016). Introduction: Toward the Anthropology of Corporate Social Responsibility. In C. Dolan & D. Rajak (Eds.), *The Anthropology of Corporate Social Responsibility,* (pp. 1–28). New York: Berghahn Books.

EEPCI (2016). *Projet de Developpement Tchad/Cameroun Mise à Jour du Projet n° 37*. Retrieved 2019, March 4, from https://cdn.exxonmobil.com/~/media/global/files/chad cam roon/chad_cameroon_project_update_37_ye2016_rpt_french.pdf.

EEPCI (2019). *Revue annuelle avec le gouvernement du Tchad pour l'année 2018*, N'Djamena Tchad.

Foucault, M. (1977). *Discipline and Punish*. New York: Pantheon Books.

Frynas, J. (2005). The False Developmental Promise of Corporate Social Responsibility: Evidence from Multinational Oil Companies. *International Affairs*, 81(3), 581–598.

Garriga, E., & Melé, D. (2004). Corporate Social Responsibility Theories: Mapping the Territory. *Journal of Business Ethics,* 53, 51–71.

Gary, I., & Reisch, N. (2004). *Le pétrole Tchadien : miracle ou mirage ? Suivre l'argent du dernier-né des pétro-États d'Afrique*. Baltimore: Catholic Relief Services et Bank Information Center.

Glencore (2016). *Revue annuelle 2015*. N'Djamena/ Tchad.

Glencore (2017). *Revue annuelle 2016*. N'Djamena / Tchad.

Gond, J-P., & Nyberg, D. (2017). Materializing Power to Recover Corporate Social Responsibility. *Organization Studies*, 38(8), 1127–1148.

Gossling, T., & Vocht, C. (2007). Social Role Conceptions and CSR Policy Success. *Journal of Business Ethics*, 74(4), 363–372.

Groupe International Consultatif (GIC) (2009). *Le Projet d'Exploitation Pétrolière et d'Oléoduc Tchad-Cameroun. Rapport final. Retrieved 2019,* October 3, from http://siteresources.worldbank.org/INTCAMEROON/Resources/GIC_Projet_Tchad-Cameroun_Rapport_Final_3-sept-2009.pdf.

Hanlon, G. (2008). Rethinking Corporate Social Responsibility and the Role of the Firm: On the Denial of Politics. In A. Crane, A. McWilliams, D. Matten, J. Moon, & D. Siegel (eds.), *Oxford handbook of corporate social responsibility* (pp. 156–172). Oxford: Oxford University Press.

Idemudia, U. (2011). Corporate Social Responsibility and Developing Countries Moving the Moving the Critical CSR Research Agenda in Africa Forward. *Progress in Development Studies* 11(1), 1–18.

Olivier de Sardan, J.-P. (2008). *La rigueur du qualitatif: Les contraintes empiriques de l'interprétation socio-anthropologique*. Louvain-la-Neuve: Academia-Bruylant.

Petry, M. & Bambé, N. (2005). *Le pétrole du Tchad, rêve ou cauchemar pour les populations?* Paris: Karthala.

Porter, M. E., & Kramer, M. R. (2002). The Competitive Advantage of Corporate Philanthropy. *Harvard Business Review*, 12: 1–15.

Rajak, D. (2011a). Theatres of Virtue: Collaboration, Consensus and the Social Life of Corporate Social Responsibility. *Focaal*, 60, 9–20.

Rajak, D. (2011b). *In Good company. An Anatomy of Corporate Social Responsibility.* Stanford, California: Stanford University Press.

Reed, K. (2009). *Crude Existence. Environment and the Politics of Oil in Northern Angola.* Berkeley: University of California Press.

Ritu, K., David, F., Murphy, V. B. (2001). *Understanding and Encouraging Corporate Responsibility in South Asia: Update One. Altered Images: the 2001 state of Corporate Responsibility in India Poll.* Tata Energy Research Institute, New Delhi, India.

Shamir, R. (2005). Mind the Gap: The Commodification of Corporate Social Responsibility. *Symbolic Interaction*, 28, 229–253.

Shever, E. (2010). Engendering the Company: Corporate Personhood and the "Face" of an Oil Company in Metropolitan Buenos Aires. *PoLAR: Political and Legal Anthropology Review* 33(1): 26–46.

Vallentin, S., & Murillo, D. (2012). Governmentality and the Politics of CSR. *Organization*, 19, 825–883.

Vogel, D. (2005). *The Market for Virtue: The Potential and Limits of Corporate Social Responsibility.* Washington: Brookings Institution Press.

Watts, M. (2005). Righteous Oil? Human Rights, the Oil Complex, and Corporate Social Responsibility. *Annual Revue of Environmental* Research, 30, 373–407.

Liste des entretiens au Tchad

(pour garder l'anonymat des enquêtés (es), nous avons nommé les interlocuteurs par les lettres de l'alpabet français).
Entretien E, Bebedjia, 2015
Entretien M, Koudalwa, 2015
Entretien F, N'Djamena, 2016
Entretien G, Doba, 2016
Entretien P, N'Djamena, 2015
Entretien E, Bebedjia, 2015
Entretien B, N'Djamena, 2016
Entretien Q, Doba, 2015
Entretien O, Komé 2016
Entretien M, Koudalwa, 2015
Entretien Y, Koudalwa, 2016

8

Tullow Oil, Corporate Social Responsibility and Dis/Entanglement in Uganda's Oil Industry

Laura Smith and James Van Alstine

1 Introduction

Oil exploration has pushed into new frontier locations; ultra-deepwater drilling in the world's oceans, exploration into remote, ecologically sensitive, and previously inaccessible locations; the Arctic, further into the Amazon, and into so-called fragile states in sub-Saharan Africa. East Africa saw a flurry of exploration activity in the early 2000s; Uganda, Kenya, Tanzania, and Mozambique were among those countries at the forefront of a much-hyped East African oil and gas boom (Frynas & Paulo, 2007). Oil discoveries in Uganda are one of the biggest on the continent in 30 years; an estimated 6.5 billion barrels of oil are thought to lie beneath the Lake Albert basin, in the western part of the great East African Rift system. Initial exploration activity in the Albertine Graben - considered a high-risk outlier prior to exploration success - was subsequently taken over by major oil players.

Uganda's oil industry has remained in a state of "not-yet-ness" since discoveries of commercial oil in 2006 (Witte, 2018). Tullow Oil planned to start an Early Production Scheme to produce 4000–5000 barrels of oil per day in 2009, but this never happened. A series of setbacks and delays followed for the industry and for Tullow. During this time, Tullow took Uganda over the commercial threshold for oil in 2009, changed from junior wildcatter exploration company to an oil producing company, and brought in major oil players CNOOC and Total E&P to develop the oil project towards production in a joint venture partnership (JVP). Oil Production is still some years away, with Total announcing a possible target of 2025 for first oil (Musisi, 2021).

This chapter focuses on the Corporate Social Responsibility (CSR) and community engagement activities of Tullow Oil in Uganda, throughout the pre-oil stage and towards the development and production phases of the industry. Tullow Oil is the only oil company that was present in Uganda from the early oil exploration stages to the development phase and during this time Tullow Oil's CSR and community engagement changed considerably. Through the lens of dis/entanglement and standardisation work that takes place in

 DOI:10.1163/9789004530065_009

contemporary extractives contexts, we analyse Tullow's changing approach to CSR and community engagement as the company transitioned from a wildcatter to an oil producing company. At the beginning of the oil exploration period, Tullow's concentration of CSR investment in a small number of villages in the Albertine Graben entangled the company and created patron-client relationships. Then, as Tullow Oil moved towards the oil production phase, they began to use CSR strategically as a means both to minimise social and environmental impacts on local communities and minimise the potential for reputational and operational risk to Tullow. The use of international industry norms and standards to guide CSR in this phase enabled Tullow to distance themselves from the complexities of the local context, however, complex entanglements were inevitable. The case of Tullow Oil highlights the challenges inherent in oil companies relying on CSR to earn trust locally by providing benefits, and at the same time maintain distance to minimise impacts.

The data for this chapter were collected during several field visits to Uganda's oil region and Kampala between 2012 and 2016. We conducted semi-structured interviews, focus group interviews, and follow up interviews with a range of actors, including community members, village leaders, local government officials, oil company representatives, Civil Society Organisations (CSOs) and beneficiaries of Tullow Oil's CSR projects. We observed CSO workshops, oil company stakeholder engagement meetings and multi-stakeholder workshops on oil and gas. We also drew on newspaper sources, CSO documents and oil company CSR reports.

The rest of the chapter is organised as follows. The next section outlines the literature on standardisation, dis/entanglement work, and CSR to frame our discussion. We then present the background and context for oil exploration in Uganda, before going on to show Tullow's changing approach to CSR and community engagement from the period of wildcatter oil exploration, to Tullow's transition to an oil producing company and partner of Total and CNOOC. The section that follows analyses Tullow's changing CSR and community engagement through the dis/entanglement lens.

2 CSR as Dis/Entanglement

Corporate Social Responsibility (CSR) in the extractive industries emerged in response to a crisis of legitimacy facing the sector in the early 2000s, amid increasing social conflict and overwhelming evidence that so-called host communities continued to suffer significantly from the negative effects of resource extraction. At the same time, growing demand for fossil fuels from newly emerging markets coupled with the early 2000s commodities boom raised new hopes of the potential for extractives-based development in the Global South. The 2009 Africa Mining Vision placed Africa's natural resource wealth central to Africa's development in the 21st century (African Union, 2009), while Latin America's "new extractivism" promised a more equitable extractives model. Therefore, how the extractive industries contribute to development continued to be the subject of contentious debate.

In response to increased scrutiny of the sector, industry assessments of the extractive industries' role in development, such as the Extractive Industries Review and Global Mining Initiative, placed greater responsibility on the private sector for ensuring more positive outcomes. The World Bank acknowledged that host governments and communities were demanding that benefits from extractives projects, including jobs, infrastructure, and community development are shared with local people (Mayorga Alba, 2009). Corporate Social Responsibility emerged as a solution for addressing these challenges; seen as both a means to improve legitimacy of the sector and as a tool for creating positive value and contributing to local development (Smith et al., 2018). CSR definitions vary, but generally CSR is a form of self-regulation by which a corporation incorporates social and environmental concerns into their business operations on a voluntary basis (UNIDO, no date). The inherent tension between the aims of ensuring legitimacy and a social licence to operate, while creating positive value through CSR is what this chapter seeks to explore.

In the context of increased global scrutiny of oil operations and changing expectations of stakeholders, the need to demonstrate detachment has become important for oil companies to gain the social licence to operate, which broadly denotes societal acceptance of the company and the oil project (Joyce and Thomas, 2000). The success of the global human rights movement in exposing oil MNC complicity in human rights abuses means that oil companies must demonstrate that they are distant from the locality that might be experiencing conflict, corruption and violence (Barry, 2006). With environmental concerns increasing, high standards in health and safety and a clean image have become important to reassure shareholders, especially in the aftermath of disasters such as the 1989 Exxon Valdez spill (Appel, 2012). CSR in the form of international norms and performance standards provided the means for companies to demonstrate a commitment to social and environmental responsibility (Buxton, 2012). The Voluntary Principles on Security and Human Rights, the Extractive Industries Transparency Initiative (EITI), the Global Reporting Initiative (GRI), IFC performance standards, and the Equator Principles are standards that aim to guide companies to improve (or minimise) their social and environmental impacts (Slack, 2012). Barry (2006) argues that this shift towards standardisation in the industry enables oil companies to demonstrate detachment by creating spatial separation from the local space by establishing "zones of standardisation;" spaces within which differences between technical practices have been reduced or common standards have been established. Appel (2012) has also shown that standardisation in the oil industry is a form of deliberate disentanglement work, which enables companies to demonstrate distance from the "unruly surroundings" of extraction sites. As such, CSR in the oil and gas sector has been employed to distance and disentangle oil MNCs from the contexts in which they are deeply enmeshed. As Witte (2018) points out, adherence to international standards of conduct is closely related to managing risk (both to reputation and to operations), and to minimise negative effects on shareholder value, on which oil companies depend. CSR programmes thus serve the dual purpose of ensuring legitimacy at the international level by demonstrating that companies are responsible global citizens and helping to gain local acceptance of the company (a social licence to operate) (Billo, 2015).

However, the use of CSR to secure an oil company's local presence has raised numerous problems, both for the company and host communities. So-called first-generation CSR by extractives companies was characterised by philanthropy and gift giving, for example in the form of donations and infrastructure projects (Frynas, 2009). A key critique of this type of CSR was that it blurred the line between the role of extractives companies and the role of the state, causing local people to make rights demands to companies and creating patron-client relations (Rajak, 2011). This was a challenge facing many extractives companies operating in marginalised and impoverished locations where social development investment was lacking (Owen & Kemp, 2013). To establish their presence, companies provided what are conventionally seen as "public goods": health infrastructure, education, roads, income projects. In some cases, the state was failing to deliver development, such as in Nigeria where oil companies effectively took over the delivery of state functions (Frynas, 2009), and in Chad, where oil companies filled the void where the state has pushed the responsibility for social service provision onto companies (Cash, 2012). CSR in these contexts risked undermining the state's capacity as local development agent and created community dependency on companies to deliver public services (Campbell, 2012). Further, CSR programmes unwittingly became part of local socio-political dynamics, exacerbating existing social tensions and causing divisions within communities between those that benefitted from CSR and those that did not (Gilberthorpe & Banks, 2012). Because companies' motivations for delivering social development were for reputation management and to secure a social licence, community development benefits were incidental.

Given the great variance in development benefits to communities, high levels of dependency and social unrest, the operational and reputational risk to companies increased and undermined legitimacy in the long run (Frynas, 2009).

To address the potential for CSR to increase rather than decrease risk to companies, second-generation CSR sought to avoid the kinds of activities that were said to lead to dependency and generate community discontent. Approaches moved away from gift giving and philanthropy towards strategic CSR, which involved "empowering" or "nurturing" approaches to CSR to promote community self-reliance (Frynas, 2005; Rajak, 2011; Billo, 2015). This has been inspired by the business case approach to CSR which flags not only compatibility, but synergies between doing good and profitability:

> Approached strategically, [CSR] generates opportunity, innovation, and competitive advantage for corporations—while solving pressing social problems.
>
> PORTER AND KRAMER, 2006, p. 1

These types of CSR projects aim for sustainability and tend to be delivered in partnerships with the community or a local NGO. A proliferation of standards, guidelines and tool kits emerged to help companies implement more participatory and empowering CSR that aimed for "win-win" outcomes. However, while these approaches sought to minimise dependency and avoid companies becoming patrons, critics argued that through projects emphasising partnership and participation, companies pushed responsibility onto those who were meant to benefit, while at the same time demonstrating they were being good corporate citizens (Billo, 2015; Gardner et al., 2012).

Furthermore, Billo (2015) and Shever (2010) showed that nurturing and empowering CSR were used as techniques to "manage" local communities and were directly related to the mitigation of operational risk to the companies. Himley (2010) also showed that partnering and "self-help" forms of CSR were being used to shape and contain community resistance against extractives projects. He argued that CSR was used by the company to co-opt sections of the community, whilst at the same time enabling the company to remain detached and unaccountable for outcomes. However, Gardner et al. (2012) highlighted that conversely, it was through such CSR projects that companies became active in the process of creating entanglements to the local space, even though the standards and guidelines that inform CSR seek to ensure distance. CSR and standards as disentanglement work overlooks that the extractive industries are inevitably deeply entangled in local spaces, and further, the role that CSR plays in fostering the entanglements.

3 Uganda's Oil Journey

Uganda's oil deposits lie in the Albertine Graben, in the remote western region of the country which forms the western part of the great Eastern African rift system. In the early 2000s, oil exploration in Uganda was an era of wildcatter exploration activity on the shores of Lake Albert; small oil exploration companies drilled wells in the hope of encountering hydrocarbons in a previously unexplored region that had little interest from bigger players at that time. These wildcatter oil companies were UK Heritage Oil, Australian Hardman, and South African Energy Africa. In 2004 Tullow Oil acquired wildcatter Energy Africa, marking its entry into Uganda. In 2006, after Hardman Resources found oil in three wells in block 2 Tullow Oil purchased Hardman and began to develop block 2 with 100% operating interests and blocks 1 and 3a alongside Heritage Oil in a Joint Development Agreement. Tullow Oil had a run of considerable success from early 2006 and planned an Early Production Scheme for 2009. In 2010 Tullow purchased Heritage's Uganda interests for $1.35 billion. As a stipulation of the Heritage purchase, the Ugandan Government required Tullow to bring in major oil players with the finance and technical know-how to develop the oil project to production.

Tullow began to work on a deal with French oil major Total SA and CNOOC, the Chinese state-owned China National Offshore Oil Corporation. However, as the stakes in Uganda's oil were raised, the industry became mired in controversy and setbacks. A dispute over Heritage Oil's unpaid capital gains tax from the Heritage sale led the Ugandan government to withhold the expired Kingfisher license in block 3a and pursue Tullow for the payment. This meant that Tullow Oil became embroiled in two lengthy legal disputes; Tullow was pursued by the Uganda Revenue Authority for the tax bill of $434 million, which Tullow paid to the Government; and then Tullow proceeded to sue Heritage Oil in a London court to recover the money. This case dragged on for much of 2011 and 2012 (Patey, 2015). In a further setback, Tullow Oil executives were accused by MPs of bribing three Ugandan ministers; allegations which Tullow Oil denied (Edwards, 2012).

In early 2012, the agreement to bring in the two oil majors Total and CNOOC in a "farm down" deal was finalised. Tullow sold two-thirds of its Uganda interests to the two companies; Tullow, Total and CNOOC each shared a third operating interests in all three blocks, with Total lead operator in Block 1, Tullow in Block 2 and CNOOC in block 3a. There were several contentious issues about industry developments that further delayed the oil project. By the time that Total and CNOOC joined Tullow in Uganda in the joint venture partnership (JVP), President Museveni was directly involved in negotiations with oil companies

FIGURE 8.1 Map of Uganda with area of exploration activities highlighted. Editors' illustration based on UN map no. 3862
SOURCE: HTTPS://WWW.UN.ORG/DEPTS/CARTOGRAPHIC/MAP/PROFILE/UGANDA.PDF

and was pushing the plan to build a large domestic oil refinery. The oil companies thought this an uneconomical and unfeasible project, but Museveni continued to lobby for Uganda to develop its own refining capacity, finally reaching an agreement for a 60,000 barrels per day refinery (Anderson and Browne, 2011). The negotiations then shifted to the pipeline, which is necessary to pipe Uganda's waxy crude across the country and out to the Indian Ocean. Tullow Oil favoured the initial plans for the pipeline to connect with the South Sudan pipeline and go through Kenya to the port of Lamu. However, this plan was then scrapped in favour of the Government and Total's preferred route through Tanzania to the port of Tanga, which was agreed upon in 2015 (Hickey & Izama, 2017).

Negotiations continued about the best way to develop the Albertine Graben basin. While CNOOC was awarded the production licence to develop the Kingfisher basin in 2013, Total and Tullow Oil did not receive the production licenses from the government until three years later, in August 2016 (Smith & Van Alstine, 2018). In the meantime, the oil price fell to below $50 per barrel in 2014. Tullow Oil, the smaller company of the JVP, was particularly affected by the price drop, which compounded the financial difficulties Tullow was already experiencing from the Heritage and Uganda Revenue Authority tax battle, as well as the ongoing delay to receiving the Uganda production licence. Tullow's earnings and stock market valuation were tied to the price of oil, and Tullow's share price fell drastically. Tullow Oil began to restructure, cutting back Uganda staff and focusing on its more profitable West African oil production and its interests in Kenya. In early 2017 Total announced that they would purchase a further 21.75% interest from Tullow Oil for $900 million, making Total the lead partner in the Uganda oil project and confirming rumours that Tullow may be planning to leave Uganda (Smith & Van Alstine, 2018). Tullow sold its remaining stake in Uganda to Total for $575 million in April 2020, marking its complete exit from the project (Nasralla, 2020).

After further delays to the planned oil pipeline, in December 2021 the Ugandan parliament passed the bill approving the oil pipeline construction, amid growing concerns about the environmental and human rights impacts of the project (Tumuhimbise, 2021). The East African Crude Oil Pipeline (EACOP) as it is known, will be a heated pipeline snaking 1,443 km through Uganda and Tanzania, carrying crude from Lake Albert to the Indian Ocean. It will start at the Tilenga and Kingfisher oil production sites in Hoima District in midwestern Uganda and end at Chongleani terminal, at Tanga port in Tanzania.

4 Tullow's Early CSR and Community Engagement in Uganda

In the early period of oil exploration by wildcatter exploration companies, CSR and community engagement was concentrated in the villages hosting the industry at the bottom of the steep escarpment on the shores of Lake Albert (figure 8.2). This region is physically isolated, and economically and politically marginalised

(De Kock & Sturman, 2012). The remote location added to the operational challenges facing wildcatters; interview respondents in the villages noted that oil companies brought equipment by boats down the lake to reach exploration sites not yet connected by road. Community engagement by wildcatters in these villages was ad hoc and informal; driven primarily by the need to access communal land and resources needed for exploration activities. Exploration work required temporary and permanent use of land to build company worker compounds, construct access roads to oil sites and carry out seismic work. The managers of the wildcatter oil companies liaised directly with village leaders to negotiate land access and resource use (interviews, village leaders, July 2014).

Oil companies made cash payments to village leaders and distributed opportunities to other local people: "They gave handouts, they hired locals as porters, they were getting food and good money. The companies were looked at as saviours" (interview, local government respondent, February 2015). Company personnel lived and worked in close contact with people from the villages whom they referred to as "neighbours" (interview, village elder, July 2014). In this phase therefore, wildcatter oil companies engaged in paternalistic types of CSR practices reflective of the first generation of CSR (Frynas, 2009).

While industry requirements of land and resource access were the main driver of interactions at this stage, the material conditions of the Albertine Graben were also influential. Tullow Oil, along with wildcatters Heritage Oil and Hardman Resources were hosted by communities in fish-landing sites (places where fish are collected and traded) along the lake. Sanitation is poor, outbreaks of cholera are frequent and social infrastructure is very minimal. Tullow Oil, Heritage Oil and Hardman Resources contributed to improving social amenities in their respective areas. However, because the companies implemented CSR at their own discretion, the support ranged from donations of materials in some villages to millions of dollars invested in infrastructure in others. Hardman gave a small wooden building (a former mess hall for Hardman workers) to one village to use as a school, Heritage Oil built a primary school and a health clinic in another village, and Tullow Oil built health clinics and schools in two other villages. Community respondents noted additional support including bore holes, and donations of educational and medical supplies. Interview respondents commented on improvements in basic hygiene and sanitation in the fish-landing sites; "the oil areas were no go zones, you have to appreciate the benefits" (interview, civil society organisation, July 2014). CSR and community engagement were not guided by the industry norms and standards for CSR that would shape engagement in the next phase of the oil project life cycle, but rather by the immediate needs of the industry to access land and the material conditions of the Albertine Graben.

FIGURE 8.2 The steep escarpment leading to the oil sites in Hoima District
IMAGE SOURCE: AUTHOR'S OWN

Due to Tullow Oil's emphasis on social development in its CSR strategy, Tullow went beyond what was usual for an oil exploration company by implementing several explicitly development-focused CSR projects in Uganda. This level of investment was partly because Tullow Oil planned for longer-term engagement in Uganda and partly due to the ambitions of Tullow Oil founder and then-CEO Aiden Heavey. Heavey's mission to make CSR a core Tullow value shaped Tullow's approach to CSR across the company in the early 2000s; he wanted to "do things differently," and ultimately gain competitive edge by being a CSR leader (Tullow Oil plc, 2010). Heavey intended to address what he saw to be key development needs of local people in the host communities in the Albertine Graben. In an interview with the Telegraph newspaper in 2007 Heavey commented:

> You find there are 30 people a month around the lake dying of cholera and you can do something by drilling a well for water. On average, 25 per cent of the babies would die at birth due to lack of hygiene, but it was the simplest thing in the world to solve: we built a little clinic.
>
> AIDEN HEAVEY, THEN CEO TULLOW OIL, QUOTED IN THE NORTHEDGE, 2007

Under Heavey's direction, Tullow Oil constructed a health centre, two schools and a maternity centre, and built a lifeboat station in the villages hosting its operations. Other CSR initiatives by Tullow in neighbouring villages included donating school supplies and mosquito nets, and training community peer educators to deliver health education in the villages. In 2012 Tullow reported expenditure of $4.8 million on social investment in Uganda since 2006 (Tullow Oil plc, 2012), most of which was planned in the context of record sales and growth, and high confidence in the Uganda oil project following the string of oil discoveries throughout 2006 and 2007. Tullow had expected to move towards development of the Ugandan oil fields by 2009.

Part of this social investment included creating several community focused projects that Tullow intended to become self-sustaining community enterprises. This CSR project was inspired by practices in international development that aimed to encourage community empowerment, and was typical of second-generation CSR (Billo, 2015). In 2005 Heavey won the Ernst & Young Entrepreneur of the Year award (Creaton, 2005). At the awards ceremony corporate leaders were challenged by the founder of international aid charity GOAL "to visit developing countries and see if they could make a difference by focusing their skills on helping communities to help themselves" and "to develop new commercial initiatives in addition to health and educational support projects" (Tullow Oil plc, 2010). It was in response to this challenge that Tullow implemented the community enterprise projects in one host village on the shores of Lake Albert in 2007.

The projects included a vegetable garden, an apiary, and a women's sewing project that would provide income generating opportunities to the community (Tullow Oil plc, 2010). Tullow Oil staff worked alongside community members to establish the projects, which were intended to eventually be taken over by the community and stand-alone from Tullow support (interviews, community members and Tullow CLOs, July 2014 and February 2015). This meant that during the early stages of oil exploration, in addition to ad hoc interventions, a "self-help" CSR project shaped by international development practice was implemented in a remote corner of Uganda.

The enterprise projects also played a strategic role for Tullow in terms of the company's goal of boosting its image and making a positive impact in Africa in an industry notoriously criticised for its negative impact (Tullow Oil plc, 2010). Tullow won an international CSR award for the enterprise projects in 2010, indicating the important role CSR played in shaping Tullow's international reputation (Nakaweesi, 2010). However, the CSR projects deeply entangled Tullow in what would be a temporary encounter between Tullow Oil and the Albertine Graben communities. As Tullow progressed towards becoming an oil producing company in Uganda, the company's CSR and community engagement strategy changed, with implications for local level relationships and local perceptions of Tullow Oil as a responsible company.

5 Tullow's Transition to Oil Producing Company

Tullow Oil passed the threshold for commercial oil in 2009 and was the only company to remain in Uganda throughout the period of transition to the development phase of the oil project. Tullow began negotiations with Total, CNOOC and the Government of Uganda to secure the deal to farm-down two thirds of its assets to the oil majors. Tullow's own transition from a wildcatter exploration company to an oil producing company meant that its CSR and community engagement strategy began to change to reflect industry norms and standards. Tullow's membership of the FTSE100 in 2007 increased its visibility to external stakeholders and opened it up to new regulations and standards in terms of its environmental and social responsibilities. At the same time, as the global interest in Uganda's oil industry increased, so did the scrutiny from international donors and NGOs concerned about oil governance in Uganda. Tullow began to draw on international industry standards and norms around CSR and social engagement to inform its strategy in Uganda and demonstrate to shareholders and stakeholders that it was a responsible operator.

One of the key changes to Tullow's approach was the introduction of Community Liaison Officers (CLOs) in 2009 to manage the community engagement function in Uganda. CLOs are Ugandan nationals originating from the oil region and possess in-depth knowledge of the local area, cultural and social practices, and local languages (in addition to English). The use of CLOs has become a standard practice in the oil and gas industry, and these roles (sometimes referred to as the social affairs or community relations function) are themselves central to the implementation of international industry standards of good practice (Bebbington et al., 2017). CLO interviewees discussed a range of international industry standards including International Finance Corporation (IFC) standards, UN guidelines and social performance norms to guide them in relation to human rights, community development and stakeholder engagement.

By 2012 Tullow's Ugandan community engagement team had grown to approximately eleven CLOs and field staff, a sign of Tullow's continued growth as well as a response to the increasingly demanding operational environment. At the local level, issues relating to land and compensation were becoming more challenging as the impacts of oil exploration accelerated. A large proportion of CLO work was around land acquisition and responding to grievances relating to land and compensation issues (interviews, Tullow Oil, July 2014, February 2015, August 2016).

The narrative and practice of Tullow's CSR also changed, with evidence that CSR was being used strategically and informed by international "best practice" on CSR. In interviews Tullow CLOs said that the new approach to CSR aimed to move away from CSR as a "one off" towards social investment and a "collaboration and partnership approach" which would be about "creating value" (interviews, Tullow Oil, July 2014 and February 2015). This contrasted with the earlier ad hoc and "hands on" approach to CSR. The change also reflected Tullow Oil's plans for longer-term engagement in Uganda as an oil producing company. As part of this shift, Tullow began to rely increasingly on external expertise to inform the Uganda strategy. In 2012 Tullow employed an international consultancy firm from the UK to evaluate Tullow Oil's existing CSR projects in Uganda and advise on CSR strategy going forward. The consultancy helped Tullow to "retro-fit" exit strategies for the village level CSR projects (interview, Tullow Oil, July 2014). The plan was to "scale up" CSR and focus on the wider district, on agri-business and agro-forestry, rather than continue to focus on village level initiatives. As a result, the village level CSR and community enterprise projects were no longer part of Tullow's vision for social investment in Uganda and were discontinued.

Tullow's community engagement strategy was further influenced by Tullow becoming embroiled in Ugandan politics. The tax litigation cases and bribery allegations were crises which prompted the focus more explicitly onto reputation management and engagement with a wider number of stakeholders. The allegations of bribery made against Tullow Oil resonated with ideas about oil and corruption and fuelled the concerns of Ugandans and the wider international community about the potential for a "resource curse" in Uganda. In this context the adherence to industry standards and norms to guide its operations in Uganda was important to maintain confidence among Tullow's shareholders and other powerful stakeholders.

In line with social performance norms and an attempt to demonstrate transparency, Tullow began to carry out formal quarterly stakeholder meetings with stakeholders at the district level in the oil region. Subnational government leaders, civil society organisations (CSOs) and media representatives, religious leaders and the Bunyoro Kingdom attended the respective stakeholder engagement meetings in Hoima town during which Tullow provided updates on oil exploration and explained any upcoming activities. Whereas Tullow had previously prioritised building support at the village level through relationships with village leaders, the shift to strategic CSR meant a geographical shift to the main town in the district for social engagement. In 2012 Tullow opened a "liaison office" in Hoima town, 90km away from the villages and this became the base in the oil region for Tullow's CLOs, enabling informal as well as formal engagements to take place at the district level. The geographical shift had implications for those living in the host villages in the oil region, as to reach the Tullow Oil office now required them to make a journey of over two hours on an unpaved road.

The focus of Tullow's CSR projects became explicitly tied to supporting operations. In interviews Tullow CLOs explained: "CSR is driven towards impact mitigation, towards social issues management [and is] geared towards addressing impacts" (interview, Tullow CLO, July 2014). Tullow's narrative around CSR changed to reflect this strategic approach; "we will not do anything that doesn't support our operations," a Tullow social engagement manager explained (interview, July 2014). In practice this meant that CSR became refocused on creating shared value through social investment, as per the business case (Porter & Kramer, 2006), or "Creating Share Prosperity" as Tullow framed it in their corporate responsibility report (Tullow Oil plc, 2012).

In accordance with the strategy developed by the international consultancy firm, Tullow implemented a district level agri-enterprise project called TraidLinks, which aimed to train farmers from the district to produce high quality vegetables and fruits to supply the oil and gas industry. In interviews Tullow Oil CLOs explained that the TraidLinks project was created in response to increasing demands among stakeholders in the district to benefit from the oil industry. TraidLinks was developed and implemented in partnership with an Irish NGO and a local farmers' association, and therefore was an example both of partnership working and a project of local empowerment. Tullow Oil provided the funding and the local partners implemented the project, providing training and capacity building for farmers and a collection point for produce to be quality checked and delivered to Tullow Oil's worker camps.

The shift to social investment and the "shared prosperity" approach therefore changed which people benefitted from CSR in the oil exploration period. From an initial concentration of CSR and community engagement at the village level centred on improving welfare and providing income opportunities, strategic CSR focused on creating longer-term value. This was directly linked to managing the oil project, both in terms of ensuring that Tullow Oil maintained shareholder confidence as a responsible operating company, and by meeting the expectations of a wider range of local stakeholders to secure a longer-term presence in Uganda.

6 Continuing Entanglements

Tullow Oil's early CSR and community engagement approach during the period of wildcatter oil exploration created entanglements at the village level. The instrumental use of CSR in this phase (in the form of handouts of money, donations, and social service provision) to gain access to land and resources established Tullow as a "patron" (Rajak, 2011). Local people began to relate their welfare to Tullow's presence in the villages. Interview respondents noted that improvements in sanitation, health and educational provision were because of Tullow, and it was clear that Tullow Oil had undertaken actions which encouraged the community to look to Tullow for support. For example, a village leader recalled that a Tullow manager said, "we are neighbours, and you can't see a neighbour suffering" (interview, July 2014).

Tullow's implementation of the community enterprise projects was explicitly linked to improving the welfare of the community by providing income opportunities. This CSR project established Tullow as a development actor in the region and further embroiled the company at the village level. While Tullow expected the enterprise projects to become self-sustaining as per modern and self-help approaches to CSR (Billo, 2015), the projects became caught up in the politics of the village which further entangled Tullow. Interview respondents noted that one of the enterprises was taken over by village elites and politicised (interviews, July 2014), a challenge that is common to development projects (Mosse, 2013). The people in the community turned to Tullow to resolve the issues because Tullow had implemented the project.

The extent of Tullow's entanglement at the village level was revealed when Tullow's CSR and community engagement strategy changed, and Tullow's presence in the villages reduced. Some interviewees within villages claimed to have been "left behind" by Tullow. For the village leaders accustomed to interacting with Tullow management, the introduction of Ugandan CLOs by Tullow symbolised an increasingly distant relationship. In contrast to the frequent interaction with managers during the earlier stage in the oil project life cycle, village respondents said: "We have missed out because we don't see the Tullow reps" (interview, July 2014). Indeed, village leaders no longer received the benefits and opportunities they had done in the wildcatter period. Other interviewees within the villages expressed concern that without Tullow's support the improvements made in education and health had reversed. The perceived gap left by Tullow's departure demonstrates the extent to which Tullow had fostered patron-client relationships in the village. The quotes also reflect the psychological distance that those in the villages perceived to exist between the bottom of the escarpment and the town 90 km away, reflecting the isolated and marginalised nature of the communities there.

Tullow's shift to strategic CSR enabled Tullow to detach from the village level. The use of the international consultancy firm to retrofit exit strategies to existing CSR projects can be seen as an effort to deliberately disentangle Tullow from the community enterprise projects that failed to become self-sustaining. According to respondents in the village, the exit strategies appeared to have led to an immediate removal of the projects; the sewing machines, beehives and other equipment "disappeared" (interviews, village members, July 2014). Even the lifeboat provided by Tullow was removed and the station locked (figure 8.3). The removal of the CSR enterprise projects from the village and closure of the lifeboat station further added to the sense of the community being left behind by Tullow. The disappearance of the CSR projects came to define the relationship between the village and Tullow Oil and this experience was mentioned by all respondents in the village during interviews in 2014, and was a story recalled many times in discussions with CSOs and other researchers in the region. Tullow's receipt of the CSR award for the community enterprise CSR projects in Uganda raises the question of who benefitted from Tullow's CSR? While village residents struggled to understand why the projects were taken away, Tullow secured a reputation at the regional and international level as a socially responsible oil company.

The shift to strategic CSR and social investment was also a means to minimise potential negative impacts by enabling Tullow to maintain a distance from the oil communities and the complexities of CSR. This demonstrates the blurred line between the aim of minimising impacts on the communities in terms of social and environmental harm, and minimising impacts on the company in terms of reputational and operational risk. Tullow's CSR investment during the wildcatter period was concentrated in only a few villages at the bottom of the escarpment. This led to claims by people in the surrounding villages that they were excluded from the benefits of the oil industry. Tullow Oil's CSR projects were providing social services and opportunities for some communities, which in the context of high poverty and marginalisation served to highlight the relative exclusion of others. Interview respondents in neighbouring villages perceived themselves to be impacted indirectly by oil exploration, by increased traffic, noise, and dust. Here, the negatives of oil exploration were being experienced without the benefits, therefore contestations around CSR began to emerge and the potential for community discontent increased. In interviews, district leaders and CSOs also criticised Tullow Oil's heavy investment in a small number of villages in the context of high needs and growing negative impacts of oil exploration (interviews July 2014 and February 2015).

FIGURE 8.3 The closed down Tullow Oil-funded lifeboat station in one of the host villages
IMAGE SOURCE: AUTHOR'S OWN

Tullow's social investment strategy aimed to broaden the number of local people that would benefit from the oil industry and reduce the risk of community discontent. At the same time, social investment through local partners was also a way for Tullow to maintain distance from the local context. However, the experience of Tullow's TraidLinks agriculture project shows the potential for complex entanglements to occur through strategic CSR. This is especially the case in the context of the short-term horizons for oil and gas, which conflict with the promise of longer-term empowerment through social investment and raises expectations that cannot be met. Tullow was providing 100% of the Traidlinks project funding for the first three years, known as phase one, and had promised funding for a further two years to fund phase two, which would have enabled farmers to supply to the oil industry in the future. In an interview in 2014, the TraidLinks project officer claimed that after six months of training some local farmers were already successfully supplying a small amount of farm produce to the oil camps (interview, TraidLinks, July 2014).

However, after the oil price crash in 2014 and restructuring within Tullow, the Uganda oil project was on hold and the number of Tullow workers living in the camps had reduced significantly. Tullow discontinued funding for the next phase (phase two) of the TraidLinks project. Therefore, while Tullow Oil had

FIGURE 8.4 Entrance to the Tullow Oil-funded Traidlinks agri-enterprise farmer training centre in Hoima town, Uganda
IMAGE SOURCE: AUTHOR'S OWN

continued to invest in CSR during the delays in the Uganda oil project throughout 2012 and 2013 due to the commitment to CSR across the company, Tullow's status as a small independent oil company meant that subsequent financial constraints experienced by the company impacted its ability (and willingness) to maintain the levels of CSR spend in Uganda. In a follow up interview with TraidLinks in 2016 the project officer explained with regret that without the demand for food in the worker's camps and no guarantee of further funding from Tullow, the TraidLinks project had collapsed (interview, Traidlinks August 2016).

The Traidlinks case shows that strategic CSR is tied to the business case and therefore the profitability of the oil project, meaning it becomes tied to the vagaries of the global oil industry. The shift to Tullow focusing on value for money from CSR and shared prosperity meant that social investment was delivered in phases, therefore avoiding the long-term commitment that social investment requires. Indeed, the short-termism of CSR that is tied to the political economy of oil and gas contradicts the aims of social investment to create empowerment and lasting value. Modern CSR delivered through partnerships enables distance by pushing responsibility onto the partners for the delivery and success of CSR, but when partners such as TraidLinks are relying 100% on funding from the company, CSR projects become linked to the boom-and-bust nature of oil. The failure of the TraidLinks project left another bitter CSR legacy in Uganda, this time among project partners and local farmers who were promised improved livelihoods by Tullow Oil.

7 Conclusion

Using the case of Tullow Oil in Uganda this chapter explored CSR from the analytical perspective of dis/entanglement in an emerging oil state. Tullow's Uganda journey was one of entanglement and disentanglement as the company went from wildcatter to oil producer and finally to scaling back and discontinuing CSR.

Tullow created entanglements by using CSR and community engagement to establish the oil project. At first, this was done through the instrumental use of CSR to build relationships at the village level and negotiate land access and resource use. Then Tullow sought to secure a longer-term presence in Uganda and increase shareholder confidence by implementing oil industry standards and strategic CSR. As the oil project life cycle progressed, these approaches became more important to manage the anticipated impacts of oil and enable Tullow to remain distant from the dynamics of the local context. The problem, however, was that Tullow was already deeply entangled. The shift to strategic CSR enabled Tullow to detach from its initial concentration at the village level, however this shift revealed the extent to which Tullow was entangled and impacted Tullow's local level legitimacy.

Tullow's transition to an oil producing company in Uganda meant that there was an associated change in which groups benefitted from CSR and community engagement. Tullow focused CSR and engagement in the wider district as the pressures on Tullow increased and the company needed support from a wider number of stakeholders. However, social investment in this later phase continued to entangle Tullow through the partnership approach and promise of long-term social investment. The strategic approach to CSR was tied to the business case and therefore undermined Tullow's ability to deliver longer-term value when the oil price dropped.

While Tullow Oil aimed to do things differently as an oil company in Uganda, gain competitive edge through CSR and provide social development, there were complex factors which challenged this ambition. This case highlights the contradictions inherent in the process of establishing an oil project. Standardised approaches and contemporary CSR seek to maintain distance and minimise impacts both on local communities in terms of adverse social and environmental harm, and on the company in terms of reputational and operational risk. However, companies become active in the process of creating entanglements to the local space through CSR, which in the context of the short-term horizons and boom-and-bust nature of the oil industry can undermine the legitimacy which is crucial for an oil companies' social licence to operate.

References

African Union (2009). *Africa Mining Vision*. African Union, Addis Ababa.

Anderson, D. M. & Browne, A. J. (2011). The Politics of Oil in Eastern Africa. *Journal of Eastern African Studies*, 5, 369–410.

Appel, H. (2012). Offshore Work: Oil, Modularity, and the How of Capitalism in Equatorial Guinea. *American Ethnologist*, 39, 692–709.

Barry, A. (2006). Technological Zones. *European Journal of Social Theory*, 9, 239–253.

Bebbington, C., Wilson, E., Smith, L. & Van Alstine, J. (2017). *Community Liaison Officers: Exploring the Frontline of Corporate Practice in the Oil and Gas Sector*. London: Audire and ECW Energy Ltd.

Billo, E. (2015). Sovereignty and Subterranean Resources: An Institutional Ethnography of Repsol's Corporate Social Responsibility Programs in Ecuador. *Geoforum*, 59, 268–277.

Blowfield, M. (2005). Corporate Social Responsibility: Reinventing the Meaning of Development? *International Affairs*, 81, 515–524.

Buxton, A. (2012). MMSD+ 10: Reflecting on a Decade of Mining and Sustainable Development. IIED Sustainable Markets Discussion Paper, International Institute for Environment and Development (IIED). London, June 2012.

Campbell, B. (2012). Corporate Social Responsibility and Development in Africa: Redefining the Roles and Responsibilities of Public and Private Actors in the Mining Sector. *Resources Policy*, 37, 138–143.

Cash, A. C. (2012). Corporate Social Responsibility and Petroleum Development in Sub-Saharan Africa: The Case of Chad. *Resources Policy*, 37, 144–151.

De Kock, P. & Sturman, K. (2012). *The Power of Oil Charting Uganda's Transition to a Petro-State*. SAIIA Research Report 10.

Edwards, J. (2012, April 13). Tullow Refutes Bribery Accusations in Uganda. *Reuters*.

Frynas, J. G. (2005). The False Developmental Promise of Corporate Social Responsibility: Evidence from Multinational Oil Companies. *International Affairs*, 81, 581–598.

Frynas, J. G. (2009). Corporate Social Responsibility in the Oil and Gas Sector. *The Journal of World Energy Law & Business*, 2, 178–195.

Frynas J. G. & Paulo, M. (2007). A New Scramble for African Oil? Historical, Political, and Business Perspectives. *African Affairs*, 106, 229–251.

Gardner, K., Ahmed, Z., Bashir, F. & RANA, M. (2012). Elusive Partnerships: Gas Extraction and CSR in Bangladesh. *Resources Policy*, 37, 168–174.

Gilberthorpe, E. & Banks, G. (2012). Development on Whose Terms? CSR Discourse and Social Realities in Papua New Guinea's Extractive Industries Sector, *Resources Policy*, 37, 185–193.

Hickey, S. & Izama, A. (2017). The Politics of Governing Oil in Uganda: Going Against the Grain? *African Affairs*, 116, 163–185.

Joyce, S. & Thomson, I. (2000). Earning a social licence to operate: Social acceptability and resource development in Latin America. *CIM bulletin*, 93, 49–53.

Mayorga Alba, E. (2009). Extractive Industries Value Chain: A Comprehensive Integrated Approach to Developing Extractive Industries. Africa Working Paper Series, 125. World Bank, Washington. http://hdl.handle.net/10986/18400. [accessed 13 Feb 2021]

Mosse, D. (2013). The Anthropology of International Development. *Annual Review of Anthropology*, 42, 227–246.

Musisi, F. (2021, April 12). New Crude Oil Pipeline Deals Signed, Production for 2025. *The Daily Monitor*.

Nakaweesi, D. (2010, May 13). Tullow Oil Wins CSR Award. *The Daily Monitor*.

Nasralla, S. (2020, April 23). Tullow exits Uganda project, sells stake to Total for $575 million. *Reuters*.

Northedge, R. (2007, October 14). Independent Irishman Shows Rivals the Way. *The Telegraph*.

Owen, J. R. & Kemp, D. (2013). Social Licence and Mining: A Critical Perspective. *Resources Policy*, 38, 29–35.

Patey, L. (2015). Oil in Uganda: Hard Bargaining and Complex Politics in East Africa. The Oxford Institute for Energy Studies. OIES Paper WPM, 60.

Rajak, D. (2011). *In Good Company: An Anatomy of Corporate Social Responsibility*, Stanford University Press.

Slack, K. (2012). Mission impossible? Adopting a CSR-based Business Model for Extractive Industries in Developing Countries. *Resources Policy*, 37, 179–184.

Smith, L., Tallontire, A. & Van Alstine, J. (2018). Development and the Private Sector: The Challenge of Extractives-led Development in Uganda. In: Fagan, G. H. & Munck, R. (eds.) *Handbook on Development and Social Change*, (pp. 69–88), Edward Elgar Publishing.

Smith, L. & Van Alstine, J. (2018). Neoliberal Oil Development in Uganda. In: Wiegratz, J., MARTINELLO, G. & Greco, E. (eds.) *Uganda: The dynamics of neoliberal transformation*, (pp. 234–248), London: Zed Books.

Tullow Oil PLC 2010. (2009). Corporate Responsibility report: Building Africa's leading responsible independent oil company, London.

Tullow Oil PLC 2012. (2012). Corporate responsibility Report: Creating Shared Prosperity, London.

Tumuhimbise, A. (2021, November 7). 'No Power to Stop It': Optimism Turns to Frustration Over East Africa Pipeline. *The Guardian.*

UNIDO. (no date). What is CSR? www.unido.org/csr/072054.html [accessed 13 Feb 2021].

Witte, A. (2018). *An Uncertain Future - Anticipating Oil in Uganda*, Göttingen: Göttingen University Press.

PART 3

Oil Communities and Rural-Urban Transformations

9

"I Have a Vision of a Modern City, a Properly Planned City": Neoliberal Planning and Speculative Practices in Ghana's Oil City

Geertrui Vannoppen

1 Introduction[1]

The Ghanaian harbour city of Sekondi-Takoradi is currently undergoing a major transformation as a result of the discovery of large offshore oil reserves in 2007 and oil extraction that has been ongoing since 2010. The discovery generated a national discourse of hope. In the city of Sekondi-Takoradi—the closest city to the offshore oil fields—oil extraction has resulted in the creation of a new corporate identity, Ghana's Oil City, with its vision of a highly planned, world–class city sporting a modern infrastructure "befitting of an oil city". In this way, Sekondi-Takoradi is an example of petrolic semiosis (Appel et al., 2015) at work, equating oil with a highly planned, "modern" city. Oil has often been used as a metonym, where oil is understood as "oil as modernity, oil as money, oil as geopolitics, oil as violence, oil as ur-commodity, the mother of all commodities that enables other commodities" (Appel et al., 2015, p. 10). In Takoradi oil is not only a metonym for money or modernity in the form of a modern city, but also for global and urban citizenship. While oil remains an invisible commodity in the cityscape of Takoradi due to the location of oil–related infrastructure outside the urban centre, it impacts upon discourses of land, property, authority and (urban) citizenship which are increasingly competed over and sought after. The case of the new town development King City, set in the larger setting of Ghana's newest oil city, provides an analysis of the impact of oil on everyday life, with a focus on urban citizenship, urban planning, and neotraditional chieftaincy. Even in its continued absence and invisibility, the new town development King City project becomes a "dream zone" or a "gateway to citizenship" (Cross, 2014). As the new town development suffers from delays to a total suspension, it is in that gap between start and completion that processes are set into motion, new mobilities are generated,

1 This chapter is based on the author's ethnographic research conducted in Ghana from 2012 to 2016 and subsequent PhD thesis submitted in 2016.

 | DOI:10.1163/9789004530065_010

identities are transformed, and futures are re-imagined. On the one hand, the King City project is capitalised upon by urban planners and traditional leaders in the interests of their modern, orderly and highly planned vision of the city. Applying futuristic images that are borrowed from global oil cities, they project these images onto Takoradi. On the other hand, farmers and landowners who are directly impacted by the project equally instrumentalise the King City project to claim rights and recognition as urban citizens.

This chapter is broadly divided into two sections. The first analyses the speculative practice of envisioning Takoradi as an oil city and the diversification of actors in its urban management. The second section interprets the curious role played by the chief of Takoradi in the King City project, and analyses how peri–urban villages are utilising the project to voice their demands for urban citizenship.

2 Sekondi-Takoradi: The Oil City

The city of Sekondi-Takoradi's vibrant history is coloured by the presence of colonial infrastructures such as the harbours in Sekondi and Takoradi and the railways. The construction of the harbour and railways contributed to the highly spatially structured development of Takoradi township and the cosmopolitan nature of the city. The spatial legacy of segregated colonial planning means that the city of Sekondi-Takoradi does not necessarily flow. It is marked by contradictions as the functional zones of the city are isolated. Next to the two urban nodes of Sekondi and Takoradi, the peripheries contain competing and barely linked urban villages where the main source of income is farming. The recent oil discovery in 2007 has significantly changed the dynamics and atmosphere in Sekondi-Takoradi.

As a secondary city and with its new-found oil city identity, Sekondi-Takoradi is standing at the threshold of its adulthood, still grasping to combine its contrasting elements to graduate to the dreamed-of world class (oil) city. While oil is being heralded as the natural resource which brings investor-led development, inhabitants of the oil city experience the day-to-day impacts, including forced relocations to make way for the vision of a modern urban centre, loss of livelihoods and increasing living costs. The invisible presence of oil, and its inherent uncertainty, is imposing a new spatial and temporal logic on the city; it re-orders space—at times a contested practice—and re-orients the future gaze of planners and inhabitants. The petrolic semiosis (Appel et al., 2015) equating oil with modernity and with wealth becomes apparent in the popular discourse in the city. Oil is money and everybody wants some of it.

Power is increasingly fragmented and contested in the oil- city. Yet, Takoradi also offers spaces of growth, dreams and imagination through its new-found identity as the oil city. The friction (Tsing, 2005), or perhaps growing pains of Sekondi-Takoradi is a result of the city's sudden graduation into a frontier city in the oil and gas industry.

With the onset of oil exploitation, Takoradi has become part of the global economy of oil, or as a planner at the Sekondi-Takoradi Metropolitan Assembly expressed it: "The oil discovery has put us on the international radar!" The planner at the Assembly clarified: "Our vision for the city is to make it an investment destination for the whole of West Africa. To do that we need to make sure the infrastructure is in place to make it an investment-friendly climate. With the emerging of the oil industry, it is paramount that we invest in roads, electricity and water. That is the dream for our city. We want it to be aesthetic, a beautiful city."[2] On the level of urban planning, oil is a metonym for a modern, highly planned, world-class city with a befitting infrastructure. The harbour, railways and roads are being rehabilitated and there are ambitious plans to overhaul the central business district and to replace the residential living blocks with office complexes. New hospitals and schools are being constructed. A street naming and house numbering exercise was completed in 2014, and the road network is earmarked for modernisation with flyovers replacing the existing roundabouts. The oil city vision further materialises in speculative, gated communities and new towns, grotesque shopping malls and the restructuring of the city, rendering those elements invisible that do not match with the vision of Sekondi-Takoradi as a world class city. An example of erased infrastructure is the Tanokrom Kokompe, a car mechanics site the city centre, which has been (forcefully) relocated to the periphery of the city to make way for the Tanokrom shopping mall.

The global struggle for natural resources is shaping Sekondi-Takoradi's urban landscape with a boom in real estate projects and the introduction of the new town concept, as "oil is converted into the less mutable materials of concrete and steel" (Reeves, 2013, p. 513). Resources are generative as their inherent potential wealth produces possible futures (Ferry & Limbert, 2008, p. 6). The affective impact of oil on a city can be discussed as a *Petropia*, when oil only conjures hope, anticipation and expectations not materialized. Shatkin (2011) defines landscapes of anticipation in his description of Kolkota as a city with fenced-off spaces showcasing the yet-to-come on billboards, while in actuality there is relatively small progress. Weszkalnys (2016) similarly analyses the multiplicity of affective registers emerging from the futurity of oil, "translated into

2 Assembly Planner, personal communication, January 2014.

FIGURE 9.1 Tanokrom shopping mall billboard in front of cleared and walled plot of land, in Takoradi centre (picture by author). Car mechanics and related stores were removed and relocated to a less accessible site outside the city centre, which resulted to street protests in February 2014.

a doubtful hope, comprised of ambiguous visions of material betterment, personal and collective transformation, as well as anticipations of failure, friction, and discontentment" (Weszkalnys, 2016, pp. 141–142). Cross (2014) describes dreamed-of futures in relation to large-scale industrial infrastructural projects of Free Trade zones in India. He discusses the economy of anticipation set in motion by the potential presence of foreign investment discussing the "divergent ways of knowing about, imagining and living towards the future that play out in these sites, restructuring relations of power in familiar and ambiguous ways" (Cross, 2014, pp. 5–6).

Additionally, natural resource exploitation, especially oil, are central to "becoming modern" and modernity (Apter, 2005; Coronil, 1997; Ferguson, 1999). The envisioned African urban modernity present in the oil city vision is the result of a conflux of—locally and globally informed—rationalities, and is therefore not only shaped by Western urban forms. In creating the vision of a modern, African oil city, Sekondi-Takoradi's city authorities apply tactics of place marketing and rely on a diversification of governing authorities.

The vision of Sekondi-Takoradi as an oil city is a worlding practice (Roy & Ong, 2011), in which the city is imagined as part of the global economy of oil, a West-African trade hub, a modern African city. Takoradi's spatial development plan anticipates and imagines the future as an oil city. Foreign capital influences the new spatial development plan of the city and drives up land and rental prices. Speculative practices in the form of real estate projects for "projected" growth restructure power in the city, and a host of new players have entered the urban management scene in Sekondi-Takoradi.

The volatile, speculative nature of the investments results in a new architecture of urban governance with a variety of governing institutions. The municipal assembly works side-by-side with NGOs and speculative investors in the making of the city. As city councils no longer receive (enough) budget allocations from the central government, they look for funding in public-private partnerships, sales of land, property taxation and collaborations with NGOs. The future is (re-)imagined by authorities in the city by branding the city as an oil city to attract the necessary investors and private investors who bank on the image of the yet-to-come in the form of speculative infrastructure development projects, such as the King City new town development. In addition to the governing authorities of private speculative investors, city councils and NGOs, there is another strong local force that shapes Takoradi's particular case: neotraditional authorities grasp the space of growth offered by oil to transform and reinvigorate the chieftaincy structure.

The presence of oil has generated alternative social configurations and transformed processes of meaning-making in the city with the overarching oil city vision and discourse now influencing how people relate to land and land ownership. Traditional authorities are renegotiating expired (colonial) land leases in order to claim back land from the government. Large plots of land are being sold on the periphery for industrial purposes and new town developments. Land speculation and the imagination of Takoradi's future as an oil city not only leads to increased property prices and rapid conversions of agrarian land to residential land, but also to alterations in how land is valued. Alternative valuations of land in land negotiations are the result of the seemingly infinite imagined possibilities that one's little plot of land suddenly has in the oil-city, setting in motion the anticipation of alternative futures. In land sale negotiations, compensation no longer revolves around a single payment. More and more demands are now included in sale negotiations, regarding education, infrastructure, employment, yearly payments or even requests to become shareholders.

In this chapter I will continue to discuss the case of the King City project: a new town development in the peri–urban belt of Takoradi, a public-private partnership between the chief of Takoradi, Nana Bosumokura III and his community, and the foreign investor Rendeavour, which has similar projects across Africa. In Takoradi, in addition to the archetypal responsibility of a chief to safeguard tradition and gatekeep land access, the neotraditional socio-political institutions now claim a role in areas of development, business, urban governance and urban planning. In the city's palimpsest of past, present and future, the chief of Takoradi has different faces: he actively mobilises his identity as a traditional ruler to create his capacity as an urban planner and the driving force behind the King City project.

3 King City within the Oil City

Before we dive further into the figure of the neotraditional chief Nana Bosumokura III, a discussion on the King City project is necessary. The King City project is a new town development in the farmlands on the periphery of the city, which pushes farmers deeper in the forest and potentially urbanises the (rural) periphery with the creation of a "third urban node," as King City is described in the municipal's structure plan. King City is promoted within Takoradi by the urban developer Rendeavour as a public-private partnership with the chief of Takoradi Nana Bosumokura III, who had long held a vision of a modern and planned town, and the government which provides the developmental framework and an "enabling environment." The proposed site is 1018 hectares in size, located within 10 km of Takoradi's urban centre. The mixed-use new town concept is projected for 90,000 residents with highly desired industrial areas, and residential areas for all social backgrounds. The communities closest to the chosen site are the peri–urban communities of Adientem, Mpatado, Whindo and Assakae, where inhabitants predominantly make a living out of farming.

The developer behind the project is Rendeavour, which defines itself as a Pan-African land developer that has similar real estate projects in various stages of development elsewhere in Africa. Rendeavour is a subsidiary of the Russian investment group Renaissance Group, which promotes the satellite urban environment model as a solution to decongest urban centres and to drive growth and development. Rendeavour's first successful project of this kind was Roma Park in Lusaka, Zambia, followed by other town development projects such as Kiswishi in Lubumbashi, Congo, Igna and Lekki in Nigeria, and Tatu City in Kenya. The company now has two projects in Ghana: Appolonia in Accra, and King City in Takoradi. There is a high level of uniformity

FIGURE 9.2 Screenshot of Rendeavour's King City visualization from 2022-07-03, playing with the involvement of the Chief of Takoradi with a dominant statue of a traditional stool
SOURCE: HTTPS://WWW.RENDEAVOUR.COM/PROJECTS/KING-CITY/

among Rendeavour's urban projects in Africa, such as the company's template for mixed-use town development as the foundation to propel growth and wealth in the creation of the modern African city.

The King City development, and other new town developments outside of Takoradi's city-borders, are all branding themselves as modern and planned, in an attempt to attract (oil) expats. The narratives of such new town developments are marked by optimism and brim with ambitions to create ultramodern projects (Watson, 2013). Computerised images play a central role in these futuristic projects, and the King City imagery references "world-class" cities such as Dubai, Singapore or Shanghai elsewhere, indexing the modernity that is associated with them. Watson (2013, p. 1) addresses the power of the futuristic and virtual images:

> The proposed new urban master plans for many of Africa's larger cities are now to be found on the websites of international architectural, engineering and property development companies, and they depart even further from African urban reality than did the post-colonial zoning plans. Visions for these future cities reflect images of Dubai, Singapore or Shanghai, although iconic building shapes from elsewhere in the world may be thrown in for good measure.

While the images indeed draw from a similar vocabulary, I would like to challenge Watson's assertion that they are foreign concepts far removed from African urban reality. The fact is that the King City plans are not mere copy-paste projects from elsewhere in the world. The King City project is an excellent example of this emerging African modernity, where desired futures merge with local realities to merge tradition and modernity to create a new urban space. The chief of Takoradi, Nana Bosumokura III, had a considerable voice in the design of the King City plans—virtual renderings showcase a monumentally large stool, a strong symbol that references traditional indigenous chieftaincy structures.

While eventually these type of real estate developments and infrastructures may remain invisible and impose their own spatial and temporal logic on the city, they also "generate alternative spheres of social interaction, and different coping strategies and regimes of knowledge and power" (De Boeck, 2012). It is precisely these alternative strategies and regimes of power we can observe in the chief's involvement in the King City project. King City is not only exemplary of the attempt to marry local and culturally traditionally elements with a modernistic view of urban living, the case also illustrates the way in which the chief is challenged to reinvent his traditional role in the evolving urban context of Sekondi-Takoradi. With his involvement in the project, the chief of Takoradi acts as a businessman speculating upon the possible impacts of oil in Takoradi. As the future is brought into the present with spectral and spectacular visions of urban development, the past plays an equally important role in the city. There is a transformation of traditional authority in the urban context, where the chief is sourcing from the past: reinforcing customary rule and reinventing his traditional role.

4 Two Faced Chief

Neotraditional chiefs in Ghana play a hybrid role: they are expected to advance development within their community, while also protecting cultural heritage, tradition and custom (Beall, 2006; Bob-Milliar, 2009; Odotei & Awedoba, 2006; Ubink, 2007). The chief of Takoradi, Nana Bosumokura III, is a perfect example of this Janus–faced authority (Ubink, 2008). In exercising his authority, he builds on tradition and custom, wearing customary chieftaincy regalia and insisting on established regulations, but he actively attempts to grow and develop his community through his role in the King City project and his attempts to attract investors to Sekondi-Takoradi city by banking on the presence of oil.

In Southern Ghana the traditional authority's role as gatekeeper for land access explains the chiefs' prominence in local governance and land speculation, as Berry (2013) explains: "Land plays a central role not only in the nexus of wealth and power in Ghana, but also in the unusual prominence of 'traditional authority' in the country's governing system. Citing ancient historical precedents to define and legitimate their prerogatives, traditional authorities wield influence in ways that owe more to colonial practices of indirect rule than to pre-colonial institutions or political realities" (Berry, 2013, p. 37). The omnipresence of traditional authorities in Ghana's governing system equally lies in the centrality of land in power and wealth, as traditional authorities control land access and ownership to a certain extent (Berry, 2013).

The figure of the chief Nana Bosumokura III acting as an urban developer in addition to his traditional role, is an excellent case of the malleability and fluidity of traditional authority systems. The renegotiation of customary relations or reinvention of customary roles is not new, nor peculiar. The institute of chieftaincy is embedded in the larger political economy of the city and the democratic state. It is influenced by social, political and economic processes and events, such as the offshore oil discovery in the case of Takoradi. In the uncertain context of petro-urbanism marked by speculative practices of the Oil City, historical and spatial identities are negotiated in relation to the plurality of governing institutions. The chief of Takoradi attempts to consolidate his authority and influence by adapting and changing his role and identity (Hobsbawm & Ranger, 1983).

In his discourse and actions, the chief of Takoradi actively portrays himself as a "traditional" leader. In Akan culture the chief is known as *odekro* which means "the one who owns the community". As the owner he is not only charged with the protection of the community, but he also must add value to the community. When a chief is enstooled (enthroned), there are several private and public rituals, including the public swearing of an oath in which the chief promises to pursue the welfare and progress of the people. It is his identity as a "father of the people" that the chief of Takoradi actively applies in his discourse as a neotraditional leader in a rapidly changing urban context: he sees himself as the gatekeeper to the community, the first port of call for local government and investors. This reflects the importance of traditional leadership structures in the everyday lives of people ranging from dispute settlement, religious and ritual tasks to development, even when modern state structures are present at the local level (Ubink, 2008).

When Nana Bosumokura III was enstooled in 2003 he set himself the mandate "to bring order," as he reflected in 2014.

> I have a vision of a modern city, a properly planned city. The whole of Takoradi was bought in 1930 for the harbour and was properly planned—just look at the road structure. My intent is to bring order (again).[3]

The bringing of order not only refers to the physicality of bringing order in the form of planning for a modern city. It also refers to the exercise of his chiefly authority and ensuring that customary rules are followed. It is a self–imposed mandate that captivates his two–faced position between past and future with his task to protect cultural heritage, but also his obligation to develop the community. In making a point of being recognised as the traditional ruler, he started a crusade by way of litigation to "set things straight" and ensure that customary rules, particularly those related to land sales, were upheld. These actions aimed to respect the most crucial rule: that as a customary land owner, the chief is entitled to receive a percentage of land sales in the city. To add to the intrigue, Nana Bosumokura III has been the subject of several ongoing court cases that debate his legitimacy as chief. The chief also started building a magnificent palace–cum–community centre close to the central business district of Takoradi to emphasise (and make more visible) his position as the chief of the oil city.

The references to "bringing order" not only entails the recognition of the chief's authority as a traditional ruler. Just like the urban planners of the municipality, the chief has a vision for his city: a properly planned city, with an infrastructure scaled to equal its new identity as the oil city. The discourses of the developer Rendeavour and the Oil City discourse of Sekondi-Takoradi's planners situate planning as central in this imagery. It is important to note the explicit reference to Takoradi as the first fully planned city of the Gold Coast Colony.[4] There are a number of similarities between the language used at the time of the development of Sekondi-Takoradi in the 1920s, and the current discourse of the oil city, with the same emphasis on infrastructural upgrades and the conviction that planning equals structure, order and urban modernity (also see Plageman, 2013).

On the fifth anniversary of his reign in 2008, the chief's new role as an urban planner and development broker led him to launch the Osahene Sustainable Development Programme for Takoradiman, in an effort to make his vision for Takoradi reality. At the time, his aim was to raise funds through this self-established Development Programme to realise the various projects himself, instead of selling the land to investors. He attempted to find investors, and visited Ghanaian banks:

---

3 Nana Bosumokura III, personal communication, March 2014.

4 Current Ghana was a British Crown Colony, the Gold Coast from 1821 until its independence in 1957.

> But nobody understood why a chief wanted to build a city ; they think it is the role of government. They are used to give 50 or 100 acres to real estate agents to be developed, but a chief himself initiating a project like that, they thought it was too ambitious. All the other chiefs sell land to investors to sell, and that is it. They don't get involved as into the planning, they don't have the vision like that.[5]

A chief wanting to invest in real estate turned out to be unconventional, and banks were not prepared to support his project.

The chief's attempts to attract investors finally paid off; Rendeavour was interested in his vision of a modern Takoradi. The chief proposed the King City concept to the involved communities, discussed it with the landowners and family elders, and convinced them to sell the land. The area where King City will be developed is currently used as farmland. Using his position as negotiator between Rendeavour and the community, land compensation, crop compensation and alternative demands for compensation were agreed on. In the negotiations, the chief emphasised the customary land rules and his traditional role as the caretaker and owner of the land. The chief convinced the family heads and farmers of the benefit of collectively selling plots for a better price than individual plot sales, an act that reflected his role as the caretaker of common good, bringing development to the community:

> King City is benefiting everybody. One of the reasons to do the project was that normally chiefs or people will sell one plot here, one plot there, and they end up selling 1000 acres without having any substantial money to do anything. I had to do this on the behalf of the community.[6]

In his collaboration with the developer Rendeavour, the chief made several demands, for example, the inclusion of a university. In addition, it was agreed that the land lease would be for 90 years, as is customary, and that the community would be a shareholder:

> The land is leased of course, it is for the next 90 years. After 90 years the land will come back to us. We are supposed to have members on the management board so we can regulate expenditure. It also means that at the end of every year, as a shareholder, profit comes to the stool. It goes to the local people.

5 Nana Bosumokura III, personal communication, March 2014.

6 Nana Bosumokura III, personal communication, March 2014.

Whenever a land sale is made, the chief and the community receive a percentage of the sale. The community's share is transferred to a trust that can be used for community development. The managing role of the chief goes even further as he distributes the compensation to the landowners and people farming on the land. Beside fair compensation, other key elements in the land-sale negotiations were demands on local sourcing of labor (including training by Rendeavour in construction work) and a general call for development of the community with a demand for Corporate Social Responsibility activities. The demand on local sourcing of labor is locally referred to as local content, referencing Ghana's Local Content and Local Participation Regulations in relation to the petroleum industry (established in 2013). The regulations have as aim to ensure knowledge transfer, job creation, and ultimately, national development.

With the current delays in the King City project (as of 2022), the chief is experiencing the insecurity and volatility of capital. Even though the agreement between the chief of Takoradi and the developer Rendeavour are now being renegotiated into an equity agreement due to financial cutbacks, the chief remains hopeful as he banks on the inevitable land value increase. In this task he adopts a speculative logic, like many other businesspeople captivated by the promise of oil money and the hike in land prices.

The King City project is a materialisation of the potential future envisioned by the chief of Takoradi for his city, a future in which his authority as chief in/of the city and on land matters is recognised. While planning and infrastructure play a central role in Takoradi's vision of a modern city, the temporalities of planning not only entail an anticipation of the future, but also negative temporalities. Even though large-scale infrastructure projects such as King City may indefinitely linger in the virtual (non-physical) world as a concept or in computerized images they still have an impact as people act on it. In that way there is productive value in the suspense and delays that characterise these speculative projects when the possible and the not-yet result in anticipatory activities with people selling land, building, starting businesses and claiming urban citizenship.

Now that we have an insight into the dominant actors of the developer and the chief of Takoradi, let's turn our attention to the community members.

5 The Road: Perspective from Community Members

In the context of the rapid urbanisation and increasing living costs in Sekondi-Takoradi, the King City project is seized upon by the people in the surrounding communities as an opportunity for development, to voice their own demands for their visions for the future. A farmer framed it as follows: "We too we want development, and the best thing is if the road to the farmlands is constructed, so the people can take a car to their land. We all want development."[7]

The one road leading from Takoradi to Assakae is a graded dust road, but due to heavy–duty trucks the road quickly disintegrates into gullies and manholes between which traffic must manoeuvre itself. The road is a vital infrastructural connection between Assakae, the farmlands in the hinterland and the city of Sekondi-Takoradi. It was striking that in my conversations about the King City project, and urbanisation in Takoradi in general, the topic of roads always came up. In the absence of notable action from the government or the municipal authority, the community of Assakae turned to other power players active in the city, namely the chief and speculative real estate projects, to bring development to their community. The King City project is not only appropriated and incorporated by urban planners and leaders into their vision of the city, farmers and landowners who are directly impacted by the project also grasp it to imagine possible (urban) futures for themselves.

In the King City negotiations between the chief and Rendeavour, the community of Assakae and land-owning families formulated several infrastructure-related requests, in addition to monetary compensation: a new cemetery; an extension of the village school; a public sanitation facility; streetlights; and an assurance that 85% of labour for the construction of the new town development would be sourced locally from the communities. The most important request, however, was the rehabilitation of the roads in the communities and the construction of an access road between Assakae and the hinterland farms. The request was not only formulated by the local farmers who experienced hardships in getting their harvests to the market. People who had bought land in the area equally anticipated the construction of the King City access road, as it would facilitate their own building projects. Abraham, a cement shop owner, explained that the community was very excited about the King City project as they expected it would bring jobs and an accessible road to the farms:

> The community is very excited for the King City project, They are expecting jobs and the construction of the road. Some areas are very muddy; trucks or cars cannot go there. Some of the people living here are farmers, so when they make that place motorable they can take the car to go to their farm. That is the expectation of the community.[8]

7 Anonymous farmer, personal communication, December 2013.

8 Abraham, personal communication, December 2013.

The announcement of a new town development on the periphery of Sekondi-Takoradi put the long–standing villages on the urban map. The urban peripheral (farming) communities suddenly had a platform to voice their demands and views for the future. From being a run-down, unimportant village–community, the community of Assakae suddenly found itself at the centre of negotiations. They were no longer more village than city, more rural than urban. With the virtual presence of the modern King City, the affected peri–urban communities saw an opportunity to make demands to become urban citizens, and they perceived road access and infrastructure as central to their urban identity. The potential (urban) future seemly offered in the construction of the King City project shapes the present to an extent. Nielsen (2014) formulates it eloquently: "The virtual coexistence of different pasts and futures in the present actualised a particular form of differentiation (or becoming) through which new social positions potentially became accessible" (Nielsen, 2014, p. 177).[9]

The notion of infrastructure shapes the discourse of urban citizenship. The road connecting the rural to the urban, creating access to the urban market and physically incorporating the urban villages into the urban fabric is important and linked to general development. In his *Politics and Poetics of Infrastructure*, Larkin (2013) makes a call for a systemic analysis of infrastructure beyond its technical functioning, to include the "forms of desire and fantasy" that are stored within them as well as the political rationality that underlies infrastructural projects (Larkin, 2013, pp. 328–329). People living in the peri–urban environments and farming on land that is rapidly increasing in value, can imagine themselves as new kinds of "political and economic subjects, who can make claims upon the state for protection, rights and entitlement" (Cross, 2014, p. 70). Roads, and cement by extension, can reveal "the material traces of state intervention and withdrawal" (Harvey, 2010, p. 36). The state presence in the forms of a road, hospital, school, bank or prison can be experienced as oppressive, or it can be a materialisation of state presence actively sought after by local people (Harvey, 2010). While local government permits a certain level of self-government by neotraditional authorities in Assakae, the road turns out to be politically contested. When it comes to the road, the traditional authorities have no alternative but to turn to central government. "The government does not allow us to do the road, because that is the constitution here in Ghana,

9 The compacting of past, present and future is discussed by Hirsch and Stewart (2005) as historicity. By providing a discussion of the term historicity, they aim to develop it into a tool for an alternative temporal focus, away from the standard Western concept of 'history', for ethnographic research.

every road belongs to the government," one community member connected to the royal family explained. "Even if we have billions, they will say 'Give the money to us'. They will not allow us to do it."[10]

In Assakae the lack of a road and the history of failures in attempting to get a road illustrate the absence of the state in this urban village. Roads can invoke the "presence and the absence of the state," but they also reveal multiple agencies "used and claimed in ways that planners and politicians never envisaged" (Harvey, 2005, p. 131). Roads entail fantasies, desires and dreamed-of futures of individuals and societies (Larkin, 2013). The affective qualities of roads range from expectations of progress and development, transformation, speed, stability, political integration and economic connectivity, what Harvey and Knox (2012) term "the enchantments of infrastructure."

The claiming of citizenship or a voice, through an infrastructural element such as a road, is not unique to the case of Assakae. Elsewhere in Takoradi, the need for proximity and connectivity to the urban centre via a viable road was a recurring demand, and lay at the core of people's rejections of other new urban developments that the city carried out in their process of creating a modern oil city.[11] In these various demands and evolving discourses around infrastructure, definitions are shaped on what it means to be urban, what it takes to become an urban citizen. Elements such as proximity with an incorporation into the urban market, closeness to certain services (hospitals, schools) and a promise of modern, urban living with electricity and water certainly seem to be key.

6 Postscript: Delay and Suspension

Time passed, deadlines were extended, and the King City project remains invisible in Takoradi (as of 2022), the project has stagnated. The King City project was officially launched in July 2012. The project was expected to start in 2013, but in late 2012, Rendeavour Ltd, which was the African Land Business arm of Renaissance Group, broke away from Renaissance Group after a hostile takeover of RenCap, the investment bank of Renaissance Group. Not long

10 Community member Assakae, personal communication, December 2013.

11 Examples are the earlier mentioned development of the Tanokrom shopping mall with a forced relocation of a group of car mechanics to a less centrally located and less accessible site outside the city. This was heavily protested at the time as mentioned above. When the shopping mall was inaugurated, there was again a demonstration. Another relocation that incited protest was that of the abattoir from the city centre to the periphery.

after Rendeavour's breakaway from Renaissance Group, the King City website underwent changes. A "website under construction" message appeared against a background image of the iconic stool landmark, implying that project's vision still lingered. After one year, the "under construction" page was replaced by an equally static holding page.

The vision of the planners caught up with the everyday reality of volatile venture capital and chieftaincy issues stirred up in the Oil City, amongst others. There are multiple explanations and reasons given for the delays of the King City project, ranging from the effect of the global economic crisis, to the effect of local events such as the 2012 elections and a subsequent national court case, as well as spiritual explanations. The various actors involved in the King City project explain and frame the delays differently. The business rationality of the chief and developer is not shared by the communities on the ground. The various explanations also attest to variations in scale, moving from the local arena with chieftaincy disputes and spiritual issues, to the national and the global with economic crises.

One of the major reasons for delay given is the global economic crisis and the internal organisational restructuring at Rendeavour, which resulted in the favouring of the Appolonia project in Accra over the riskier investment of King City. It is framed purely as a business decision. Compared to Appolonia, King City has no pre-existing infrastructure such as connectivity to electricity, water and road networks. The provision of basic infrastructure to the King City site, such as the access road, exceeded the designated budget. Alternative access roads are now being investigated in collaboration with the government and in connection to the planned upgrading of infrastructure in Takoradi.

The chief of Takoradi equally frames the experienced delays as "business is business." Since the signing of the agreement in 2011, the chief of Takoradi had been receiving annual compensation. It was his role to redistribute the funds among the landowners as their compensation for selling the land. As he believed in the longevity of the project, he channeled those funds to other projects. The chief refers to the "financial crisis in Europe" as the reason behind the delays of the King City project and the negotiation of a new equity agreement between the chief of Takoradi and Rendeavour. In this way, the chief sought to place the explanation for the King City delays in the national economic crisis and global economic instabilities.

Quite interestingly however, is the perspective from the involved communities in Takoradi where the delays and standstill are explained very differently, using cultural vocabularies and local realities. As De Boeck (2015, p. 47–48) explains, the relation between speculative urbanism projects and the occult is not surprising:

> The speculative and volatile nature of capital, profit-making, and accumulation runs parallel with and can easily be incorporated into the cultural vocabularies of the occult and the oneiric that people continue to use both to capture extravert sources of material well-being (…) as well as to exorcize the nightmarish abysses of material and spiritual insecurity that constantly open up in the realities of their everyday life.

Information on the King City project that reaches Takoradi is often incomplete and filtered, partly because of the distance between the developer's headquarters in Accra and the communities in Takoradi. As a result, local events within Takoradi are grasped by local actors to explain the delays in compensation and the start of the King City project. The post-election national court case (in March 2013) which questioned the authority of the chief, is also presented as an explanation for the delays. Explanations are also sought in the spiritual realm, as rumours circulate that the chief did not honour customary rites, for which he and his community are now being punished with the halt of the project and the curtailment of the(ir) fantastic and speculative visions for the city's future and its inhabitants.

Despite the delays, multiple players—the chief of Takoradi, the traditional authorities in the village of Assakae, and Rendeavour—are all confident the project will take off (as of 2022). The landowners and farmers are not fully convinced. The majority of the people are, however, hopefully awaiting the infrastructural improvements such as a viable road to their farmlands, which they are convinced the King City project will bring. Even though the project might never become a reality, the mere possibility of a different urban future sets in motion various processes and dreamed-of futures, such as a new palace for the chief of Takoradi and a new road for the peri-urban farmers. While perhaps doomed to remain a fantasy plan (Watson, 2013), King City still has a speculative effect as it impacts the imagination of the future.

Large-scale infrastructure projects such as new town developments are constantly under construction, yet they are unpredictable, incomplete, incoherent and unknowable. In his piece on "suspension," Gupta (2015) draws attention to the temporality of infrastructure. He advocates for a theorisation of suspension: "not between past and future, between beginning and end, but constitut(ing) its own ontic condition just as surely does completion." Gupta (2015) attempts to nuance the teleology of infrastructure leading to a modern future. While the future plays a central role in long-term infrastructural investments as they contain the aspirations, anticipations and imaginations of the future, infrastructural projects are not always completed or there is a gap between promise and performance. The temporal space of delays, suspensions, break-down or removal is to be analysed as well. Cross (2015), for example, writes that "Even when these projects fail to realise the hopes and expectations invested in them," they "continue to relay past promises into the present, producing new dreams, desires and aspirations" (Cross, 2015, p. 453). Despite the ongoing invisibility of the King City project in Takoradi, it provides a new arena in which people can re-imagine themselves, their lives and their livelihoods, creating new dreamed-of futures. The delays of the King City project are in that sense productive. The road and the palace are materialisations of a possible urban future, where the road is a materialisation of an aspiration to become an urban citizen, and the palace is a speculative practice given that that the chiefly authority of Nana Bosumokura III is currently being challenged. What happens when the urban future does not materialise? It is, as Appel, Anand, and Gupta (2015) write, "By attending to the formation, maintenance, and breakdown of roads, water pipes, or electricity grids in everyday life, we can ask how infrastructure helps us to theorise key anthropological questions about affect, aspiration, and imagination; about modernity, development, and temporality; and about the production of states and markets, the public and the private." Or in the case of Takoradi, the delays in the King City project, together with the formulation of an oil city vision, help us to understand the concepts of modernity, development, the urban and the rural.

7 Conclusion

In the ongoing interplay between tradition and modernity in Takoradi's urban context, the identity and roles of chieftaincy are equally changing. Despite the presence of a harbour and upcoming industrial infrastructure, the city differs significantly from larger Ghanaian urban centres such as Accra and Kumasi. Sekondi-Takoradi finds itself at the brink of changing into a middle-class city. While gated communities are thriving in cities such as Kumasi and Accra, they are hardly present in Takoradi. The King City project is the first real estate project of its kind in Takoradi. The context and reception of the King City project differs largely from other new town developments elsewhere in Africa, which I believe is the result of two factors that define Takoradi's peculiar situation. The first factor is the presence and strength of the chieftaincy structure in Ghana. The Takoradi chief presents himself as the landowner and there are no land disputes, which can be contrasted with the Tatu City development in Nairobi, also constructed by Rendeavour. In the context of King City, the struggle over assets such as land and power play out on a different level, namely via chieftaincy disputes. A second factor is the urban identity of Takoradi. Although Takoradi is the third biggest city of Ghana, it is of a much smaller scale than Accra and Kumasi, and urbanisation processes and population growth have only recently surged in Takoradi alongside the discovery of oil. Takoradi is in that respect incomparable to Nairobi, Accra or Kinshasa where similar new town developments are constructed; it is only recently that real estate developers have shown interest in Takoradi. The city of Takoradi therefore does not have the debris of imaginations that past/incomplete real estate projects leave behind.

The virtual and perhaps indeed fantasy images of modern cities are the kinds of urban futures to which planners of Sekondi-Takoradi, and other African cities aspire. The enchanting images play a role in the "economy of appearances" (Tsing, 2005). The spectacular images are part of the "dramatic performance" and "spectacular conjuring" that are essential for the Rendeavour's economic performance, in order to gather the necessary investment funds (Tsing, 2005). Harvey and Knox (2012, p. 524) argue that "Where promises and ideas which circulate with sufficient affective force [they] can have very powerful and profound material effects." King City's spectacular images conjure a variety of dreamed-of futures that materialise in various forms throughout the city. The chief of Takoradi is claiming and strengthening his position as a neotraditional chief, illustrated by his construction of a colossal palace that conveys his aspiration to be chief in the oil city. For community members in the peri–urban areas of Takoradi, the potential of the imagined future put in motion by the King City project takes the form of a connecting road, which in turn, promises them urban citizenship.

Acknowledgements

I am indebted to the people in Sekondi-Takoradi who have humored me and my many questions. My gratitude goes out to the Traditional Council in Busua, the Western Regional House of Chiefs in Sekondi, and the chiefs I was honored to interview, most grateful to Nana Bosumokura III. Jacob Ntiamoah and Nana Osei also deserve acknowledgement, I would truly have been lost in the city without them.

References

Appel, H., Anand, N., & Gupta, A. (2015, September 24). *The Infrastructure Toolbox*. Retrieved from http://www.culanth.org/fieldsights/725-the-infrastructure-toolbox [last accessed 13.2.2022].

Appel, H., Mason, A., & Watts, M. (2015). *Subterranean Estates: Life Worlds of Oil and Gas*. Ithaca: Cornell University Press.

Apter, A. (2005). *The Pan-African Nation : Oil and the Spectacle of Culture in Nigeria*. Chicago: University of Chicago press.

Beall, J. (2006). Cultural Weapons: Traditions, Inventions and the Transition to Democratic Governance in Metropolitan Durban. *Urban Studies*, 43(2), 457–473.

Berry, S. (2013). Questions of Ownership: Proprietorship and Control in a Changing Rural Terrain - A Case Study from Ghana. *Africa*, 83(Special Issue 01), 36–56.

Bob-Milliar, G. M. (2009). Chieftaincy, Diaspora, and Development: The Institution of Nksuohene in Ghana. *African Affairs*, 108(433), 541–558.

Coronil, F. (1997). *The Magical State : Nature, Money and Modernity in Venezuela*. Chicago : University of Chicago press.

Cross, J. (2014). *Dream Zones: Capitalism and Development in India*. London: Pluto Press.

Cross, J. (2015). The Economy of Anticipation Hope, Infrastructure, and Economic Zones in South India. *Comparative Studies of South Asia, Africa and the Middle East, 35*(3), 424–437.

De Boeck, F. (2012). Infrastructure: Commentary from Filip De Boeck. *Cultural Anthropology*, Art.No. 3. https://journal.culanth.org/index.php/ca/infrastructure-filip-de-boeck [last accessed 12.9.2022].

De Boeck, F. (2015). Dreams, Magic, and Mirrors: More Histories of Extraversion and Speculation in Central Africa. In Rao, V. V., Krishnamurthy, P., & Kuoni, C. (Eds.), *Speculation, Now: Essays and Artwork*. Duke University Press.

Ferguson, J. (1999). *Expectations of Modernity: Myths and Meanings of Urban Life on the Zambian Copperbelt*. Berkeley: University of California press.

Ferry, E. E., & Limbert, M. E. (2008). *Timely Assets*. School for Advanced Research Press.

Gupta, A. (2015, September 24). *Suspension. Theorizing the Contemporary*. Retrieved from https://culanth.org/fieldsights/suspension [last accessed 13.2.2022].

Harvey, P. (2005). The Materiality of State-Effects: An Ethnography of a Road in the Peruvian Andes. In C. Krohn-Hansen & K. G. Nustad, *State Formation: Anthropological Perspectives* (pp. 123–141). London: Pluto Press.

Harvey, P. (2010). Cementing Relations: The Materiality of Roads and Public Spaces in Provincial Peru. *Social Analysis*, 54(2), 28–46.

Harvey, P., & Knox, H. (2012). The Enchantments of Infrastructure. *Mobilities*, 7(4), 521–536.

Hirsch, E., & Stewart, C. (2005). Ethnographies of Historicity. *History and Anthropology*, 16(3), 261–274.

Hobsbawm, E., & Ranger, T. O. (1983). *The Invention of Tradition*. New York: Cambridge University Press.

Larkin, B. (2013). The Politics and Poetics of Infrastructure. *Annual Review of Anthropology*, 42(1), 327–343.

Nielsen, M. (2014). A Wedge of Time: Futures in the Present and Presents without Futures in Maputo, Mozambique. *Journal of the Royal Anthropological Institute*, 20(S1), 166–182.

Odotei, I. K., & Awedoba, A. K. (Eds.). (2006). *Chieftaincy in Ghana: Culture, Governance and Development*. Accra, Ghana: Sub-Saharan Publishers.

Plageman, N. (2013). Colonial Ambition, Common Sense Thinking, and the Making of Takoradi Harbor, Gold Coast. *History in Africa*, 1–36.

Reeves, M. (2013). Clean Fake: Authenticating Documents and Persons in Migrant Moscow. *American Ethnologist*, 40(3), 508–524.

Roy, A., & Ong, A. (Eds.). (2011). *Worlding Cities: Asian Experiments and the Art of Being Global*. Oxford: Blackwell Publishing Limited.

Shatkin, G. (2011). Coping with Actually Existing Urbanisms: The Real Politics of Planning in the Global Era. *Planning Theory*, 10(1), 79–87.

Tsing, A. L. (2005). *Friction: An Ethnography of Global Connection*. Princeton: Princeton University Press.

Ubink, J. (2007). Traditional Authority Revisited: Popular Perceptions of Chiefs and Chieftaincy in Peri-Urban Kumasi, Ghana. *The Journal of Legal Pluralism and Unofficial Law*, 39(55), 123–161.

Ubink, J. (2008). *Traditional Authorities in Africa: Resurgence in an Era of Democratisation*. Leiden: Leiden University Press.

Watson, V. (2013). African Urban Fantasies: Dreams or Nightmares? *Environment and Urbanization*, 26(1), 1–17.

Weszkalnys, G. (2016). A Doubtful Hope: Resource Affect in a Future Oil Economy. *J R Anthropol Inst*, 22, 127–146.

10

L'enclave pétrolière de Diffa ? La théorie de la malédiction des ressources et le désenclavement social et économique d'une commune pétrolière au Niger

Mahamidou Aboubacar Attahirou

1 Introduction

> Du pétrole béni à N'Gourti ? Serait-ce possible ? Peut-on sérieusement parler de la bénédiction du pétrole à N'Gourti, en Afrique ou partout ailleurs ? Cela ressort plutôt d'une simple et hasardeuse imagination, de la moquerie, voire d'une pure provocation.

Ceci présente un condensé de réactions auxquelles j'ai fait face lors de mes échanges avec mes interlocuteurs. Que ce soient des étudiants, des chercheurs ou tout simplement des ressortissants de la région pétrolifère de Diffa. La plupart de mes interlocuteurs s'étonne plutôt de ne pas entendre l'expression « malédiction du pétrole ». D'autant plus qu'au Niger – tout comme dans la plupart des pays pétroliers au demeurant –, il y a un discours qui renforce l'idée que le pétrole est une malédiction en termes politique, économique et sociale et que le Niger va souffrir avec l'aggravation de sa situation socio-économique, l'inflation, le surenchérissement du coût de la vie à toutes les échelles et notamment à l'échelle des zones d'extraction du pétrole. Ce type de discours issu de certains résultats de recherche dans d'autres contrées (Hoinathy, 2013), mais aussi promu par certaines ONG et structures de la société civile au Niger (e.g. GREN, ROTAB, PWYP), est importé des zones ayant des contextes qui ne sont pas forcément identiques à celui de la commune de N'Gourti et greffé à ce contexte précis par les ONG et la société civile qui, souvent, ne manquent pas d'argument fort à cet effet. Toutefois, ce discours est repris dans une large proportion par les médias qui interviennent dans ce secteur et qui cherchent tantôt à préserver les populations des effets néfastes de l'extraction des ressources naturelles en attirant l'attention des acteurs producteurs, tantôt à assurer leur gagne-pain en critiquant systématiquement l'État et les multinationales pétrolières (Schritt, 2020). Mais N'Gourti étant déjà une localité

 | DOI:10.1163/9789004530065_011

en souffrance économique, délaissée par l'État (Moussa, 2009, 2013), elle est également une zone saharienne très peu peuplée où les superficies cultivables sont quasiment inexistantes. Elle présente ainsi moins de risques de conflits ou de revendications territoriales sérieuses.[1] Le pétrole est au contraire arrivé à N'Gourti à un moment où toutes les autres opportunités se fermaient à la jeunesse de cette commune complètement enclavée, ce avant même la coulée du pétrole.[2]

L'essentiel de la littérature sur les industries extractives en général et sur le pétrole plus spécifiquement fait davantage ressortir des aspects liés aux enclaves et aux effondrements économiques (Auty, 1993; Karl, 1997). Appel (2012) montre comment, en Guinée Équatoriale, une compagnie pétrolière américaine essaye, dans une logique capitaliste, d'enclaver ses installations, en isolant ses services et ses employés expatriés dans une enclave qui se veut détachée de l'environnement social, culturel et économique du milieu dans lequel elle s'est implantée. Au sein de cette enclave, tout est prévu pour garantir un bien être aux agents expatriés de cette entreprise alors qu'à l'extérieur des murs de l'enclave, la population environnante qui accueille le projet pétrolier n'arrive même pas à avoir assez d'eau courante pour étancher sa soif. Ainsi, en enclavant ses propres installations, cette compagnie pétrolière isole de fait le reste de la ville au sein de laquelle elle s'est installée. Le degré d'isolement de cette enclave est tel qu'elle est même inaccessible pour les autorités de la Guinée Équatoriale. Au Tchad, Hoinathy (2013) fait remarquer à quel point la production pétrolière dans le bassin de Doba a exacerbé le coût de la vie pour les citoyens tchadiens, en favorisant ainsi la précarité dans laquelle vit la population, hôte du projet.

Toutefois, la théorie de la malédiction des ressources ou « malédiction du pétrole » (Ross, 2012) a ses propres limites. Presque toutes les causalités qui ont été établies par les tenants de cette théorie entre l'existence des ressources extractives et la survenance du déclin économique, politique et social sont aujourd'hui contestées par bien d'auteurs (Basedau & Lay, 2009; Brunnschweiler & Bulte, 2008; Cavalcanti et al., 2011; Haber & Menaldo, 2011; Leong & Mohaddes, 2011; Ross, 2009). Si dans certains pays, dans certaines situations, ils ont pu montrer des causalités qui semblent évidentes, cela ne fut pas le

1 En effet, dans le cadre de l'exploitation des ressources naturelles, les terres qui, grâce à leur potentiel agricole ou autre, procuraient aux communautés locales un avantage économique (notamment) avant l'installation d'un projet d'exploitation, sont plus susceptibles de vivre des contestations que celles qui n'en présentaient pas (Magrin & Vliet, 2005).

2 Je fais allusion aux conflits en Libye et au Nigéria qui sont les principales destinations de commerce et d'exode de cette jeunesse et qui sont jusqu'à aujourd'hui difficilement accessibles.

cas ailleurs. Certains pays ont su au contraire exploiter et profiter de leurs ressources pétrolières dans la prospérité (Karl, 2007; Kauffman et al., (n.d.); Montazer-Zohour, 1978; Rosser, 2006).

Le pétrole n'est pas un mal en soi. « The 'resource curse' is not due to the resource itself, which is simply a black and viscous substance, and it is not inevitable. A resource boom can be beneficial or detrimental » disait Karl Terry (2007, p. 3) malgré son penchant pour la théorie de la malédiction des ressources. S'il est assez fréquent ou vrai de compter en nombre ces pays pétroliers pauvres et instables, il est tout aussi vrai qu'il existe des pays producteurs riches et prospères qui ont bénéficié ou qui bénéficient toujours des bienfaits du pétrole. Ainsi, le pétrole n'est pas forcément une source de malédiction pour les pays producteurs, cela dépend plutôt des conditions dans lesquelles il est exploité (Humphreys et al., 2007). Le pétrole peut même être une bénédiction, une aubaine pour les populations et les pays producteurs en fonction des décisions utiles que ces derniers prendraient pour une gestion et une utilisation positive de cette manne (Humphreys et al., 2007; Magrin & van Vliet, 2005).

Sur la base d'une série d'enquêtes socio-anthropologiques réalisée entre 2012 et 2016 dans la région pétrolifère de Diffa, ce chapitre explore les induits de l'exploitation du pétrole sur la situation socio-économique des populations de la commune rurale de N'Gourti, populations riveraines des sites d'extraction. N'Gourti étant une zone désertique située à l'extrême Est du Niger, oubliée par les politiques publiques de l'État central et particulièrement enclavée avant l'avènement du pétrole, elle présente depuis le début du projet pétrolier des perspectives encourageantes qui ont abouti à un élan de désenclavement de la région toute entière. Même si le discours de la malédiction des ressources a fait son entrée dans la région et que certaines attentes ont été déçues, au point que quelques plaintes concernant l'exploitation pétrolière se font entendre (Schritt, 2018), on peut constater que la région dans son ensemble a bénéficié de cette exploitation, même si, évidemment, certains en profitent plus que d'autres. Ce chapitre essaye de montrer que, contrairement aux prédits de la théorie de la malédiction du pétrole et aux contextes dans lesquels l'extraction pétrolière a été assimilée, souvent sans retenue, à la pauvreté et à l'enclavement, le pétrole a ici favorisé le désenclavement socio-économique de la population, hôte d'étude. Ainsi, je soutiens d'une part que la théorie de la malédiction du pétrole est plutôt aveugle pour les micros dynamiques observées autour des zones d'extraction du pétrole et d'autre part que, ce que cette théorie défend, dépend en effet du contexte social, politique et économique dans lequel est extraite cette ressource, de sa situation géographique et aussi des acteurs en jeux (les compagnies pétrolières, les investisseurs, la population locale, etc.).

Le chapitre décrit tout d'abord la commune de N'Gourti avant l'ère pétrolière. Ensuite, il fait état des facteurs contribuant à l'amélioration de sa situation socio-économique avec l'avènement du pétrole. Suivra en conclusion une analyse sur les enseignements tirés du cas de N'Gourti par rapport aux prédictions de la théorie de la malédiction du pétrole.

2 N'Gourti pré-pétrolière

2.1 *N'Gourti, zone désertique enclavée*

La commune rurale de N'Gourti est située dans une zone désertique très aride à plus de 1.600 kilomètres à l'est de la capitale Niamey et à environ 270 kilomètres au nord-est de la ville de Diffa en extrême orient du pays. La commune de N'Gourti partage ses frontières ouest avec le département de Tesker en région de Zinder. Au nord elle fait frontière avec le département de Bilma dans le grand nord et au sud avec les départements de Maïné-Soroa et N'Guigmi. A l'est, elle fait directement frontière avec la République du Tchad.

N'Gourti couvre une superficie de 98 000 km^2, soit près de 2/3 de la région de Diffa entité administrative au sein de laquelle elle est logée. Mais ce vaste territoire de 98 000 km2 reste très faiblement peuplé. En 2012 le plus récent recensement général de la population et de l'habitat du Niger (RGPH – 2012) fait état d'une population de 51 767 individus disséminés à travers tout l'espace territorial, soit une densité d'un habitant au km2. Les conditions difficiles de vie dans cette localité caractérisées par une très faible pluviométrie, sa désertification et son inaccessibilité expliquent le faible enthousiasme exprimé à N'Gourti par les Nigériens en général et même par les ressortissants de la zone. N'Gourti accueille une moyenne pluviométrique annuelle de 5 millimètres, ce qui ne favorise pas du tout la production agricole. Le pastoralisme est l'activité phare pratiquée par la population composée majoritairement des Toubou, Arabe et Peulh. Aux côtés de ces ethnies majoritaires vivent des Touareg, des Haoussa et des Zarma qui sont pour la plupart des fonctionnaires (militaires, administrateurs) et des commerçants.

En raison du très mauvais état de la route, l'accès à N'Gourti coûte cher en temps comme en argent. Le trajet Diffa - N'Guigmi fait seulement 130 kilomètres, mais pour parcourir cette distance, un véhicule Pick-up met en moyenne quatre heures du fait du mauvais état de la route. Pour se rendre de N'Guigmi à N'Gourti, il faut attendre en moyenne une semaine pour trouver une place libre dans un véhicule de transport passager. Pour l'acheminement de marchandises, ce délai d'attente est facilement rallongé à trois, quatre semaines. Proportionnellement à la distance parcourue (140 km), les tarifs

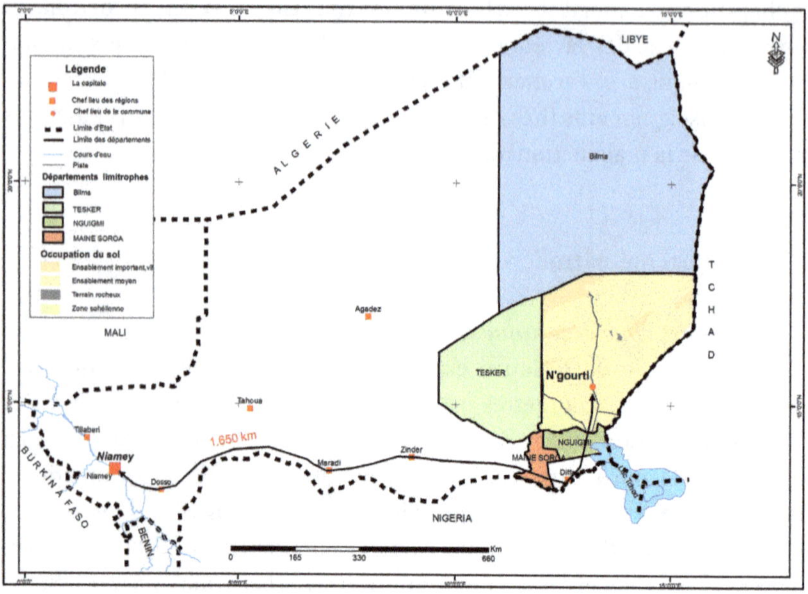

FIGURE 10.1 Carte de localisation de la commune rurale de N'Gourti
SOURCE : INSTITUT NATIONAL GÉOGRAPHIQUE DU NIGER (IGNN)

locaux de transport sont tout aussi onéreux. Les frais pour un voyageur sans bagage de N'Guigmi à N'Gourti s'élèvent à 5000 FCFA (7,60 Euro) pour un aller simple. Cent kilogrammes de Mil (une denrée alimentaire très consommée par les habitants de cette localité) sont acheminés pour 4000 FCFA de N'Guigmi à N'Gourti. Pour se rendre de N'Gourti à Diffa (270 km), il faut débourser le double de cette somme. De plus, en raison de toutes ces difficultés, il est pratiquement impossible pour la population de s'approvisionner en certaines denrées alimentaires tels que les fruits et autres légumes qui périssent rapidement. L'éloignement et le désert ne sont pas à eux-mêmes les seuls facteurs qui minent le développement de cette zone. Le manque d'investissement de l'État central ainsi que des natifs économiquement et politiquement bien nantis joue un rôle qui n'est pas des moindres.

2.2 *N'Gourti abandonné par l'Etat et par ses ressortissants*

La population de N'Gourti explique l'abandon de sa commune par le gouvernement central par l'éloignement de celle-ci du centre décisionnel du pays, à savoir Niamey, et par le désintérêt de l'État central pour N'Gourti. Cette marginalisation par le pouvoir politique central est observable dans presque toutes les communes excentrées du pays, notamment dans les communes situées au nord (dans les régions de Tahoua et d'Agadez) et à l'est (région de Diffa) du pays. Elle est souvent caractérisée par l'insuffisance ou l'absence d'investissements de l'État central dans les secteurs de l'hydraulique, de la santé, de l'éducation, de l'environnement, de l'élevage, de l'économie, de la sécurité et des infrastructures routières, etc.

Le secteur sanitaire à N'Gourti se résume à l'existence d'un centre de santé intégré (CSI), situé dans le chef-lieu de la commune, dépourvu d'électricité, d'eau potable, des médicaments et matériels nécessaires pour une population de plus 50.000 individus. L'insuffisance voire l'indisponibilité des agents de santé se fait également criarde. Les évacuations sanitaires, dans les cas où les véhicules du chef de poste administratif, de l'inspection d'enseignement de base (IEB) ou de l'armée ne viennent pas à la rescousse, coûtent la somme de 150.000 FCFA (229 Euro) pour une distance de 140 kilomètres en direction de l'Hôpital de District de N'Guigmi. Cette population se voit également privée par ce dernier de tout stock de vaccins en raison du manque d'électricité dans son CSI. Dans le cas où les véhicules du Chef de poste, de l'armée ou de l'IEB sont disponibles, ces coûts sont réduits à 100.000 FCFA (152 Euro). Cette somme d'argent représente une fortune pour une population sahélienne qui vit dans l'extrême pauvreté et dont le revenu moyen journalier est loin d'atteindre un (1) Euro.

Sur le plan des ressources humaines, très peu d'agents affectés dans cette zone y restent. Le personnel dudit CSI se trouve fréquemment en déplacement vers l'Ouest afin de, dit-on, « respirer l'air frais » des villes de l'ouest, loin des conditions de vie difficiles de N'Gourti. Les abandons de poste des services étatiques sont légion dans cette localité. Moussa (2009, p. 306) rapporte que :

> Les affectations dans la zone de Diffa – généralement assimilée à un département de la République du Tchad – sont toujours considérées par les fonctionnaires comme une punition administrative. Ceux qui sont dotés de ressources relationnelles importantes n'y viennent presque pas. On a souvent recensé des cadres ayant abandonné leur poste, faute d'une intervention pouvant les muter ailleurs, dans des régions du pays jugées plus "clémentes".

Le secteur de l'hydraulique, tout comme celui de la santé, souffre d'énormes insuffisances tant du point de vue des infrastructures que du point de vue des ressources humaines. Le service de l'hydraulique est géré par une association de volontaires locaux dénommée : AUSPE (Association des Utilisateurs de Services Publics de l'Eau). C'est un secteur presque complètement abandonné par l'État dont la seule contribution pour le fonctionnement de ce service s'est limitée à une formation technique élémentaire faite au profit du comité de gestion. Le mètre cube d'eau à N'Gourti coûte 500 FCFA (0,76 Euro). C'est le tarif le plus cher du Niger. S'agissant de l'hydraulique traditionnelle, on dénombre quatre (4) puits modernes dont deux (2) fonctionnels, un forage non fonctionnel dans le chef-lieu de la commune et un puits moderne à Meleck, un campement de pasteurs arabes situé à 50 kilomètres au nord-ouest du chef-lieu.

Dans le secteur éducatif, on dénombre en tout quatre infrastructures scolaires construites en matériaux définitifs dans le département. Il s'agit d'une école primaire créée en 1954, d'un collège d'enseignement général, d'un complexe franco-arabe construit en 2008 et financé par Muammar Kaddafi (Président libyen jusqu'en 2011) dans le chef-lieu de la commune, et d'une classe située dans le campement de Meleck. Les infrastructures routières sont pratiquement inexistantes ou en voie de l'être. La seule infrastructure perceptible dans cette zone est la relique de la voie bitumée Diffa - N'Guigmi, dite « Route de l'unité », bâtie en 1975.

Les conditions de vie particulièrement difficiles dans la zone de Diffa en général et dans celles de N'Guigmi et N'Gourti en particulier ont été sources de bien des frustrations collectives qui ont conduit soit à l'abandon de la localité par ses propres natifs, soit à la création des mouvements armés. L'une des premières rébellions armées au Niger a vu le jour dans le Manga (partie sud-est de la région de N'Gourti) en 1990 sous la dénomination du Front Démocratique

FIGURE 10.2 État de la route Diffa - Nguigmi avant les travaux de bitumage (dans les environs de la commune de Kablewa)
SOURCE : AUTEUR, OCTOBRE 2014

pour le Renouveau (FDR). Cette rébellion avait pour mission de dénoncer et de rétablir l'exclusion socio-économique et politique (par le gouvernement central) à laquelle faisait face les populations du Manga et même celles du Kawar (frontière nord de N'Gourti avec le département de Bilma) (Hamit & Abdrourahamane, 2013). Pour le FDR, la centralisation étatique ou « l'Ouestisation »[3] des programmes de politiques publiques et des projets de développement nuit gravement à l'émancipation sociale, économique et politique de la population du Manga et il est nécessaire d'intervenir pour y remédier. Toutefois le pouvoir central n'est pas le seul acteur critiqué concernant l'abandon de N'Gourti. Les personnes fortunées et autres hauts cadres de l'administration publique et privée issus du terroir sont également mis en cause dans l'observance de la léthargie socio-économique caractéristique de la région, et cela par refus d'investir ou d'attirer des partenaires pour le développement dans la localité. Moussa (2009, p. 291) relève que :

> Les ressortissants de N'Gourti, dispersés dans plusieurs régions du pays et particulièrement dans la capitale, interviennent très peu dans le débat public local. On est d'ailleurs frappé par leur étrange détachement vis-à-vis de toutes les questions d'intérêt général du poste administratif. N'Gourti, nous dira-t-on, a pourtant produit des cadres ayant occupé de hautes responsabilités dans l'administration publique nigérienne : ministres, députés, directeurs généraux.... Mais beaucoup d'observateurs ont l'impression que ces fonctionnaires fuient leur zone, où ils viennent peu, et s'impliquent peu ou pas du tout dans les affaires locales.

Tout comme le désert, le manque d'investissement de l'État et des personnes fortunées locales, le commerce local n'aide pas assez à la promotion du développement socio-économique régional. Les ressources économiques traditionnelles de N'Gourti avant l'ère pétrolière étaient dans un état assez léthargique.

2.3 *N'Gourti et ses activités économiques traditionnelles*

Les principales sources de l'économie de la commune de N'Gourti sont l'élevage, le commerce, l'exode et la rente des projets de développement. Cette dernière se manifeste par l'intervention des structures internationales telles que le PAM, le PNUD, Save the Children, la Fondation Aicha Kaddafi et des Programmes de développement tels que le PAC (Programme d'Action Communautaire), le PSSP

3 Le terme "Ouestisation" fait référence ici au fait que le gouvernement central concentre l'essentiel de ses investissements et programmes de développement dans les régions ouest du pays.

(Projet de Sécurisation des Systèmes Pastoraux N'Gourti-Termit), le PADL-N (Programme d'Appui au Développement Local – N'Guigmi), etc. Ces structures interviennent globalement dans le secteur éducatif, hydraulique, sanitaire et pastoral. Le PADL-N est beaucoup plus intervenu dans la promotion de la gouvernance locale à travers l'accompagnement des structures décentralisées.

En ce qui concerne le commerce local, il est essentiellement constitué de la vente des produits de premières nécessités comme les céréales, le sucre, le thé, le savon, les tissus, et autres petits articles de consommation à l'image de la plupart des zones rurales nigériennes. Le type de commerce qui s'est développé en particulier est celui de l'exportation de dromadaires vers les pays magrébins. L'élevage local est pratiqué dans une large mesure afin de soutenir cette activité transnationale.

L'élevage, les échanges commerciaux dans le chef-lieu de la commune, le commerce transsaharien des dromadaires et l'exode sont les principales sources de revenu pré-pétrolières de N'Gourti. Ces sources d'économies traditionnelles soumises aux aléas climatiques, à l'isolement de la commune et au désintéressement du pouvoir central, ainsi que des ressortissants locaux n'avaient pas réussi à favoriser le développement socio-économique de la commune tant espéré par la population. L'avènement du pétrole va-t-il jouer un rôle pour le changement de la situation ? C'est ce que nous allons essayer de voir à travers les lignes qui suivent.

2.4 *N'Gourti, zone pétrolière et qualité de vie de la population locale*

Comme je viens de le décrire, avant l'exploitation du pétrole, N'Gourti était une localité très enclavée géographiquement et économiquement. Mais, depuis le début du projet pétrolier, cette commune présente des perspectives encourageantes qui ont abouti à un élan de désenclavement de toute la région. Le pétrole a apporté, dans une certaine mesure, des changements dans plusieurs secteurs de la vie socio-économique de la population locale. Les secteurs dans lesquels le pétrole a su faire profiter les populations locales sont entre autres : le commerce, l'emploi, les infrastructures drainées par la production pétrolière, etc. Ces avantages et facilités accordés par l'exploitation pétrolière constituent maintenant le point de départ du désenclavement de la commune et même, de toute la région de Diffa.

2.5 *Pétrole et désenclavement économique de la région*

A N'Gourti, le commerce a connu une certaine prospérité pendant la phase de construction du projet ainsi qu'après cette phase. Le développement de l'activité pétrolière a en effet induit des mouvements intenses de personnes dans l'Agadem. Le territoire de N'Gourti qui jadis souffrait du manque de présence humaine intense a vu sa situation métamorphosée, passant d'une zone « proscrite » à un eldorado pour les jeunes employés des entreprises pétrolières et autres chercheurs d'opportunités qui viennent d'autres localités nigériennes.

Cette ruée vers la zone pétrolière de N'Gourti a drainé des opportunités d'affaires aux commerçants locaux. Le site du marché du chef-lieu de la commune qui, avant, était composé d'un nombre très restreint de boutiques s'est en effet agrandi. Le mouvement démographique à travers la commune de N'Gourti était tellement important que les activités commerciales avaient pris de l'ampleur. De nouvelles boutiques ont été ainsi construites sur ledit site ainsi que sur un autre site situé à l'entrée du village. Des commerçants ayant des boutiques intégrées à leur maison les ont déplacées à la place du marché. D'autres, ayant déjà des boutiques sur la place du marché, ont senti, face à la forte demande, la nécessité d'en construire d'autres sur le site situé à l'entrée du village. La population de la commune de N'Gourti a profité du développement de l'économie locale pour améliorer relativement ses conditions de vie. Des produits manufacturés tels que le lait en poudre, les tomates en boîtes de conserve, les sardines, les produits pharmaceutiques et autres articles en provenance de sites pétroliers étaient disponibles sur le marché local et à moindres coûts. Ceci a apporté un réconfort dans le quotidien des habitants de N'Gourti qui étaient habituellement en manque de ces produits de première nécessité considérés comme du luxe à l'échelle locale.

Cette nouvelle dynamique commerciale n'a pas profité qu'aux petits commerçants locaux. Les principales entreprises locales tirent également profit de la présence du pétrole dans la région. Après son implantation, la CNPC-NP a décidé de collaborer avec les principales entreprises locales pour supporter ses activités. Certaines de ces entreprises appartiennent aux ressortissants de N'Gourti et N'Guigmi (Entreprise ZOUWAYA par exemple) et d'autres aux autres localités de la région (BARKA, AZIMA, STT, SANE, etc.). Ces entreprises interviennent essentiellement dans la fourniture de biens alimentaires (viande, légumes, boissons, etc.), le transport des agents et du matériel de la CNPC-NP, le terrassement, l'approvisionnement en hydrocarbures, la construction de bâtiments, le fonçage de puits, les forages d'eau et autres prestations de services. Cette participation des entreprises locales au développement de l'activité pétrolière aux côtés de la CNPC-NP leur a permis non seulement de faire énormément d'affaires, mais aussi d'apprendre et d'avoir de l'expérience dans le rude métier du secteur pétrolier. C'est pourquoi, pour elles, la production pétrolière a non seulement contribué au développement économique et social de leur région, mais elle a aussi contribué à leur propre rayonnement. Un de ces entrepreneurs locaux me notifie ceci :

> Maintenant la région de Diffa a beaucoup changé, les activités économiques marchent beaucoup. Les camions de transport se comptent par centaines chaque jour que Dieu fait. Et c'est au moins trois à cinq personnes par camion. C'est déjà un plus pour l'économie parce que ces personnes vont dépenser dans la localité auprès de nos populations. Maintenant, partout, c'est des restaurants qui fleurissent dans la ville, même vous, c'est parce qu'il y a du pétrole dans la région que vous êtes là, et vous allez dépenser. Notre entreprise a démarré avec seulement 140 millions, maintenant ça ne fait qu'évoluer. En 2005 nous étions à 4 milliards, maintenant nous sommes à 15 voire 16 milliards. Extrait d'entretien avec Elhadji Ali Gagaré, un des responsables de l'Entreprise Barka.[4]

Aux côtés des petits commerçants et entreprises locaux, les jeunes sont eux-aussi concernés par les bienfaits de l'arrivée du pétrole.

2.6 *Pétrole et emploi des jeunes*

Parmi les changements positifs induits par la production du pétrole dans la région de Diffa, on peut retenir l'opportunité d'emploi offerte aux Nigériens en général et à la jeunesse locale en particulier. Au début de la production en 2008 les sociétés chinoises ont fait appel à un grand nombre d'ouvriers nigériens (dont une partie est réservée aux ressortissants de la région) destinés à travailler dans l'industrie pétrolière. Après 2008 et 2009, cette offre d'emploi était restée constante avant de chuter entre 2010 et 2013, période qui coïncide avec la fin de la construction du projet. En effet, à chaque début d'installation d'un projet pétrolier, il faut procéder à la construction et mise en place de l'infrastructure nécessaire, et cette mise en place requiert un grand nombre d'ouvriers qualifiés et non qualifiés. Ainsi, afin de satisfaire ce besoin, les sociétés productrices procèdent à un recrutement de masse. Cela a permis à beaucoup de jeunes de trouver de l'emploi et en conséquence, d'améliorer leur situation socio-économique. Toutefois, en 2010–2011, la phase de construction et d'installation de l'infrastructure pétrolière est pratiquement achevée sur le site principal d'Agadem à Tantammardé (Djaouro), dans l'actuel département de N'Gourti. Ainsi, les compagnies pétrolières chinoises GWDC et DAGANG spécialisées respectivement dans le forage et la construction de pipeline, n'avaient plus besoin d'une masse de main-d'œuvre. Elles ont alors procédé à la mise en stand-by et/ou au licenciement de leurs employés. Ceci a fait observer une

4 Entreprise spécialisée dans les BTP (Bâtiments et Travaux Publics).

perte importante d'emplois chez cette jeunesse. La situation de l'offre d'emploi dans le secteur pétrolier est ainsi restée en baisse ferme jusqu'en 2013, année durant laquelle elle a connu une croissance importante avant de rechuter à nouveau en fin 2014 sous la menace de Boko Haram.

Selon l'inspection du travail de la région de Diffa, depuis 2008 (année qui coïncide avec le contrat entre la CNPC et le gouvernement du Niger pour l'exploitation pétrolière), les demandes et offres d'emploi ne font que croître dans la région de Diffa. Mieux, sur toutes les offres, c'est en moyenne plus de 80% d'entre elles qui sont offertes dans la branche d'industries extractives. En 2013, la demande a monté de plus de 80% (5918 demandes contre 2980 en 2008). La même année, l'offre d'emploi a aussi augmenté de plus de 100% (1989 postes offerts contre 951 en 2008) en raison du démarrage des activités de la compagnie britannique Savannah Petroleum S.A sur une partie du site d'Agadem.

L'offre d'emploi a permis à beaucoup de jeunes de la région d'améliorer leurs conditions de vie socio-économiques. L'argent qu'ils ont gagné dans l'industrie pétrolière en travaillant généralement comme ouvrier leur a permis de faire beaucoup d'économie, de s'acheter des motos, des véhicules, des parcelles et même de construire des habitats. Le niveau de chômage a été considérablement réduit de telle sorte que le problème de sécurité interne lié au vagabondage de la jeunesse (vol, coupures de route, consommation de drogue, etc.) se posait de moins en moins dans la région comme le témoigne Matadawou Ibrahim Bagara, ancien président de l'association monde rural Diffa :

> Cette affaire d'exploitation pétrolière nous a beaucoup plu. Le fait que nos enfants arrivent à trouver du travail dans l'industrie pétrolière a réduit nos souffrances. Le chômage diminue de plus en plus ainsi que la délinquance. Quand tu as un enfant qui part travailler dans l'industrie pétrolière et gagne de l'argent, il construit une maison à Diffa, il se marie avec ses propres moyens, il nourrit sa femme. Et, toi son père, tu es au village, il te trouve là-bas et t'offre un billet de 1000 francs, mais que voudras-tu de plus ?

Malgré la baisse des activités pétrolières de 2011 à 2012 ayant conduit au licenciement de beaucoup de travailleurs locaux, malgré aussi le conflit lié aux incursions répétées de Boko Haram, l'industrie pétrolière a visiblement permis à un nombre important de jeunes Diffalais de se réaliser et de subvenir aux besoins de leurs familles. Maintenant voyons ce qu'il en est du désenclavement géographique de la zone.

2.7 *Pétrole et désenclavement géographique de la région*

Grâce à l'exploitation pétrolière, des infrastructures sont bâties dans la région de Diffa. Certaines sont l'émanation directe de certains acteurs principaux impliqués dans le processus de production (entreprises pétrolières, État), d'autres sont l'initiative d'acteurs privés qui les ont construites afin de profiter des opportunités offertes par l'extraction pétrolière. Les entreprises pétrolières chinoises et sous-traitantes nigériennes, conformément à leur politique de Responsabilité Sociétale de l'Entreprise (RSE), ont construit des centres des soins, des classes, foré des puits, bitumé des routes, etc. L'un des investissements les plus importants pour les populations locales reste le bitumage de la route Diffa - N'Guigmi - Frontière Tchad (distante de 185 kilomètres) appelée aussi « Route du pétrole », financée par l'État du Niger à hauteur de 11 milliards de FCFA et exécuté par une entreprise chinoise. Cette route revêt une importance capitale pour les populations locales et même sous-régionales. Elle devait non seulement lier Diffa à N'Guigmi et à la République tchadienne, mais aussi N'Guigmi à N'Gourti et à Bilma.

FIGURE 10.3 Travaux de bitumage de la route Diffa - N'guigmi - Frontière Tchad (tronçon Garin Dogo – Gaguam)
SOURCE : AUTEUR, OCTOBRE 2014

La maire de la commune rurale de N'Gourti notifie ceci :

> Avec mon véhicule Pick-up je passe quatre heures de temps pour faire le trajet Diffa - N'Guigmi. Et ceux qui utilisent les voitures de transport public prennent non seulement plus de temps, mais payent aussi 10.000 FCFA pour les 130 kilomètres. Donc, avec la route du pétrole, non seulement la durée de transport va diminuer, mais les coûts baisseront aussi. On espère même voir les compagnies de transport "Rimbo"[5] par-là. Extrait d'entretien avec Koubra Kadallah Boutrane, Maire de la commune de N'Gourti.[6]

La région de Diffa est en effet un carrefour international. Plusieurs nationalités transitent par cette région, particulièrement entre la Komadougou et le Lac Tchad. Vers le lac Tchad, le principal point de transit est N'Guigmi. Les exodants, les commerçants, les éleveurs, les pêcheurs et autres affairistes venus du Bénin, du Tchad, du Soudan, de la Centrafrique, etc. transitent par la commune de N'Guigmi pour leurs activités. Comme le souligne le secrétaire général du gouvernorat de la région de Diffa, la remise en état de la route est d'une importance capitale pour la population.

> C'est une route très utilisée dans la sous-région. C'est la route des "véhicules 10 roues" en partance et en provenance du Tchad. Presque tous les véhicules "neufs" (véhicules d'occasion) en provenance de Lomé, de Cotonou et à destination du Tchad transitent par-là malgré la longue distance (plus de 2600 kilomètres). Les marchands de bétails en provenance du Tchad, du Soudan, du Cameroun et de la Centrafrique et à destination du Nigeria transitent par là en passant par N'Guigmi, Diffa, Tam, Maïné avant d'atteindre Gaydam au Nigéria. Ils préfèrent contourner et passer par là parce que c'est une voie plus sûre que d'aller directement au Nigeria bouleversé par Boko Haram» Extrait d'entretien avec Hassan Ardo Issa, Secrétaire général du gouvernorat de la région de Diffa.

D'aucuns pensent même que la réalisation de ladite infrastructure pourra jouer un plus grand rôle dans l'échange international et dans l'exécution de certains cultes.

---

5 Rimbo est le nom d'une des plus importantes compagnies de transport public modernes au Niger.

6 Le bitumage de cette route a été interrompu fin 2015 sous la menace des incursions de Boko Haram.

> Avec le rétablissement de cette route, même le coût de transport pour La Mecque pourrait baisser. Les gens pourront faire leur voyage à travers Diffa, Tchad, Soudan jusqu'à La Mecque et faire leur Hadj.[7] Extrait d'entretien avec Maï Wandara, deuxième vice-président du conseil régional de Diffa.

Auparavant, se rendre à N'Guigmi et notamment à N'Gourti était assimilable à une mission impossible du fait de l'inaccessibilité de la zone. Mais, avec l'exploitation pétrolière, la situation a changé dans ce secteur. Le délai d'attente pour se rendre de N'Guigmi à N'Gourti est passé d'une semaine à moins d'une journée pour le transport des personnes et de quatre semaines à quelques jours pour le transport des marchandises. Les coûts ont également baissé de 50 % pour le transport de passagers et de marchandises. Ceci parce que les « pétroliers »[8] participaient au transport public. La population pouvait ainsi effectuer ses déplacements presque quotidiennement et à moindre coût. Les commerçants locaux pouvaient alors facilement introduire plusieurs variétés de marchandises et autres aliments qui manquaient à la population.

Par ailleurs, un autre avantage important pour la population de cette zone est l'implantation des réseaux de téléphonie mobile grâce au pétrole. Pour le besoin de leurs communications et de sécurisation de leurs activités, les entreprises pétrolières ont incité certains opérateurs de téléphonie mobile à s'implanter dans le département. Cette implantation a été en effet d'un grand soulagement pour les locaux parce que ce fut un moyen supplémentaire qui a contribué à leur désenclavement, en faisant d'abord baisser les coûts de la communication téléphonique et en leur permettant désormais de pouvoir utiliser les réseaux de téléphonie cellulaire pour envoyer ou recevoir de l'argent. Il y a lieu de noter qu'avant le pétrole, cette opportunité n'était pas du tout à la portée de la population. Cette dernière utilisait l'appareil cellulaire satellitaire Thuraya pour communiquer à raison de 1000 FCFA la minute. Or avec ce coût, seule l'élite locale était en mesure d'utiliser ce service. Maintenant, avec l'extension du réseau téléphonique dans la zone, chacun est en mesure d'émettre et de recevoir un appel, la minute n'excédant guère 60 FCFA.

2.8 *Nouvelle situation économique, nouveau regard !*

Dans le cadre de la répartition de « l'argent du pétrole », la constitution du Niger prévoit que l'État central rétrocède aux communes concernées 15% des recettes fiscales tirées de l'industrie pétrolifère. Ces 15% sont ensuite repartis entre toutes les communes de la région. Des indices tels que le poids

7 Pèlerinage à la Mecque.

8 Les conducteurs des véhicules des entreprises pétrolières principales et sous-traitantes.

TABLE 10.1 Tableau de répartition des 15% des recettes fiscales pétrolières aux 12 communes de la région de Diffa au titre de l'année 2014

TOTAL MONTANT A ALLOUER PAR COMMUNE								
Communes	**Démographie**	**Environment**	**Ress Locales**	**Equipement**	**Superficie**	**Vol Invest**	**Fonc COM.**	**Total**
Mainé	108 400 659	21 801 600	42 935 526	46 812 627	8 175 600	29 508 735	12 616 667	270 251 415
Foulatari	42 615 427	21 801 600	37 029 755	7 329 361	8 175 600	8 450 993	12 616 667	138 019 403
N'Guelbely	30 256 086	21 801 600	24 202 268	-	8 175 600	4 542 000	12 616 667	101 594 221
Goudoumari	138 447 475	21 801 600	22 407 749	44 467 347	32 702 401	28 257 918	12 616 667	300 701 157
CU Diffa	77 701 251	43 603 201	53 275 373	132 552 182	8 175 600	75 236 497	12 616 667	403 160 771
Chétimari	90 108 780	21 801 600	45 859 927	83 671 551	8 175 600	49 166 827	12 616 667	311 400 953
Gueskerou	52 091 793	21 801 600	32 776 080	33 767 666	8 175 600	22 551 422	12 616 667	183 780 829
Bosso	89 520 895	21 801 600	80 183 661	46 413 616	16 351 200	29 295 929	12 616 667	296 183 569
Toumour	16 126 207	21 801 600	28 133 119	-	5 450 400	4 542 000	12 616 667	88 669 994
N'Guigmi	64 981 194	65 404 801	17 375 500	3 463 892	8 175 600	6 389 409	12 616 667	178 407 064
Kablewa	36 038 555	43 603 201	19 835 645	10 301 768	19 076 400	10 036 276	12 616 667	151 526 513
N'Gourty	71 271 695	218 016 005	4 747 404	-	136 260 003	4 542 000	12 616 667	447 453 775
total	817 560 018	545 040 012	408 780 009	408 780 009	272 520 006	272 520 006	151 400 003	2 876 600 063

Le Rapporteur **Le Président**

SOURCE : ABOUBACAR ATTAHIROU M. NOVEMBRE 2014

démographique, la proximité aux principales zones d'extraction, le degré d'exécution du budget propre de la commune, l'étendue territoriale de la commune, etc. servent de critères de base à la répartition de cette manne.

Ces critères tirent leur origine du Décret no 2007-184/PRN/MI/D du 25 mai 2007 fixant les modes de calcul des recettes minières attribuées aux communes des régions concernées.[9] Ainsi, ce sont environ trois (3) milliards de FCFA qui ont été redistribués aux douze communes de la région de Diffa pour la première année d'attribution, l'année 2014.

En effet, c'est avec ces ressources que lesdites communes essayent désormais de planifier et d'assurer le progrès économique et social qu'elles n'avaient jamais réussi à réaliser. D'importants investissements sont ainsi programmés dont les infrastructures sanitaires, hydrauliques, éducatives, etc. Il faut noter que ces sommes redistribuées représentent des sommes colossales pour la plupart de ces communes dont les recettes habituelles ne dépassent guère le quart de ce que « leur pétrole » leur donne. A titre d'exemple, la commune de N'Gourti, qui a bénéficié de près de 450.000.000 FCFA de rente pétrolière au titre de l'année 2014, avait un budget en recettes de 28.434.000 FCFA en 2010 et dont les recettes réelles étaient de moins de 5.000.000 FCFA cette même année. Au titre de l'année 2015, cette commune a reçu plus de 280.000.000 FCFA et un peu plus de 300.000.000 FCFA l'année suivante. La qualité des dépenses effectuées avec ces fonds chaque année par la mairie détermine l'importance de la répartition au titre de l'année suivante. Ainsi, avec l'argent reçu, la mairie de N'Gourti a fait construire des infrastructures éducatives, sanitaires et hydrauliques.

Il convient de noter que cette politique gouvernementale consistant à rétrocéder constitutionnellement une partie des recettes fiscales pétrolières aux communes de la région pétrolière peut être assimilée à un nouvel intérêt politique porté à cette région par le gouvernement central grâce, effectivement, à la manne du pétrole.

3 Conclusion : N'Gourti et la théorie de la malédiction du pétrole

Les ressources naturelles, le pétrole en particulier, sont largement vues comme une source inévitable de déclin économique à cause d'une économie enclavée,

---

9 Ce décret a été originellement pris dans le cadre de l'exploitation minière et non pétrolière. Il vient de faire l'objet d'une révision par le gouvernement suite au conseil des ministres tenu le 02 septembre 2022 pour préciser davantage les termes d'utilisation des recettes pétrolières et de raffinage allouées aux collectivités territoriales.

détachée de l'environnement économique, politique et sociale dans lequel elle s'est installée. La littérature qui en fait cas est de loin la plus importante par rapport à celle qui exploite d'autres facettes des conséquences de ces ressources, certes. Toutefois il ne serait pas juste ou simplement neutre, quand on envisage les choses d'un point de vue scientifique, de fondre sous le coup de la masse savante, et de s'empêcher d'explorer ces autres pistes tout aussi parlantes. Et c'est bien l'exercice auquel je me suis livré à travers ce chapitre fondé sur une recherche socio-anthropologique, sur une observation du vécu de ma communauté d'études au-delà de tout discours conformiste. Il est vrai que comme à l'image de certaines théories savantes et de discours véhiculés çà et là par les médias présentant souvent sans aucune réserve le pétrole comme source de malheur, les communautés hôtes des projets pétroliers ou miniers ont tendance à reprendre mimétiquement les mêmes discours. Ces discours sont aussi liés aux attentes excessives sur la production du pétrole par la population comme sur les avantages du pétrole très inégalement redistribués entre ceux qui profitent et ceux qui n'arrivent pas à en profiter. Mais le discours de la malédiction du pétrole n'est pas pour autant toujours la représentation stricte de la réalité observable à certaines échelles. Comme le notifie Le Meur (2016, p. 4) :

> La contribution de l'anthropologie, et particulièrement de la démarche ethnographique – à la fois méthode et épistémologie – qui la sous-tend est de sortir des explications unilatérales, mono-causales ou réductrices, souvent très normatives, qui souvent dominent les champs académiques et politiques, comme par exemple la notion fourre-tout de "Malédiction des ressources".

Ainsi, la portée positive des réalisations (construction d'écoles et leurs équipements, dotation de ces écoles en matériel didactique au profit des apprenants et des professeurs, réalisation des forages d'eau, désenclavement géographique, économique et social de la commune, rétrocession d'une partie des recettes fiscales issues de l'extraction pétrolière aux collectivités concernées, offres d'emploi, etc.), occasionnées par la manne pétrolière à l'échelle de la commune de N'Gourti et même au-delà à l'échelle régionale de Diffa ne saurait être ignorée.

Pour comprendre la portée de ce point de vue ici avancé, il suffit également, et entre autres, de faire un playback sur ce qu'était N'Gourti, sur sa situation socio-économique pré-pétrole. En effet, avant l'ère pétrolière, N'Gourti (et au-delà toute la région de Diffa) était une localité économiquement et géographiquement déconnectée du reste du pays, une zone réellement enclavée qui était susceptible d'être abandonnée, même par ses natifs. Il fut une époque où enseignants, agents de santé et autres fonctionnaires de l'État natifs de cette localité la fuiyaient quand ils y étaient affectés du fait de son enclavement, de sa sécheresse climatique et économique.

Néanmoins, le pétrole produit bien sûr des effets négatifs. L'environnement est le pan le plus susceptible de subir les impacts néfastes de l'activité pétrolière. Ainsi, les plus importants dégâts enregistrés en ce sens portent notamment sur l'effondrement, lors de la phase de la construction du projet pétrolier, de puits traditionnels et la perturbation de la faune. La commune rurale de N'Gourti abrite une importante réserve faunique, dont l'emblématique gazelle Dorcas et l'Addax, située sur des paysages propices au tourisme. Mais cette faune est en voie de disparition du fait notamment de la chasse opérée par les militaires présents dans cette zone bien avant l'ère pétrolière, et qui continue encore aujourd'hui (Meynier, 2009; Moussa, 2009). Il est tout aussi raisonnable de s'interroger sur l'instabilité sécuritaire au Nord du pays depuis 2011, au Sud et dans la zone du Lac Tchad depuis 2014. Cette instabilité sécuritaire sur pratiquement toutes les frontières du pays serait-elle totalement étrangère à l'activité pétrolière au Niger et à ses enjeux ? Le terrorisme au Nord, Boko Haram dans la zone du Lac Tchad seraient-ils purement et simplement l'œuvre d'un fait de hasard ou plutôt d' une stratégie de certains groupes d'intérêts afin d'influer sur la redistribution des cartes dans le cadre du contrôle des ressources énergétiques tel que cela a été prévu par la théorie de la « malédiction des ressources »?

Remerciements

Je tiens à exprimer mes vifs remerciements au LASDEL et à l'Université de Göttingen pour m'avoir fourni les moyens nécessaires à la réalisation de cette recherche à travers le Programme SPP 1448 financé par la DFG. Je tiens également à remercier tous mes collègues de ce programme, notamment Jannik Schritt et Annika Witte, pour leur lecture des premières versions de ce texte et leur contribution.

Références

Appel, H. C. (2012). Walls and White elephants: Oil Extraction, Responsibility, and Infrastructural Violence in Equatorial Guinea, *Ethnography*, 13(4), 439–65.

Auty, R. M. (1993). Sustaining Development in Mineral Economies: The Resource Curse Thesis. London: Routledge.

Basedau, M. & Lay, J. (2009). Resource Curse or Rentier Peace? The Ambiguous Effects of Oil Wealth and Oil Dependence on Violent Conflict. *Journal of Peace Research*, 46(6), 757–776.

Brunnschweiler, C.N. & Bulte, EH. (2008). The Resource Curse Revisited: A Tale of Paradoxes and Red Herrings. *Journal of Environmental Economics and Management*, 55(3), 248–64.

Cavalcanti, T. V. V., Mohaddes, K., & Raissi, M. (2011). Does Oil Abundance Harm Growth? *Applied Economics Letters*, 18 (10/12) , 1181–1184.

Hamit, A., & Abdrourahamane, MM. (2013). *Rapport d'étude sur la prévention et la gestion des crises : études de cas de N'Guigmi et N'Gourti dans région de Diffa*, PNUD, Niger.

Humphreys, M., Sachs, J., & Stiglitz, J. E. (2007). *Escaping the Resource Curse*. New York: Columbia University Press.

Karl, T. (1997). *The Paradox of Plenty: Oil Booms and Petro-States*. Berkeley: University of California Press.

Karl, T. (2007). Oil-led Development: Social, Political and Economic Consequences. *CDDRL Working papers*, 80.

Kauffman, I., Aimé, C. & Edel, A. (n.d.). *TPE: Pétrole et conséquences géopolitiques*. http://tpe-petrole.lo.gs [Last accessed 31.1.2022].

Haber, S. & Menaldo, V. (2011). Do Natural Resources Fuel Authoritarianism? A Reappraisal of the Resource Curse. *American Political Science Review*, 105(1), 1–26.

Hoinathy, R. (2013). *Pétrole et changement social au Tchad : rente pétrolière et monétisation des relations économiques et sociales dans la zone pétrolière de Doba*. Paris: Karthala.

Le Meur, P.Y. (2016). *Énergie, pouvoir et société : approches anthropologiques*. Papier JTD Danang du 8 au 16 juillet 2016.

Magrin G., & van Vliet, G. (2005). Greffe pétrolière et dynamiques territoriales : l'exemple de l'on-shore tchadien. *Afrique contemporaine*, 216 (4): 87–105.

Meynier, A. (2009). *Réserve Naturelle et exploitation pétrolière dans la Zone du Massif de Termit et du Désert du Tin Touma (Niger) : perceptions et représentations des nouveaux enjeux. Approche par acteurs et par campements*. Mémoire de Master 2, Université Denis Diderot Paris VII, Paris, France.

Leong, W. & Mohaddes, K. (2011). Institutions and the Volatility Curse. *CWPE*, 1145. Retrieved from https://www.econ.cam.ac.uk/research-files/repec/cam/pdf/cwpe1145.pdf [last accessed 13.2.2022].

Montazer-Zohour, M. (1978). *Pétrole et développement au Moyen-Orient*. Paris: De Gruyter Mouton.

Moussa, H. (2009). Les pouvoirs locaux à N'gourti. In J-P. Olivier De Sardan & M. S. Tidjani Alou (eds.), *Les pouvoirs locaux au Niger : Tome 1 : A la veille de la décentralisation* (pp. 279–307). Paris: Karthala.

Moussa, H. (2013). *Enjeux de l'exploitation pétrolière : etude de cas à N'Gourti.* Présentation à la conférence ECAS à Lisbonne.

Ross, M. L. (2009). *Oil and Democracy Revisited.* Retrieved from http://www.michaelross.info/papers/working/Oil%20and%20Democracy%20Revisited.pdf [last accessed 13.2.2022].

Ross, M. L. (2012). *The Oil Curse: How Petroleum Wealth Shapes the Development of Nations.* Princeton: Princeton University Press.

Rosser, A. (2006). The Political Economy of the Resource Curse: A Literature Survey. Brighton, IDS, *IDS Working Paper*, 268.

Schritt, J. (2018): Crude Controversies: Disputes along Niger's Petro-Infrastructure. *History and Anthropology*, 29(5), 645–669.

Schritt, J. (2020). Crude Talking: Radio and the Politics of Naming, Blaming and Claiming in Oil-Age Niger. *Journal of Contemporary African Studies*, 38(3): 415–436.

11

De l'argent facile ? Pétrole et transformation rurale-urbaine dans la région de Zinder (Niger)

Salissou Oubandoma and Jannik Schritt

1 Introduction

L'exploitation du pétrole est souvent anticipée par une grande partie de la population comme source de richesse et de bien être en dépit des conséquences négatives qu'elle pourrait engendrer. Alors que les effets de la production de pétrole sont discutés par des experts et dans une grande partie de la littérature académique comme une malédiction des ressources (Auty, 1993; Karl, 1997; Ross, 2012), les pays africains en collaboration avec les compagnies pétrolières transnationales ne cessent d'explorer le sous-sol dans la perspective de trouver de nouveaux gisements. Particulièrement, au cours des deux dernières décennies, l'Afrique a été de plus en plus entraînée dans une nouvelle course aux réserves de pétrole inexploitées (Frynas & Paulo, 2007; Ghazvinian, 2007; Klare, 2012). Dans ce processus, un certain nombre de pays africains sont devenus de nouveaux États producteurs de pétrole. L'un de ces pays est le Niger.

Au Niger, l'existence de cette ressource ne date pas d'aujourd'hui, mais des considérations d'ordre économique et politico-stratégique ont empêché son extraction face à d'autres ressources jugées plus rentables ou stratégiquement plus importantes, notamment l'uranium (et l'or). Le Niger avait une histoire de 50 ans d'exploration pétrolière, mais comme d'autres pays sahélo-sahariens, avec sa position enclavée et son environnement difficile limitant la rentabilité, il est longtemps resté sous-exploré dans la recherche de nouvelles réserves de pétrole (Augé, 2011). A partir de 1958, inspirées par les découvertes majeures faites en Algérie voisine deux ans auparavant, ce sont principalement des compagnies pétrolières françaises et américaines qui ont exploré le Niger à la recherche de pétrole. Bien que les premiers résultats positifs de ces explorations pétrolières aient été connus dans les cercles politiques nigériens au début des années 1980, le pétrole est resté dans un état d'attente, un état qui allait durer plus de trois décennies au Niger. Encore en 2006, Esso et Petronas ont jugé que le bloc Agadem, situé à l'extrême est du Niger, n'était pas économiquement viable en estimant les réserves à 324 millions de barils de pétrole et 10 milliards de mètres cubes de gaz.

 | DOI:10.1163/9789004530065_012

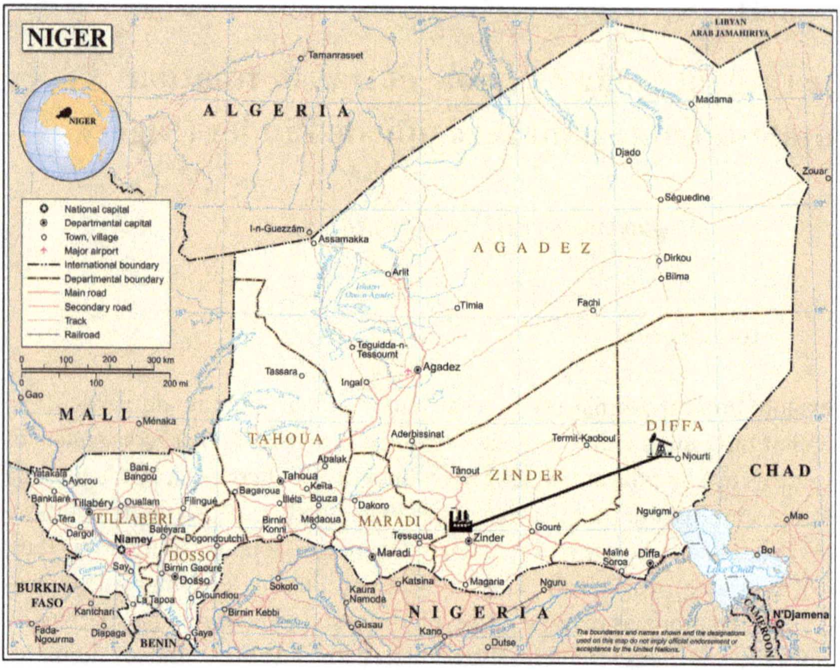

FIGURE 11.1 L'infrastructure pétrolière au Niger montrant les puits et la raffinerie
SOURCE : ILLUSTRATION DE JANNIK SCHRITT BASÉE SUR LA CARTE DES NATIONS UNIES N° 4234, (HTTPS://WWW.UN.ORG/GEOSPATIAL/CONTENT/NIGER)

Le regain d'intérêt suscité par le pétrole ces dernières années s'explique entres autres raisons par l'irruption en Afrique de la Chine populaire mue par sa soif de ce précieux combustible (Jiang, 2009; Klare & Volman, 2006; Soares de Oliveira, 2008). De plus, avec la crise des subprimes américains de 2007 et la crise financière mondiale de 2008, la valeur du baril de pétrole léger et doux trouvé au Niger est passée d'environ 30 USD en 2006 à 147 USD en juillet 2008 (Moussa, 2012). Dans ce contexte, le gouvernement nigérien a signé un premier accord de partage de la production avec la China National Petroleum Corporation (CNPC) en 2008 sur le bloc Agadem située dans la région de Diffa. Trois ans plus tard, la première raffinerie de pétrole du pays, située à Bakin Birgi, à environ 50 km au nord de la deuxième plus grande ville du Niger, Zinder, est entrée en production. Peu de temps après, la CNPC a réévalué les estimations des réserves à 744 millions de barils de pétrole et 16 milliards de mètres cubes de gaz et a prévu d'exporter le brut par un oléoduc de raccordement à l'oléoduc Tchad-Cameroun existant (Moussa, 2012).[1]

1 Entre 2008 et 2014, la CNPC a fait d'autres découvertes de pétrole, débloquant deux milliards de barils de pétrole et 2,5 trillions de mètres cubes de gaz naturel sur le permis original d'Agadem (Liu et al., 2015). En 2014, the British Savannah Petroleum a acquis 50 % du bloc pétrolier.

Dans ce contexte, l'avènement de cette raffinerie a suscité beaucoup d'espoir pour le peuple nigérien en général et pour la ville de Zinder et la communauté locale de Bakin Birgi en particulier. Dans des discussions informelles avant même le début de la production en 2011, beaucoup de gens espéraient que la raffinerie transformerait Zinder en une « ville pétrolière » comparable au luxe et aux richesses que de nombreux Nigériens avaient vus de « leurs propres yeux » en se rendant dans les États arabes lors du pèlerinage ou en travaillant dans la Libye de Kadhafi. Cependant, les attentes élevées et, dans certains cas, les promesses faites par les politiciens à la population risquent de se transformer en une grande déception. C'est ainsi que depuis sa mise en exploitation, des débats politiques houleux au parlement et dans les médias, des grèves et des manifestations de tous genres ont émaillé l'espace public nigérien exprimant des griefs, des espoirs déçus et de nouvelles demandes (Schritt, 2018; 2019; 2020).

Ainsi, la prise en compte de cette nouvelle ressource implique logiquement des mutations non seulement à l'échelle nationale mais aussi sur le plan régional et local. Cette contribution se focalise sur les processus de transformation socio-économique déclenchés par la raffinerie et qui se déroulent entre la commune d'Olléleoua et la ville de Zinder. En nous penchant sur cette question, nous soutenons que les processus de transformation socio-économique sont mieux compris dans l'interaction entre les milieux ruraux et urbains. Nous montrons que les processus de transformation socio-économique tels que l'expropriation et l'indemnisation, le travail dans l'industrie pétrolière, la spéculation immobilière et foncière ainsi que les activités économiques connexes doivent toujours être compris en relation avec le paysage et la ville, deux configurations entre lesquelles il n'y a pas seulement un échange de biens et de personnes, mais aussi de perceptions et de plaintes mutuelles.

Pour élaborer notre argumentation, nous esquissons brièvement la littérature sur la transformation rurale-urbaine dans un contexte de la production pétrolière avant d'analyser les différents processus de transformation dans leur interaction dialectique.

2 Pétrole et transformation sociale en milieu rurale et urbaine

L'installation d'une unité industrielle dans une zone rurale entraîne toujours une certaine transformation dans les relations sociales de la communauté qui y réside. Pour le cas du Nigeria, Paraut (2009) constate que dans le contexte de production de pétrole, « l'idéologie individualiste et la logique capitaliste ont atomisé la structure des sociétés traditionnelles en rompant l'équilibre mis en place depuis des siècles ». Même si le constat de Paraut ressemble à une romantisation et à une image fixe de vie rurale, partout dans le monde, les bouleversements liés à la révolution industrielle et l'exploitation du pétrole font naître des réflexions nouvelles sur le devenir des sociétés. De la même manière, l'écrivain Beti (Audition de M. Mongo Beti, écrivain, 1999) parle du pétrole au Cameroun en termes d'appauvrissement vertigineux de la population, d'abandon scolaire des enfants et de privatisation du système de santé.

Dans la littérature, on trouve nombre d'exemples qui montrent comment l'espoir s'est développé en désolation. Hoinathy (2013) a montré comment, dans une économie agraire avec des niveaux de revenus relativement peu élevés, l'argent du pétrole a bouleversé, grâce aux compensations versées aux paysans et aux salaires perçus mensuellement par ceux qui travaillent pour le projet, le mariage, les réseaux de parenté et les rapports de pouvoir dans la société. Behrends et Hoinathy (2017) soutiennent que le pétrole génère une forme d'inflation locale particulièrement perturbatrice. Pour Petry et Bambé (2005) également, c'est comme si on peignait un tableau assez sombre du bouleversement du mode de vie des populations locales du Tchad et du Cameroun par les infrastructures pétrolières. Pour l'extrême-Est du Niger, à Diffa, Moussa (2013, p. 3–4) constate que :

> En lieu et place de prospérité, ces dernières [les populations riveraines] vivent un « naufrage » matérialisé par la prostitution et la propagation du Sida, la pollution des sols, le déplacement des populations et du cheptel, le développement des violences et du brigandage, etc.

D'autre part, il y a un nombre important de personnes qui, soit trouvent directement du travail dans l'industrie pétrolière, soit bénéficient indirectement des opportunités économiques qui entourent cette industrie. Vannoppen (2016, cet ouvrage) montre, pour la « ville pétrolière » de Sekondi-Takoradi au Ghana, comment les capitaux attirés par la découverte du pétrole ont un impact sur la ville en influençant un nouveau plan de développement spatial de cette dernière et un boom des projets immobiliers engendrant l'augmentation des prix des terrains et des loyers, créant des pratiques urbaines spéculatives. Les recherches sur les villes en plein essor qui émergent souvent spontanément autour des ressources naturelles ont également montré que l'argent gagné rapidement grâce à l'or, aux saphirs ou à d'autres ressources peut être uniquement dépensé à des fins spécifiques excluant ainsi certains principes moraux et éthiques de redistribution (Walsh, 2003 ; Werthmann, 2009). Les villes en plein essor sont aussi souvent des endroits où la méfiance l'emporte sur la confiance, même parmi les amis et la famille (Walsh, 2003).

Cependant, le rural et l'urbain ne sont pas des dichotomies isolées. Elles se caractérisent par des flux et une fluidité réciproques (Lynch, 2008). La contribution de Mangarella dans cet ouvrage a donc montré que les questions relatives à une mentalité rentière ne touchent pas seulement les élites urbaines, mais aussi les communautés rurales. Se concentrant principalement sur la production culturelle au Nigeria, Apter (2005) a illustré la « politique d'illusion » du gouvernement revenant à utiliser la production pétrolière pour aider à construire une identité nationale. Cela a conduit à un « champ de significations instable » dans lequel les gens ont d'abord pensé au pétrole comme une manne de Dieu qui soulagerait la pauvreté, mais qui s'est ensuite transformé en une « malédiction », le pétrole étant devenu un signe du diable et des régimes corrompus (pour le cas du Tchad, voir aussi Seign-Goura, 2017). Weszkalnys (2016) a théorisé l'espoir et les attentes « de l'argent facile » d'une part, et les frustrations et exclusions de sa richesse d'autre part, comme des réponses affectives inhérentes à tout projet capitaliste d'exploitation des ressources naturelles. Néanmoins, il reste important de retracer empiriquement les processus socio-économiques de transformation induits par le pétrole. C'est la seule façon de garantir une approche différenciée qui mette en contraste les simples images en noir et blanc avec des recherches bien fondées.

3 Les transformations socio-économiques dans la région de Zinder

Lors de plusieurs entretiens de groupes de discussion avec des villageois expropriés menés indépendamment par les auteurs dans des villages proches de la raffinerie de pétrole en 2011, 2013 et 2014, les villageois se sont plaints, non seulement des expropriations de leurs champs, mais aussi qu'après la phase de construction de la raffinerie de pétrole en 2011, leurs fils avaient été licenciés, certains d'entre eux ayant alors migré en Libye à la recherche de travail. Leurs fils étant maintenant sans travail, les villageois n'ont pas vu d'impact positif de la raffinerie de pétrole. Au contraire, ils ont invoqué une perte de fertilité des sols, ainsi que la fumée et la pollution de l'air, et des problèmes avec les forces de sécurité qui limitent leurs déplacements, notamment la nuit, car les Chinois avaient à plusieurs reprises accusé leurs enfants de voler de la ferraille et d'autres choses dans la zone de la raffinerie. De plus, ils déplorent un afflux d'étrangers en quête de moyens de subsistance qui apporteraient des maladies et des valeurs culturelles différentes. En outre, les villageois se sont plaints qu'aucune des améliorations promises par l'État en matière de santé, d'eau potable ou d'éducation n'ait été réalisée. Lors de ces discussions de groupe, les habitants se sont également plaints du fait que la vie était devenue plus chère, en particulier le prix des terrains et des maisons, ainsi que les tarifs des transports. Du point de vue des villageois, ce sont les habitants de la ville de Zinder qui reçoivent tous les bénéfices de la raffinerie alors qu'eux en subissent les effets négatifs. Non seulement le nouveau centre résidentiel des travailleurs du pétrole a été construit dans la ville de Zinder et non à Bakin Birgi, mais le centre de soins de santé promis n'a pas été construit, de sorte qu'ils doivent encore se rendre à Zinder pour se faire soigner. Enfin, ils ont critiqué le gouvernement et la société civile car aucun représentant ne leur a rendu visite ou n'a manifesté un réel intérêt pour comprendre leur situation.

Dans ce qui suit, nous examinons de plus près certains domaines de transformation socio-économique : (3.1) l'expropriation et l'indemnisation, (3.2) le travail dans l'industrie pétrolière, (3.3) la spéculation immobilière et foncière et (3.4) les activités économiques connexes.

3.1 *L'expropriation et l'indemnisation*

Dans le cadre de l'exécution des travaux de construction de la raffinerie de Zinder, des paysans se sont vus expropriés de leurs terres. Au total, 598 hectares soit 167 champs ont été pris par l'État dans onze villages riverains de la raffinerie. De plus, selon le rapport de mission d'enquête publique dans le cadre de l'expropriation des propriétaires coutumiers mené par le gouvernement en novembre 2009 (Laminou & Amadou, 2009),[2] un jardin de manioc, quatorze habitations traditionnelles, quatre habitations en banco, trente-six greniers, un forage collectif et vingt-trois sites de cimetières ont été expropriés.

Bien que des représentants du gouvernement soient venus identifier les villageois touchés, le processus et le montant de l'indemnisation auxquels les villageois avaient droit n'a été publié ni dans le rapport, ni dans le décret. Selon les villageois, il leur avait seulement été demandé d'attendre et d'être patients. Dans une interview radiophonique réalisée en 2011, deux villageois ont parlé de leurs souffrances, déclarant qu'ils avaient perdu leurs champs et que, avec cela, « leur joie et leur espoir s'étaient transformés en fatigue et en désespoir ». Ils ont appelé le Président de la République à l'aide, expliquant qu'on leur avait dit que les paiements de compensation avaient déjà été transférés par le gouvernement, mais non qui devait leur remettre les paiements.

---

2 Le rapport a été validé dans un atelier à Zinder du 09 au 14 Novembre 2009 avec des représentants de l'enquête, des ministères, des expropriés et leurs avocats, le chef de canton, le préfet et le maire. En 19 août 2010, le président du Niger, Salou Djibo, a publié le décret n°2010-629 pour convertir le rapport en loi.

FIGURE 11.2 L'un des onze villages expropriés sur fond de la raffinerie nouvellement construite
PHOTO DE JANNIK SCHRITT

Deux avocats ont pris en charge leur dossier d'indemnisation, en contrepartie de 17% de l'indemnité finale (selon certains expropriateurs). D'après les informations des avocats, trois tranches de transfert des fonds de compensation étaient prévues. L'un des avocats avait été un militant de la société civile bien connu lors des « mouvements contre la vie chère » en 2005, et entretenait des relations étroites avec quelques dirigeants de la société civile de Zinder. Quand les expropriés ont été indemnisés par l'État, ce furent les avocats qui leur virèrent l'argent sur des comptes bancaires individuels ouverts à la Banque Internationale pour l'Afrique (BIA). Dans une économie agraire avec des niveaux de revenus relativement peu élevés, ces populations ont perçu des montants assez intéressants selon l'étendue des champs. Au cours de la première phase de dédommagement, ils perçurent de 1.000.000 à 50.000.000 FCFA (environ 1.500 à 76.000 €).[3] C'est pourquoi, au début, la plupart des villageois étaient satisfaits du montant de la première tranche. C'était en 2011.

3 Taux de change de mars 2011.

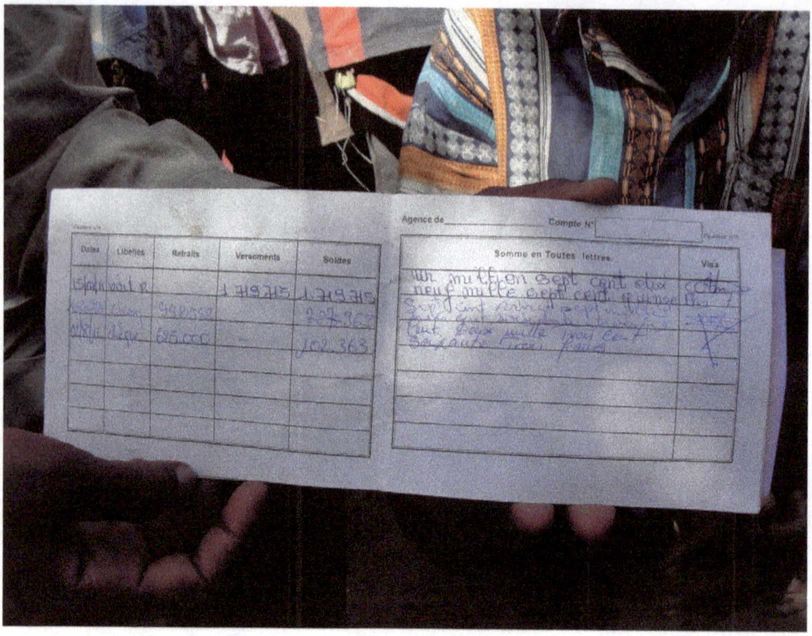

FIGURE 11.3 Le livret de gestion du compte indique les versements des indemnités et les retraits
PHOTO DE JANNIK SCHRITT

Cependant, ils ne savaient pas combien de tranches d'indemnités seraient versées, ce qui les a déçus par la suite.

Lorsque les agriculteurs expropriés ont reçu le deuxième des trois paiements d'indemnisation en 2013, seule une partie de l'argent est effectivement arrivée. L'avocat proche de la société civile de Zinder a rapidement été accusé d'avoir détourné l'argent et a été interpellé par la police, comme un exproprié de Rougaguen Ruwa a expliqué :

> On nous a escroqués. Tout le monde pense que l'argent est avec nous alors que ce n'est pas ça. Au premier paiement, tout s'est bien passé, mais au second tout a chamboulé. Même nos propres frères héritiers ne nous comprennent pas sur l'irrégularité de ce paiement.
>
> Entretien réalisé par Salissou Oubandoma le 27–06-13

Au lieu de défendre et de soutenir les villageois qui avaient accusé l'avocat, les membres de la société civile de Zinder ont affirmé que l'arrestation de l'avocat était politique, et ont exigé sa libération immédiate. Tout au long du conflit, les villageois expropriés n'ont pas eu une voix en public, ce qui a également été observé dans d'autres pays comme l'Ouganda (Witte, 2018, p. 149).

De plus, il est important de noter que la plupart des bénéficiaires de ces compensations individuelles, ont été accusés par des représentants de l'État, de la société civile et des non-bénéficiaires d'avoir mal géré les compensations du fait du manque d'encadrement. Ils disent que cet argent dû par les bénéficiaires a été source de problèmes du fait qu'ils n'avaient pas l'habitude de posséder des sommes aussi importantes. Certains ont acheté des motos, d'autres sont partis en pèlerinage, d'autres encore se sont mariés ou ont multiplié leurs épouses. Il est intéressant de noter que ce discours n'est en aucun cas unique au Niger. Des accusations similaires ont été faites en Ouganda, par exemple (Witte, 2018, p. 152). Toutefois, certains ont acheté des champs pour remplacer les terrains perdus ou ont remplacé leurs cases par des maisons en banco amélioré. Mais dans l'ensemble, les paiements des compensations ont été jugés, en 2013 et 2014, insuffisants, ce qui a également été observé dans d'autres pays comme le Nigeria (Oluduro, 2012), l'Angola (Reed, 2009, p. 104–136) ou l'Ouganda (Witte, 2018, p. 149).

Le conflit lié à la question d'indemnisation du foncier se situe en particulier à trois niveaux. D'un côté, un conflit a opposé les expropriés et les avocats ; les premiers estiment qu'il y a un manque de transparence dans le paiement des ressources qui leur sont allouées. De l'autre côté, le conflit est familial et local car il oppose les membres d'un village et même d'une famille à propos du partage des fonds d'indemnisation. A ce niveau, il faut préciser que la terre n'est généralement pas une propriété privée mais un bien commun que les familles individuelles ont le droit de gérer en vertu du droit coutumier. Pour l'expropriation et l'indemnisation, l'État a délivré des titres privés pour les terres après négociation avec les chefs traditionnels,[4] ce qui a donné lieu à des litiges entre les familles, notamment avec les chefs de village et de canton. L'argent reçu à cette phase de paiement n'était pas à la hauteur des attentes des bénéficiaires et cela a engendré un sentiment de méfiance auprès des autres ayants droit. Ces derniers ont même accusé leurs frères qui les ont

4 Au niveau rural, l'État se traduit par « le groupement » pour les groupes nomades et « le canton » pour les groupes sédentaires. Chacune de ces unités est dirigée par des chefs administratifs ou « chefs traditionnels », respectivement le « chef de groupement » et le « chef de canton ». Ces chefs supérieurs commandent les chefs inférieurs, le « chef de tribu » pour les groupes nomades et le « chef de village » pour les groupes sédentaires. Le pouvoir politique de ces chefs repose, d'une part, sur l'autorité de l'État (comme le droit de percevoir des impôts) et, d'autre part, sur la légitimité généralement acceptée, bien qu'un peu faible, de l'héritage aristocratique.

représentés d'avoir détourné une partie des sommes. Leur chef de canton a en particulier été accusé de complicité avec l'avocat. Une troisième dimension de conflit concerne leur relation avec l'État. Les expropriés n'auraient pas su combien et à quelle fréquence ils devaient être indemnisés. Lors des discussions de groupe, il s'est avéré que certains villageois s'attendaient à recevoir des indemnités annuelles. Selon leur point de vue, ils devaient subir des pertes de récoltes annuelles en raison des expropriations. Il semble que différentes logiques économiques soient ici à l'œuvre. D'une part, la logique des agriculteurs selon laquelle les pertes de récolte annuelles devraient également être compensées par des dédommagements annuels. D'autre part, il y a la logique de compensation, qui semble également coïncider avec la logique de l'entreprenariat au Niger, selon laquelle des jeunes entrepreneurs reçoivent un versement initial de leur famille (par exemple, 1 million FCFA) pour créer leur propre entreprise. Dans ce contexte, l'utilisation des paiements d'indemnisation sous la forme de dépenses de consommation plus élevées en prévision de la compensation annuelle, au lieu de dépenses d'investissement, ouvre une perspective différente.

En résumé, cette partie a montré que l'expropriation n'est pas seulement un phénomène purement rural, mais qu'il se déroule dans une dialectique entre ville et campagne. L'expropriation et l'indemnisation des champs pour la construction de l'infrastructure pétrolière implique non seulement les villageois mais aussi les entreprises qui construisent l'infrastructure, l'État central qui fournit le cadre juridique pour l'expropriation et qui est responsable de la mesure et de l'indemnisation des terres, l'État local et les autorités administratives qui fournissent les titres fonciers, les avocats qui plaident la cause des agriculteurs ainsi que les militants de la société civile et les journalistes qui (ne) rendent (pas) les affaires publiques et politiques. On peut observer quelque chose de similaire pour le travail dans l'industrie pétrolière.

3.2 *Le travail dans l'industrie pétrolière*

Au Niger, la China National Petroleum Corporation (CNPC) effectue son travail par l'intermédiaire de plusieurs filiales qui emploient les travailleurs nigériens. Même si nous n'avons pas de chiffres officiels, nous estimons que plusieurs centaines de Nigériens et de Chinois travaillaient seulement dans la construction de la raffinerie. Au début de la construction, beaucoup de travailleurs vivaient à côté des sites de la raffinerie dans des camps séparés selon leur nationalité et protégés par les militaires. Par la suite, la Société de la Raffinerie à Zinder (SORAZ) a entrepris de construire une cité à Zinder pour les ouvriers. Aussi, au tout début, les entreprises chinoises employaient directement les travailleurs nigériens pour la construction de la raffinerie. Mais comme les litiges sont

FIGURE 11.4 Une image des sous-traitants chinois sélectionnés lors de la cérémonie d'ouverture de la raffinerie
PHOTO DE JANNIK SCHRITT

devenus plus nombreux, ils ont externalisé leurs tâches à des agences privées de travail intérimaire comme la SOPLAMO qui prenait une partie du salaire mensuel des travailleurs pour leur service de recrutement.

La question du recrutement des employés à la raffinerie a mis en lumière certains conflits. L'article 22 du code pétrolier de 2007 stipule que les compagnies pétrolières doivent se conformer aux réglementations nationales. Néanmoins, lors d'entretiens, les travailleurs nigériens du secteur pétrolier ont accusé les Chinois de mauvaises conditions de travail, de sous-paiement, d'absence d'équipements de sécurité appropriés, de manque de procédures adéquates pour le traitement des produits chimiques (ce qui a entraîné de graves problèmes de santé et même des décès), de soins de santé inadéquats (y compris le traitement de maladies graves avec des antidouleurs), de licenciements injustifiés en cas de maladie, de mise à disposition de logements insalubres et d'un manque de transfert des connaissances. De plus, au début de la phase de construction de la raffinerie, de nombreux jeunes des villages environnants ont été recrutés comme manœuvres. Après la phase de construction, les travailleurs villageois, pour la plupart sans éducation, ont été licenciés, et les emplois de la raffinerie, désormais en activité, sont allés à des citadins lettrés. Dans la phase opérationnelle, seuls 265 jeunes Nigériens diplômés universitaires hautement qualifiés en pétrochimie et en mécanique seraient nécessaires pour la maintenance, la surveillance et le raffinage.[5] L'agence de recrutement privée SOPLAMO est aussi dénoncée par les travailleurs du pétrole pour deux raisons. Premièrement, parce qu'elle prélève une partie du salaire des travailleurs pour son service de recrutement. Deuxièmement, parce qu'elle est perçue comme collaborant avec et corrompu par les Chinois afin d'obtenir leur part. Puis, les uns et les autres s'accusent mutuellement sur le (non)respect des engagements pris.

Pour les jeunes de Bakin Birgi en particulier, la SORAZ n'a pas honoré ses engagements envers la commune rurale préférant la ville de Zinder, comme l'explique le Président de l'Association des Jeunes de Bakin Birgi (AJB) :

> Au moment de la construction, ils nous ont fait travailler comme des animaux en nous promettant un recrutement massif et prioritaire de tous les jeunes du village. Nous avons rendu publique une déclaration pour une prise en compte totale de nos doléances par la SORAZ en ce qui concerne le recrutement. Et comme si cela ne suffisait pas, nous avons appris que même la construction de la cité SORAZ qui pouvait créer de l'emploi a été transférée à Zinder.
>
> Entretien réalisé par Salissou Oubandoma le 26-06-13

En général, les jeunes cherchaient leur fortune dans le secteur pétrolier en espérant un emploi à long terme et un peu d'argent supplémentaire pour l'épargne, la construction de maisons, le mariage, etc. Dans la plupart des cas, ces attentes n'ont pas été satisfaites. Le salaire et la durée du contrat de travail des travailleurs nigériens varient en fonction des tâches, des fournisseurs de services et des conditions de sécurité. Alors que certains d'entre eux ont dit, dans les groupes de discussion qu'ils avaient gagné environ 70.000 FCFA (environ 105 €), un manœuvre nigérien a montré à Jannik Schritt son contrat avec l'entreprise de construction chinoise CPSCC qui était limité à 6 mois et stipulant un salaire mensuel de 35.984 FCFA (environ 55 €) pour une semaine de 40 heures. Par rapport à leurs collègues chinois, les travailleurs nigériens se sont notamment plaints du fait que les Chinois gagneraient beaucoup plus pour le même travail. Et c'est à juste titre que l'Inspecteur du travail de Zinder affirme :

5 Pendant sa phase opérationnelle, la raffinerie de pétrole emploie 548 personnes à son siège (265 Nigériens et 283 Chinois).

> Par rapport aux conditions de travail, l'aspect le plus litigieux qui concerne les travailleurs c'est le niveau de salaire. Les travailleurs de la SORAZ estiment que le niveau de salaire qui leur est payé pour le moment est en deçà de leur expérience.
>
> Entretien réalisé par Salissou Oubandoma le 01-07-2013

Cette situation fait ressortir la question du non-respect de la réglementation du travail en vigueur au Niger selon laquelle « tout employeur est tenu d'assurer, pour un même travail ou un travail de valeur égale, l'égalité de rémunération entre les salariés quels que soient leur origine, leur sexe, leur âge et leur statut » (article 148, Code du travail, 2000).

Cependant, le point de vue des anciens du village diffère de celui des jeunes villageois. D'une part, ils se sont plaints que seuls les jeunes avaient trouvé du travail pendant la construction de la raffinerie et qu'eux-mêmes n'avaient pas eu la possibilité de travailler. D'autre part, ils voient aussi le problème chez les jeunes qui soit sont insatisfaits du salaire, soit n'ont pas l'habitude de travailler très dur. Lors de la tenue d'une assemblée villageoise à propos du recrutement des jeunes de Bakin Birgi, le Chef dudit village a constaté :

> Nos jeunes ont été recrutés au tout début, mais après, ils ont cessé d'aller au travail soi-disant qu'ils ne sont pas bien rémunérés pour certains et que c'était trop dur pour d'autres.
>
> Entretien réalisé par le Salissou Oubandoma le 26-06-13

De plus, les anciens du village ont jugé que seuls certains jeunes étaient dévoués et qu'ils distribuaient le salaire au sein de la famille. D'autres, en revanche, dépenseraient l'argent principalement pour la prostitution ou les cigarettes.

Une perspective similaire se retrouve chez les fonctionnaires de l'État et la SOPLAMO qui présentent les Chinois comme des gens « travailleurs » alors que « les ouvriers nigériens n'ont pas l'habitude de travailler dur ». Il est à nouveau intéressant de noter que ce discours n'est en aucun cas unique au Niger. Des constats similaires ont été faits en Ouganda, par exemple (Witte, 2018, p. 142–143). D'une manière similaire, l'interprète chinois responsable des conditions de travail de la SORAZ a attribué un fatalisme islamique aux travailleurs nigériens afin d'expliquer par leur passivité les conflits inhérents aux conditions de travail. Dans une conversation informelle avec Jannik Schritt en 2011, il a expliqué que les problèmes dans les relations de travail étaient dus à « la mentalité » des Nigériens. Selon lui, « les Nigériens pensent que tout vient de Dieu, mais ils ne voient pas qu'ils doivent travailler dur pour s'aider eux-mêmes ».

Du côté de la SORAZ, l'entreprise estime que le recrutement du personnel nigérien s'est fait normalement et de la façon la plus régulière, conformément à la loi. De leur propre aveu, ils ont recruté fin décembre 2012, pendant la phase de production, 236 Nigériens au total. Suite à une évaluation du personnel recruté, ceux qui n'ont pas respecté la discipline de la société ou qui ont failli dans l'évaluation à l'issue de la période d'essai (dix-huit personnes) ont été licenciés. Six Nigériens ont démissionné volontairement (SORAZ, 2012). Ce nombre plutôt faible de personnes ayant démissionné ou ayant été licenciées montre que la comparaison des « Chinois travailleurs » et des « Nigériens paresseux » ne correspond pas à la réalité, mais constitue plutôt une stratégie visant à légitimer les déséquilibres de pouvoir et les mécanismes d'exploitation. De plus, pour les travailleurs nigériens du pétrole, la situation est totalement différente. Peu d'entre eux ont déclaré avoir abandonné leur emploi en raison de la pénibilité du travail. Au contraire, ils se sont plaints du « racisme » de leurs supérieurs chinois. Cela se reflète, entre autres, dans le comportement apparemment très répandu des Chinois qui frappent les travailleurs nigériens sur la tête en guise de punition lorsqu'ils commettent des erreurs. En outre, il existe de nombreuses histoires de comportement discriminatoire de la part des Chinois. Par exemple, un travailleur nigérien a déclaré que, lorsqu'ils travaillaient dans le désert, ils étaient obligés de dormir la nuit à côté des « toilettes turques » des Chinois. D'autres se sont plaints de problèmes de santé dus à la manipulation non protégée de produits chimiques, des problèmes de santé que les Chinois se contentaient de traiter avec des antidouleurs.

Alors que la plupart des travailleurs nigériens ont déclaré qu'ils ne se plaignaient pas officiellement des problèmes parce qu'ils craignaient de perdre leur emploi, certains parmi ceux qui l'avaient déjà perdu ont poursuivi les grèves et les litiges, particulièrement sous forme de plaintes collectives. Ils ont invoqué des violations du code du travail par l'inégalité salariale, le licenciement illégitime, le non-paiement des heures supplémentaires et la réduction illégitime des salaires par la SOPLAMO. Compte tenu de ces plaintes, il n'est pas surprenant que les travailleurs nigériens aient cherché à former un syndicat. Cependant, ce n'est qu'en janvier 2013, soit plus de quatre ans après le début de la construction et un an après le début de la production, qu'un syndicat national des travailleurs du pétrole a été autorisé. Le Syndicat National des Travailleurs de Pétrole (SYNATRAP) a été créé pour couvrir les travailleurs du bloc pétrolier Agadem, tandis que la sous-section SYNATRAP/SORAZ a été créée pour les travailleurs de la raffinerie de pétrole. Les ingénieurs nigériens travaillant à la raffinerie (SYNATRAP/SORAZ) se sont mis en grève à plusieurs reprises. Leurs revendications s'articulaient autour de cinq points : (1) le renouvellement des contrats à durée déterminée, (2) la conversion des contrats à durée déterminée en contrats à durée indéterminée, (3) l'augmentation et l'harmonisation des salaires entre Chinois et Nigériens, (4) l'amélioration des logements et de la prestation de services, et (5) le développement d'un programme de formation du personnel nigériens de haute qualité. Les négociations entre le syndicat, le SORAZ, l'inspecteur du travail de la région de Zinder et le ministère du pétrole et de l'énergie ont eu lieu en mars 2014. Ils ont convenu d'une nouvelle procédure d'évaluation des contrats de travail, de nouveaux logements avec eau courante et électricité, d'une augmentation générale des salaires et d'un changement de prestataires de formation. Cependant, le syndicat a organisé des grèves répétées en 2014, 2015 et 2016, accusant la direction chinoise de ne pas respecter les accords.

En résumé, le domaine des relations de travail comprend divers acteurs des zones rurales et urbaines. Non seulement les villageois se plaignent du traitement préférentiel dont bénéficient les citadins lettrés, mais les différents acteurs ou groupes d'acteurs s'accusent aussi mutuellement. En général, les fonctionnaires de l'État et la SOPLAMO identifient les besoins illimités des travailleurs nigériens et leur manque d'habitude de travailler dur comme le problème central dans les relations de travail. De la même manière, les Chinois identifient un fatalisme islamique parmi les travailleurs nigériens. Il s'agit ici d'une sorte de gestion des attentes pour bloquer les demandes des travailleurs comme c'est actuellement en vogue dans l'industrie pétrolière (UNDP, 2011 ; Weszkalnys, 2016, p. 137–141 ; Witte, 2018, p. 136–137).

3.3 *La spéculation immobilière et foncière*

L'avènement de la raffinerie a contribué à la revalorisation du loyer et du foncier, à l'émergence de nouveaux types d'habitat et au déplacement des populations étrangères à la recherche d'emploi. Partout dans la ville de Zinder, on peut voir des villas à moitié achevées et des terrains clôturés dans le but de les mettre en valeur. Même si le processus de construction a commencé avant le pétrole, les habitants de Zinder se sont plaints dans plusieurs conversations informelles que le prix des maisons et des terrains avait au moins doublé, voire avait été multiplié par dix depuis la construction de la raffinerie.

Une augmentation des prix est le cas même si l'État vend des terrains à un prix fixe. À Zinder, c'est la mairie qui vend des parcelles de taille standardisée de 400 m^2 pour 800 FCFA/m^2, soit un total de 320.000 FCFA. Le prix du terrain n'a pas été augmenté depuis plus de 15 ans dans les centres urbains du Niger et n'a pas été augmenté à Zinder depuis la construction de la raffinerie. Néanmoins, avec la construction de la raffinerie, il y a eu une spéculation sur les parcelles de terrain car les hommes d'affaires ont acheté de plus grandes quantités de parcelles de l'État et les ont ensuite revendues à un prix plus élevé.

FIGURE 11.5 L'une des nombreuses villas à moitié achevées à Zinder
PHOTO DE JANNIK SCHRITT

La course aux nouveaux terrains à bâtir a également encouragé une pratique illégale consistant à vendre une même parcelle à plusieurs personnes en même temps à leur insu. Cette pratique des titres fonciers multiples est devenue une préoccupation publique et a même été portée devant le gouverneur de la région de Zinder.

En effet, plusieurs facteurs ont concouru à l'enchérissement du loyer et du foncier dans les localités de Bakin Birgi et de Zinder. À Zinder, nous avons constaté que les personnes les plus aisées du pays ont investi dans l'acquisition de terrains et la construction de nouvelles résidences de luxe mus par la vision d'une future ville pétrolière. Les bâtiments de luxe, construits dans les zones résidentielles plus aisées ainsi que dans les zones périphériques de la ville, étaient également motivés par des significations sur les Chinois en accord avec les expériences locales avec les Occidentaux. Selon ces expériences, les coopérants occidentaux louent généralement des maisons entières, pour lesquelles ils emploient souvent un large éventail de personnel local (gardiens de jour et de nuit, cuisiniers et nounous) (Spies, 2009). Mais au grand dam de nombreux investisseurs qui en partie se sont endettés pour bâtir des somptueuses villas, les Chinois s'arrangeaient pour louer une maison à 30 ou 50 employés. Pire, les Chinois ont déménagé, au bout de six mois seulement, pour être logés dans des conteneurs nouvellement construits par la SORAZ dans l'enceinte de la raffinerie. Lors de la visite d'une des maisons abandonnées par des Chinois, Jannik Schritt a découvert des lits superposés installés dans des chambres pour accueillir un maximum de personnes. En outre, ils avaient non seulement fortifié et entretenu les maisons, mais ils les avaient aussi détruites peu de temps avant de les quitter. Par conséquent, les propriétaires se sont plaints que les maisons étaient devenues difficiles à louer à d'éventuels successeurs. Peut-être que ces histoires donnent également naissance à la rumeur persistante à Zinder selon laquelle de nombreux Chinois travaillant à la raffinerie seraient des prisonniers qui exercent pour le compte de l'État Chinois.

À Bakin Birgi, nous avons constaté un processus similaire. Ici, le déplacement des populations dans ces localités a eu des répercussions sur le loyer, d'autant plus que l'offre ne suit pas la demande. A titre illustratif, ce sont des dizaines de citernes qui débarquent et attendent souvent pendant des jours voire des semaines avant de repartir. Pour ce qui est de la revalorisation du foncier, il faut noter que certains paysans qui ont perdu leurs champs à la suite de l'expropriation de leurs terres ont procédé à l'achat de nouveaux terrains grâce aux indemnités perçues. Par ailleurs, l'installation de la raffinerie à Bakin Birgi devient source de spéculation du foncier. Dans un entretien avec un élu local et commerçant de Bakin Birgi, il voit avant tout un changement positif pour le village de Bakin Birgi, dû à l'augmentation du commerce et aux nombreuses personnes venues des pays voisins comme le Nigeria, le Burkina Faso, la Côte d'Ivoire et le Cameroun. Pour lui, l'augmentation du prix de foncier est un exemple particulièrement révélateur des effets positifs de la raffinerie. Selon lui, le prix du mètre carré de terrain est passé de 75–100 FCFA (0,11€–0,15€) avant la raffinerie à 300–400 FCFA (0,46€–0,60€) dans le village de Bakin Birgi et à 200–250 FCFA (0,30€–0,38€) dans la périphérie, ce qui signifie que beaucoup plus d'argent circule qu'auparavant.

> Par exemple si quelqu'un vient payer dix terrains à 600.000 FCFA [915€] le terrain, donc dix fois 600.000, ça fait déjà six million [9.145€]. C'est un ajout !
>
> Entretien réalisé par Jannik Schritt le 21-3-2014

En effet, en prévision d'une ville pétrolière de Bakin Birgi, certaines personnes anticipent en achetant de nombreux terrains morcelés dans les champs autour du village. D'ores et déjà, on constate un début de mise en valeur de ces terrains par la construction d'habitations plus ou moins modernes. Dans l'ensemble, un « petro-urbanisme » (Vannoppen, cet ouvrage) ne se manifeste pas seulement dans la grande ville de Zinder, mais s'étend aussi à la périphérie. Le village de Bakin Birgi, juste à côté de la raffinerie, n'est pas à l'abri de la spéculation immobilière et foncière.

3.4 *Les activités économiques connexes*

Sur le plan économique, la présence de la raffinerie a favorisé la création de plusieurs activités économiques. Tout d'abord, l'arrivée du pétrole a déclenché l'émergence de nouvelles sociétés de transport nigériennes. Ensuite, des stations d'essence privées ont vu le jour dans tout le pays. Dans la ville de Zinder, le nombre de stations-service est passé de six en 2011 à vingt-et-un en octobre 2015. Les commerçants nigériens approvisionnent en outre les entreprises chinoises en légumes, viande, poisson et boissons.

De plus, l'installation de la raffinerie a stimulé l'économie informelle au Niger en fournissant des opportunités d'emploi supplémentaires. La nouvelle activité dans le domaine des transports a par exemple incité un homme d'affaires local de Zinder à ouvrir un parking privé en dehors de la ville. Cette zone est gérée par le syndicat des conducteurs de transport et attire des détaillants, des petits commerçants, des vendeurs de nourriture, des professionnelles du sexe et d'autres prestataires de services qui essaient tous de vendre leurs produits et services aux centaines de camionneurs qui attendent pendant des jours pour charger leurs camions-citernes à la raffinerie. Ajouté à cela, le boom de la construction de nouvelles maisons, notamment de villas, a employé des centaines de manœuvres, de charpentiers et de maçons dans la ville de Zinder. Tous ces acteurs n'ont pas de relation directe avec la SORAZ, mais la présence de la raffinerie a ouvert des nouvelles perspectives économiques. Ces activités connexes ont toutes leur implication dans l'économie locale. La mairie gagne dans les taxes que payent ces acteurs, ce qui lui procure des ressources additionnelles pour son bon fonctionnement. Comme l'affirme le 1er Vice-président du Conseil Régional de Zinder :

> Par rapport à l'aspect économique, il y a à peu près 80 citernes qui chargent chaque jour ; regardez la vendeuse de beignets, le petit boulanger, à coté on a les cireurs des chaussures et bien d'autres encore, tous trouvent de quoi satisfaire leurs besoins. Comme je dis, ça peut transformer rapidement la société.
>
> Entretien réalisé par Salissou Oubandoma le 01-07-2013

L'avènement de la raffinerie a également apporté une modification considérable sur le plan de la transformation du village. Ainsi, on constate l'apparition de nouveaux types d'habitats non seulement à Zinder mais aussi à Bakin Birgi, notamment l'ouverture de restaurants et de débits de boisson (bars), la floraison de

FIGURE 11.6 Quelques-uns des nombreux kiosques et boutiques qui ont été nouvellement installés sur le parking des camions-citernes à Zinder
PHOTO DE JANNIK SCHRITT

vidéoclubs et l'utilisation des groupes électrogènes comme source d'énergie tout en attendant l'électrification annoncée. Toujours en termes de changement, il faut ajouter les opportunités d'emploi créées même si les ouvriers continuent de se plaindre de l'insuffisance des salaires. Au village de Bakin Birgi, des acteurs se transforment en commerçants ambulants, ce qui leur procure des revenus supplémentaires et leur permet d'épargner des ressources et d'agrandir leurs activités, puis d'ouvrir des boutiques. En effet, depuis l'installation de la raffinerie, les activités génératrices de revenu pratiquées surtout par les femmes qui assurent notamment l'approvisionnement en nourriture se sont considérablement développées. On constate aussi le développement des initiatives des jeunes notamment par l'ouverture de petites boutiques de vente de produits divers, de petits salons de coiffure et de points de vente de cartes de recharge téléphoniques. D'autres jeunes ont porté leur préférence sur la pratique de motos-taxi, plus connues sous l'appellation de « kabou-kabou ». Il en résulte donc des effets économiques tels que la création de nouvelles activités génératrices de revenus, la diversification et la disponibilité des produits de première nécessité ainsi que d'articles divers font des villages environnants des lieux attractifs, ce qui insuffle un dynamisme certain à la vie économique de la zone.

Cependant, comme de nombreux travailleurs nigériens du secteur pétrolier ont perdu leur emploi à la fin de la phase de construction et que de nombreuses maisons nouvellement construites attendent toujours d'être occupées, parler de pétrole révèle plus souvent une déception qu'une aubaine. Tout d'abord, l'exploitation de la raffinerie a également induit un déplacement des populations étrangères à la recherche d'un emploi non seulement vers la ville de Zinder mais aussi vers le village de Bakin Birgi. Cette situation est susceptible de provoquer des accidents de citernes et d'entraîner la propagation et l'accroissement des infections sexuellement transmissibles. C'est ce qu'évoque le conseiller municipal et directeur de l'école de Bakin Birgi lors de notre entretien. En effet, il nuance le progrès sur le plan social dû à la présence de la SORAZ en ces mots :

> C'est vrai cette raffinerie a bien changé les choses à Bakin Birgi car il y a beaucoup d'étrangers ; mais il y a des risques énormes d'accidents avec l'afflux des citernes ; les nombreux chauffeurs qui débarquent apportent avec eux la débauche et bien d'autres choses comme les maladies.
>
> Entretien réalisé par Salissou Oubandoma le 03/12/2012

De plus, la population du village de Bakin Birgi est rurale et a des niveaux de revenus relativement peu élevés. Aujourd'hui, comme dans d'autres pays comme le Tchad (Hoinathy, 2013), l'avènement de la raffinerie fait naître des réflexions et des comportements nouveaux comme la monétarisation des relations sociales. Cependant, il y a lieu de nuancer ce fait car les changements au stade actuel ne sont pas totalement perceptibles en raison des fortes attentes. Le chef de Canton de Olléleoua témoigne à ce propos :

> Je te dis que depuis un certain moment, la vie est devenue chère chez nous ; tout est devenu argent ; si tu n'en as pas, eh bien personne ne t'approche ; avant la raffinerie, nous payions 1.000 FCFA pour aller à Tanout. Aujourd'hui, c'est 3.000 FCFA ; pour aller à Zinder, nous payions également 1.000 FCA. Aujourd'hui, il faut payer 1250 FCFA. Malgré cet état de fait, les gens continuent à venir.
>
> Entretien réalisé par Salissou Oubandoma le 30/11/2012

Il est intéressant de noter ici qu'à Diffa, la région située à l'est de Zinder, là où le brut est extrait, l'évolution inverse se produit. En raison de la construction d'une nouvelle « route du pétrole », les prix du transport y ont considérablement baissé comme le montre la contribution de Mahamidou Aboubacar

Attahirou dans cet ouvrage. Une fois de plus, c'est le contexte qui influence les processus de transformation socio-économique.

Face à la réalité des promesses non tenues dans les domaines de l'emploi, des compensations et des réalisations socio-économiques (écoles, routes, santé), les déceptions des populations sont énormes. En outre, les avantages et les bénéfices de la raffinerie ne sont pas perçus en soi, mais principalement par les autres. C'est ainsi que les femmes membres du groupement « Haddin kay Yarda » expliquent que le changement lié à l'avènement de la SORAZ se fait attendre. Selon la Présidente du groupement :

> Lorsque la société voulait s'installer, ils ont recruté nos enfants pour le travail physique et après ils les ont lâchés pour exiger des lettrés. Et voilà qu'ils sont partis en exode nous laissant leurs femmes.
>
> Entretien réalisé par Salissou Oubandoma le 28-06-13

En effet, les entretiens font ressortir un mécontentement général consécutif à l'avènement de la raffinerie. Sur la question de la manne pétrolière, le discours reste partout le même : « le pétrole coule toujours pour les autres » (Moussa, 2013). Les populations de Diffa disent que c'est Zinder qui profite du pétrole, celles de Zinder estiment que ce sont les gens de Niamey qui sont recrutés en lieu et place de leurs enfants. Par ailleurs, les habitants de Bakin Birgi accusent Zinder de dévier à leur profit les avantages sociaux que procure la raffinerie (citée des travailleurs, hôpital, etc.) (Schritt, 2018).

4 Conclusion

La construction de la raffinerie a impliqué un grand nombre d'acteurs ruraux et urbains avec des intérêts divergents. Il s'agit de l'État, des autorités régionales et des habitants de la ville, des chefs administratifs et de la population villageoise, des avocats, des compagnies pétrolières chinoises, des sociétés de transport, des organisations de la société civile et des commerçants. Ces acteurs développent des stratégies différentes pour faire valoir leurs intérêts (accès aux revenus pétroliers, accaparement de terres, recherche de positions politiques, etc.) (voir la contribution d'Abdoutan Harouna dans cet ouvrage). À titre d'illustration, sur la question de l'emploi, l'entreprise SORAZ met l'accent sur la qualification des travailleurs, tandis que les villageois se plaignent des licenciements et les travailleurs des mauvais salaires et des conditions de travail difficiles. En outre, l'État a créé le cadre juridique et institutionnel pour la construction de la raffinerie, les compagnies pétrolières chinoises ont fourni l'expertise et les ressources financières nécessaires, et les villageois ont abandonné leurs terres sous contrainte ou dans l'espoir d'une vie meilleure.

En effet, les processus de transformation provoqués par le pétrole montrent que les zones urbaines et rurales ne peuvent être considérées séparément. Le domaine de l'expropriation et le versement d'indemnités montrent non seulement l'implication des acteurs de la ville et de la campagne, mais aussi leur interdépendance et la façon dont la confiance et la méfiance façonnent leurs relations mutuelles. Le domaine du travail dans l'industrie pétrolière montre comment les travailleurs de la ville et de la campagne ont été montés les uns contre les autres dans une certaine mesure, se considérant comme les véritables perdants. Le domaine de la spéculation immobilière et foncière a montré comment les visions d'une future ville pétrolière et l'afflux de personnes différentes à la recherche d'une vie meilleure, de loyers et de prix des terrains peuvent monter en flèche. Le domaine du développement économique autour de la raffinerie a montré que de nouvelles possibilités de revenus apparaissent à la campagne comme à la ville, mais que celles-ci ne peuvent généralement pas être à la hauteur des espoirs et des attentes suscités par le pétrole, surtout pour la population à faible capital économique. En bref, l'ensemble des processus de transformation a conduit à une augmentation du coût de la vie et à une monétarisation des relations sociales qui touche tout le monde dans la région de Zinder, mais frappe particulièrement ceux qui ne peuvent tirer aucun bénéfice de la production pétrolière.

Remerciements

Nous tenons à rendre un hommage mérité à tire posthume à l'enseignante et premier encadreur de Salissou Oubandoma, feue Dr Hadiza MOUSSA dont, hélas, la disparition précoce l'a empêchée de voir ce travail accompli. Que son âme repose en paix ! Nos remerciements vont également au deuxième encadreur Dr Amadou Oumarou, à l'UAM qui n'a ménagé aucun effort dans l'encadrement de ce travail. Nous disons ensuite merci au Pr Mahaman Tidjani Alou pour les conseils indispensables qu'il nous a prodigués. Ces conseils sont autant d'éléments de la réussite de ce travail. Nous nous devons aussi de dire merci à la fondation DFG à travers le LASDEL pour le soutien financier dans le cadre du Programme de Recherche « Oil and Social Change in Niger and Chad - Adaptation and Creativity in Africa ». Un grand merci à nos informateurs, interlocuteurs et amis sur le terrain pour leurs précieux conseils sans lesquels ce travail n'aurait pas été possible. Finalement, merci à nos épouses et à nos enfants pour la joie, l'inspiration et le soutien qu'ils nous apportent.

Références

Apter, A. (2005). *The Pan-African Nation: Oil and the Spectacle of Culture in Nigeria.* Chicago: University of Chicago Press.

Audition de M. Mongo Beti, écrivain. (1999, March 24), https://www.voltairenet.org/article7974.html [last accessed 13.2.2022].

Augé, B. (2011). Les nouveaux enjeux pétroliers de la zone saharienne. *Hérodote - Revue De Géographie Et De Géopolitique* (142), 183–205.

Auty, R. M. (1993). *Sustaining Development in Mineral Economies: The Resource Curse Thesis.* Routledge.

Behrends, A., & Hoinathy, R. (2017). The Devil's Money: A Multi-Level Approach to the Disordering in Oil-Producing Southern Chad, *Social Analysis*, 61(3).

Frynas, J. G., & Paulo, M. (2007). A New Scramble For African Oil? Historical, Political, and Business Perspectives. *African Affairs*, 106(423), 229–251.

Ghazvinian, J. H. (2007). *Untapped: The Scramble for Africa's Oil.* Harcourt.

Hoinathy, R. (2013). *Pétrole et changement social au Tchad: rente pétrolière et monétisation des relations économiques et sociales dans la zone pétrolière de Doba.* Paris: Karthala.

Jiang, W. (2009). Fuelling the Dragon: China's Rise and It's Energy and Resources Extraction in Africa. *The China Quarterly* 199, 585–609.

Karl, T. L. (1997). *The Paradox of Plenty: Oil Booms and Petro-States.* Berkeley: Univ. of California Press.

Klare, M. T. (2012). *The Race for What's Left: The Global Scramble for the World's Last Resources.* New York: Picador.

Klare, M. T., & Volman, D. (2006). America, China & the Scramble for Africa's Oil. *Review of African Political Economy*, 33(108), 297–309.

Laminou, S., & Amadou, A. (Novembre 2009). *Rapport de mission: enquête publique dans le cadre de l'expropriation des propriétaires coutumiers concernés par les travaux de construction de la raffinerie de Zinder.* Ministre de Mines et de l'Energie (MME).

Oluduro, O. (2012). Oil Exploration and Ecological Damage: The Compensation Policy in Nigeria. *Canadian Journal of Development Studies/Revue Canadienne D'études Du Développement,* 33(2), 164–179.

Ordonnance no 96-039 du 29 juin 1996 portant Code du travail (2000). http://www.ilo.org/dyn/natlex/docs/WEBTEXT/44750/66561/F96NER01.htm.

Liu, B., Wan, L., Mao, F., Liu, J., Lü, M., & Wang, Y. (2015). Hydrocarbon Potential of Upper Cretaceous Marine Source Rocks in the Termit Basin, Niger. *Journal of Petroleum Geology*, 38(2), 157–175.

Lynch, K. (2008). Rural-Urban Interaction in the Developing World. In V. Desai & R. B. Potter (eds.), *The Companion to Development Studies*, (pp. 268–271). Hodder Education.

Moussa, O. (2012, November 9). Le pétrole nigérien: d'Agadem à la SORAZ. *Sahel Dimanche*, p. 12.

Moussa, H. (2013). *Enjeux de l'exploitation pétroliere: etude de cas à N'gourti* [Paper presented at ECAS]. Lisbon.

Paraut, B. (2009). *Le pétrole au Nigeria: un instrument au service de quel développement? : pillage, crise identitaire et résistance dans le delta du Niger*. L'Harmattan.

Petry, M., & Bambé, N. (2005). *Le petrole du Tchad: reve ou cauchemar pour les populations?* Tropiques. Karthala.

Reed, K. (2009). *Crude Existence: Environment and the Politics of Oil in Northern Angola.* Berkeley: University of California Press.

Ross, M. L. (2012). *The Oil Curse: How Petroleum Wealth Shapes the Development of Nations*. Princeton: Princeton University Press.

Schritt, J. (2018). Crude Controversies: Disputes along Niger's Petro-Infrastructure. *History and Anthropology*, 29(5), 645–669.

Schritt, J. (2019). Well-Oiled Protest: Adding Fuel to Political Conflicts in Niger. *African Studies Review*, 62(2), 49–71.

Schritt, J. (2020). Crude Talking: Radio and the Politics of Naming, Blaming and Claiming in Oil-Age Niger. *Journal of Contemporary African Studies*, 38(3), 415–436.

Seign-Goura, Y. (2017). Representations of Oil in Chad: A Blessing or a Curse? *Africa Spectrum*, 52(1), 65–83.

Soares de Oliveira, R. (2008). Making Sense of Chinese Oil Investment in Africa. In D. Large, C. Alden, R. S. de Oliveira, & C. Alden (eds.), *China Returns to Africa: Superpower and a Continent Embrace* (pp. 83–109). London: Hurst.

SORAZ. (2012). *Bilan des activités de l'année 2012 et le plan des activités de l'année 2013.*

Spies, E. (2009). *Das Dogma der Partizipation: Interkulturelle Kontakte im Kontext der Entwicklungszusammenarbeit in Niger*. Köln: Köppe.

UNDP. (2011). *Getting it Right: Lessons from the South in Managing Hydrocarbon Economies.* New York. United Nations Development Programme.

Vannoppen, G. (2016). *Fueling the Future with Concrete, Paper and Discourse: Competing Claims in the Making of an Oil City, Sekondi-Takoradi, Ghana*. Thesis, KU Leuven.

Walsh, A. (2003). 'Hot Money' and Daring Consumption in a Northern Malagasy Sapphire-Mining Town. *Amercian Ethnologist*, 30(2), 290–305.

Werthmann, K. (2009). *Bitteres Gold: Bergbau, Land und Geld in Westafrika*. Köln: Köppe.

Weszkalnys, G. (2016). A Doubtful Hope: Resource Affect in a Future Oil Economy. *Journal of the Royal Anthropological Institute*, 22(S1), 127–146.

Witte, A. (2018). *An Uncertain Future - Anticipating Oil in Uganda*. Göttingen: Universitätsverlag Göttingen.

Index

www.ingramcontent.com/pod-product-compliance
Lightning Source LLC
Chambersburg PA
CBHW071430230926
51846CB00001B/171
* 9 7 8 9 0 0 4 5 3 0 0 5 8 *